The Development of Behavior

The Development of Behavior

A Synthesis of Developmental and Comparative Psychology

Bill Seay
Nathan Gottfried
Louisiana State University

Houghton Mifflin Company
Boston
Dallas   Geneva, Illinois
Hopewell, New Jersey   Palo Alto
London

Printed in the U.S.A.

Library of Congress Catalog Card Number: 78-50639

ISBN: 0-395-24747-0

Contents

Preface

A course in the development of behavior should be an interesting and pleasant experience for both the students and the teacher. In our experience as teachers we have missed this mark when a coherent framework was not provided for the diverse and sometimes fragmentary information in this broad area. Specific research articles are sometimes necessarily fragmentary in content. An undergraduate textbook must provide a general framework to enable the student to understand, appreciate, and retain the essential features of important research findings. The major goal of this book is to help students and teachers realize the potential intellectual pleasure inherent in a consideration of behavioral development.

The point of view expressed in the text has developed from two related concerns. One of these is our need to communicate with our students. The other is our need to understand our own research and that of other scientists who study human and animal behavior. Since our research and teaching interests span developmental and comparative psychology, it was clear to us that our concept of the development of behavior should involve a synthesis of these two closely related areas of psychology.

A number of recurrent themes run through our presentation of a coherent framework for understanding the development of behavior. One is the explicit recognition that any behavior has multiple determinants. Any behavioral outcome is seen as the result of interacting biological, psychological, and individual behavioral determinants. The implications of evolutionary theory for behavioral science provides another general theme for our point of view. The behavior of successful species, cultures, and individuals is adaptive in an evolutionary sense. Adaptation implies behavioral organization and effective interaction with the environment at every level from individual to species. These considerations underlie an organized background for presenting the basic information about development to the undergraduate student. We feel that the perspective given here is an attractive alternate to age-stage or topical presentations of similar material.

The sources of basic research information presented here are from several disciplines, primarily psychology, anthropology, psychiatry, genetics, and zoology. The methods used by scientists whose work is reported included laboratory experiments, clinical case studies, observational studies in the field and in contrived environments, and survey research of various kinds. We feel strongly that a multidisciplinary, method-independent view of behavioral science is most appropriate for the student's introduction to studies in development.

Our desire to develop a textbook for the undergraduate student precluded other goals that could better be achieved in a different way. We have made no attempt to provide a comprehensive review of the vast literature available in the area of development. Instead, we have presented a highly selected sample of research results from this area. In many cases we have used older studies when more recent research efforts were considered to be too specific or too technically complex for our purposes. Similarly, we have made no effort to provide the student with conflicting theoretical views on many of the topics presented in the book. Some teachers may find presentation of other information and other ideas one source of lectures to accompany this text.

The emphasis of the text is clearly developmental, but this should not discourage its use in an undergraduate comparative psychology course. In a sense, comparative and developmental psychology are interdependent and mutually supportive areas of our discipline. The basic information usually included in a comparative psychology course is presented here. The developmental orientation and the interest in human behavior included in this book have proved valuable in generating and maintaining interest in the authors' own comparative psychology classes.

The text has several features intended to augment its effectiveness as a teaching tool. Terms that may be unfamiliar to the student are defined within each chapter and are also included in a glossary. An annotated list of suggested readings will be found at the end of each chapter. These range from nontechnical short books that would be of interest to most students to highly technical basic sources that dedicated students will choose to pursue.

Additional aids to teaching will be found in the teacher's manual, which includes class and individual project suggestions, suggested essay and multiple choice examination items, and other recommendations drawn from our own teaching experience. All of the information in the teacher's manual has been prepared by the authors of the text, which will ensure compatibility between the manual and the text.

In a work of this sort our intellectual debts are many and in some instances probably unconscious. We are unable to mention all individuals and groups that have influenced our thinking, but would like to take this opportunity to recognize a few major sources of help to us. First, there are those among our teachers and colleagues whose influence has stayed with us over the years. These include Harry F. Harlow, Eva Goodenough, E. Mavis Hetherington, John Horrocks, Delos Wickens, Horace B. English, and Paul Rosenblum. These individuals and many others have aided our development through personal interaction as well as through their own published research. Others are known to us through their work, and as the reader will see, have strongly influenced our thinking. These include T. C. Schneirla and his colleagues, who developed the epigenetic view of behavioral development; Harriet Rheingold, who has called for a developmental-comparative psychology for some time; Konrad Lorenz, Iranus Eibl-Eibesfeldt, and other outstanding contributors to ethology; Jean Piaget and Barbel Inhelder and other followers of Piaget; and a number of contributors to modern psycholinguistics.

Specific help with our project has ranged from patient and helpful reading of rough drafts of early chapters by Peter Klopfer, J. R. F. Stadden, and Sandor Friedman of Duke University to the careful line-by-line reviews provided by Merrill F. Elias, Syracuse University; Judith Langlois, University of Texas; William A. Mason, University of California, Davis; and Gary Mitchell, University of California, Davis. Our thanks to the many individuals who have contributed. We are of course fully responsible for the errors and misconceptions that may appear in the completed work.

A special thanks goes to the members of our families who have contributed directly and indirectly to this work. Our wives and children have supported our preoccupation with a task that has taken our effort and theirs. Nedra Seay contributed far above and beyond any wifely duty. She typed the manuscript, did preliminary editorial work, created and maintained the permissions file, and tried to teach us to copy references accurately and legibly. Without her there would have been no book.

This book has provided a great deal of intellectual stimulation and pleasure for the authors. We hope that it is now a source of pleasure and interest for the student. Like any interpretation of data, our interpretations go beyond the data, and like any interpretations ours are fallible. We would like to encourage the student who reads this book to use it and other sources of information to develop his or her own interpretation of the nature of behavioral development. May that student have as much fun (and a little less work for it) as we have had.

Part I
The
Determinants of
Behavior

Chapter 1
An Introduction

The development of a new individual is a fascinating process. Our attention is held by the orderly changes that occur as an organism develops, and we may spend hours simply observing the behavior of a puppy, kitten, or child. If we carefully consider the behavior of organisms, a number of characteristics will be evident in their development. For one thing, development is *species typical.* That is, any animal will behave in some respects like all other members of its species. A kitten will slink and stalk toys, litter mates, and the mother's tail in the same way the mother stalks rats. A puppy will wag its tail, chew and mouth everything, and play tug-of-war with anyone who will cooperate. A child will smile, attempt to talk, look for its mother and perhaps become distressed and cry if she is not in view.

The behavior of developing organisms is related to their level of maturity. The week-old kitten is unable to walk well, cannot see, and does little except eat and sleep. At six weeks of age it is a bundle of activity, plaguing its mother and vigorously exploring its world. A four-week-old child indiscriminately responds to adults; the child's needs may be satisfied by anyone. By eight months children may be shy of strangers and may cry unless familiar adults care for them. At a year the child has a vocabulary of two or three words and communicates nonverbally (although not nonvocally) most of the time. By four years of age he or she has a vocabulary of about fifteen hundred words and effectively communicates with adults and peers. In the above examples, age has been used as a crude indicator of maturation. It must be understood that while age and level of maturity are related, they are not perfectly related. In many respects, one four-year-old child may be more mature than another. The average four-year-old is, of course, more mature in all respects than the average three-year-old.

Developing organisms continuously interact with the environment, and their past experience always influences their present behavior. In some cases, the particular time at which an experience occurs may have important consequences. If a puppy has no experience with human beings before twelve weeks of age, it will be afraid of people and difficult to tame. If it has attention from humans when it is between three and seven weeks of age, it will be affectionate toward people and respond well to opportunities to interact with them. Cats are also difficult to tame if they are isolated from human beings until weaning. Children reared in minimal care orphanages

Figure 1.1
Development

smile less and later than children who receive affectionate attention early in development. Past experience is an important determinant of present behavior.

For children, and perhaps for other primates, the individual's culture also influences the behavior he or she exhibits. For example, the frequency and consequences of aggressive behavior differ among cultures and social classes. The kind and amount of interaction between the child, peers, older and younger children, and adults also varies with the culture. Basic child-rearing practices are an important influence on the child's behavior. For example, the duration of breast feeding or whether breast feeding is practiced varies widely. In some societies, the child may nurse at least occasionally until seven or eight years of age. In contrast, bottle feeding is common in middle-class America. In this culture, breast feeding is usually terminated by six months of age.

The careful observer will note that each organism is unique. A litter of kittens provides an excellent example of individual variability. Although members of a litter share at least one parent and have lived in the same box from birth, the individuals show obvious behavioral differences. A single litter might include timid, adventurous, and placid individuals. In a litter of five kittens, three might be finicky eaters alongside two with good appetites. Four might love attention from humans, while one seems never to relax when held or petted. Although of the same age and raised in the same setting, the individuals in the litter are not, nor do they become, behaviorally homogeneous.

These individual differences have many sources. For one thing, each kitten has a unique genetic composition that influences its behavior. Other bases for individuality include subtle differences in experience. Although the social and physical environments were apparently shared with litter mates, each kitten found unique experiences within that common environment. All kittens were raised by a family that included a four-year-old child, but the four-year-old stepped on only one of them. All were raised in a box with 9-inch sides, but only one climbed out before it was four weeks old. All have the same mother, but only one bit the mother's tail too hard and was swatted by her.

Individual differences can also be observed within a human family with several children. Although some genetic similarity is typical, the actual degree of genetic similarity in siblings can vary from an improbable perfect similarity to an equally improbable complete difference. The odds for either of these occurrences is about 1 in 70 trillion.[1] So there is almost always a potential genetic basis for behavioral differences within a group of siblings. There are also differences in individual experiences that could produce variability in the children's behavior. A mother does not provide the same social environment for her first and for her fourth child. Among other things, she is younger and inexperienced as a mother during the infancy of her firstborn.

The Determinants of Behavioral Development

Throughout this book the determinants of behavior will be described as sets. A *set,* as used here, is a predisposing influence on behavior that either increases or decreases the probability of a developmental or behavioral event. Behavior is never the outcome of the influence of one set alone. Behavior is always the outcome of interaction among the sets we are about to describe.

Phylogenetic Set

An organism inherits genetic codes that under normal circumstances interact with the environment to produce species typical physical and physiological characteristics. Strictly speaking, the only thing inherited is the genotype. The *genotype* is the genetic material an individual organism receives from its parents, from which physical and behavioral traits develop. The *phenotype* refers to the physical and behavioral traits exhibited by an organism. *Phylogenetic Set* is determined by that part of the genotype shared by all members of a species. The expression of this genetic endowment is always a function of the environment. Phenotypes are the result of interactions between genetic and environmental influences. A disturbed prenatal environment may prevent expression of species typical physical characteristics. It is known, for instance, that certain chemicals such as thalidomide will interfere with the limb development of human fetuses.[2] However, in a wide range of circumstances, the most probable result of prenatal development in humans is an infant with fully

1. J. Hirsch, "Behavior Genetics and Individuality Understood," *Science,* 142 (1963), 1436–1442.
2. H. Sjostrom, *Thalidomide and the Power of the Drug Companies,* Penguin Books, Baltimore, 1972.

formed limbs, hands, and feet as programmed by the inherited genetic code. If the prenatal environment is deficient in some respect, the anatomy of the new organism will fail to develop normally. In some cases, children whose mothers took thalidomide during the first three months of pregnancy were born without limbs or with malformed limbs. This example is a particularly unfortunate instance of the dependence of inherited traits upon appropriate environmental conditions for expression.

In this text the word "inherited" will refer to traits that are the typical consequence of development of individuals with particular genotypic traits. Any genetically programmed trait is dependent on a supportive environment for expression.

In a similar fashion, members of a species share genetic codes that have a potential influence on behavior. Inherited behaviors include simple reflexes, which are as resistant to environmental pressures as are physical structures. Knee jerk, startle, plantar, and palmar reflexes are examples. Dysfunction in these basic reflexes is usually indicative of physical, usually neurological, impairment. Some authorities feel that human beings have no inherited behavioral characteristics other than reflexes of this sort.[3] We believe otherwise.

Another kind of inherited behavior is the *fixed action pattern* (FAP), that is, a relatively stereotyped behavior pattern in which an organized sequence of responses is made to a particular stimulus. The FAP was first described and labeled by zoologists, including the Nobel Prize winning ethologists Konrad Lorenz and Niko Tinbergen, who studied birds and fish. These animal forms characteristically demonstrate relatively stereotyped behavior patterns in which an organized sequence of muscle movements is repeated by all normal members of a species in response to a particular stimulus. A stimulus that initiates a fixed action pattern is called a *releaser,* or releasing stimulus. For example, an adult male three-spined stickleback will exhibit a stereotyped form of fighting whenever he is approached by a fish or fishlike object with a red belly. The attack behavior is an FAP and the red belly is the releaser.[4] Another example of an FAP is provided when a nesting goose attempts to

3. A. Montagu, *Culture and the Evolution of Man,* Oxford University Press, London, 1962.

4. N. Tinbergen, *The Study of Instinct,* Oxford University Press, London, 1951.

retrieve any egg that is outside her nest.[5] The egg retrieval response illustrated in Figure 1.2 is a species typical behavior. That is, geese retrieve the egg by means of a predictable sequence of movements. The goose will stretch her neck out until her bill is touching the far side of the egg. She then draws the egg toward the nest while wagging the bill from side to side. If the egg rolls out of the way of the bill, she still completes the stereotyped response, pulling her

5. K. Lorenz and N. Tinbergen, "Taxis and Instinctive Action in the Egg-retrieving Behavior of the Graylag Goose," in *Instinctive Behavior,* ed. and trans. C. H. Schiller, International Universities Press, New York, 1957, pp. 176–208.

Figure 1.2
Egg Retrieval Response of Graylag Goose
(From K. Lorenz and N. Tinbergen, "Taxis und Instinkthandlung in der Eirollbewegung der Graugans," Zeitschrift für Tierpsychologie, 2, 1938, Verlag Paul Parey; pp. 1– 29.)

head all the way back to the nest before she makes another attempt. In this case, stretching out the neck and bringing the head slowly back to the nest is the FAP, and the egg outside the nest is the releaser.

Fixed action patterns in human beings are most evident in infants and young children.[6] The rooting and feeding responses of young infants are excellent examples of highly coordinated sequences of motor movement typically seen in response to specific stimuli. The hungry infant turns its head and body in a way that moves the infant from side to side. When the face contacts a stimulus similar to an erect nipple, the infant quickly takes it into the mouth and begins to nurse. The precision and vigor of this organized sequence of behavior is amazing to the observer or participant expecting an infant to be clumsy, poorly directed, and weak.

Another behavior frequently identified as a human fixed action pattern is smiling, as seen in Figure 1.3. Developing human infants smile at faces and at facelike stimuli from as early as three weeks of age.[7] As infants grow older, visual stimuli must be more and more like a human face to elicit smiling; eventually, particular familiar individuals most readily release smiling. There is considerable dispute over the existence of FAPs in older human beings, but some reported adult FAPs will be described in Chapter 2.

Other species typical behavior patterns may be more environmentally dependent than reflexes or FAPs. Behavior patterns such as male sexual behavior in rhesus monkeys are clearly species typical, but develop only in some environments.[8] Specifically, a male rhesus monkey must have social experience with other monkeys or he will not show normal sexual behavior. One way to interpret this kind of environmental dependence is to conclude that monkeys learn appropriate sexual behavior. This interpretation is incomplete and probably inaccurate. Any other monkey or monkeys appear to provide enough environmental support for adequate development of sexual behavior. The infant monkey can be reared by his mother

6. I. Eibl-Eibesfeldt, *Ethology,* trans. E. Klinghammer, Holt, Rinehart, and Winston, New York, 1970.

7. P. Wolff, "Observations on the Early Development of Smiling," in *Determinants of Infant Behavior,* ed. B. M. Foss, John Wiley, New York, 1963, vol. II, pp. 113–134.

8. B. Seay and N. W. Gottfried, "A Phylogenetic Perspective for Social Behavior in Primates," *Journal of General Psychology,* 92 (1975), 5–17.

Figure 1.3
Smiling Baby
*(Erika Stone from Peter
Arnold.)*

and not allowed contact with other monkeys. He can be removed from the mother and raised in a cage with other infants. He can be raised alone and permitted contact with other babies for thirty minutes a day. In all of these situations, he develops species typical sexual behavior. He need never see adult sexual behavior or, indeed, an adult male to show the appropriate behavior pattern for his species. In a strongly supportive environment that includes a mother and other babies he may exhibit an adult pattern mount before reaching six months of age.

A supportive environment that includes other monkeys appears necessary for the development of male sexual behavior in monkeys.

This does not mean that male sexual behavior is learned. It does help us realize that behavior develops within an environment. The environment necessary for the development of sexual behavior in male rhesus monkeys is always present for a wild-born rhesus monkey. For several months, he must have maternal care or he will die. Typically, he has playmates of his own species as well, since the rhesus is a troop-living monkey. There appears to be a delicate and effective match between inherited behavioral tendencies of the animal and the environment within which he will normally develop. In the case of rhesus male sexual behavior, natural environments that would not support the development of sexual behavior would also not support life.

The development and maintenance of reasonably effective adult behaviors in humans, as in monkeys, requires a supportive social environment. Some of these behaviors are commonly described as learned. Parents arrange for their children to play with age mates so that "they will learn to get along" or "learn to play with other children." The word "learn" describes adequately what the parents mean. It would be a mistake to assume that "learning" as used by these parents refers to the same process as the learning studied by the experimental psychologist in the laboratory. The parents are providing a supportive environment for the development of adequate social behavior. Learning does play a role in human social development, but other processes are also involved.

Species specific *learning dispositions* are another aspect of Phylogenetic Set described by ethologists.[9] As a result of evolutionary development, a member of a given species learns quickly and easily about behaviors that will be important for survival or reproductive success. One species of gull is particularly adept at discriminating slight differences in the mottled pattern of gull eggs.[10] These gulls will learn readily to choose one pattern and reject another. Other related gulls that produce monochromatic unmarked eggs cannot learn such discriminations. The importance of the ability to discriminate between eggs for the first species is clear. The gulls of this species recognize and protect their own clutch of eggs but readily eat those of other members of their species. One psychologist maintains that associations between stimuli and responses are either prepared,

9. Eibl-Eibesfeldt.
10. N. Tinbergen, *The Curious Naturalists,* Basic Books, New York, 1958.

unprepared, or contraprepared in any given species.[11] A *prepared* relationship between stimulation and response patterns is one that is easily learned by the organism. An *unprepared* relationship between stimulation and response patterns is one that can be learned slowly through extensive experience. A *contraprepared* relationship is one that cannot be learned or can be learned only with great difficulty after long periods of exposure.

Learning dispositions are also characteristic of the development of human behavior. Some prepared associations, no doubt, relate to social behavior vitally important for all social primates. A dramatic and important learning disposition in man is the ability to develop speech.[12] More than any other species, human beings have the ability and desire to make noise with the mouth. A person readily imitates the noises other human beings make. Most important, human beings learn to associate these noises with meaning. This unique ability is by no means a simple product of the human intellectual capacity. Very dull human beings learn to speak (although not very well in some cases) and very bright chimpanzees cannot. Recent evidence indicates that chimpanzees can acquire the rudiments of a communication system, but only a gestural or pictorial system, not a spoken one.[13] This suggests that the ability to develop speech is contraprepared in chimpanzees.

Communication skills represent an area of high achievement for the human species. Language greatly simplifies the passage of learned skills from one generation to another. Written language, which is a recent extension of spoken language, permits the storage of information for long periods of time. These unique skills account in large measure for the cultural and technological development of our species.

Ontogenetic Set

Ontogenetic Set is the influence of level of maturation on behavior. As an organism develops, the number and kind of possible patterns of

11. M. E. P. Seligman, "On the Generality of Laws of Learning," *Psychological Review,* 77 (1970), 406–418.

12. C. F. Hackett, *A Course in Modern Linguistics,* University of Chicago Press, Chicago, 1958.

13. A. J. Premack and D. Premack, "Teaching Language to an Ape," *Scientific American,* 227 (1972), 92–99; and R. A. Gardner and B. T. Gardner, "Teaching Sign Language to a Chimpanzee," *Science,* 165 (1969), 664–672.

behavior change. Some changes are primarily the result of physical or physiological development. Others are closely associated with particular environmental characteristics necessary for adequate development. In many instances, a specific level of physical and physiological development and a particular event or series of events are necessary for optimal behavioral development. Frequently, optimal development requires the coincidence of internal and external conditions, that is, a specific level of development must have been attained when a particular external situation is encountered. In this text, the term "ontogenetic development" is used to refer to the development of the individual organism as a function of time and time-related processes.

Although environments influence all behaviors, ontogenetically determined behaviors vary in their degree of environmental dependence. Some behavior patterns, such as locomotion, show minimal dependence on particular environments or experiences. In salamander tadpoles *(amblystoma)*, swimming is relatively independent of preswimming movement experience.[14] In a classic study of motor development, tadpoles were anesthetized before any voluntary movements occurred. They were permitted to recover from anesthesia just after untreated tadpoles of the same age began to swim. Within thirty minutes the previously anesthetized tadpoles were swimming so well that very careful observation would be needed to detect any differences between their behavior and that of untreated tadpoles.

Three aspects of this study are important. First, practice is not necessary for the development of locomotor behavior in this species. Second, the untreated tadpoles show orderly changes in behavior that might lead the unwary observer to conclude that swimming is learned. At first they move clumsily and ineffectively, then they develop slow and ineffective forward motion, and finally, they swim swiftly and efficiently. In this case, orderly progressive changes in behavior are the result of physical maturation rather than the product of practice or experience. Finally, one must remember that anesthesia has some slight effects on tadpole swimming. These effects were not detected in the earliest studies, but more recent

14. L. Carmichael, "The Development of Behavior in Vertebrates Experimentally Removed from the Influence of External Stimulation," *Psychological Review,* 33 (1926), 51–58.

investigations show a slightly reduced efficiency in the swimming of previously anesthetized tadpoles.[15] In behavioral development, maturational and environmental factors are never completely independent.

Studies of locomotor behavior in children also reveal substantial, but not complete, environmental independence. About forty years ago two patterns of child rearing were practiced by Hopi Indians.[16] Some parents used the traditional Hopi practice of keeping babies on cradle boards similar to the one illustrated in Figure 1.4 for much of the day. Other families did not use cradle boards and permitted infants and young children more freedom of movement. The cradle board children had less opportunity to creep, crawl, stand, and walk than did those reared without the use of cradle boards. Yet all the children walked at about the same age. Within rather broad limits, practice or experience was of little importance in the development of walking. It should be remembered, however, that a cradle board permits limb movement. Furthermore, all children were permitted to move about freely for some part of the day. Within these conditions, the onset of walking in children was determined primarily by neuromuscular maturation and depended only minimally on environmental support.

Other ontogenetic aspects of behavioral development are related to interactions with the environment. In *precocial* birds and mammals that are relatively physically mature at birth, social attachment is a rapid process. For example, ducklings, who can walk shortly after hatching, tend to form an attachment to the first moving object they see. This process is called imprinting. In ducks and geese many objects will serve as an imprinting stimulus and need not resemble the mother. The ducklings must form an attachment within a short time after hatching, or no attachment is formed. For a particular species of duck, imprinting can only occur within a specific period of time, for example, eight to twenty hours after hatching. Before that period, the ducklings are unable to follow the mother or other imprinting object. After that period, they not only fail to follow a new object but show fear of new objects, including mother ducks.

15. A. Fromme, "An Experimental Study of the Factors of Maturation and Practice in the Behavioral Development of the Embryo of the Frog *Rana pipiens*," *Genetic Psychology Monographs*, 24 (1941), 219–256.

16. W. Dennis, *The Hopi Child*, John Wiley, New York, 1940.

Figure 1.4
Child on Cradle Board
*(Photo by A. C. Vroman.
Reproduced by
permission of Southwest
Museum.)*

This period within which a behavior or characteristic develops if it is going to develop at all is called a *critical period*. There is some variability in how readily a duckling can imprint within the critical period, and a low probability that it could imprint before eight or after twenty hours. Because the change in capacity for imprinting is not absolute, some authors prefer the term *sensitive period* for this phenomenon. In any case, optimal periods for the development of particular behavior patterns are common.

Sensitive periods can be demonstrated for such diverse phenomena as the development of species specific bird songs in finches, the attachment of dogs for human beings, the development of social behavior in monkeys, and sex role identification in human beings.[17] These very different processes are of course based on different underlying maturational factors. The descriptive term "sensitive period" does prove useful in organizing our thoughts about development. More detailed coverage of this concept will be included in Chapter 3.

Another concept linking ontogenetic development and reactions to the environment is *readiness,* that is, a level of physical and psychological maturity before which particular behavior patterns can be acquired with great difficulty or not at all. In some instances, the bases of readiness for a particular kind of learning experience are clearcut. A child simply cannot be toilet-trained until neuromuscular development has progressed to the point where voluntary control of the sphincter muscles that control urination and defecation is possible. Training before the maturation of the capacity for voluntary control is a waste of time. In fact, such premature training attempts may have unfortunate consequences. If the child is physically unable to accomplish a task of considerable importance to the parent, it will experience some frustration and disturbance. Training that is attempted too early may interfere with toilet training when the child is physically capable of control.

The readiness concept is also used in reference to more complex tasks with less clearcut maturational bases. "Reading readiness" is a frequently used term.[18] While the characteristics of a child who is ready to learn to read are difficult to specify completely, a number of time-dependent processes are involved. The child's perceptual capacity must develop to the point that *b, d, p,* and *q* are seen as different. She or he must be able to attend to a task long enough for teaching to be effective. The child must be able to translate the written symbols into sounds or words. There is, then, a minimal level of maturity that must be reached before one can learn to read. Special techniques may be used to teach reading, or something similar to reading, to children at a lower level of maturity. These

17. J. P. Scott, "Critical Periods in Behavioral Development," *Science,* 138 (1962), 949–958.

18. J. S. Chall, *Learning to Read: The Great Debate,* McGraw-Hill, New York, 1967.

techniques are an important tool in educating children who are immature for their age. We believe these techniques are not advisable for early training of children whose maturity level is average or accelerated for their age.

In summary, attempts to teach a skill before the learner is sufficiently mature can be disastrous. If the learner is unable to perform the required task, he or she will experience failure and frustration. These unpleasant experiences may interfere with later learning when there is an attempt to teach the same tasks. Failure in one task may also influence the learner's attitude toward other learning experiences in the same setting. Because the expected tasks in reading cannot be performed, the child may feel unable to do anything the teacher suggests. In this particular situation, believing does make a thing so.

The changes in behavior that occur as the organism matures are associated with physical and physiological changes. Sometimes the relationship between behavioral and physical maturity is clearcut and simple, as in the development of bowel and bladder control. In most cases the association appears to be more complex and less direct. One of the most striking changes that occurs in ontogenetic development is associated with sexual maturity. At puberty the human organism experiences rapid modification of endocrine function, metabolism, body shape, and behavior. All of these changes occur at about the same time and are intricately interrelated. The modifications of orientation and interests that occur at puberty are among the most interesting of these phenomena. For example, a hosiery ad on television will cause different reactions from pre- and postpubescent males. In the ad, which is similar to the scene depicted in Figure 1.5, a car pulls into view and an attractive model gets out so that her legs are clearly seen. A prepubescent male might at this point comment on the make and model of the car. His father or older brother would be unlikely to recall anything at all about the car. Visual orientation to stimuli associated with sexually attractive females would prevent the mature male from focusing on the automobile. Similar shifts in orientation at maturity occur in females.

Postpubescent children also change in the activities they prefer.[19] Early maturers tend to seek out new friends if their old associates lag too far behind in physical and social development. Games and forms

Figure 1.5
Legs
(Courtesy Volkswagen of America)

---

19. E. Douvan and J. Adelson, *The Adolescent Experience,* John Wiley, New York, 1966.

of play that were interesting a few months ago are now boring and childish. Above all, orientation toward members of the opposite sex shows a striking and abrupt change. Attitudes that ranged from mild distaste to overt hostility shift to intense interest and admiration. In some cases, the shift in interests is not immediately accompanied by changes in social behavior. Pubescent boys may push, hit, or otherwise annoy girls who attract them. These behaviors, which are indices of friendship in a same-sex group, are dropped when they prove to be inadequate in the heterosexual context.

Ontogenetic influences on behavior continue to be important throughout life. Physical and physiological changes continue as long as the organism is alive. Sometimes physical change is gradual and the accompanying behavioral change not particularly dramatic, as during middle childhood or early adulthood. At other times, physical and physiological changes are more rapid and more visible. At times of rapid physical change, striking behavioral changes are also typical. The periods of early childhood, postpubescence, menopause, and advanced old age are noteworthy for rapid physical, physiological, and behavioral changes. Because each level of maturity has an idiosyncratic rhythm of physiological and psychological change, there is a need for scientific study of behavior at all levels of maturity.

Experiential Set

The past experience of an organism is almost always a partial determinant of its present behavior. *Experiential Set* is the influence of past and present environments on behavior. The specific results of a particular experience on an organism will depend on its species, level of maturity, cultural background, and individual characteristics. That is, Phylogenetic Set, Ontogenetic Set, Cultural Set, and Individual Set limit and modify the influence of the environment. The interdependence of behavioral determinants provides the fascination and frustration inherent in the scientific study of behavior.

Some examples of environmental influences on behavior have already been described. In *social animals*, animals that live in groups in the natural habitat, experience with other species members is necessary for adequate development of social behavior. In many species, social isolation creates an environment inadequate to support species typical behavioral development. In some cases, such as the male rhesus monkey described previously, elements of species typical behavior develop, but a coherent and biologically functional pattern of behavior does not develop. Another pattern of dysfunctional behavior may be observed in chickens.[20] A rooster raised in isolation will develop the complete pattern of adult male sexual behavior, including rather complicated courtship movements called "displays." He will never direct these behaviors toward a hen, however. He will display these behaviors toward some other object. If he has been raised with a good deal of experience with human beings, he may court and attempt to copulate with a human. If he has been raised in nearly total isolation, he is likely to direct his sexual behavior repertoire to a feather. In this case the development of the behavior is relatively independent of environmental influence, but appropriate orientation of that behavior is dependent on development within a supportive environment.

The necessary experiences for adequate behavioral development vary both with the species of the developing organism and with the particular behavioral process under consideration. Some patterns of behavior, such as the male sexual response in the rhesus monkey, develop adequately in a number of environments. While all of the environments that have been seen to produce a sexually adequate male rhesus have contained other monkeys, no particular set of experiences appears to underlie normal development of this particular behavior pattern. This type of environmental or experiential dependence may be said to be a nonspecific experiential dependence.

Behavior that is highly important for individual or species survival may have multiple potential bases for adequate development. If any combination of highly likely experiences can support adult reproductive adequacy in a species, that species has a higher probability of surviving than if a specific experiential pattern were required for adult reproductive behavior. Nonspecific environmental dependence would be expected for behaviors of critical importance to the individual's survival and reproductive success.

For many behavioral processes, experience determines the orientation or direction of a behavior pattern rather than the details of behavior. The behavior of the isolated rooster described previously is one example of dependence on experience for appropriate orientation of behavior. A similar, quite specific, experiential dependence

20. A. E. Fisher and E. B. Hale, "Stimulus Determinants of Sexual and Aggressive Behavior in Male Domestic Fowl," *Behaviour,* 10 (1957), 309–323.

is demonstrated in the following behavior of birds that are relatively mature at hatching. These birds will follow many different kinds of objects, but will follow most consistently the first moving object they see. If a brood of ducklings is to show the species typical pattern of following the mother wherever she goes, the mother must be the first moving object seen. For many species, this following response can be reoriented readily to another stimulus—a hen, a man, an orange football, or a rag on the end of a stick.[21] In this case, there is specific environmental dependence for appropriate behavioral orientation.

Much of the effort of scientific psychology since 1900 has been devoted to the study of learning. The treatment of the topic in this book will necessarily be somewhat superficial, and the interested reader will find a number of excellent books available to augment and clarify the material presented here.

Sometimes "learning" is used to refer to almost any experiential dependence. However, in this book the term will be used in a more restricted sense. *Learning* will be defined as a change in behavior associated with practice or experience. A behavior pattern is learned when its appearance is dependent on a particular class of experiences. As noted in the earlier discussion of swimming in salamander tadpoles, it is sometimes difficult to discriminate between behavioral changes based on learning and those that reflect the gradual maturation of neuromuscular systems.

In laboratory studies of animal learning, two major types of learning procedures have been employed. Pavlov, the Russian physiologist, described and popularized a procedure called "classical conditioning." The technique he employed is illustrated in Figure 1.6. In this procedure a stimulus that consistently produces a response pattern before training is begun is selected and labeled an *unconditioned stimulus* (UCS). The response to this stimulus is labeled an *unconditioned response* (UCR). These terms indicate that the relationship between the stimulus and the response was present before conditioning began. In Pavlov's original study, a mild acid placed on a dog's tongue was the unconditioned stimulus and the production of saliva by the dog was the unconditioned response. Meat powder, which also increases salivary flow, was used in Pavlov's studies as another unconditioned stimulus. A second stimulus that is neutral

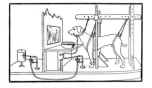

Figure 1.6
Classical Conditioning
Apparatus for Dogs
*(R. M. Yerkes and S.
Morgulis, "The Method of
Pavlov in Animal
Psychology,"* Psychological
Bulletin, *6 (1909), Fig. 2,
p. 264. Copyright 1909 by
the American Psychological
Association. Reprinted by
permission)*

21. W. Slukin, *Imprinting and Early Learning,* Aldine, Chicago, 1965.

with respect to the unconditioned response is selected and labeled a *conditioning stimulus.* A bell or buzzer might be selected as a conditioning stimulus. The procedure then calls for repeated pairings of the conditioning stimulus, the buzzer, with the unconditioned stimulus, the mild acid. The most effective procedure is to begin to sound the buzzer a half second before placing the acid on the dog's tongue, continuing the sound for that half second and while the dog is reacting to the acid.

After many repetitions of the sequence (buzzer—acid—salivation) the dog will begin to salivate after the buzzer begins to sound but before the acid is placed on his tongue. The buzzer may now be referred to as the *conditioned stimulus* (CS) and salivation in response to the buzzer is called a *conditioned response* (CR). This response is not identical to the unconditioned response but is the same kind of response. Differences might include the amount of saliva produced and a longer time between the onset of the conditioned stimulus (CS) and salivation (CR) as compared to the original time between placing acid on the dog's tongue (UCS) and salivation (UCR). After the dog is consistently responding to the CS, the UCS is sometimes discontinued. At first, the dog will respond to the CS by salivating. However, if the CS is repeatedly presented without the UCS, the CR will become weaker and finally stop. That is, the dog will no longer salivate in response to the sound of the buzzer. This procedure, repeatedly presenting the CS without the UCS, is called *extinction.* When the dog no longer salivates, the CR is said to be extinguished.

The other procedure employed in the laboratory studies of learning is called "operant conditioning" or "instrumental learning." The American psychologist B. F. Skinner is the best known scientist using this procedure. In *instrumental learning,* the organism is required to make some specific response in order to receive a reward or reinforcement. (In this text, instrumental learning and *operant conditioning* are considered roughly equivalent.) A common example is a food-deprived white rat that has been placed in a Skinner box like that seen in Figure 1.7. The Skinner box is a small cage equipped with a lever that can operate a reward-producing mechanism. In one frequently used arrangement, the lever can control the operation of a dipper. The dipper is situated so that when the lever is pressed it dips into a sugar-water solution and delivers a small amount to the rat. In a simple kind of instrumental learning, each time the lever is pressed the dipper will operate.

Most often the rat's response to the lever and dipper is *shaped* by an experimenter. When the hungry rat is placed in the Skinner box he will quickly begin to explore this new environment, sniffing the corners and moving about the small enclosure. The experimenter at this point maintains manual control of the dipper mechanism. The rat will first be *dipper-trained*. When he sniffs close to the dipper, the experimenter operates the mechanism that delivers a dipper of sugar-water to the cage. This procedure is repeated until the rat consistently drinks the sugar-water each time it is delivered.

Once dipper training is complete, the shaping procedure begins in earnest. At first, the rat is required only to approach the location of the lever to receive a reward. When he does this consistently, he may be required to touch the lever, and, finally, he must press the lever in order to receive his dipper of sugar water. The experimenter now adjusts the apparatus so that the dipper is automatically operated each time the rat presses the lever. The rat is now in control of the dipper and his lever-pressing response is instrumental in providing him with a reward or reinforcement.

Learning studies with human subjects use procedures similar to those described above. It is interesting that humans, and perhaps some other primates, will learn when the only reward is finding out whether the correct response has been made. A great deal of research has been done on human verbal learning. These investigations have been oriented toward understanding the unique human ability to assign meanings to sounds or printed words and to learn and remember relationships among sounds and words.

Part of the behavioral repertoire of most vertebrate organisms is dependent on learning. The laboratory models described previously represent tools used by psychologists to develop an understanding of this particular kind of Experiential Set. In studying the developing behavior of an organism it is often difficult to determine by observation whether a behavior pattern is the result of maturation or learning. The most common finding when this question is posed is that behaviors are the result of both maturation and learning.

Cultural Set

Cultural Set refers to the influence of a culture on the behavior of members of that culture. A thorough knowledge of a particular culture enables one to predict what most or many members of that culture will do in a given situation. Cultural influences on behavior are limited by phylogenetic and ontogenetic factors. That is, a culture can only foster development of behavioral traits that are consistent with the capacities of its members. One of the characteristics of human beings is the pliability of many behavioral capacities. Thus, cultures can and do produce many diverse behavioral prescriptions or roles. However, the nature of the species requires that certain functions must be provided or the culture will cease to exist.

For example, human beings require some sort of stable social unit to provide care and instruction for their developing young. A number of possible cultural arrangements exist. In our society, a nuclear family consisting of a mated pair and their children with occasional dependent adults is the most frequent model. An alternate model consisting of a woman, her mature daughters, and their immature offspring is found in some social groups. In still other societies, child care is the function of an extended family in which the mature offspring of one family head live close together and cooperate in most aspects of their behavior, including child care. These extended family units may be based either on male or female lineage. In male lineage extended families, child care and education are usually the responsibility of parents and/or grandparents. In female lineage extended families these responsibilities may be fulfilled by either the parents, the maternal grandparents, or the mother and her brothers. The point to remember is that in every viable culture there is a stable social group that provides child care and training.

Cultures can strain or exceed the biological limits within which they must operate. The Marquesans regarded erect breasts as a necessary characteristic for feminine beauty. This was so important that most mothers nursed their infants for a very brief time if at all, believing that nursing would ruin their figures. The infants were fed a thin gruel from birth.[22] These practices no doubt led to high infant mortality rates. One would imagine that this set of practices would lead to extinction of the culture in any but the most favorable environment. This would appear to be a culture that was approaching a biological limit and was reducing the reproductive survival of its members.

Cultures sometimes press ontogenetic limits in the same way they approach phylogenetic limits. In some Eskimo societies, work roles for men and women were prescribed in a way that required a mated pair.[23] Men were not permitted to learn the skills of some aspects of maintaining hunting equipment or preparing their catch for complete use. A marriage partner was therefore essential for economic success. At around twenty years of age this need was considered absolute for young men. If no postpubescent girls were available, the young man would marry the oldest prepubescent girl his family could help him find. However, this arrangement was less than ideal in two respects. First, the young girl acquired considerable responsibility before she was fully trained. Second, her husband was required to conform to the behavioral prescriptions and food taboos expected of adolescent girls, thus reducing his efficiency as a provider. Thus, the culture required behavior that was not consistent with the level of maturity of its members.

Our own culture may impose similar ontogenetic insult with respect to first grade entrance. Children of both sexes are expected to enter the first grade at approximately six years of age. However, it is widely recognized that boys and girls have different levels of

22. R. Linton, "Marquesan Culture," in *The Individual in His Society*, ed. A. Kardiner, Columbia University Press, New York, 1939, pp. 137–196.

23. M. Lantis, "The Social Culture of the Nunivak Eskimo," *Transactions of the American Philosophical Society*, 35 (1946), 153–223.

success in elementary school, with girls, on the average, having a more successful time of it. It is also known that boys are less mature physically than girls of the same age from birth through sexual maturity. It is not totally unreasonable to assume that males are on the average too immature at six years of age to competently handle the tasks imposed on them. Another possibility is that their inability to compete with the more mature girls has an indirect but pervasive influence on their school behavior. The boys do have more difficulty in elementary school than the girls. Some lack of cohesion or fit between the demands of the culture and the Ontogenetic Set of the boys may partially explain their problems.

Cultural Set may modify the expression of Ontogenetic Set. In the previous section, changes at puberty were discussed. Expressions of interest in members of the opposite sex vary widely. In some societies social interaction is encouraged, with the idea that heterosexual social experience is a valuable part of social learning and a good preparation for eventual mate selection. Other societies refuse to leave such important business to children, and the selection of mates is a family responsibility. In these groups, independent heterosexual social behavior is frowned upon, and the sexes may be segregated socially between puberty and marriage. In societies where mate selection is an individual prerogative, at least for one sex, a number of patterns are observed. In our society, courtship is usually an individual matter between the couple, with varying degrees of advice and consent from parents. In some societies, the young man negotiates with the girl's father, with or without her consent. In a number of other societies, a third party is required to approach the girl, to negotiate between families, or to negotiate between the boy and the girl's father.

Individual Set

Individual Set refers to the unique characteristics of the organism that make its behavior unlike that of any other organism. There are two bases of Individual Set. One basis for individuality in behavior and behavioral development is genetic variability. Unless two siblings are produced by the same fertilized egg they will almost never have the same genetic inheritance from their parents. From the moment of conception, the interaction between a unique genetic endowment and an environment results in a developing being that in some respects is different from all other members of its species.

The second basis of individual behavioral variability is related to Experiential Set but refers to specific effects of the environment on the developing organism. Although an animal may share a history of environmental changes with other animals, the effective environment will have been somewhat different for each animal. It is not usually possible, of course, to determine exactly what aspects of a present or past environment have influenced the behavior and development of an individual organism. Differences in the past and present effective environments for individual organisms constitute the second basis for Individual Set.

One procedure that has been used to study genetic influences on the behavior of laboratory animals is selective breeding. In a classic study by Tryon, a University of California psychologist, laboratory rats were selectively bred for their ability to run a seventeen-unit, automated, multiple T-maze.[24] A group of rats learned to run the maze for food reward, and the fastest and slowest learners were selected from the group. Fast learners were bred with fast learners and slow learners with other slow learners. After the original selection, each generation was tested. The fastest of the fast learners were bred with siblings who were also fast learners, while the slowest of the slow learners were bred with slow-learning siblings. After several generations two strains of rats were produced. The descendants of the fast learners, the maze-bright strain, all learned the maze faster than almost any of the descendants of the slow learners, the maze-dull strain, could learn it. The progressive separation of the two strains is illustrated in Figure 1.8. It is important to note that this difference in learning ability was specific to the maze used for selecting the strains. In other learning tasks, even other kinds of mazes, the maze-dull strain was sometimes brighter than the maze-bright strain. The selection was for some trait advantageous in that particular maze but not effective in other situations.

Similar selective breeding studies using various animal species show that most behavior that varies within a species can be the basis for successful selective breeding. However, there are some limits; for example, one attempt to selectively breed rats for activity level was abandoned when the inactive strain became so inactive that it failed to reproduce. Occasionally, when a strain has been selected for one

24. R. C. Tryon, "Individual Differences," in *Comparative Psychology,* ed. F. A. Moss, Prentice-Hall, Englewood Cliffs, N.J., 1942, pp. 409–448.

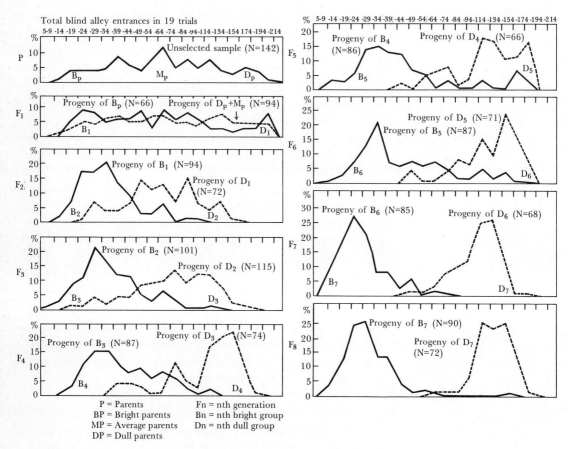

Figure 1.8
The Performance of Maze
(From R. C. Tryon, "Individual Differences," in F. A. Moss, Ed. Comparative
Psychology, *1942. Adapted by permission of Prentice-Hall, Inc., Englewood
Cliffs, New Jersey.)*

trait, other characteristics will be developed that prove undesirable
or, as in the case of the inactive rats, not viable.

Another technique used in the study of genetic influences on
behavior is to compare the behaviors of existing strains. A number
of strains of rats and mice are commercially available. Within each
strain, after many generations of inbreeding there is relatively low
genetic variability. Two or more strains might be tested on some
particular behaviors of interest such as activity level, learning ability,

or any other measurable response. The two strains may then be crossed, and the offspring bred to each other and back to the two parent strains. Studies of this sort help to determine the degree of genetic influence on a particular behavior and the pattern of inheritance associated with particular behavioral influences.

Genetic influences on behavior are also demonstrated in various domestic animals. Inherited differences in behavioral traits are particularly evident in different purebred dogs.[25] No experienced hunter would buy a new dog that was not of a breed known for its ability to learn hunting readily. Further, the hunter would prefer a dog whose parents were known to have the behavioral traits he wanted. For some dog breeds, an understanding of the traits of the breed are essential for an owner to appreciate and enjoy the pet.

While genetic influences on animal behavior appear to be well documented and widely accepted, there is a great deal of controversy concerning genetic influence on human behavior. Part of this controversy is oriented around race and racial differences in behavior and in particular racial differences in intelligence. While this topic will be dealt with in more detail in later chapters, a few comments seem appropriate here.

There is a great deal of difference between "race" as the term is used in classical genetics and "race" as socially defined in the United States and some other countries. In genetics, "race" has sometimes been used as a synonym for subspecies. A *subspecies* is a relatively isolated breeding group within a species. A large number of generations of exclusive breeding within some subpopulation of a species is necessary to produce a subspecies that differs in some respects from the rest of the species. It is obvious that blacks in the United States do not constitute a subspecies. Race in this country is socially defined. Any degree of recognized African ancestry is usually considered the basis for assignment to this social grouping. Furthermore, the original sources of African ancestry for many American blacks derive from more than one area of that continent. That is to say that even an individual of pure African descent is likely to be descended from several different breeding populations. Many American blacks have genetic backgrounds that derive from European, African, and

25. J. P. Scott and J. L. Fuller, *Genetics and Social Behavior of the Dog,* University of Chicago Press, Chicago, 1965.

American Indian ancestors. Therefore, any hypotheses concerning racial inheritance that are based on the assumption that American blacks are a race in the genetic sense of subspecies have no basis in fact.

Flaws in many discussions of the inheritance of intelligence involve some misunderstanding of both inheritance and intelligence. Briefly, one does not inherit a trait, such as intelligence, from the parents. One inherits a biochemical code that interacts with and is dependent upon the environment for expression. There is no gene for intelligence. There are specific genetic codes that if expressed may tend to increase or decrease the intellectual capacity of the organism. Intelligence is not a simple characteristic, and any measure of intelligence is subject to a number of errors. In particular, tests of intelligence are subject to cultural bias, so that individuals from different cultures will have different scores, independently of any difference in intellectual capacity. Since we know that there are cultural differences between socially defined races in the United States, it is evident that the intelligence tests presently in wide use cannot be used to determine genetically related differences in intellectual capacity between blacks and whites.

Neither blacks nor whites in the United States constitute a genetically defined race. Even if they did, intelligence tests could not be used to test for inherent differences in intellectual capacity, since the several subcultures that encompass these groups differ sufficiently to produce different test scores independently of differences in intellectual capacity. Thus, any discussion of inherited differences in intelligence between these two socially defined groups seems to have no reasonable basis.

A similar rejection of racism and of nonsensical discussions of "racial" differences has led many social scientists to reject genetic influences on human behavior. However, this is a case of throwing out the baby with the bath, for the behavior of individual human beings does reflect the influence of the individual's genetic background. If we knew, for several generations, the characteristics of the ancestors of an individual, we would be able to make a number of fairly accurate predictions concerning his or her behavior. In practice, we do not usually have this information, and the unique genetic background of the individual is therefore a source of unpredictable variability in individual behavior. We would never be able to precisely determine the genetic makeup of the individual even if we had a complete genealogy. This source of Individual Set will plague or intrigue us in every case of individual behavior.

Interacting with the unique genetic makeup of the individual are particular past and present effective environments. Any two organisms will have different experiences with the same environment. It is unlikely that the sensory systems of two individual animals would be identical in sensitivity and discriminatory power. In addition, the orientation and focusing of sensory processes is likely to differ between two organisms. Thus, the same objective environment will differentially affect different individuals. If two animals are of the same species and level of maturity, and if they have similar experiential histories, these differences may be slight but they are always present. This means that identical stimulation of two organisms is rarely, if ever, accomplished. A part of the ever present individual variability in behavior is attributed to differences in the effective environment for any two behaving organisms.

Dynamic Interaction

Any behavior in an organism is the result of dynamic interaction among the five determinants of behavior described in the previous section. These determinants, Phylogenetic Set, Ontogenetic Set, Experiential Set, Cultural Set, and Individual Set never act independently of one another. Their action is interdependent, and one determinant can augment, modify, or negate the influence of another. Behavioral determination is always probabilistic. No behavioral outcome is the inevitable outcome in every case of a particular Phylogenetic Set across all possible environments. Nor is the behavioral outcome of a particular series of experiences (Experiential Set) inevitable for every individual in a species. No behavioral prescription, however strongly sanctioned within a culture, will be followed by every individual within that culture.

The more precisely one can determine the characteristics of the individual organism, the more accurately one can predict and understand that organism's behavior. This determination can be made accurately only if information about the typical behavior of an organism of the species, as well as level of maturity, experiential history, and cultural background of the specific individual is available. In every case, variability will characterize the behavior of organisms, and some individuals will differ in their behavior from most of their fellows.

The selection of the five determinants of behavior we have used is arbitrary. Those characteristics of the organism and its environment that determine its behavior might have been organized differently. The organization of ideas presented here is intended to help the reader think about and discuss the processes involved in the development of behavior. In subsequent chapters each of these influences on behavioral development will be discussed in greater detail. In the second section of the book, the process of development will be presented in terms of this classification of behavioral determinants and the dynamic interaction among these determinants.

Human and Animal Behavior

A key issue in behavioral science is the relationship between human behavior and the behavior of other animals. There are a number of attitudes toward this issue. In this book, humankind will be viewed as a species. Like all animal species, our species has many unique behavioral characteristics. Since behavior differs between species, the behavior of one species cannot provide final answers concerning the behavior of another, even if the species are closely related. Behavioral information from one species can provide suggestions about the behavior of another, and in some cases these suggestions may be the best available information about the behavior in question. More frequently, information from one species may provide valuable supplementary information for someone trying to understand another species.

In the case of human behavior, information from other species is particularly important. Certain studies, such as a mother-infant separation study, simply cannot ethically use human subjects. Children can, of course, be observed when separation from the mother is necessary. Observational studies of this kind are important, but interpretation is often difficult because of factors other than the separation itself. If a child is in a hospital that does not permit the mother's presence, the child's behavior after separation from the mother can be observed and recorded. However, several other things may also affect the child's behavior in this situation. In addition to separation, the child faces illness, a strange place, and strange adults in forbidding costumes. This situation is depicted in Figure 1.9. On the other hand, the scientist who wants to understand the effects of mother-infant separation cannot ethically separate the child from the mother experimentally, since immediate discomfort and long-term psychological damage might result.

Figure 1.9
Children's Ward
*(Francis Laping/Design
Photographers
International, Inc.)*

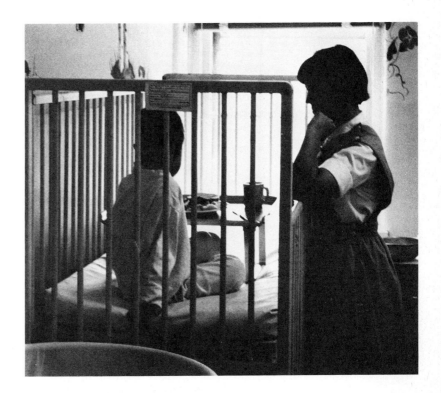

One way to approach this problem is to use both naturalistic studies of children who must be separated from their mothers and experimentally produced data from studies of mother-infant separation in other species. Experimental studies of infant-mother separation have used the rhesus and other monkey species.[26] The infant rhesus monkey reacts to maternal loss in much the same way as a hospitalized child reacts to hospitalization and separation from the mother.[27] While the monkey's behavior cannot provide absolute information about the child, the monkey data strongly support the idea that the child's disturbance is more closely related to absence of the mother than to hospitalization. The data from one species provide hypotheses and suggestions about the behavior of another, broadening our understanding of both species. These monkey separation studies provide an example of the use of animals as models in research. That is, the monkeys were used as substitutes for humans,

26. Seay and Gottfried.

27. J. Bowlby, *Attachment and Loss: Attachment,* Basic Books, New York, 1969, vol. I.

mostly because such experiments with human children would be unethical.

Another advantage of animal behavior observations as an aid in understanding human behavior is objectivity. The observer may be more objective about the behavior of the nonhuman species. When we watch human behavior we may want to see certain things and not see others. Such bias may also affect our observation and interpretation of the behavior of other animals, but it is less likely. The bias that creeps into studies of human beings can be illustrated by a dispute among psychoanalysts. The dispute concerned whether young infants direct coital-like pelvic thrusts against their mothers' bodies. Some authorities stoutly denied that presexual behavior of this sort was seen in six- to eight-month-old children. A psychoanalyst reporting the thrusting behavior contacted scientists who observed monkey mother-infant interactions and asked if this pattern was characteristic of infant monkeys. The primatologists consulted their data and discovered that the pattern was infrequent but occurred at least once in most observed babies.[28] These monkey observations, which were not considered important or exciting by the primatologists, served to increase the confidence of the psychoanalyst in her observations of the behavior in human children.

Animal subjects are frequently used in studies of genetic influences on behavior. Animals with behavioral traits of interest can be selected for controlled mating. Many animal forms have short life spans compared to that of human beings, and the time between generations is also short. In the case of laboratory rats, which reproduce at sixty days of age, studies of genetic influences on behavior spanning many generations are possible. Similar studies involving human beings might take centuries to complete.

General principles of behavioral development are even more important than are the specific behaviors or reactions discussed above. All of life is related, and it is reasonable to assume that general principles of growth and development will apply broadly to related organisms. Because of the limitations imposed by ethical considerations and the long, slow development of individual human beings, our information about human behavior is necessarily limited and imperfect. General principles based on human data should make sense in terms of more complete data derived from animal

28. H. F. Harlow, Personal Communication.

observations. The simpler explanations of human behavior are sometimes fitting when animals and human beings show the same behavioral reactions to a situation. The simpler explanations are acceptable because we believe the animals studied need not experience the complicated psychological processes attributed to human beings in the same situation. For example, it is difficult to believe that an infant monkey is upset when the mother is taken from it because it had hostile fantasies of eating the mother up and now believes that it has done so. The similarity of the reaction of the monkey and the human child raises serious questions about the validity of the more complex interpretation of human behavior. Some single set of factors should account for the disturbance seen in both species after maternal separation.

While the study of animal behavior is an aid in understanding human behavior, interest in animal behavior can be intrinsic. Any living species can be a source of wonder and delight. The more one knows about a species, the more interesting it becomes. One cannot know whether study of a particular species will or will not help in understanding another species. Many scientists study animal behavior in an attempt to increase understanding of one small part of our universe with no particular intention of illuminating any other area. Since all knowledge is interrelated, however, any new information has a potential value for other species and other sciences.

Summary

The development of behavior is a result of interactions among five behavioral determinants. These partial determinants are associated with increases or decreases in the probability of a given behavior, but one can never make absolute predictions of the behavior of an individual organism. Phylogenetic Set refers to the behavioral influences associated with the species of an organism. Members of the same species share genetically coded characteristics that partially determine their behavioral repertoire. Ontogenetic Set is the influence of maturational level on behavior: as an organism matures its behavior and behavioral tendencies change. Experiential Set is the influence of the past and immediate environment on the behavior of an organism.

Environmental dependence may be nonspecific or specific. Nonspecific environmental dependence is present when particular behaviors develop in animals within a wide range of environments but do not develop in animals exposed to environments outside this range. Specific environmental dependence requires that organisms exhibiting a particular behavioral trait share an experiential history.

Cultural Set is most clearly demonstrated in human beings. Members of a culture share a common body of environmental experiences that tend to result in similar behavioral repertoires and expectations among members. Individual Set refers to the unique characteristics of each organism that produce ever present individual variability in behavior. Individual set has two bases. First, every organism has a unique genetic makeup. Development is the result of interaction between genetic makeup and the environment. As a result of this interaction, the individual's behavior will be different in some respects from that of all other organisms. Second, the effects of any environment will be somewhat different for any two individuals. Behavior is therefore always influenced by the individual differences characteristic of all organisms.

Defined Terms

Species typical
Set
Genotype
Phenotype
Phylogenetic Set
Fixed action pattern
Releaser
Learning disposition
Prepared
Unprepared
Contraprepared
Ontogenetic Set
Amblystoma

Precocial
Imprinting
Critical period
Sensitive period
Readiness
Experiential Set
Social animals
Learning
Unconditioned
  stimulus
Unconditioned
  response
Conditioning
  stimulus

Conditioned stimulus
Conditioned
  response
Extinction
Instrumental
  learning
Operant conditioning
Shaped
Dipper-trained
Cultural Set
Individual Set
Subspecies

Suggested Readings

The short books listed here will provide the interested reader with brief introductions to human and animal behavior and development from several different points of view. Readings relevant to specific topics will be listed at the end of each chapter.

D. Elkind, *A Sympathetic Understanding of the Child: Birth to Sixteen,* Allyn and Bacon, Boston, 1974.

A general overview of mental, personal, and social development in children. The book is written for the general reader with minimal background in psychology and child development and contains an excellent brief annotated bibliography.

K. Lorenz, *King Solomon's Ring,* Crowell, New York, 1952.

A delightful introduction to animal behavior study by the Nobel Prize winning father of modern ethology. This book is written for the general reader and is highly recommended for any student of behavior.

K. Lovell, *An Introduction to Human Development,* ed. D. Elkind, Scott Foresman, Glenview, Illinois, 1971.

A discussion of human development that emphasizes the results of psychological research. Many areas are covered, and are presented from a cognitive point of view.

A. Manning, *An Introduction to Animal Behavior,* 2nd ed., Addison Wesley, Reading, Mass., 1972.

A brief introduction to animal behavior incorporating the findings of ethologists and experimental psychologists. This book contains an excellent section on the evolution of behavior.

P. Muller, *The Tasks of Childhood,* trans. A. Mason, McGraw Hill, New York, 1969.

A review of development. The first part of the book deals topically with a number of areas including intelligence and social development. The second half of the book sketches development from birth to adolescence from an age-stage perspective.

J. P. Scott, *Animal Behavior,* University of Chicago Press, Chicago, 1958.

This book presents animal behavior from the perspective of traditional American comparative psychology. Strongly recommended for psychology majors with an interest in comparative or developmental psychology.

Chapter 2
Phylogenetic Set

In Chapter 1 we stated that behavior is *species typical*—that is, an individual's behavior is likely to be similar in many respects to that of other members of his or her species and different from the behavior of members of another species. Even when behavioral patterns of different species might be equivalent in some way, their behavior is likely to demonstrate species typical elements. Fighting in sheep and goats, illustrated in Figure 2.1, provides an example of behavioral differences between species.[1] When two rams fight, they usually back off from one another, lower their heads, run toward each other, and butt heads. Male goats, called bucks, typically rear on their hind legs and hook to one side with their heads, striking their horns together as they come down. These differences in fighting patterns probably prevent fights between rams and bucks.

Fighting behavior of sheep and goats, respectively, is an expression of Phylogenetic Set. Genetically programmed differences between these two species insure, with a high probability, that individual members of each species will exhibit the fighting pattern typical for the species. Specific physical, physiological, and behavioral elements underlie the differences in fighting patterns observed in these species. The appearance of species typical fighting behavior requires adequate development of these genetic elements and also depends on a supportive early environment for the individual sheep or goat.

It is important to remember that, strictly speaking, a behavior pattern cannot be inherited. What is inherited is a particular arrangement of molecules comprising the genetic code. A part of any individual's genetic makeup is shared with all other members of her or his species. When a behavior pattern emerges as the result of maturation in most environments encountered by members of a particular species, we may conclude that the behavior in question is an expression of species general genetic coding. This is another way of saying that the behavior is partially determined by Phylogenetic Set. Phylogenetic Set is the influence of species general genetic characteristics on behavior.

In the next two sections of this chapter, several basic concepts of biological evolution and the evolution of behavior will be introduced.

1. J. P. Scott, "Comparative Social Psychology," in *Principles of Comparative Psychology*, eds. R. H. Waters, D. A. Rethlingshafer, and W. E. Caldwell, McGraw Hill, New York, 1960, pp. 250–278.

Figure 2.1
Fighting Patterns in Sheep and Goats *(Len Rue, Jr./Photo Researchers, Inc.)*

This introduction to evolution will necessarily be brief and somewhat oversimplified. A list of suggested readings at the end of the chapter will serve to augment the coverage of the topics presented here.

Introduction to Evolution

The theory of biological evolution presented by Charles Darwin, and subsequently refined, provides the central concepts for modern biological science. General principles derived from the study of the development and diversification of living forms have many implications for all branches of biological and social science. In the study of behavior and behavioral development, an appreciation of animal diversity and evolutionary processes is essential.

The Survival of the Fittest

Modern evolutionary theory differs in several respects from some generally held ideas deriving from Darwinian theory. One important key to understanding evolutionary processes is the principle that evolution is a characteristic of populations of animals and not of individuals.[2] In this context, a *population* is an interbreeding group

2. T. Dobzhansky, *Genetics and the Origin of Species,* Columbia University Press, New York, 1941.

of animals, all members of some species. The genetic composition of an individual is fixed, and the individual cannot respond to adaptive pressure by genetic modification. However, the genetic composition of a population can and does respond to adaptive pressure. Micro-evolutionary changes in a population can lead to the development of a new species. The term "survival of the fittest" is frequently inter-preted to mean a battle among competing forms, only one of which survives to reproduce. In fact, evolutionary change is rarely so abrupt and absolute. Typically, adaptive pressure produces slight differences in reproductive survival between individuals expressing a particular trait and those not expressing that trait.

The gradual nature of evolutionary change is easier to understand when one comprehends the length of time involved. In considering the time since life began, it may be helpful to use a more familiar scale than the millions of years that sometimes are hard to compre-hend. G. G. Simpson provides a helpful analogy.[3] Let us assume that life began on earth at twelve midnight last night, and it is now twelve

3. G. G. Simpson and W. S. Beck, *Life: An Introduction to Biology,* shorter ed., Harcourt, Brace, and World, New York, 1969, p. 479.

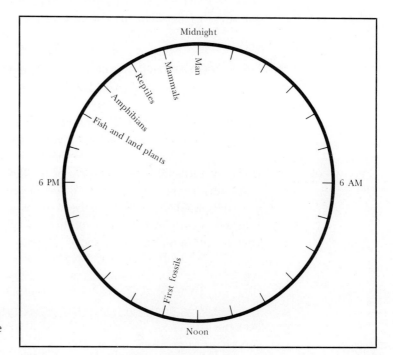

Figure 2.2
The Order of Appearance
of Living Forms

midnight again. A twenty-four-hour clock showing the order of appearance of various forms is shown in Figure 2.2. It took all morning and a little more for living forms sufficiently large and complex to leave fossils to develop. The first living forms to leave fossils appeared at 1:00 in the afternoon. Fish and land plants did not appear until nearly 8:00 P.M., and amphibians were not around until 8:30. By 9:30 P.M. reptiles were on the scene. Not until 11:00 did the first mammals develop. And just now, at 11:59 P.M., man appeared on the planet.

Variation and Change

Evolutionary development is a result of the combined effects of genetic and chromosomal mutation, adaptive pressure, and genetic drift. Genetic information is carried by long complex DNA molecules called *chromosomes. Mutations* are changes in these complex macromolecules. A location on a chromosome that is related to some specific trait is called a *gene.* A change in the precise chemical composition at such a location is a genetic mutation. Gene mutations are one kind of mutation. Chromosomal mutations include loss, duplication, inversion, or translocation of parts of chromosomes. In this chapter, only gene mutation and the evolutionary implications of this process will be considered. A more detailed presentation of genetic mechanisms can be found in Chapter 6.

For any species there is a specific number of types of chromosomes. This number is designated "N." This number indicates the number of pairs of chromosomes found in most cells of a member of a species. For human beings N equals twenty-three, and most of the cells of our bodies contain twenty-three pairs of chromosomes, or forty-six chromosomes. Cells that contain two N chromosomes are called *diploid* cells. In our species, the primary reproductive cells, the *sperm* and *ova,* contain only N chromosomes. Cells with N chromosomes are called *haploid* cells.

Actually, only female human beings have twenty-three pairs of chromosomes in diploid cells. In the place of the twenty-third pair, males have one X and one Y chromosome. The twenty-two pairs of chromosomes are distinguishably different when seen under an electron microscope. The X and Y chromosomes are also distinguishable. In sexual reproduction the new individual receives N chromosomes from each parent, and these complex molecules of DNA constitute all that is inherited.

In the simplest case of genetic influence, a trait is influenced in some way by a single gene or locus on a particular type of chromosome. For example, hairy ears are associated with a particular gene locus on the Y chromosome.[4] If a chromosome varies at a particular location, the gene at that location is said to have multiple alleles. *Alleles* are gene variants, located at the same point on a particular type of chromosome, which differentially affect the same trait. If alleles exist for a gene locus on a chromosome type, one and only one allele will be at that locus on any chromosome of that type. Two alleles of a particular gene produce three possible genotypes for that gene. In a common example, the allele for brown eye color is labeled B and the allele for the blue color is labeled b. The three possible genotypes for this gene are *homozygous* for brown (BB), homozygous for blue (bb), and *heterozygous* (Bb). In this case, the relationship between the alleles is said to be a case of Mendelian dominance. Individuals with the genotypes BB and Bb have brown eyes, and individuals with the genotype bb have blue eyes. The allele for brown eye color is said to be dominant over the allele for blue eye color. In a dominance relationship of this sort, two genotypes, BB and Bb, are expressed by identical phenotypes or appearances, while a third genotype, bb, is expressed by a different phenotype.

A simple relationship between two variants at a single gene locus expressed as a qualitative character such as eye color is rare. Many traits are influenced by *polygenetic* systems in which genes from several sites interact to influence the phenotype. Height in human beings is an example of a trait under the influence of a polygenetic system. Sometimes a gene has a relationship with more than one phenotypic trait.

A mutation is said to have occurred when there has been a change from one allele to another. If a person whose parents are both homozygous for a particular allele shows a phenotype indicating that he or she is heterozygous, then a mutation has occurred. Thus, two blue-eyed parents could produce a brown-eyed child if the mutation b → B occurred during the production of sperm or ova in one of the parents. Normally, the rate of genetic mutation is very low.

Genetic mutation provides the raw material for evolutionary change. Chromosomal mutations provide unique recombinations of genetic material, but evolutionary development is ultimately dependent on the actual modification of DNA structure, which is identified

4. R. R. Gates, *Human Genetics*, Macmillan, New York, 1946.

as genetic mutation. In a population, mutations are random and may occur in any direction. Progressive change in adaptation, which is evolution, could not take place unless some process other than random mutation occurred. This process is called *selection*.

Selective adaptive change in a population gene pool occurs gradually over a considerable period of time. If a new trait has adaptive value or if the adaptive value of present traits changes due to environmental change, the distribution of various alleles in the population gene pool will also change. Adaptive value refers to the reproductive survival of individuals possessing a trait. A very slight difference in reproductive success between individuals expressing a trait and those not expressing that trait is sufficient to change the population genetic composition. In this way, environmental pressures interact with the genetic variability already present in a population and with mutations to modify the genetic composition of an interbreeding group of animals.

New species of animals may appear through successive or divergent evolution. In successive evolution, small changes occur in successive generations of a population. Across a very long time period, these changes are sufficiently great that the organisms living at the beginning of the period are not reasonably classified as the same species as the organisms living at the end. There are, of course, intermediate forms during the period so that a point in time can be arbitrarily assigned to separate successive species. This taxonomic convention permits assignment of all animals to a reasonable number of categories.

In divergent speciation, two or more independent populations develop from one parental population. Sometimes this development begins when some members of a population migrate geographically. Whether through geographic separation or otherwise, one group of descendants of the parent population becomes reproductively isolated from another group. If the two descendent populations redevelop genetic interchange at a later time, divergent speciation may not continue, and the period of genetic independence may be a phase in sequential evolution. If independent adaptive change continues for a very long time, the two populations may come to differ sufficiently to justify classification as different species. In general, members of different species do not interbreed fertilely under natural conditions. There are a few exceptions to this general rule, particularly among primates. In many cases there is no evidence concerning mating between species, and classification is based on physical and physiological differences and similarities among populations. *Sympatric* species occupy the same general locale. *Allopatric* species occupy different geographic localities. In sympatric species interbreeding may be inhibited by behavioral differences that prevent interspecific mating or by genetic differences that prevent the development of viable hybrids. In rare cases interspecific hybrids occur in nature, but these are typically infertile or markedly less fertile than members of either parent species.

Genetic drift refers to changes in population gene pools other than reactions to selection pressure. Such changes do not reflect adaptation and may even be maladaptive. There is considerable disagreement as to the role genetic drift has played in evolution. Without selection pressure, it is very unlikely that a genetic trait will change in a large population. In small populations, genetic drift is more likely to produce changes in the population gene pool from one generation to the next. A complicating factor is that many species are divided into partially isolated breeding groups called *demes.* There is some genetic interchange between demes, but most breeding occurs within the deme. The deme may be relatively small even in a large population. Genetic drift could then change the composition of a deme, although subsequent spread in the population would still depend on adaptive pressure.

This brief summary of the processes involved in the development of animal species is necessarily oversimplified. The interested reader will find more complete coverage of this topic in the readings listed at the end of the chapter. The development of species is sometimes called microevolution. Most authorities are in agreement with the view summarized above concerning speciation. The evolution of higher taxonomic categories, such as genus, family, order, and so forth, sometimes called macroevolution and megaevolution, is the subject of more discussion and more divergence of opinion. There is general agreement, however, that evolution always involves selective pressure on genetically based variability in populations, with mutation providing the basic source of new variability.

| The Evolution of Behavior | George Gaylord Simpson the American evolutionary theorist has said that most dynamic evolutionary changes involve changes in the organism-environment interaction.[5] This statement implies that |

5. G. G. Simpson, *The Major Features of Evolution,* Columbia University Press, New York, 1953.

most evolutionary changes involve changes in behavior. Behavioral changes are particularly evident when the adaptive changes are related to the environment. The potential range of evolutionary modification of behavior is so great that it is difficult to comprehend. Behavioral reflection of genetic composition may be direct or indirect. On rare occasions, it may reflect a specific allele at one locus. Most commonly, observed behaviors demonstrate quantitative variations apparently associated with the action of many genes. Behavioral change as a function of selection pressure is gradual, involving simultaneous modification of both behavior and the physical structure of the organism.

Striking evidence for evolutionary diversification is frequently found on oceanic islands that have been populated by a few immigrant species. Darwin's observations of the animal inhabitants of the Galapagos Islands shaped his thinking concerning evolution. One group of birds, Darwin's finches, shown in Figure 2.3, provides a familiar example of structural and behavioral evolution.[6] By chance, one species came to occupy the island group. In the absence of other land birds, the single species was able to invade and utilize ecological niches not available to it in an occupied region. From the original immigrant species, fourteen distinguishable species of birds gradually developed.

The birds least divergent from the original stock constitute a genus of six species of ground finches. Three of them are seed eaters, primarily differentiated by size, beak size, and the size of the seed they eat. It is supposed that each of the three species developed on an isolated island in the group and later came to inhabit the same areas. A low degree of competition for food permits these three species to live together.

A fourth species of ground finch with a longer, more pointed beak than the seed eaters feeds primarily on the prickly pear. Two other species live on isolated islands, feeding on ground seeds and cactus. They too have sharper beaks than the three ground seed eaters.

The second major genus of Darwin's finches are tree finches. These are large, medium, and small birds, and presumably they feed primarily on large, medium, and small insects. Another species occupies humid mangrove swamps and feeds on insects. The remaining two species of the genus show remarkable behavioral and structural adaptations. One has developed a parrotlike beak, feeds

6. D. Lack, "Darwin's Finches," *Scientific American*, 188 (1953), 67–72.

on plant buds and fruit, and is totally vegetarian. The other, sometimes called a woodpecker finch, has a strong, straight beak that bores into bark for insects. Unlike the woodpecker, its tongue is too short to probe the openings in wood. To capture its insect prey, the woodpecker finch inserts a thorn or twig into the hole it has bored.

The remaining two species each constitute a separate genus. One of these occurs only on Cocos Island. The other, the warbler finch, is so similar to true warblers in appearance and behavior that it was classified for more than one hundred years as a warbler. Recent evidence indicates that the warbler finch is another example of evolutionary development from the basic ground finch stock. The warbler finch has a slender beak and picks insects from leaves. Occasionally it catches insects in flight like a warbler.

These remarkable evolutionary developments took the form of concurrent gradual modifications of behavior and structure. The transformation of a seed-eating ground finch into a jack-leg woodpecker is not a simple matter of gradual structural change. Nor is the evolutionary change primarily behavioral. Behavior and structure had to change together in minute increments, each shift making possible further modification of the organism. In the woodpecker finch we see a case in which a behavioral adaptation, the use of thorn probes, serves a function otherwise undertaken by an analogous structural adaptation, a long, sticky tongue, in true woodpeckers.

| Categories of Inherited Behavior | Inherited behaviors, like inherited morphological features, unfold in individual development. In taking this point of view we must remember that for behavior and structure, a phenotypic trait is never set by the genotype; it is potentiated by the genotype. In the following discussion of inherited behavior, the reader should keep in mind that every trait said to be inherited is in some way dependent on the environment for its development and expression. |

| Reflexes | Behavior that reflects species general genetic coding includes a wide range of responses and behavioral tendencies. Many reflexes are characteristic of most members of a particular species. A *reflex* is a more or less automatic response to a specific stimulus. These relatively simple responses to stimulation, including knee-jerk, startle, and plantar reflexes, are so stereotyped in human beings that they |

are used for diagnostic purposes by physicians. Some reflexive behavior, such as withdrawal from a pin prick, requires only an intact and normally developed spinal cord. However, other fairly automatic and consistent reflexes do not appear if the organism has developed in a nonsupportive environment. For example, chimpanzees reared in the dark for several months do not show protective eye blink responses for some time after introduction to light.[7] Interpretation of this finding is complicated by partial retinal atrophy in the dark-reared chimps. The evidence strongly indicates that the development of a species typical repertoire of reflexive responses is environmentally dependent.

Kineses and Taxes

Other more coordinated patterns of response to stimulation are called kineses and taxes. *Kinesis* refers to a change in movement in response to a stimulus. In some organisms, such as the wood louse, a kinesis results in clumping or grouping of animals in one area. In the wood louse this is a result of the influence of increasing humidity on movement.[8] As humidity increases, the number of motionless wood lice increases, so that the animals congregate in damp places. *Taxes* are directional orientations often associated with movement toward or away from a source of stimulation. Many fish are positively phototaxic, swimming toward a source of light.[9] The wood tick is negatively geotaxic, climbing to the top end of a grass stem or twig.[10] Taxes in different organisms are not necessarily based on similar underlying mechanisms. The term does, however, provide a useful category for one kind of species general stereotyped behavior.

Fixed Action Patterns

Species typical behaviors labeled as fixed action patterns have been the subject of intensive study by ethologists. Their initial concern was to use behavioral characteristics as an aid in taxonomic classification. A great deal of research has been done to demonstrate the relation-

---

7. A. H. Riesen, "Arrested Vision," *Scientific American,* 183 (1950), 16–19.

8. G. Fraenkel and D. Gunn, *The Orientation of Animals,* Dover, New York, 1940.

9. V. G. Dethier and E. Stellar, *Animal Behavior,* 3rd ed., Prentice-Hall, Englewood Cliffs, N.J., 1970.

10. J. von Uexkull, "A Stroll through the World of Animals and Men," in *Instinctive Behavior,* ed. and trans. C. H. Schiller, International Universities Press, New York, 1957, pp. 5–80.

ships between taxonomic classification and behavior. One of the underlying assumptions of such research is that certain behavioral characteristics are related to phylogenetic ancestry in the same way as are morphological characteristics. In general, consummatory behavior is thought to be sufficiently stereotyped to be of taxonomic value, and for many authorities fixed action patterns are considered to be consummatory responses. A *consummatory* response is a response that terminates a behavioral sequence and satisfies some drive or motive.

A *fixed action pattern* (FAP) is a stereotyped behavior found in members of a particular species as a response to a class of stimulation. A stimulus that is associated with an FAP is called a *releaser* or a *sign stimulus*. Although there is considerable variation in the hypothesized mechanisms underlying this kind of species typical behavior, examples of fixed action patterns may be given for many animal forms, including man. As with kineses and taxes, different mechanisms underlie this sort of behavior in various species.

Some interesting research on fixed action patterns has been conducted, using birds as subjects. In a classic study of courtship displays in ducks, Lorenz demonstrated the usefulness of behavioral traits in taxonomic classification.[11] Noting the limited taxonomic value of a single behavioral trait, Lorenz did a careful descriptive study of as many behavioral traits of an organism as was possible. In the study, he described and classified thirty-two behavioral traits as they occur in sixteen duck species. The behavioral similarity among these ducks and related water birds provides the basis for Lorenz's interpretation of phylogenetic relationships among these water fowl.

Fixed action patterns are also typical elements in intraspecific fighting and appeasement behavior.[12] In many species the pattern of intraspecific fighting makes mortal damage to an opponent unlikely. Bison bulls always charge head to head, and however impressive their mutual butting, they are unlikely to seriously damage each other. When one champion turns his head and nibbles at the ground, the fight is over, and he is permitted to walk away. African antelope, illustrated in Figure 2.4, with long saberlike horns fence

11. K. Lorenz, "Comparative Studies of Motor Patterns of Anatinae," in *Studies in Animal and Human Behavior*, trans. R. Martin, Harvard University Press, Cambridge, Mass., 1971, vol. II, pp. 14–114.

12. I. Eibl-Eibesfeldt, *Ethology*, trans. E. Klinghammer, Holt, Rinehart, and Winston, New York, 1970.

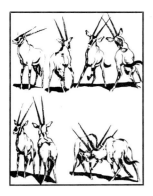

Figure 2.4
Ritualized Fighting
*(Fritz Walther, "Zum
Kampf und Paarungsver-
halten einiger Antilopen,"
Zeitschrift für Tierpsychologie,
15 (1958), abb. 21, p. 354.
Reproduced by
permission of Verlag Paul
Parey.)*

with their rivals, never realizing the lethal potential of their arma-
ment. However, the animals can and do effectively use their horns
against predators. Some ethologists believe that the more effective
the fighting behavior of a species, the more effective are its species
specific appeasement behaviors in terminating fights. In many species, appeasement behavior by the loser consists of exposure to
mortal injury by the winner, who does not press this advantage.
Wolves expose the throat to the winner of a fight, bison turn aside,
and turkey gobblers lie down before the victor. Animals with less
effective weapons appear to avoid serious injury in fights by flight
rather than appeasement.

Variability in Fixed Action Patterns   Forty years ago researchers
described fixed action patterns as identical in every respect in different individual animals. More recent studies have emphasized individual variability in species typical behavior. The degree and kinds
of variability in stereotyped species typical mating displays in goldeneye ducks seen in Figure 2.5 were the focus of one study.[13] While the

13. B. Dane and W. G. Van der Kloot, "An Analysis of the Display of the
Goldeneye Duck," *Behaviour,* 22 (1964), 282–328.

Figure 2.5
Goldeneye Ducks
(Philippa Scott)

study included observations of a number of behavior patterns in the complicated flock display setting, behaviors preceding and following copulatory behavior of a mated pair will provide an adequate example of individual variability.

Eight stereotyped behaviors are observed in the precopulatory behavior of the male of this species. The drake typically begins a precopulatory sequence by sham drinking, which is often associated with swimming away from the flock while making a ticking sound. If the pair is separated from the flock and the female assumes a prone position in the water, the male then exhibits some or all of five mating displays. These behaviors (sham drinking, head flicking, head rubbing, wing stretching, and bill shaking) do not occur in any fixed sequence. The sequence is random. The final three precopulatory patterns (the crescendo response, display preening, and precopulatory steaming) always occur in the same sequence preceding copulation. These responses also precede unsuccessful attempts at copulation. The five unordered precopulatory behaviors have different relative frequencies, and this relationship is roughly the same in all successful matings. In unsuccessful matings the relative frequency of bill shaking is reduced.

In this situation, the simplest kind of releaser–fixed action pattern relationship (described in Chapter 1) does not hold. The mating situation, including the stimuli associated with the female's prone display, appears to facilitate all five precopulatory behaviors. Each behavior is associated with a relative frequency within the total number of display behaviors produced between the initial sham drinking and the crescendo response. Postcopulatory behavior of both female and male is as stereotyped as the last three behaviors preceding copulation. The male dismounts, and still holding the female by the back of the head, rotates by swimming in a circle around her. Nearly all males dismount on the right side and swim in a clockwise direction when showing the rotating response. The male then swims around the female, exhibiting wing stretching and bathing while the female bathes.

Two kinds of variability in the mating displays of these birds are described. There is variability in the duration of particular responses, some birds being typically slow in their displays and some typically fast. The form of particular behaviors also varies. For example, a wing stretch may be to the left or right. This particular pattern is usually alternated by the drake, while head rubbing is alternated in slightly more than two-thirds of the observed cases. As noted previously, almost no variability is seen in the direction of rotating.

A frequent source of misunderstanding between psychologists and ethologists relates to the degree of similarity of fixed action patterns exhibited by different members of a particular species. Ethologists maintain that species typical behaviors classified as fixed action patterns are "items of behavior in every way as constant as are anatomical structures."[14] Many psychologists believe that this means the behavior patterns in question must be identical in every member of the species. Yet to assume that all of a species' fixed action pattern behaviors are identical is like stating that a morphological characteristic shared by all members of a species is identical. No one would question that a nose is a phylogenetically determined morphological characteristic of human beings. The next time you are with a group of people, you can readily determine by observation that this species typical morphological trait is not identical in all members of our species. As Figure 2.6 demonstrates, noses vary in length, breadth, curvature, relative nostril size, and hairiness, as well as in more subtle ways. Thus, a degree of individual variability is implied in the phrase "as constant as are anatomical structures."

Human Fixed Action Patterns   Smiling is frequently classified as a fixed action pattern in human beings.[15] The human face is the most generally recognized stimulus for infant smiling (see Figure 2.7). However, the development of smiling in early infancy has two phases that precede smiling in response to faces.[16] Smiling is first seen as a spontaneous behavior unrelated to external stimulation. A little later the smile occurs as a response to auditory stimulation, produced by high-pitched talking, wind whistles, or small brass bells. By twenty days of age, babies smile to a high-pitched human voice while awake. Some three-week-old infants smile more readily to a voice coupled with a nodding human head than to the voice alone.

14. W. H. Thorpe, "Ethology as a New Branch of Biology," in *Readings in Animal Behavior,* ed. T. E. McGill, Holt, Rinehart, and Winston, New York, 1965, p. 38.

15. Eibl-Eibesfeldt.

16. P. Wolff, "Observations on the Early Development of Smiling," in *Determinants of Infant Behavior,* ed. B. M. Foss, John Wiley, New York, 1963, vol. II, pp. 113–138.

Figure 2.6
Variation in Anatomical Structure
(a. Ginger Chek from Peter Arnold; b. Bob Adelman/ Magnum Photos, Inc.; c. Yoram Lehmann from Peter Arnold; d. George Bellerose/Stock, Boston.)

The third phase of smiling begins when the infant begins to focus on faces and particularly on the eyes of others. As early as twenty-eight days, some infants smile after focusing on the face and eyes of an observer. At about this time, the mother reports her infant to be "more fun to play with" and says that "she really sees me now." At this time, the most effective auditory stimulus that elicits smiling is the mother's voice. However, the infant shows a similar response to all faces. Smiling occurs in response to any human face that is accompanied by talking. At twenty-eight to thirty-two days, the baby will smile at any nodding head if it is accompanied by a voice, especially the mother's. By thirty-one to thirty-five days of age, the infant is less likely to respond with smiling to voice alone. A silent nodding head is the best smile stimulator. At this time, vocal stimulation from an adult is more likely to produce infant vocalization rather than infant smiling.

During the second and third months different human faces are equivalent smile stimulators. Infants will smile at pictorial or three-dimensional models of the human face. Early in the second month eyes alone will produce smiles; however, as the infant grows older, models must be more and more facelike to be effective. When the baby reaches five or six months of age, a familiar human face is the most effective visual smile stimulus. This pattern of multiple early releasing stimuli eliciting a fixed action pattern, followed by progressive specificity of stimulation as maturation proceeds, is held in common with other organisms.

Some authors classify other expressions of emotion and social behaviors in human beings as phylogenetically determined behavior. Using motion pictures of unaware subjects in several different cultures, the ethologists Eibel-Eibesfeldt and Hass have described cross-cultural consistencies in facial expressions and gestures associated with flirting, greeting, arrogance and disdain, and anger.[17]

Male observers initiated most flirting in the filmed sequences, and their subjects were female. The flirting girl smiles and lifts her eyebrows briefly. She then turns her head to the side or looks down, and the eyes nearly close. She may then cover her face with her hand and laugh or smile. She continues to look at the male out of the corner of her eyes, and may glance toward him and away several times. This pattern was consistently observed in Samoa, Papua, France, Japan, Africa, and South America. Eibel-Eibesfeldt interprets kissing to be a form of ritualized feeding behavior, although kissing is not found in all societies. As support for the interpretation, he cites the exchange of chewed pine resin or tobacco by lovers in an Austrian mountain valley.

Additional evidence for the partial determination of human facial expressions by Phylogenetic Set comes from studies of facial expressions in children born blind and blind-deaf.[18] Facial expressions of these infants and children are almost identical to those of sighted

17. H. Hass, *The Human Animal*, trans. J. M. Brownjohn, Delta, New York, 1970.
18. Eibel-Eibesfeldt.

Figure 2.7
Smiling
*(Erika Stone from Peter
Arnold)*

and hearing children. Compare Figure 2.8 with Figure 2.7. Smiling
does not require visual or auditory stimulation. In both sighted and
blind children, rhythmic touching or tickling produces smiling. As
the blind child matures, he or she develops a repertoire of facial
expressions that is somewhat more limited and stereotyped than that
of sighted individuals. However, basic expressions remain in the
behavioral repertoire of blind children and are readily recognized by
those around them.

Some ethologists maintain that human beings recognize certain
stimulus patterns as having meanings associated with specific attitudes or emotions.[19] The characteristics of the human infant are
believed to release tender, supportive feelings in the adult observer.
The specific characteristics of the infantlike stimulus pattern include
large eyes for head size, large head for body size, and rounded
contours. Cartoonists and other artists exploit these characteristics to
create cute and appealing objects. Other naturally recognized patterns are said to include neonatal crying and adult screaming. Both
of these vocal expressions use a sensitive part of the human auditory
range not of primary importance in understanding speech.

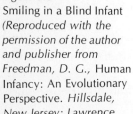

Figure 2.8
Smiling in a Blind Infant
*(Reproduced with the
permission of the author
and publisher from
Freedman, D. G.,* Human
Infancy: An Evolutionary
Perspective. *Hillsdale,
New Jersey: Lawrence
Erlbaum Associates,
Publishers, 1974.)*

19. K. Lorenz, "Part and Parcel in Animal and Human Societies," in *Studies in
Animal and Human Behavior,* trans. R. Martin, Harvard University Press, Cambridge,
Mass., 1971, vol. II, pp. 115–195.

Learning Dispositions   Another species typical behavioral trait is a *learning disposition.* Some species are especially able to learn certain discriminations or stimulus response relationships more readily than they can learn others. Norway rats will readily associate a certain taste with nausea, even if there is a long delay between ingestion and nausea.[20] After experiencing a particular taste that is followed by nausea, a rat will avoid the offending food. Other rats in the area will also avoid the food. This expression of Phylogenetic Set is well known to those who have tried to use poisoned food to exterminate rats. After a few rats receive a sublethal but nauseating dose of a poison, almost all rats in the area avoid bait with that poison. In contrast, rats have a great deal of difficulty associating a taste with foot shock. These findings indicate that all associations are not equally easy for the rat to learn. The ability to associate taste with nausea has adaptive value for rats. Associating taste with foot shock would be an unusual ability in the context of the phylogenetic history of this species. The learning capacity of each organism is related to its ecological niche and the kinds of adaptive pressure that had an influence on ancestral populations.

Another example of a learning disposition is the development of species typical songs in chaffinches and white crowned sparrows.[21] In several studies of these species, it was reported that isolated birds develop aberrant songs. However, if isolated birds hear recordings of the songs of their own species, they develop normally. In the song sparrow, the optimal period for this auditory experience is between ten and fifty days of age, several months before the bird actually sings. Chaffinches reared together without any experience with adult songs develop a group-specific song that is slightly more complex than that of single isolates but less complex than the species typical song. Both the chaffinch and the white throated sparrow respond only to recordings of the song of their own species.

Similarities to human speech development are seen in two experimental treatments conducted in the song sparrow study. Song sparrows deafened after they have heard adult songs but before they begin to sing, fail to develop songs. If the birds are deafened after they begin to sing, they continue to sing, although some distortions

20. J. Garcia, D. J. Kimeldorf, and R. A. Koelling, "The Use of Ionizing Radiation as a Motivating Stimulus," *Psychological Review,* 68 (1961), 383–395.

21. P. Marler and W. J. Hamilton, *Mechanisms of Animal Behavior,* John Wiley, New York, 1966.

eventually develop. Brain lesions in the left hemisphere terminate song in adult birds, but identical unilateral lesions in newly hatched birds have no apparent effects on subsequent song development. The effects of left hemisphere brain damage and early or late deafness has strikingly similar effects on speech in human beings. These two findings represent a remarkable parallelism in behavioral development between vocally communicating organisms with very remote phylogenetic associations.

While the neurophysiological and phylogenetic bases of bird song and human speech are quite different, both processes are an expression of Phylogenetic Set. All normal human beings have the behavioral capacities necessary for acquiring a vocal language. Vocal language is developed through exposure to aural language in the early years of life. Deaf children exhibit the initial babbling stage of language development, as do hearing children, but in deaf children babbling drops out soon after it appears. In the human species, language acquisition is facilitated by the tendency of both the child and the adults interacting with the child to repeat sequences of sounds. Once the child has begun to speak, the adults he or she talks to are likely to repeat the conversational form of any phrase the child attempts. An all-important behavioral capacity for vocal speech is the ability to associate meanings with self-produced sounds and those produced by others.

The idea that human speech is learned as a set of isolated stimulus response associations now appears untenable. One basis for this statement is the ability children demonstrate for creating new words. This is seen most clearly when children produce a regular form for irregular verbs.[22] A child will say, "I runned," rather than "I ran," or "My friend commed to my house," rather than "My friend came to my house." It may be assumed that the child generates regular rules for language and must learn irregular forms as specific associations. The acquisition of regular and irregular language forms will be discussed more fully in Chapter 4.

The point emphasized here is that rules for the regular verb forms in the child's language must be learned, but it is reasonable to classify the ability to learn such rules as a learning disposition. A two-and-one-half-year-old certainly would have difficulty expressing the language rules already mastered, and as the child grows older a

22. R. Brown, *A First Language,* Harvard University Press, Cambridge, Mass., 1973.

remarkable ability to learn a number of complicated linguistic rules is demonstrated. Some linguists have said that humans have an inherent comprehension of grammatical structure. The statement that humans possess species typical learning dispositions that enable them to readily acquire a vocal language is a slightly more conservative way of saying the same thing.

The results of attempts to teach chimpanzees to speak provide an interesting contrast to human speech acquisition. The best vocal performance produced by a chimpanzee consisted of three unvoiced lip movement approximations of three words.[23] One might conclude that chimpanzees just are not intelligent enough to learn language. Recent successful attempts to teach a chimpanzee American sign language, the gestural language of the deaf, make this interpretation untenable.[24] In this study, a chimpanzee named Washoe was raised in a house trailer by a young couple. The foster parents never used vocal speech in Washoe's presence. The chimpanzee's gestures might be said to have a chimp accent, but she communicated quite effectively. On one occasion, when her doll had fallen between the inner and outer walls of the trailer, she stood in front of the doll's location and repeatedly performed the gesture for open. Another time, apparently unaware of a nearby observer, Washoe made the signs, "Washoe climb tree," and then climbed a tree. Although one may question the name given to Washoe's languagelike behavior, her performance is certainly impressive. A moderately complex gestural-visual communication system appears to be well within this chimpanzee's capacity. The species is not capable of the rudiments of a vocal-aural communication system. The chimpanzee is not too stupid to learn a language; the species typical behavioral traits that enable a human to learn vocal speech are simply lacking in the chimpanzee.

Expressions of Phylogenetic Set

Clear examples of behavior repertoires largely determined by Phylogenetic Set may be seen in various insects. Organisms with short adult life spans cannot afford the luxury of behavioral plasticity; species survival depends on the immediate assumption of behavior

23. C. Hayes, *The Ape in our House,* Harper, New York, 1951.
24. R. A. Gardner and B. T. Gardner, "Teaching Sign Language to a Chimpanzee," *Science,* 165 (1969), 664–672.

patterns that assure reproduction and maintenance of young. However, even the stereotyped behavioral repertoire of an insect is responsive to environmental stimulation. Limited but clearcut examples of so-called higher processes such as learning and memory may be seen in their behavior.

The Digger Wasp

The behavior of female digger wasps provides an example of a pattern of species specific behavior with little experiential dependence.[25] In the spring, the wasp hatches and then mates. Next, it builds a nest, carries off the loose sand, and closes the nest with a clod of dirt. When it has killed a caterpillar, it brings it to the nest site. The wasp drops the caterpillar near the nest, crawls into the nest, and turns around. It then drags the caterpillar into the nest, deposits an egg, and closes the nest. It visits the nest frequently until the egg hatches, after which it brings caterpillars to feed the developing larvae.

The size and number of caterpillars are determined by the stage of development of the larvae. A wasp may tend fifteen nests with larvae of different ages and visits each one early in the morning. Its behavior for the rest of the day is determined by the condition of each nest at that time. If caterpillars are put into a nest by an experimenter before the wasp's first visit of the day, it will bring fewer caterpillars to that nest during that day. However, the addition of caterpillars after the first visit has no effect on subsequent behavior.

The digger wasp shows one kind of learning when it uses landmarks to help locate its nests. An artificial landmark, such as a triangle of pine cones, can be used by the wasp. If this landmark is moved several yards after the wasp's first visit of the day, it has great difficulty finding the nest. The digger wasp has an extensive repertoire of species specific behavior. In addition, it shows two kinds of so-called higher mental processes. It remembers for several hours the caterpillar needs of as many as fifteen larvae in various stages of development. It also learns the location of its nests relative to prominent landmarks around the nest.

The Rhesus Monkey

Phylogenetic Set may also be expressed in organisms whose behavioral repertoire is nonspecifically dependent on the environment.

25. N. Tinbergen, *Curious Naturalists*, Basic Books, New York, 1958.

Certain species typical behaviors develop in a wide range of environments and do not depend on specific experiences. However, even where the behavior has nonspecific dependence, some experiential histories permit development of species typical patterns while other histories interfere with development. The development of social behavior in rhesus monkeys illustrates this point. Rhesus monkeys reared in isolation from other monkeys for the first year of life fail to develop species typical social behavior.[26] In Chapter 1, male sexual behavior in isolate monkeys was described. Normal and inadequate patterns of sexual behavior are portrayed in Figure 2.9. Other behavior patterns disturbed by isolation include play, grooming, maternal behavior, and aggression. Female sexual behavior is also modified although not as drastically as is male sexual behavior.

26. H. F. Harlow and M. K. Harlow, "The Affectional Systems," in *Behavior of Nonhuman Primates*, eds. A. M. Schrier, H. F. Harlow, and F. Stollnitz, Academic Press, New York, 1965, vol. II, pp. 287–334.

Figure 2.9
Sexual Patterns in Rhesus Monkeys
(From H. F. Harlow and M. K. Harlow, "The Affectional Systems," Behavior of Nonhuman Primates, *Schrier, Harlow, and Stollnitz (eds.), Academic Press, New York, 1965, p. 326. Copyright 1965 by Academic Press, Inc.)*

William A. Mason first reported the effects of social restriction on social behavior in the rhesus monkey. The social behavior of preadolescent monkeys captured in the wild was compared with that of preadolescent monkeys reared in cages where they were able to see and hear but not touch other monkeys. The restricted animals were described as exhibiting less play and more aggression than the wild-reared monkeys.[27] The restricted monkeys also failed to groom one another and showed infrequent and inadequate sexual behavior. In later studies, monkeys were subjected to more severe restriction with even more striking results. Animals that had not seen or heard other monkeys for a year after birth were socially incompetent in virtually every respect, unable even to flee from attackers. Some animals showed a degree of recovery when allowed to interact with younger "therapist" monkeys.[28]

As indicated in Chapter 1, restricted adult male monkeys subsequently do not reproduce. Restricted females are also difficult to breed. However, mating of restricted females with wild-born males is often successful. From one-half to two-thirds of the restricted females that give birth are inadequate mothers with their first-born, either ignoring the neonate or frequently abusing it.[29] Figure 2.10 shows one of these inadequate mothers. Many of these animals are adequate mothers with later babies. Other behavioral peculiarities in adult animals subjected to early restrictions include stereotyped motor behavior such as repetitive back flipping and self-directed aggressive behavior.

These dramatic disruptions of species typical social behavior in monkeys have led many authorities to conclude that social behavior in monkeys is learned. However, the evidence from these and other studies fails to provide support for this conclusion.

Monkeys subjected to a number of different early environments develop social behavior repertoires that are quite similar to each other.[30] Infant monkeys separated from their mothers from birth may develop adequate social behavior repertoires. For example,

27. W. A. Mason, "The Effects of Social Restriction on the Behavior of Rhesus Monkeys," *Journal of Comparative and Physiological Psychology,* 53 (1960), 582–589.

28. H. F. Harlow, M. K. Harlow, and S. J. Soumi, "From Thought to Therapy: Lessons from a Primate Laboratory," *American Scientist,* 59 (1971), 538–549.

29. Harlow and Harlow.

30. B. Seay and N. W. Gottfried, "A Phylogenetic Perspective for Social Behavior in Primates," *Journal of General Psychology,* 92 (1975), 5–17.

Figure 2.10
Inadequate Monkey
Mother
*(From H. F. Harlow and
M. K. Harlow, "The
Affectional Systems,"*
Behavior of Nonhuman
Primates, *Schrier, Harlow,
and Stollnitz (eds.),
Academic Press, New
York, 1965, p. 310.
Copyright 1965 by
Academic Press, Inc.)*

infant monkeys reared with other babies in one cage develop strong attachments for their cage mates and cling to one another a great deal but they still develop species typical play and sexual behavior. Even infants reared mostly in isolation but permitted to play with other babies for twenty minutes a day show fairly normal development, without the intense clinging. Mother-reared animals develop almost normal behavioral repertoires, whether or not they have an opportunity to play with other infants during the first eight months of life. However, mother-reared, peer-restricted babies demonstrate higher levels of aggression than peer-experienced infants during their early interactions with other infants. Even when reared with adult males only, rhesus monkey infants show essentially normal social development.[31]

Across a wide range of experiential backgrounds, rhesus monkeys develop similar social behavior repertoires. No single social experience or set of social experiences appears to underlie the development of these similar social behaviors. This does not mean that the frequencies of the various social behaviors are identical in all groups. For example, some evidence suggests that infants reared by punitive mothers are more frequently aggressive than the offspring of non-punitive mothers. Even if verified, these differences related to differential maternal patterns are in the frequencies of various social behaviors. The behavior patterns seen in play, aggression, and sexual behavior in these laboratory animals are the species typical behaviors usually observed in wild rhesus monkeys.

Rhesus monkey social behavior patterns are an expression of Phylogenetic Set. The disruption produced by restricted environments shows that this species typical behavior is environmentally dependent. Socially restricted monkeys reared on moving surrogate mothers do not show the same degree of disruption as other restricted monkeys.[32] This finding suggests that it might be possible to construct a set of inanimate stimuli to provide an adequate basis for species typical social behavior in these monkeys. However, one suspects the most effective inanimate stimulus would look and act much like a rhesus mother.

Lovebirds

Sometimes it is possible to crossbreed closely related species and study the behavior of their offspring.[33] In one study, two species of lovebirds with different nest-building behaviors were crossed. One parent species carried nest materials in its beak. Members of the

31. W. K. Redican and G. Mitchell, "The Social Behavior of Adult Male Infant Pairs of Rhesus Macaques in a Laboratory Environment," *American Journal of Physical Anthropology*, 38 (1973), 523–526.

32. W. A. Mason, "Early Social Deprivation in the Nonhuman Primates: Implications for Human Behavior," in *Environental Influences*, ed. D. C. Glass, Rockefeller University Press, New York, 1968, pp. 70–100.

33. W. C. Dilger, "The Behavior of Love Birds," *Scientific American*, 206 (1962), 89–99.

other species tucked strips of leaves or paper into the rump feathers and carried the material to the nest site in this way. Hybrid birds tucked materials into their feathers, but the feathers did not hold the material. The hybrids arrived at the nest site, found no materials in their feathers, and then repeated the fruitless task. After two years most of the hybrid birds had developed a technique for carrying strips of paper. They took the material in their beak and made tucking movements, but they either kept the material in their beak or immediately removed it from the rump feathers and then flew to their nest. It is important to note that they did not acquire a new behavior but instead reordered the original sequence of acts. In virtually all of the flights, naive hybrids cut the strips, tucked them into their feathers, flew to the nest, and attempted to retrieve the material. After two years the hybrids cut the strips, tucked them into the feathers, retrieved them from the feathers, and then flew to the nest. After three years, the tucking behavior was less frequent, but in many instances hybrid birds turned in a tucking movement before flying to the nest site. When complete tucking did occur after three years, it was much more efficient than in naive birds, although the pattern never resulted in getting material to the nest.

In this example, a highly stereotyped pattern of behavior is modified by experience. The modification retains elements of the stereotyped behavior pattern but changes the order of occurrence. Another important aspect of the study of hybrid lovebirds is the clear evidence for the determination and persistence of complex patterns of behavior through Phylogenetic Set. The hybrids exhibited the behavior of their material-tucking parent but did not grow material-holding feathers. This behavior-morphology inconsistency resulted in inefficient nest building, and even though fertile, the hybrids would fall two breeding seasons behind competing birds of either parent species.

Characteristics of Phylogenetic Set

Phylogenetic Set encompasses those attributes of behavior that are typical of a given species. In some ways this concept is similar to some interpretations of instinct; however, Phylogenetic Set differs from instinct as psychologists have defined that term in several ways. For one thing, behavior that is an expression of Phylogenetic Set is a probable rather than an inevitable feature of development in a particular species. An atypical environment for a species will inhibit the development of a phylogenetically determined species typical behavior repertoire. Behavior as an expression of Phylogenetic Set is almost always partially dependent on development in a supportive environment. In some cases, environments that disrupt phylogenetically related behavior do so by inhibiting typical physical or physiological development. Retinal atrophy produced in dark-reared chimpanzees is an example of this phenomenon. In other cases, such as the social behavior of isolation-reared monkeys, clearcut physical or physiological bases for aberrant behavior are not evident.

Phylogenetic Set partially determines behavior that is related to individual and species survival. It is likely that the more important a behavior pattern is for reproductive survival, the less dependent it will be on specific experiences for its development. When a behavior is essential for reproductive survival, the necessary experiences are likely to be a consistent feature of the natural environment for the species in question. Animals evolve in environments; the behavioral traits that reflect Phylogenetic Set have developed in response to particular aspects of those environments. In this sense, Experiential Set always interacts with Phylogenetic Set in the development of behavior. Instinct is usually understood to imply little or no dependence on the environment.

The most rigid interpretation of instinct assumes little individual variability. Behavior related to Phylogenetic Set is assumed to exhibit differences among individual animals. Genetic and experiential variability among individual animals within a species interacts with Phylogenetic Set. Ontogenetic Set, discussed in the next chapter, is also inextricably entwined in Phylogenetic Set, to the extent that separation of these two determinants of behavior can be done only as a convention to simplify discussion and analysis.

The past history of an individual organism is not supposed to affect instinctive behavior, but it must affect the expression of Phylogenetic Set. The Phylogenetic Set concept allows for the influence of the organism's past history on species typical behavior. Experiential and Cultural Set may modify the expression of Phylogenetic Set, as in the culturally defined conventions associated with facial expressions. More commonly, the expression of these two environmental determinants of behavior is confined to limits imposed by Phylogenetic Set. The influence of environment differs for various species and for particular behavioral processes within a species. Grouse learn to avoid barriers and deal with three-dimensional detour problems more readily while in flight than while walking.[34]

Phylogenetic Set is characteristic of behavioral development in all species, including man. In organisms with short life spans and early reproductive maturity, a large part of the behavioral repertoire may be an expression of phylogenetically related behaviors refractory to environmental influence. Even in these organisms, exemplified by the digger wasp, some experiential determination of behavior is evident. In other organisms with relatively long life spans and late reproductive maturity, Phylogenetic Set is more frequently expressed in terms of learning dispositions, such as the unique human capacity for vocal speech. However, even in the human species, fixed action patterns, particularly early in development, provide clear evidence for phylogenetic influence on behavior.

Summary

Phylogenetic Set, the influence of species general inheritance on behavior, has been discussed in this chapter. Phylogenetic Set is a partial determinant of behavioral development and accounts for species typical behavior in most members of a species. Behavior that reflects Phylogenetic Set is partially dependent on a supportive environment.

A brief introduction to biological evolution is presented to provide a background for considering species typical behavior. Evolutionary development is the result of mutation, genetic drift, and selection. Adaptive change as a result of selection is a characteristic of populations rather than of individuals. Very slight selective advantages associated with a trait are sufficient to produce change in a population across many generations.

Behavioral changes are frequent concomitants of other genetically related changes that occur in evolution. Categories of behavior that appear to be phylogenetically related include reflexes, fixed action patterns, and learning dispositions. Examples of inherited behavioral tendencies are given for several organisms. Species typical

34. K. Lorenz, "Psychology and Phylogeny," in *Studies in Animal and Human Behavior,* trans. R. Martin, Harvard University Press, Cambridge, Mass., 1971, vol. II, pp. 196–245.

behaviors in human beings, including smiling and language development, are discussed.

Phylogenetic Set is described as a partial determinant of behavior for all species. Behavior that expresses Phylogenetic Set is susceptible to environmentally produced disruption. Phyletically related behavior patterns would be expected to exhibit individual variability as well as environmentally produced variability. In subsequent chapters, the interaction of Phylogenetic Set with other partial determinants of behavior will be emphasized.

Defined Terms

Species typical	Allele	Reflex
Population	Homozygous	Kinesis
Chromosome	Heterozygous	Taxes
Mutation	Polygenetic	Consummatory
Gene	Selection	Fixed action pattern
Diploid	Sympatric	Releaser
Sperm	Allopatric	Sign stimulus
Ova	Genetic drift	Learning disposition
Haploid	Demes	

Suggested Readings

D. Lack, "Darwin's Finches," *Scientific American,* 188 (1953), 67–72.

This reading describes a good example of divergent evolution. It is written for the general reader.

K. Lorenz, *Evolution and Modification of Behavior,* University of Chicago Press, Chicago, 1965.

D. S. Lehrman, "A Critique of Konrad Lorenz's Theory of Instinctive Behavior," *Quarterly Review of Biology,* 28 (1953), 337–363.

The short book by Lorenz presents a classic ethological view of the inheritance of behavior. The article by Lehrman is a criticism of Lorenz's views from the point of view of traditional American experimental psychology. The two fields are closer in thought today than at the time these selections were written, but the student will gain an understanding of the conflicts between the fields from these readings.

A. Manning, "Evolution of Behavior," in *Psychobiology,* ed. J. L. McGaugh, Academic Press, New York, 1971.

This is a good brief introduction that goes beyond the coverage of Chapter 2. The writing is somewhat technical but not difficult.

P. Marler, "Birdsong and Speech Development; Could There Be Parallels?" *American Scientist,* 58 (1970), 669–673.

A description of the development of species typical song patterns in birds. Strikingly similar experiential and neurological phenomena in birdsong and human speech are described. This article is written for the general reader.

J. M. Savage, *Evolution,* 2nd ed., Holt, Rinehart, and Winston, New York, 1969.

A brief introduction to evolutionary theory for the general reader.

M. E. P. Seligman, "On the Generality of the Laws of Learning," *Psychological Review,* 77 (1970), 406–418.

This article provides a brief historical review of animal learning research and suggests that the search for general laws of learning that apply to all problems for all species is not feasible. Seligman introduces the notion that animals are phylogenetically prepared, unprepared, or contraprepared for specific learning tasks. The article is recommended for psychology majors and others with a serious interest in animal learning.

G. G. Simpson, *The Major Features of Evolution,* Columbia University Press, New York, 1953.

A classic discussion of evolutionary theory. Recommended for the student with a serious interest in evolution. The first two chapters are the most difficult. The reader might choose to scan these chapters lightly the first time through and then reread them after completing the book.

Chapter 3
Ontogenetic Set

As a developing organism grows older, its behavior changes. Some time-dependent changes in behavior are clearly and directly related to physical maturation. As nerves and muscles develop, the human infant becomes more capable of coordinated movements. His or her motor development shows an orderly and predictable sequence. Other age-correlated changes in behavior demonstrate strong environmental influences. As the individual reaches sexual maturity changes are likely in speech patterns, standards of dress and personal grooming, preferred companions, and activities. While these changes are clearly associated with physical and physiological maturation, they are also related to the particular subculture to which the developing individual belongs. Change in behavior at about the time of puberty is a general phenomenon, but the specific details of behavioral change vary considerably among cultures, subcultures, and social classes.

Maturationally related changes in the developing individual affect her or his impact on the environment, particularly the social environment. In the last chapter we saw that the mother's new feeling that the baby is "more fun to play with," was associated with the infant's new tendency to focus on the mother's eyes. This development in the infant's behavior modified the character of interactions with the mother. Similar interactions between the developing individual and the social environment may be found throughout life.

Prenatal
Development

The newborn infant seen in Figure 3.1 is a remarkably complex, complete, effective organism. At birth, the baby assumes several new functions previously accomplished for him or her in the protected uterine environment. He or she must now breathe, ingest and digest food, eliminate wastes, announce pain or discomfort, and maintain body temperature. At the same time, sensory systems that were minimally stimulated before birth are now subjected to what must amount to massive stimulation.

William James likened the initial sensory experiences of the neonate to "one great buzzing booming confusion."[1] However, more recently, observers have found a good deal more organization of the newborn's sensory systems than James's statement suggests. While

1. W. James, *The Principles of Psychology*, Henry Holt, New York, 1890, p. 488.

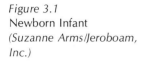

Figure 3.1
Newborn Infant
(Suzanne Arms/Jeroboam,
Inc.)

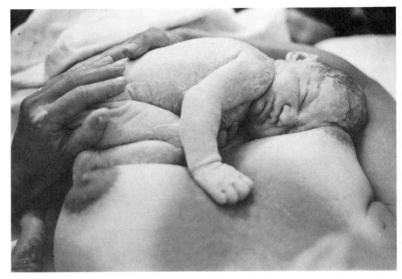

our general impression of the newborn is one of frailty and ineptitude, the neonate is quite sturdy and, within limits, superbly competent. For example, the newborn taking the breast is like a big bass taking a surface lure—forceful, sudden, and effective.

Some authorities, including the psychoanalyst John Bowlby and the ethologist Konrad Lorenz, believe that the adult's impression of infant frailty and helplessness is an inborn reaction important to the survival of our species. The infant is, of course, limited in its capacities. The baby must be brought to the breast, cleaned, moved about, and protected from temperature extremes. He or she needs care and protection for a long period of time. The point is that no infant or child is quite as helpless and vulnerable as it appears to be.

The human infant may be compared with altricial animals and birds, like the rat and the robin, which are born or hatched at an immature stage of development. Precocial animals, such as the goat and the duck, are born or hatched with the ability to locomote and to react effectively to sensory input from the environment. Human babies differ from the infants of most altricial species in that their sensory capacities are well developed at or near birth. One might say that the human infant is motorially altricial but sensorially precocial. As a consequence the human infant identifies familiar adults long before he or she is able to move toward or away from them.

Behavioral development does not begin at birth. In one sense, the development of behavior begins at conception, the starting point of individual development. From another point of view, behavior begins when maturation of nerves and muscles permits movement in response to external stimuli. Regardless of the exact time of behavioral origin, the behavioral repertoire of the newborn organism has undergone a considerable period of prenatal development.

Our knowledge of prenatal behavioral development comes primarily from three kinds of studies.[2] A great deal is known about development in other animals prior to birth or hatching. Information about normal development can be obtained easily from birds by removing a portion of the egg shell, which has little effect on the developing chick. In mammals, surgically removed fetuses have been studied, especially those of rats and guinea pigs. A second source of information about prenatal development is found in surgically removed human fetuses. While these studies tell us about the behavioral capacities of the fetus, they do not accurately represent the behavior of the normal fetus in the uterus. Formerly, these fetuses were available only in cases where maternal health required removal of the fetus. Recent changes in attitudes and laws respecting abortion have made fetal subjects more readily available. The behavior of an aborted fetus is abnormal in two ways: the fetus is in an abnormal environment and it is dying. The third source of information concerning prenatal life is the fetus while it is being carried by the mother. Maternal reports of fetal activity and recordings of movement from the mother's abdomen have served as a limited source of information concerning normal development.

Several features of prenatal human development can be derived even from the limited information available. First, the sequence but not the timing, of particular behavioral developments is relatively consistent among members of a species. Second, a response repertoire develops well in advance of normal functional demands. The adaptive value of this advanced preparation is obvious.

The mouth and facial area are the first to produce responses to tactile stimulation. At eight or nine weeks after conception the embryo responds to stimulation of the facial area with a whole body

2. L. Carmichael, "Onset and Early Development of Behavior," in *Carmichael's Manual of Child Psychology,* ed. P. H. Mussen, John Wiley & Sons, New York, 1970, vol. I, pp. 447–563.

flexion, the result of contraction of long muscles of the neck and body. Nine- to ten-week-old fetuses show spontaneous movements of the arms and legs. These movements are described as slow, asymmetrical, arrhythmical, and noncoordinated. The area of skin sensitivity spreads until by thirteen weeks of age only stimulation of the top and back of the head fails to produce a response. At fourteen weeks spontaneous activity includes most body parts and is described as graceful and delicate. Except for respiration, vocalization, and the grasp reflex, the human fetus shows most of the behavioral repertoire of the newborn by this time.

At around sixteen weeks, the developing fetus shows some reduction in activity. Paradoxically, the mother is likely to first report fetal movement at about this time, probably because the fetus has reached the size where its movements are perceptible. The reduction in activity is associated with a relatively lower level of oxygen for the fetal nervous system, also a consequence of this growth. By the sixth month, breathing movements occur. Some infants born at this age survive. By the seventh month the infant has a greater than fifty-fifty chance of survival, and after eight months the probability of survival is quite high.

As previously mentioned, the developing infant responds distinctly to sensory stimulation, sometimes uncomfortably so for the mother. The infant's startle response to loud noises, such as music, applause, or laughter, can be felt by the mother. Other sensory systems are functionally mature prior to birth, but except for the vestibular senses, which respond to motion, they are rarely stimulated.

A casual observer might conclude that environmental influences on organisms begin at birth, assuming that behavior present at birth is "purely" genetically determined. This is a misconception; interactions between the individual and the environment commence at conception rather than at birth. In fact early in life, following conception, the developing organism is so sensitive to departures from the typical environment for her or his species that it does not survive many kinds of environmental variation. The effects of environmental variation on fetal development are usually drastic and tragic, as seen in the children whose mothers had rubella or other viral diseases during the first three months of fetal life. Most early prenatal environmental manipulations that affect later behavior affect gross structural development as well.

A fertilized ovum of any species interacts with its environment throughout prenatal development. Thus the newborn of any species is structurally and behaviorally the product of its species general and individual genetic characteristics interacting with a species typical prenatal environment. A great deal of behavioral variability between species is evident when newborns are compared. These differences are consistent with the species typical social environments that the neonate must now exploit.

Neonatal
Development

A newborn kitten appears to be a particularly helpless creature.[3] Eyes and ears are closed and locomotor capacity is limited. However, this squirming, blind creature is so well adapted to its new environment that the first-born of a litter frequently nurses before all of its siblings are born. Within two days of birth, a kitten is likely to have fixated on a particular nipple and will consistently nurse from it. Should a kitten attach to a sibling's nipple, it quickly releases it when pushed by the rightful owner. However, if it is attached to its personal nipple, a pushing sibling has a hard time disengaging it.

During the first three weeks of life, nursing in cats is a mother-initiated activity. The mother approaches the litter, lies down, and arches her body around the kittens. As the kittens grow older, they become increasingly capable of rapid attachment to their preferred nipple. After three weeks, the kittens, now more physically competent, sometimes initiate nursing. At this age, the mother readily responds to the kittens' attempts to suckle, actively joining her offspring in initiating a bout of nursing. By five or six weeks of age, the kittens almost always initiate nursing, but the mother is frequently unresponsive. With time, maternal indifference and rejection increase. By eight weeks, the kittens are likely to be primarily dependent on other sources of food and may be completely weaned.

The behavior of the developing kitten cannot be interpreted as an automatic, predetermined sequence, dependent solely on maturation. From the moment of birth, the kitten interacts with the social environment provided by the mother. The mother stimulates the kitten, and the kitten in turn stimulates the mother. If the kitten is removed from the mother for several days, it will not easily fit back

3. T. C. Schneirla, J. S. Rosenblatt, and E. Tobach, "Maternal Behavior in the Cat," in *Maternal Behavior in Mammals*, ed. H. L. Rheingold, John Wiley & Sons, New York, 1963, pp. 122–168.

into the litter-mother social unit. However, the kitten's behavior is not determined entirely by the environment. The newborn kitten is phylogenetically and ontogenetically prepared to adapt to a particular kind of environment. The most important features of that environment are provided by the mother and the litter mates. The behaviors of the mother and litter mates are in turn influenced by the behavior of the kitten. Phylogenetic and Ontogenetic Set together determine the kitten's behavior, so that at each stage of development the kitten is capable of exploiting an environment usually available to a member of its species.

The behavior of the newborn goat provides a sharp contrast to the apparent aimlessness and helplessness seen in the newborn kitten.[4] Like many mammalian mothers, the goat mother may begin to interact with the kid before birth is complete. As soon as the head of the infant is presented, the mother begins to lick it. Licking continues for some time, with intermittent pauses during which the mother may eat the placenta or begin to lick a second kid. Twins are common among goats, and the mother alternately licks both babies. The kid stands on all fours within five to ten minutes of birth but is likely to totter and fall on the first attempts to stand. The mother usually stands and the infant orients to her, nuzzling her ventral surface.

Kids frequently attempt to nurse clumps of hair or the attached afterbirth. After a period of persistent nuzzling, the kid will find the teat and begin to suckle. The initial bout of nursing may be brief, and it may take the kid a few minutes to regain the teat. Once the kid has fed, it will usually go to sleep. By the second day the kids follow the mother easily and nurse with vigor and skill. If other adult females are present they attempt to nurse from them, but after two or three attempts they learn to select their own mother. Mother goats are infant specific and violently reject other infants. The kid's early locomotor independence and its ability to learn to attempt to nurse from only one adult female appear to provide a clear contrast to the physical incompetence seen in the cat and human being. It is sometimes difficult to remember that the kid is no more nor less competent in its typical postnatal environment than is the kitten or the human infant in its respective species typical postnatal environment.

4. P. H. Klopfer, "Mother Love: What Turns it On?" *American Scientist,* 59 (1971), 404–407.

An example of unique adaptation to the postnatal environment is seen in infant marsupials like the opossum or the kangaroo.[5] Marsupials are born at a remarkably immature stage of development and crawl from the vaginal opening to the pouch, where they stay for some time. At birth, the opossum is almost embryonic in physical development, except for its front limbs (see Figure 3.2). Unlike the rest of its body, its front limbs are well formed, complete with relatively large claws. Precocial development of forelimbs and associated neural structures equip this almost unformed creature for a relatively long journey. At a comparable stage of development, placental mammals show only simple and uncoordinated reflexes.

The behaviors of neonatal cats, goats, and marsupials just described result in changes in the physical and social environment that facilitate the neonate's development and ultimate survival. These behaviors also release in the mothers and siblings behavior patterns that further ensure successful adaptation of the neonate. The behavior of a human newborn is similar in this respect. Even at birth, the infant is prepared to turn the face toward a source of

5. G. Gottlieb, "Ontogenesis of Sensory Function in Birds and Mammals," in *The Biopsychology of Development*, eds. E. Tobach, L. R. Aronson, and E. Shaw, Academic Press, New York, 1971, pp. 67–128.

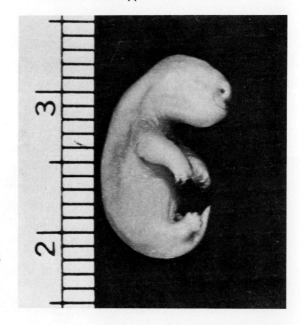

Figure 3.2
Newborn Opossum
(Specimen 71414
obtained with the
cooperation of the
Michigan Department of
Natural Resources and the
support of NIH grant NS
05982. Photo courtesy of
J. I. Johnson.)

physical contact, grasp a protrusion with the mouth, and suck. The mother will generally respond to distress by picking up her crying infant and placing it close to her ventral surface. Thus, the postnatal interactions of human mother and infant construct the environmental supports necessary for infant development.

Furthermore, a number of maternal behaviors are elicited by infant fixed actions such as sucking, grasping, distress cries, smiling, and visual scanning.[6] These include maternal vocal and verbal responses, smiling, and visual attention to the infant. Soon after birth the infant's attention is captured when a human face is within 2 feet of its eyes. The human voice also arouses interest more than other competing stimuli. While the exact age of onset for human socialization is not known, the sights and sounds of the child's caretakers are surely essential releasers of social behavior in the first two years after birth.

The newborn of different species exhibit widely variable behavioral repertoires. Their species typical behaviors are the result of the interactions of the individual's genetic potential with the prenatal environment. Development in this protected and predictable environment produces an organism capable of exploiting and interacting with the postnatal environment typical for the species. The behavior of the newborn represents a stage rather than a beginning point in the development of behavior. This stage is particularly important, for it demonstrates the interdependence between the behaving organism and the environment it must exploit to survive.

Maturation and Behavioral Development

The behavioral processes that begin at conception and continue throughout life defy convenient categorization. The terms "genetic versus environmental," "nature versus nurture," "innate versus acquired," all represent attempts to force upon events differences that may reflect the point of view of the observer. From the perspective of population genetics and evolutionary theory, it is obvious that human intelligence is genetically determined, and indeed it is, in part. From the point of view of those who study the effect of environment on development and are interested in early childhood education, human intelligence is a product of the environment, and

6. J. Bowlby, "The Nature of the Child's Tie to the Mother," *International Journal of Psychoanalysis,* 39 (1958), 350–373.

that also is true. Every process, including cell differentiation, requires permissive genetic coding. Every process, including cell differentiation, requires a supportive environment. The development of behavior, like the physical development of the organism, is an expression of the genetic characteristics of the individual organism in dynamic interaction with the environment. Recognition of the influence of genetic traits on behavior need in no way negate or overlook environmental influences. In a very real sense, innate determination of behavioral development and environmental influences on behavioral development are two sides of the same coin.

Temporal changes in behavior usually follow characteristic patterns. A particular sequence (for example, the development of prehension in young children) will have a species typical order.[7] First, the child will reach in the general direction of objects, then sweep at them with the forearms and hands used as a unit, then grasp them clumsily with the hand used as a unit, and finally will pick up objects with the thumb and finger. This sequence is repeated by all normal infants. The precise age at which each succeeding pattern of behavior is shown varies among individuals. One source of this variability is undoubtedly the direct and indirect influence of individual genetic differences. It is possible to demonstrate environmental influences on the development of prehension. If infants reared in an almost object-free environment are compared with infants presented with a carefully designed, stimulating, object-rich environment, substantial differences in the age of development of prehension can be demonstrated.[8] What determines the development of prehension?

For almost all individuals, the sequence of behavioral change is an expression of Phylogenetic and Ontogenetic Set. Within the sequence, the specific age of achievement of a behavioral competency is an expression of Ontogenetic Set interacting with Individual and Experiential Set. In the case of environmental influence on prehension, infants in an orphanage were the subjects. In the usual situation in that orphanage, infants spent most of their time on their backs looking at the most interesting things in their meager environ-

7. A. S. Espenschade and M. M. Eckert, *Motor Development,* Charles Merrill, Columbus, Ohio, 1967.

8. B. L. White, *Human Infants: Experience and Psychological Development,* Prentice-Hall, Englewood Cliffs, N.J., 1971.

ment, their own hands. In this setting, manipulations of the environment produced dramatic effects. In other, more typical, environments where infants are generally subjected to some moderate level of stimulation, the influence of more stimulation would be less important and perhaps negligible. In theory, an optimal environment, one that matched the maturity level of each individual, would permit differences among the subjects to be attributed to individual genetic characteristics.

Ontogenetic influences on behavior constitute the focus of this chapter. In the perspective of the chapter and in the examples provided, the regularity and species general nature of behavioral development are emphasized. In every case of ontogenetic development to be described, the organisms will be normal members of their species developing in an adequate environment. However, individual differences are assumed to exist in any behaviors described, and the description is presented as a subjective average of the behavior of individual organisms.

Maturational factors influence behavior. Some behavioral phenomena cannot occur until a specific level of physical and physiological maturity has been reached. The past experiences of the organism and the specific environmental situation when this level of maturity is achieved will also modify behavior. This is further complicated by the fact that environmental conditions affect maturational rates. For example, it is known that diet, which is correlated with socioeconomic level, influences the age of human sexual maturity.[9] The timing in development of this important process has far reaching effects on the behavior of the child, influencing her or his behavior toward others and their behavior toward the child.

The Endocrine System in Behavioral Development

One aspect of maturation that has profound effects on behavior is a series of changes in endocrine system activity.[10] The endocrine system is made up of the ductless glands that release *hormones* directly into the bloodstream. These chemical products, which are related in form and structure to some proteins, regulate or modify

9. J. M. Tanner, "Physical Growth," in *Carmichael's Manual of Child Psychology*, ed. P. H. Mussen, John Wiley, New York, 1970, vol. I, pp. 77–155.

10. J. H. N. Brown, *Basic Endocrinology for Students of Biology and Medicine*, F. A. Davis, Philadelphia, 1966.

Table 3.1   The Major Endocrine Glands

Gland	Hormones	Functions
Pituitary		
Neurohypophysis	Oxytocins	Uterine contractions
		Milk cell contractions
	Vasopressins	Water conservation
		Blood vessel constriction
Adenohypophysis	Somatotrophin	Promotes general body growth
		Regulates metabolism of fat, protein, and carbohydrates
	Prolactin	Stimulates milk production
	Follicle stimulating hormone	Stimulates growth of ovarian follicles
		Stimulates growth of seminal vesicles
	Leutinizing hormone	Stimulates estrogen production and ovulation
		Stimulates androgen production
	Thyrotrophin	Regulates thyroid gland function
	ACTH	Stimulates adrenal cortex to produce adrenal hormones
	Intermedin	Unclear
Thyroid	Thyroxin and other thyroid hormones	Regulate metabolic rate
		Act with somatotrophin to produce skeletal growth
		Regulate neural functioning
Parathyroid	Parathyroid	Regulates calcium and phosphorous metabolism
Pancreatic isles	Insulin	Regulates carbohydrate metabolism

Table 3.1   The Major Endocrine Glands (*cont.*)

Gland	Hormones	Functions
Adrenal		
Medulla	Epinephrine	Supports stress reaction
		Releases stored blood sugar
	Norepinephrine	Maintains blood vessel tonus and blood pressure
Cortex	Steroid hormones including cortisone, cortisol, corticosterone, aldosterone, androgens and estrogens	Regulates metabolic processes
		Provides resistance to stress
		(See below for specific effects of sex hormones)
Gonads		
Testes	Androgens	Stimulate development of primary and secondary sexual characteristics
	Estrogens	May act as growth hormones for tissues of reproductive importance
Ovaries	Estrogens	Stimulate development of primary and secondary sexual characteristics; may act as growth hormone for tissues important for reproduction
	Androgens	Unclear
	Progestogins	Maintain pregnancy

Glands and Hormones

cellular activity in one or several *target organs.* Target organs are specific for a given hormone. Many hormones are essential for survival and are associated with particular metabolic processes. The adrenal cortex, for example, produces hormones necessary for salt metabolism. If the adrenal glands are removed, large quantities of salt must be ingested or the organism will die. Table 3.1 provides a list of the major endocrine glands and the hormones produced by these glands. Some of the functions of these hormones are also included in the Table. The endocrine system is best understood as a part of the regulatory and reactive functional unit that includes the nervous system. Striking behavioral changes associated with sexual maturity and reproductive functioning are related to endocrine function.

Androgens and Estrogens

Much of our knowledge about hormones and behavior comes from studies of sex hormones in nonhuman subjects. The male and female sex hormones, *androgens* and *estrogens* respectively, have been studied extensively. Their primary sources in the body can be removed without seriously weakening the animal. In contrast, removal of other endocrine glands may lead to rapid physical deterioration or death.

A great deal of the research on this topic has involved rats and guinea pigs. Sexual behavior in these rodents is dependent on hormones. Castrated males show no sexual behavior toward a receptive female unless injected with an androgen such as testosterone proprionate. Females whose ovaries have been removed come into estrus only when injected with an estrogen similar to the hormones produced by the ovaries around the time of ovulation.

Much individual variability exists in the relationship between hormones and sexual behavior in other animals. After observing a castrated chimpanzee that was quite active sexually, one authority in the field stated that simple mammals such as rats are hormonally dependent, but that complex animals such as primates are much less dependent on hormonal influences.[11] This statement is enthusiastically accepted by most of us, since we are sometimes hesitant to accept hormonal regulation of human behavior. In fact, the statement is commonly interpreted to mean that most human behavior, whether sexual or not, is independent of hormonal influences. As we shall see, this is not true.

When a large number of animal forms ranging from fish through reptiles, amphibians, birds, carnivorous mammals, nonhuman primates, and human beings is considered, rats and guinea pigs appear to be somewhat unique.[12] The castrated male rat or guinea pig

11. F. A. Beach, *Hormones and Behavior*, Harper, New York, 1948.
12. L. A. Aronson, "Hormones and Reproductive Behavior," in *Comparative Endocrinology*, ed. A. Gorbman, John Wiley, New York, 1959, pp. 98–120.

quickly loses interest in receptive females and is not subsequently interested without hormone therapy. Other species show similar patterns of response, but the pattern is by no means typical of all species. A more common reaction to castration involves a gradual reduction in sexual interest and vigor, with loss of some, but not necessarily all, components of sexual behavior.

Within a species there may be a great deal of individual variability. In a study of sexual behavior in castrated cats, three patterns of reactions were described.[13] All cats studied were sexually experienced adult males. One reaction was a ratlike cessation of all sexual behavior soon after castration. Another pattern of response involved complete sexual behavior for about two months and interest and mounting without intromission for a year. A third kind of castrate behavior included complete sexual behavior for a year and interest and mounting for five or more years. (The experimenter gave up before the cats did.) Large individual variation in reaction to castration is also found in clinical reports of human sexual behavior following removal of the testes.

Hormones are more clearly involved in the development of an adult repertoire of sexual behavior than in its maintenance. Prepubescent castration typically precludes the development of sexual behavior. However, rare cases of adultlike sexual behavior in prepubescent children have been reported.[14] Folk knowledge emphasizes the importance of gelding a horse after its testes descend but before it has any sexual experience.

The chimpanzee whose sexual prowess was so impressive was a prepubescent castrate. In this case, sexual behavior was observed after the chimpanzee had taken part in a study that involved injections of androgens. However, no androgens were injected near the time of the observed sexual behavior. In general, sex hormones are most clearly associated with the instigation and organization of adult sexual behavior. Hormones may or may not be necessary for maintenance of sexual behavior once initiated. In some species, all individuals appear to be dependent on hormonal support for continued maintenance of sexual behavior. In other species, including our own, individuals vary in their dependence on hormonal support.

13. Ibid.
14. W. Simon and J. H. Gagnon, "On Psychosexual Development," in *Sexuality: A Search for Perspective,* eds. D. L. Grummon and A. M. Barclay, Van Nostrand, New York, 1971, pp. 67–88.

Prenatal Hormonal Influences   The influence of sex hormones on behavior and structure do not begin at puberty. If pregnant guinea pigs or monkeys that are carrying genetic female fetuses are given intramuscular androgen injections, the fetuses will be masculinized.[15] The injections are most effective when given during the first trimester of pregnancy. External genital structures of the treated female infant at birth are almost identical to those of normal males. Even more important from the point of view of this book is the masculinization of the behavior of these *pseudohermaphrodites*. Pseudohermaphrodites are animals with both male and female genital traits who are members of a normally bisexual species. Guinea pigs given prenatal androgens may be masculinized behaviorally even if they appear structurally female. That is, they respond to injections of androgens given at maturity by displaying male sexual behavior patterns. Females not given prenatal androgen are much less likely to exhibit this reaction to androgen given at maturity. Masculinized females are also unresponsive to estrogens as adults, or at least are no more responsive to the female sex hormones than are normal males.

The behavior of monkey pseudohermaphrodites is even more striking, because masculinization of behavior occurs prior to sexual maturity and without additional hormonal injections. Genetic female monkeys given prenatal androgen show masculine play behavior. They threaten, mount, and play fight at about the same rates as normal male monkey infants. Normal female monkeys perform these behaviors less frequently than males.

Hormonal Changes at Sexual Maturity   In humans, the hormonal events occurring just prior to and during sexual maturity affect changes in metabolism rates, body shape and size, interests, and activities. Some changes in behavior that accompany sexual maturity are indirect results of hormonal activity. The attitudes and expectations of adults toward a child often reflect the child's apparent

15. C. H. Phoenix, R. W. Goy, A. A. Gerall, and W. C. Young, "Organizing Action of Prenatally Administered Testosterone Propinate on the Tissues Mediating Mating Behavior in the Female Guinea Pig," *Endocrinology*, 65 (1959), 369–382; and W. C. Young, R. W. Goy, and C. H. Phoenix, "Hormones and Sexual Behavior," *Science*, 143 (1964), 212.

Figure 3.3
Variations in Physical
Maturity in Children of the
Same Age
*(Reproduced by
permission of J. M.
Tanner.)*

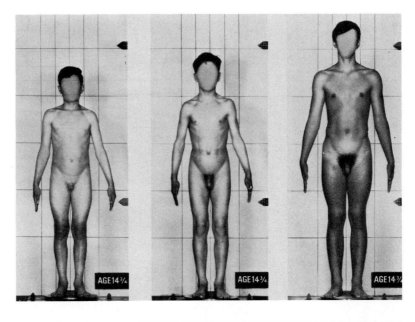

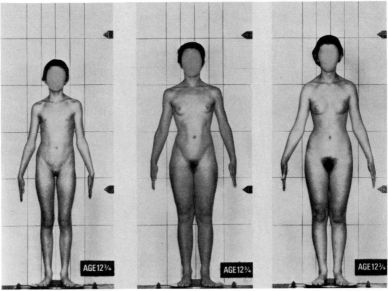

physical maturity rather than the child's actual age. As seen in Figure 3.3, age and physical maturity are not perfectly correlated. To some extent adult expectations shape the child's behavior. However, some changes in activity levels and objects of interest are more directly the result of hormonal activity.

Hormonal activity influences behavior throughout life. However, the most obvious effects occur at or near the time of puberty. At this time, the pituitary increases its output of growth hormones and gonadotrophins. Responses to these increases are rapid general body growth and rapid maturation of the testes or ovaries. The ovaries or testes begin to secrete high levels of estrogens or androgens, which affect specific growth processes. Interactions among the gonadal, pituitary, and thyroid hormones eventually inhibit the rapid growth characteristic of the prepubertal period. Behavioral changes accompany these complex hormonal and morphological events. The effects of these behaviors are seen directly in changes in sexual interest and activities and indirectly in modifications of social role and self-concept.

The changes occurring at puberty are not the result of sex hormone changes alone. The endocrine glands and their hormones are a complicated and interrelated system. Androgens and estrogens functionally interact with thyroxin, which affects activity levels, metabolic rate, and production of growth hormones. Puberty can be viewed as a period of change from one kind of hormonal balance to another. The hormonal changes associated with sexual maturity encompass the entire endocrine system, not just an isolated part of that system.

Expressions of
Ontogenetic Set

Sexual Identity and
Sex Role Behavior

At some time during late infancy or early childhood the developing human individual forms a personal gender identity.[16] The self is identified as male or female and the child consistently refers to itself as a boy or a girl. Gender identity is not totally determined by genital, hormonal, chromosomal, or genetic sex. Most individuals, of course, develop gender identity congruent with their apparent sex at birth.

16. J. Money, "Intersexual and Transexual Behavior," in *American Handbook of Psychiatry,* eds. S. Arieti and E. B. Brody, Basic Books, New York, 1975, pp. 334–351; and E. M. Maccoby and C. N. Jacklin, *The Psychology of Sex Differences,* Stanford University Press, Stanford, Cal., 1974.

Personal genital identity is attained early in development and is permanent in most individuals. Sex role behaviors, which are a partial expression of genital identity, are different for different ages, cultures, and experiential backgrounds. An individual's sex role behaviors are much more subject to change than is his or her core sexual identity.

One way to discuss sex role behaviors is to describe behavioral differences between the sexes. In a discussion of this sort it is important to keep in mind that average differences imply an overlap between groups. If males are on the average more aggressive than females, one should still expect to encounter individual females who are more aggressive than many males and individual males who are less aggressive than many females. It is also important to recognize that variability of this sort is a valuable characteristic of living organisms and should not be considered abnormal in any psychological sense.

Sex Differences in Behavior Patterns of masculinity and femininity show considerable variation across cultures, subcultures, and social classes. In this section we will present traits that appear to yield sex differences most often. Within a particular social group, other behavioral traits would also be likely to yield sex differences.

The tendency for males to be more aggressive than females is a pervasive behavioral sex difference. Sex differences in aggressive behavior may be observed as early as two years of age and are evident for all ages for which adequate data are available. Aggression has been found to be a masculine trait in every culture studied. Other characteristics associated with maleness are superior visual-spatial ability and superior mathematical ability. These differences do not appear until late childhood or early adolescence and they continue into adulthood. Females have superior verbal ability. Like mathematical ability, sex differences in verbal ability become evident in late childhood or early adolescence and continue into adulthood.

Girls are reported by themselves and their teachers to be more timid and anxious than boys. However, observational studies of fearful behavior do not support these reports. The widely held belief that males are more active than females is confirmed by some studies, while other studies have failed to find greater male activity. On balance, we disagree with Maccoby and Jacklin's interpretation that males are no more active than females. Sex differences favoring males in activity are reported from birth or shortly thereafter.[17] Differences in activity level are also evident in the social play behavior of males and females. We conclude that higher average male activity and need for activity is a probable, if disputed, sex difference in behavior.

Developing males appear to be more interested in social dominance than are females. Behaviors associated with dominance are a characteristic of all-male play groups. Such groups tend also to be larger than the social groups preferred by developing females. In older, mixed sex groups, male dominance is not universal.

Female children are more likely than male children to comply with adult demands, directions, and restrictions. However, female compliance may be limited to interactions with adults. Another trait attributed more frequently to females than to males is a tendency to be interested in and supportive of young children. Most of the evidence for this difference comes from more or less informal observations of young girls in many cultures.

The differences we have just described are one basis of sex role behavior. Other components of an individual's expression of masculinity or femininity are derived from specific cultural ideals. One focus of interest in this area has been the mechanisms involved in an individual's acquisition of sex role behavior. In the next section we will discuss these mechanisms.

The Development of Sex Role Behaviors   Psychological processes often used to account partially for sex role behaviors include identification, observational learning, and differential reinforcement. Identification is a complicated concept from psychoanalytic theory. Briefly, *identification* refers to a tendency on the part of the child to take on the personality characteristics of another person. In the context of sex role development, the child would tend to take on the characteristics of a same-sex adult. *Observational learning* refers to the same sort of process as identification, except that observational learning means imitation of the behavior of the same-sex adult

17. J. E. Garai and A. Scheinfeld, "Sex Differences in Mental and Behavioral Traits," *Genetic Psychology Monographs,* 77 (1968), 169–299; and Maccoby and Jacklin.

model, whereas identification refers to the internalization of under-lying personality traits as well as the behavioral patterns. A third process used to explain the development of sex role behaviors is that of *differential reinforcement*. This concept refers to the tendency of adults and other children to encourage behaviors in a developing child that conform to appropriate sex role standards and to discourage behaviors that do not conform to these standards. The precise contribution of hormonal factors, personality development within the child, external stimulation provided by models for observational learning, and social reinforcement cannot be determined from the research currently available.

Some idea of the importance of particular same-sex and opposite-sex adults in the child's social environment can be derived from studies of single-parent families. For research purposes, it would be interesting to study children reared exclusively by adult females and those reared exclusively by males. However, as in all deprivation studies, both moral and practical limitations must always prevail over any purely scientific purposes. Until recently, Western legal practice has usually placed children with mothers instead of fathers if at all possible. Even when death or abandonment left the child with only a father, a female relative or other mother substitute was almost always provided for the child. The available studies, then, concern children raised by their mothers when the fathers were either permanently absent through death or divorce or gone for long periods, as in time of war.

These studies of children reared only by mothers do not imply total absence of male figures. Male friends and relatives often serve some paternal functions for the child. Furthermore, older children and peers may also serve functions similar to parents. In any case, children raised principally by their mothers have been the focus of the studies to be discussed.

Slight differences are found between children raised by their mothers only and those raised in two-parent families.[18] Males raised only by mothers tend to show slightly less aggression and dominance than those raised by both parents. These males show more reactions of fear and dependence than do males raised in two-parent families.

18. E. M. Hetherington and R. D. Parke, *Child Psychology*, McGraw Hill, New York, 1975, pp. 354–379.

The differences in girls are slighter. In general, girls raised without available fathers show some differences in their approach to heterosexual relationships in adolescence. These differences may consist of withdrawal from heterosexual contacts or at the other extreme a slightly more aggressive and more widely dispersed search for heterosexual contact than is found in adolescent girls raised by both parents.

In summary, the males raised primarily by mothers exhibit behavior slightly less masculine in the conventional sense. For females, the effects of rearing by mothers only shows during adolescence in slight difficulties in making heterosexual adjustments.

Again, the point needs to be made that most children raised in single-parent homes differ only slightly or not at all from other children. The increase in single-parent homes in our society means that the social disapproval formerly associated with single parenthood is likely to fade. This should facilitate the adjustment of children in such families. Finally, we must emphasize that the quality of the child's family is more strongly influenced by the affection and care given by the adult family members than by their gender. Affectional relationships and emotional stability are the most important features of this environment.

Identification, observational learning, and role modeling account for some sex role behaviors. However, these concepts do not explain all of the masculine and feminine patterns observed in developing children. Another way to look at the development of sex role behavior is to assume that the child develops a mental or cognitive structure that defines patterns of masculinity and femininity. At the same time, the child incorporates one of these patterns into his or her view of the self. The very young child's ideas of masculinity and femininity tend to be rigid and frequently idiosyncratic. As the child grows older the personal definition of femininity or masculinity becomes more like the culture's stereotypes of masculinity and femininity. The child will to some extent shape his or her behavior in terms of the mental picture of sex-appropriate behavior he or she has developed.

Problems in Sexual Identity The importance of an early and unambiguous sexual identity is most clearly seen in individuals whose genital development at birth is ambiguous. Two rare conditions produce genetic females who have partially masculinized genitals. One of these conditions is produced by artificial hormones formerly given to pregnant women to help maintain pregnancy.[19] The artificial hormone given in these cases is not an androgen but is chemically similar to testosterone and apparently had testosterone-like effects on the developing fetus. The other condition is due to an inborn error in cortisone biosynthesis that results in an excess of fetal androgen in genetic females.[20] Both groups of girls are born with ambiguous external genitals. In the cases reported, surgical modification produced essentially normal genital appearance early in development.

The authors of these reports emphasize the importance of early sexual identification of the child. Patients with unclear or ambiguous personal gender identity tend to experience considerable adjustment difficulties throughout development. Early and expert determination of the best sexual choice for the child is very important. As far as the child's psychological adjustment is concerned, very early surgical treatment also appears to be preferable to later treatment.

Prenatal masculinization in these girls appears to have included a degree of behavioral masculinization as well as genital modification. Self-reports and mother accounts indicate that more of the girls in these two groups are tomboys and more prefer boys' toys and active "masculine" play behaviors than do girls with normal fetal genital development. The tomboy role assumed by these girls is one accepted feminine role in our society. The point here is that human beings, like the monkeys discussed in the previous section, are behaviorally influenced by the early hormonal environment.

Despite the difficulties presented by prenatal masculinization, these girls developed a feminine personal gender identity. As a result of appropriate surgical treatment coupled with counseling for the girls and their parents, twenty-four of twenty-five girls developed an unambiguous female self-identification. Their sex role

19. A. A. Ehrhardt and J. Money, "Progestin-induced Hermaphroditism: IQ and Psychosexual Identity in a Study of Ten Girls," *The Journal of Sex Research,* 3 (1967), 83–100.

20. A. A. Ehrhardt, R. Epstein, and J. Money, "Fetal Androgens and Female Gender Identity in the Early Treated Andrenogenital Syndrome," *The Johns Hopkins Medical Journal,* 122 (1968), 160–167.

behavior had a somewhat masculine flavor, which was identified by themselves and their parents as tomboyish. This expression of femininity is a culturally acceptable pattern in our society and is in no way inconsistent with successful adjustment to traditional feminine sexual and maternal roles.

Changes in Sex Role Behavior   There appears to be a trend toward some breakdown of rigidly defined behavioral stereotypes for masculinity and femininity in our society. This is certainly to be applauded when it leads to greater acceptance of individual variability. In dealing with young children, it is important to discriminate between permitting variable expressions of sexuality and confusing the child with respect to its sexual identity. The authors believe that the development of an unambiguous personal gender identity is very important for later adjustment. The particular behaviors that express that identity are less important and more subject to change.

Honeybee Work Roles

The development of work roles in an adult honeybee is an excellent example of the influence of age-dependent processes on behavior.[21] When the young worker honeybee first comes from her cell she assumes housekeeping duties, cleaning cells as new bees develop and leave them. After a few days she acts as a nurse, feeding older larvae honey and pollen. As her nurse glands develop, she begins to feed young larvae and larvae destined to become queens the special fluid they require. While bees at this age may fly about the hive, they do not forage. The nurse glands atrophy as the wax glands develop and begin to function. At the same time the bee's activities shift. She now takes honey and pollen from foragers, stores it or feeds it to other bees, and builds new wax cells. She also functions as a garbage collector, taking trash and even dead bees out of the hive. Her next function is that of a guard, and she inspects many bees as they come into the nest. The last two or three weeks of the bee's six-week life are spent foraging for nectar and pollen.

Some of the older foragers also serve as scout bees, informing other bees about the location and quality of sources of nectar and

21. M. Lindauer, *Communication Among Social Bees,* Harvard University Press, Cambridge, Mass., 1961.

pollen. This information is communicated to bees in the hive in a dance performed by returning foragers on the vertical face of a honeycomb. As seen in Figure 3.4, other foragers follow the dancing scout. The direction of a source of food is communicated by the orientation of the dance. If the long axis of the waggle dance is directed straight up, the nectar supply is in the direction of the sun. Any angle with respect to the vertical corresponds to an equivalent angle with respect to the sun. The taste and odor of the nectar is directly communicated by feeding samples to the bees following the scout in her dance, and in some cases this appears to be all that is necessary. The distance of the source appears to be correlated with

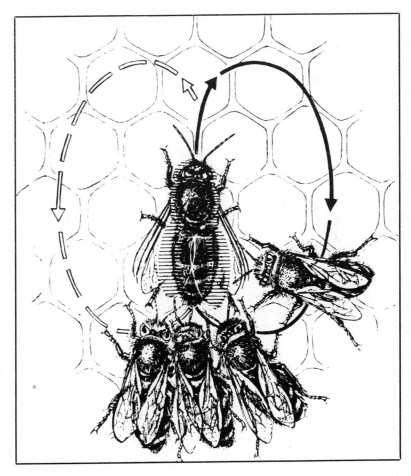

Figure 3.4
Dancing Bee
(*Karl von Frisch*, Aus dem Leben der Bienen, *Springer-Verlag, Heidelberg, 1927. Reproduced by permission of the author and the publisher.*)

the number of abdominal movements made by the scout in the straight part of the dance. Nearby sources of nectar are indicated by a simpler round dance that does not include directional cues. The quality of a source of nectar is indicated by the duration of the scout's dance. Duration of the dance also influences the number of recruits she sends to the source. In many cases, foragers may simply follow the scout to the new source, but the source can be located by other bees from the dance alone. Scout bees also communicate information concerning hive sites when the bees are about to swarm. At this time dances may continue for several hours, and the long axis of the dance changes to compensate for movement of the sun.

As we have seen, the roles of worker honeybees change as they grow older, and these changes are associated with structural and physiological changes. The activities of the bees are not independent of environmental influences. If the young bees are removed from a hive, some foragers will regenerate nurse or wax glands and assume care of the developing larvae. If the foragers are removed from a hive, young bees will begin to forage. To the writers' knowledge there is no information on dancing in young bees forced to forage.

One would suspect that dances performed by young workers forced into a scout role would be less precise and effective than is usual in communications of scout bees. In these social insects, typical behavioral development is strongly associated with maturational processes. This influence of Ontogenetic Set is modified by environmental pressures but permits prediction of a bee's activity under normal conditions.

Locomotor Development in Children

One obvious expression of Ontogenetic Set in human development is the development of locomotor ability.[22] This process, although called "learning to walk," is actually an expression of maturation that is minimally dependent on the environment. While there is considerable individual variability in the time a given response is seen in an infant, the sequence of development illustrated in Figure 3.5 is generally the same for different infants. Only occasional exceptional individuals may show sequence reversals. The infant may be able to raise the head while in a prone position shortly after birth, and most infants show this response by one month of age. By two months he

22. Espenschade and Eckert.

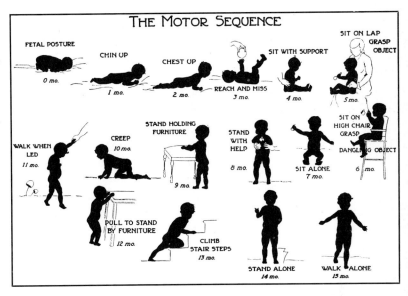

Figure 3.5
The Motor Sequence
*(From M. M. Shirley, The
First Two Years: A Study of
Twenty-Five Babies, vol.
II, 1933, University of
Minnesota Press,
Frontispiece. Reprinted by
permission of the
University of Minnesota
Press, Minneapolis.)*

or she can raise the chest as well as the chin. Many four-month-olds can sit with support, and by six months babies are able to sit in high chairs or other supporting furniture. The seven-month-old may sit alone, and within a month he or she can stand with support. The nine-month-old can stand holding onto furniture and will shortly begin to creep on all fours. By a year the child is pulling up to stand with support and may have been walking when led by the hand for a month or more. A few babies walk independently at one year, but thirteen to fifteen months is the most typical age for this accomplishment. Usually the child stands and learns to crawl up stairs prior to walking alone. The combination of walking and climbing brings about interesting experiences for the family of the newly competent explorer.

This sequence of progressive motor competence appears to be resistant to environmental manipulation. While severe restriction can delay development, a very wide range of opportunities to practice locomotor skills produces equivalent locomotor development. There is some evidence of genetic influence on the rate of physical and locomotor development. In some parts of Africa, children show rapid physical development during the first two years of life. The rapid early development seen in these children appears to be associated with lower rates of maturation in the period from two to five years, so that differences are not apparent at six years of age.

Social Attachments in Birds and Mammals

In social birds and mammals, one of the most important events of life is the development of attachment toward other organisms of the same species. In most species the first attachment is developed for the mother, or in the case of some birds that share parental responsibilities, for both parents. In many species affectional development within a litter or with unrelated age mates is important, but the greatest amount of information is available for infant-mother interactions. It is in the context of infant-mother interaction that the term critical period has been most often used, particularly with respect to imprinting.

The term *imprinting* was initially used to describe the attachment of precocial birds to mothers or mother substitutes.[23] Konrad Lorenz first popularized the concept in his descriptions of greylag geese that imprinted on him. In many species of birds that hatch in a relatively mature state, there is a tendency to follow the first moving object the bird encounters. The little bird will persist in following that object and may emit distress cries if separated from the imprinted object. The immediacy of imprinting, its relative permanence, and the wide range of potential imprinting objects have caught the attention of many scientists. Imprinting is limited to a very narrow period early in the bird's life, a striking feature of the process. The beginning of the imprinting period appears to be determined by the bird's ability to follow, that is, to visually orient to the imprinting object and walk toward it. The end of the imprinting period was originally thought to be associated with the development of fear of novel objects. However, eliminating fear responses extends the imprinting period only slightly. Species differences in imprinting in birds have already been described and will be considered in greater detail in Chapter 11. Our concern in this chapter is primarily in the ontogenetic development of imprinting as a general phenomenon.

Imprinting is not irreversible. The younger the bird, the greater the likelihood of a shift of allegiance to a new object. The likelihood of a shift is increased if the new object is an adult female of the appropriate species. If the initial imprinting object is an adult female of the right species, shifts are very unlikely.

Similar patterns of early attachment with minimal experience is characteristic of mammals with very precocious locomotor ability. Mary's lamb is too trite an example of imprinting in mammals (see

23. W. Slukin, *Imprinting and Early Learning,* Aldine, Chicago, 1965.

Figure 3.6). In goats the newborn kid appears to be attracted to any adult goat, but it will be rejected by any female that has not interacted with the kid or its siblings within five minutes of giving birth. There is a highly sensitive period for maternal olfactory imprinting, and apparently this is associated with hormonal changes accompanying the birth process. The little goat subsequently learns to identify its mother as a function of violent rejection by all other females. This pattern of maternal specificity is certainly not true for herding mammals generally. Roe deer provide one example of a more permissive system in which alien young are permitted to nurse. The effects of hand-rearing in some ungulates is similar to alien imprinting in birds, in that the alien-imprinted adults may be socially incompetent.

The term "imprinting" has also been applied to early social attachments in altricial species, although it loses much of its original meaning in this context. Social attachment occurs over a much longer period in finches and cats than in ducks and goats. The processes involved in altricial species are more likely to include associative learning. This implies a wide range of stimuli and a longer period of development. Surely, many periods of exposure to the litter mates and mother are experienced before the end of a

Figure 3.6
Following in a Goose
(Mary Thacker/Photo
Researchers, Inc.)

sensitive period for attachment. Still, there are a number of points of similarity in the development of attachments in precocial and altricial organisms. The most striking is the existence for most species of a period of sensitivity to attachment objects followed by a relatively strong resistance to attachment. Scott identified the period up to ten to fourteen weeks as highly important for attachment of dogs to human beings.[24] Puppies isolated from human beings for this period are almost impossible to tame. Many readers will be familiar with the common difficulty of taming a kitten whose mother kept it away from humans until it was half grown. If the information from birds is a good indication, one would expect dogs and cats to be able to form attachments to members of their own species even after they are too old to attach to humans. Eventually, however, a pattern of fear and avoidance toward even their own species would develop.

It is an error to consider social attachment as a fairly mechanical outcome of maturation alone. As mentioned earlier in this chapter, developing kittens interact with the mother and litter mates, stimulating them and initiating behaviors that provide stimulation in return. The mother is not a passive producer of visual, tactual, and gustatory stimulation but is a dynamic and reactive part of the kitten's environment. The development of attachment is determined in large part by Ontogenetic Set, but the maturational processes underlying attachment can only function adequately in the interactive and supportive environment provided by a mother and litter mates. An American zoologist, T. C. Schneirla, saw the dynamic interrelationships between mother and litter as a functional mosaic and emphasized the role of the environment in determining the behavior of the kitten.[25] Our emphasis on the ontogenetic development of attachment carries with it no implication that specific characteristics of the environment are not essential for adequate affectional development.

A similar kind of interdependence between maturation and environment may be seen in infant-mother interactions in rhesus monkeys. Monkeys reared without social experience with other monkeys

24. J. P. Scott, "Critical Periods in Behavioral Development," *Science,* 138 (1962), 949–958.

25. T. C. Schneirla, J. S. Rosenblatt, and E. Tobach, "Maternal Behavior in the Cat," in *Maternal Behavior in Mammals,* ed. H. L. Rheingold, John Wiley, New York, 1963, pp. 122–168.

for six to twelve months are socially inadequate.[26] Rearing with either the mother or peers alleviates much of the effect of this restriction. If restricted monkeys are given later experience with younger peers they show a degree of recovery from the effects of restriction. One might ask, "At what age would reunion with the mother alleviate the effects of isolation?" But this turns out to be a moot question. Many rhesus monkeys that have previously had babies readily adopt infants that are taken from their own mothers and then caged with the foster mother. The female monkeys hold the baby, groom it, permit it to suckle, and within a few days begin to produce milk. However, if a baby has been isolated for a month or more it is unlikely to be adopted. The prospective foster parent will approach the infant and attempt to pick it up. The baby resists, screams, and behaves in an altogether unmonkeylike fashion. The adult frequently recognizes its error in thinking that this object was a baby monkey and makes no further attempt to interact with it.

The point here is that the mother and infant, and litter mates if they are present, mutually stimulate each other. Appropriate behavior on the part of one actor initiates and maintains appropriate behavior on the part of the other. Since the babies of brutal monkey mothers persist in attempting to cling to them, it appears that the mother's behavior is somewhat more dependent on her early experience than is the infant's behavior on adequate stimulation. However, sufficient deficit in stimulation so modifies the infant's behavior that the infant no longer functions as a generator of maternal behavior. Development in atypical environments produces atypical behavior. These inappropriate behavior patterns may preclude or markedly interfere with subsequent species- and age-typical behavior.

In both precocial and altricial social organisms, early attachments are significantly related to later social behavior. The organisms less mature at birth or hatching are probably somewhat more flexible and their early attachment outcomes more susceptible to later modification. For most species there appears to be a point in development that terminates a period of ready social attachment. This point is usually associated with the appearance of indications of fear of novel

26. H. F. Harlow and M. K. Harlow, "The Affectional Systems," in *Behavior of Nonhuman Primates*, eds. A. M. Schrier, H. F. Harlow, and F. Stollnitz, Academic Press, New York, 1965, vol. II, pp. 287–334.

objects or situations. However, there is no clearcut causal relationship between fear of novelty and the end of a sensitive period for attachment.

Most authorities agree that a capacity for affection is an important aspect of normal human adjustment. The human infant, as was seen in the last chapter, begins to respond socially within the first month of postnatal life. John Bowlby a British psychoanalyst feels that there is a sensitive period for human maternal attachment.[27] The failure to develop an early attachment is presumed to have profound effects on later development. It is difficult to specify a sensitive period for human maternal attachment. Ethical and moral considerations prevent isolation studies of human infants. Another complicating factor is that some children show two periods of fear of novel social stimuli, one at about eight or nine months and another at eighteen months to two years. Even if some maximally sensitive period for affectional development were specified—say between eight and eighteen months of age—some individuals would undoubtedly develop adequate affectional ties after this period.

Other authorities place the sensitive period for human affectional development between six weeks and six months of age, basing their ideas on the maturation of learning capacities by six weeks and the initial appearance of fear of strangers soon after six months. The most general statement that can be made is that the development of social attachment typically occurs during the first two years of human life, and that failure to develop affectional ties during this period will be associated with subsequent atypical development. The generality of this statement is based on a great deal of ignorance. At this point it would seem essential to provide infants with adequate social stimulation throughout the first two years and thereafter.

It should be emphasized that while mothers are the most common affectional object, they are not the only adequate social stimulus, as indicated in Figure 3.7. Any older human being is a great deal better than a bare crib. In one study, retarded adolescent girls provided affectionate care for a group of institutionalized infants.[28] Followup reports after thirty years indicated remarkable differences between the "mothered" babies and a contrast group. A partial cause of many

27. J. Bowlby, *Attachment and Loss: Attachment,* Basic Books, New York, 1969.
28. H. M. Skeels, "Adult Status of Children with Contrasting Early Life Experiences," *Monographs of the Society for Research in Child Development,* 31, No. 3 (1966).

Figure 3.7
Social Stimulation
(Erika Stone from Peter
Arnold)

of the differences was that most of the "mothered" babies were later adopted, while only a few of the contrast group were selected for adoption. One suspects that prospective adoptive parents were able to discriminate, without knowing what they were discriminating, between infants who had developed affectional ties and those who had not.

In summary, the timing and course of social attachment are expressions of Ontogenetic Set. Within a particular species, there is a period of maximal probability of attachment. There are differences between species in the consequences of initial attachments. The degree of recovery of social and affectionate capacity after the passing of the sensitive period varies among species and among individuals within a species. The development of social attachment exemplifies the interactive nature of behavioral determination.

Intellectual Development in Children

During the past two decades our understanding of intellectual development has changed greatly. Only a few years ago, the prevailing studies in this field described the average age of attainment of certain sensory, motor, and verbal behaviors. These behavioral components were believed to be a representative sample of intelligence. In addition, the correlation of individual differences in these components with sex, socioeconomic, and ethnic variables was investigated.

Recently, considerable interest has been accorded to the theories and observations of the Swiss child psychologist Jean Piaget.[29] Piaget, seen in Figure 3.8, and other cognitive psychologists have been interested in the processes underlying adult intelligence and in their ontogenetic course during childhood and adolescence. Moving away from the study of individual differences, the cognitive psychologists have turned their attention to intellectual structures and functioning shared by all humans.

In this section we will present an overall view of intellectual or cognitive development based on the work of Piaget and other psychologists of this tradition. Since the work is based on studies of human subjects, we will restrict our discussion to this species. However, as will be seen in Chapter 9, there is no reason to believe that the underlying psychological processes in human beings are basically different from those in some other animals. For many species the differences may be more apparent than real.

At every stage of development, intellectual processes may be understood by using the same principles that apply to other biological phenomena. One principle is the classification into structure and function. As applied to the development of intelligence, the functions of intellect are constant over time. These functions include the organization of behavior and adaptation to the environment.

29. J. Piaget and B. Inhelder, *The Psychology of the Child*, Basic Books, New York, 1969.

Figure 3.8
Jean Piaget
(Yves de Braine/Black Star)

The function of organization is to relate intellectual activities to each other within the organism. Adaptation relates thinking to things and events in the external world. These functions of organization and adaptation remain basic to intellectual processes from infancy on. Piaget calls them *functional invariants* since they do not change with maturation.

The bridge between functional adaptation and changing intellectual structures is provided by the processes of assimilation and accommodation. As said previously, adaptation refers to the relationship between thought and things. The mechanisms of accommodation and assimilation balance the characteristics of objects and the person's understanding of these objects. In *assimilation,* new experience with an object utilizes an intellectual structure already available to the organism. In *accommodation,* no existing structure provides an adequate match with the new object or experience, and so a new structural arrangement is made to provide a better fit to the experience. Together, assimilation and accommodation are the mechanisms for adaptation, the balance of thought and experience.

While the functional invariants of organization and adaptation remain stable over the life span, the content and structures of thinking are constantly changing during maturation. These structures and the contents of thinking must change for the organism to adapt to the environment. The organization of abilities must also change to reflect maturation and experience.

The direction of the changes in intellectual structures is toward balance. Like other biological growth, intellectual development is directed toward balancing the structures within the organism and between the organism and its environment.

The direction of intellectual functioning at every age is toward *equilibration,* the ultimate balance of all forces, external and internal. The particular compromise between the organism and environment made at any given moment, a kind of trial balance, is called an *equilibrium.* Equilibration is unattainable during life, because the end of the road cannot be precisely described. Because equilibration is unattainable, developmental changes in intellectual processes continue throughout the life span.

This discussion of intellectual development as a process directed toward achievement of balance between the organism and its external environment will be clarified by the following example. In reaching for an object, a child of six months usually closes the hand only after making initial palmar contact. This strategy permits the child to grasp stable objects such as wooden blocks. However, very light objects like sheets of paper are often displaced by the initial contact. To effectively grasp a light object, the fingers must be prepositioned so that closure is almost instantaneous upon contact. Indeed, the developmental sequence of grasping behavior from postcontact closure to instantaneous closure is seen during the first six months of life, as a part of the development of visually directed grasping. This example involves sensory and motor behavior but is being used to illustrate intellectual development. Many developmental psychologists believe that sensory and motor behavior reflect intellectual development as surely as does verbal and mathematical functioning.

Maturation and experience interact to produce age changes in the modes of behavioral expression of intellectual functioning. A sequence of stages is one useful way of describing these changes.

The sequence is universal, but timing varies from one individual to another. The reader will recall that locomotor behavior shows this pattern of variation—that is, an individual may pass through one stage quickly, but the next slowly. In the example given above, as the mode of expression of grasping changed, there was concomitant change from reflexive to voluntary control. An individual's behavior may also be described as fitting one stage in a particular environment and a different stage in another environmental situation.

The labels and descriptions offered below are meant to familiarize the reader with Piaget's ideas. Detailed consideration of these stages will be discussed in Chapters 8 and 9, which cover the orientation and organization of behavior. Piaget classifies intellectual development into four major stages: sensory-motor, preoperational, concrete operations, and formal operations. Piaget believes that the sequence—sensory-motor, preoperational, concrete operations, and formal operations—describes the course of intellectual development of all members of the human species during the preadult years. More detailed discussions of intellectual development require a large number of substages, which will not be discussed here.

The *sensory-motor stage* is the easiest of the stages to describe and understand. Behavioral indices of intellectual activity are found in sensory-motor functions like grasping an object in the visual field or showing surprise when a moving object fails to reappear after going behind an obstruction.

The *preoperational stage* is that period during which the cognitive structures necessary for concrete operations develop. An example of achievement during the preoperational stage would be the differentiation of verbal labels to specific referents. For example, whereas the two-year-old may call any four-legged animal a "cow," the five-year-old is able to use appropriately the words "cow," "horse," and the like. In the domain of numbers, the two-year-old may have the idea of "oneness" and "manyness" but cannot yet match number names with sets of objects. By the age of seven, the child can match any set of objects up to about fifteen in number with the appropriate number names. An explanation of how this elegant triple correspondence between idea of number, name of number, and application to an actual numerical situation comes about will be reserved for later chapters.

The stage of *concrete operations* is characteristically marked by the ability to manipulate several dimensions of real-world objects at the same time. For example, the ten-year-old can integrate length, width, and depth so that he or she is not tricked by appearances when liquid is poured from one container to another of a different size or shape. The ten-year-old can perform the mental gymnastics required to compensate for these perceptual tricks by knowing the rules governing estimation of volume, mass, and number. He or she can apply these rules to liquids, solids, and collections whether or not the specific objects are present or absent.

The stage of *formal operations* is the final stage described by Piaget. From about age twelve onward the person can extrapolate from all earlier experiences—sensory-motor, preoperational, and concrete operational—to situations that are hypothetical, including probabilistic situations. For example, the adolescent may talk about a weather forecast predicting a 60 percent likelihood of showers with some understanding. In our opinion, human adults typically function at the stage of concrete operations. Some individuals use formal operations some of the time. A schematic representation of intellectual development is provided in Figure 3.9.

The stages of intellectual development sketched in Figure 3.9 show an orderly progression that each individual follows. Attainment of the competencies of one stage presupposes attainment of previous competencies. The adult, then, easily shifts from one stage of behavioral expression to another as he or she goes about daily activities. In the course of a day, an adult may consider the chances

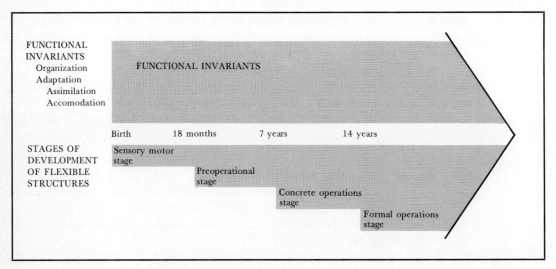

Figure 3.9
Intellectual Development

of settling the latest international dispute (formal operations, verbal expression) while reading the newspaper. On purchasing a new shotgun, the buyer carefully assesses the relationship between weight and balance while sighting imaginary game with various models (concrete operations, nonverbal mode of information). Finally, the adult may grasp a glass of his or her favorite beverage after a single cursory glance in its direction with only minimal awareness of the size, shape, and weight of the glass, its location with respect to his or her position, or the location of the arms and hands (sensory-motor, nonverbal mode of information).

When buying groceries, the adult symbolically manipulates the contents of the pantry and refrigerator and the checking account in terms of the available items and their prices. These functions are performed at the level of concrete operations. Many interactions with the environment, such as playing poker or bridge, can be accomplished at the level of concrete operations, but striking increases in performance and experienced pleasure accompany applications of formal operations to these pursuits.

It has been pointed out that quite intelligent adults behave in a preoperational manner when dealing with areas of personal ignorance. A gifted historian will, for example, apply childlike concepts of causality to the phenomena of atomic physics. Such findings emphasize the progressive nature of intellectual maturation and the fact that the accomplishments of one level of development are necessary for the expression of the next level. Piaget describes the child's developing capacity to deal with its environment and the orderly changes that accompany intellectual maturation. His findings are to some degree culture specific, in that the exact timing of the stages appears to vary among different societies.

Intellectual development is a function of Ontogenetic Set. The child interacts with the environment, and the style of this interaction is determined by maturation and previous experiences. In the normal environment, the effects of the child's manipulations shape subsequent individual development. A species typical sequence of stages of intellectual functioning is expressed as the child's genetic potential is realized via maturation in a supportive environment.

Characteristics of Ontogenetic Set

Ontogenetic Set is the influence of life-span developmental processes on behavior. Sequences of development and characteristic rates of development are species typical traits. Ontogenetic Set, therefore, functions within limits determined by Phylogenetic Set. Ontogenetic Set and Phylogenetic Set are joint expressions of the influence of the biological history of a species on the behavior of current members of that species. Ontogenetic Set cannot be expressed without an organism-environment interaction, and therefore the effects of Ontogenetic Set are always partially dependent on the environment. Typical development for a particular species is dependent on some environment within the limits of viability for that species. Developmental norms may be violated, as when young honeybees become foragers, but this probably reduces the viability of the particular individuals or group so influenced.

An important aspect of Ontogenetic Set is the effect of age-related physical and physiological change. As an organism matures, its potential range of behavior changes, and its capacity to receive information from the environment changes. Structural and hormonal influences on behavior tend to dramatize the biological nature of Ontogenetic Set. The developing honeybee feeds larvae when her nurse glands mature and begin to function. In human beings, members of the opposite sex become objects of particular interest to pubescent children. These evidences of structural or physiological behavioral determination must not be interpreted to indicate independence from environmental influences. We know that if no young adult bees are present, nurse glands regenerate and older bees feed larvae. We do not fully know what triggers puberty in human beings, but environmental influences cannot be ruled out at this time.

Cultural Set may modify the expression of Ontogenetic Set. As a child grows older, physical and intellectual capacities change. These changes may be associated with an introduction to formal education in one society, the assumption of responsibility for younger children in another, or the assignment of specific work roles in a third. The adolescent may enjoy a temporary vacation from required tasks or may be required to begin to make decisions with long-term consequences for adult life. In no case can the expression of Ontogenetic Set be isolated from the underlying maturational processes. Human behavioral development is the product of the interaction between a maturing organism and a particular physical and sociocultural environment.

Individual variation in behavioral development is usually characterized by rate rather than sequence variation. That is, the developing organism expresses a species typical sequence of behavioral maturation. The timing of these sequential changes is quite variable and is susceptible to experiential influence. Some reversals in the usual sequence of behavioral events will occur, but most individual variation will be expressed in relative speed or slowness in going through a normal sequence of development.

Summary

Ontogenetic Set is the influence of maturational processes on behavior. It is a partial determinant of behavior that, like Phylogenetic Set, is an expression of the biological determination of behavior. In the course of individual development, members of a species exhibit behavioral sequences that are species typical. Individual variation in sequential rates is typical.

The influence of Ontogenetic Set can be modified by environmental events. In some cases environmental effects are associated with physical or physiological alterations. In other cases, behavior may be altered without other apparent effects. The sociocultural environment modifies the expression of Ontogenetic Set in developing children.

Hormonal influences on behavior have been presented in this chapter as an example of physiological determination of ontogenetic characteristics. As the organism matures, the endocrine system balance changes. The results of endocrine system activity modify the developing organism structurally and psychologically. These modifications directly and indirectly influence behavior. Such changes permit rather than cause changes in behavior, and the specific behavioral concomitants of hormonal changes are in part due to the environment.

Examples of expressions of Ontogenetic Set were given for several behavioral processes in insects, birds, and mammals. Species typical sequences are evident in work roles in honeybees, social attachment in birds and mammals, and locomotor, intellectual, and social development in human beings. In every case, the typical expression of Ontogenetic Set interacts with other partial determinants of behavior in the development of individual organisms.

Defined Terms

Hormone	Estrogens	Identification
Target organ	Pseudohermaphro-	Observational
Androgens	dites	learning

Differential reinforcement	Assimilation	Sensory-motor stage
Imprinting	Accommodation	Preoperational stage
Functional invariants	Equilibration	Concrete operations
	Equilibrium	Formal operations

Suggested Readings   J. Piaget, "Piaget's Theory," in *Carmichael's Handbook of Child Psychology*, ed. P. H. Mussen, John Wiley, 1970, pp. 703–732.

This is the most succinct presentation Piaget has made of his ideas. While his work never provides easy reading, the student should not miss the opportunity of reading the core ideas of a major figure in psychology in less than thirty pages.

E. Salzen, "Imprinting in Birds and Mammals," *Behavior*, 28 (1967), 232–254.

A fine review of imprinting phenomena in many species. While the writing is somewhat technical, it is recommended for psychology and biological sciences majors.

J. P. Scott, "Critical Periods in Behavioral Development," *Science*, 138 (1962), 949–958.

This article reviews the concept of critical periods and provides examples for many species, including human beings. While the term "sensitive period" is now preferred for many of these phenomena, Scott's presentation is well worth the student's attention.

B. L. White, *The First Three Years of Life*, Prentice-Hall, Englewood Cliffs, N.J., 1975.

A well-balanced, complete, nontechnical presentation of the findings on physical and intellectual development in infancy and early childhood. The author's ideas about optimal physical environments and behavioral management are his own but should challenge the reader.

Chapter 4
Experiential Set

The development of behavior is continuously influenced by forces arising within the organism and those originating in external inanimate objects and other organisms. In the previous chapters, the influence of species characteristics (Phylogenetic Set) and the timing mechanisms of maturation (Ontogenetic Set) was emphasized. External influences are termed the "environmental aspects" of behavior. Objects, both living and nonliving, provide external stimulation to the organism and are in turn the recipients of its actions. For the purposes of this discussion the "environment" will include all elements regarded as independent of the organism. All elements in the environment do not directly influence behavior.

Individual Behavioral Settings

A given environment represents a very different set of stimuli for individuals of different maturity. The baby's room in Figure 4.1 has recently been decorated by the parents of its newborn occupant. Walls displaying mother goose characters, the mobile hanging from the ceiling, the music box that plays "Mary Had a Little Lamb" have been carefully arranged to provide pleasure and rich stimulation for the neonate.

The infant probably can focus only on objects within 3 feet of its head. In prone or supine posture the child is usually drowsy the first month or so.[1] Infants are alert when placed head upright during feeding, and they focus on the mother's face. When the father or grandmother feeds the infant, its behavior manifests its inability to tell the difference for some time. For two months, the baby's small world consists of the mother's face, its own hands, and whatever else is within 2 or 3 feet of its head.

Substantial indirect effects of the decorated infant's room should be noted. The mother recalls with pleasure her own memories of nursery rhymes as she enters the room and interacts with the baby several times each day. As she handles the infant, she recites the rhymes suggested by the wall decorations and sings to the infant as the music box plays. She blows on the mobile while holding the child in a supported upright position and turns the baby's head toward the moving objects suspended from the mobile. While the mother

1. T. G. R. Bower, *Development in Infancy*, W. H. Freeman, San Francisco, 1974, pp. 83–84.

Figure 4.1
Baby's Room
(Suzanne Arms/Jeroboam)

may be more or less knowledgeable about the timing of milestones in her child's development, she provides for the child effective stimulation of at least a minimum variety and complexity. From this array of objects and person-object interactions the child selects experiences to fit developing perceptual, motor, and cognitive organization.

The point is that the objective environment is only partially effective in stimulating the infant. The mother responds and is capable of responding to many features of the nursery that do not exist for the infant. The effective environment for the mother is based on the present setting and her previous experiences. As the child develops, its behavior in the setting will be influenced by increasing maturation of sensory and motor systems and interaction with the environment. The mother's behavior is an important aspect of this developmental process.

Environmental objects releasing or reflecting energy patterns within the potential range of the organism directly influence behavior. The composite of all of these stimuli comprise the *effective environment* for the organism. The effective environment changes as the organism matures, reflecting the influence of Ontogenetic Set on Experiential Set. Phylogenetic Set also limits the range of the effective environment. For example, sounds of 25,000 cycles per second are audible to a dog but not to a person. These sounds are part of the effective canine environment but are excluded from the effective human environment since they do not register on the human sensory system. Other stimuli might influence one species more than another. The scents emitted by *conspecific* individuals (those of the same species) are usually a powerful stimulus to dogs, which have an elegant olfactory coding system. However, olfactory sensitivity is extremely limited in our species, and little of the dog's olfactory world is apparent to humans.

It is easy to see how changes in the *objective environment* and species differences in sensory capacity determine the effective environment. Less obvious is the effect of the internal state of the organism. The organism selects stimulation from the environment to suit needs and to fit expectations. An individual in a crowd may be spotted because he or she is very tall, distinctively dressed, or has a loud voice. On the other hand, an individual may be singled out because the observer is looking for him or her or wants to hear what he or she says. The fact that two observers of a crowded room will report seeing different individuals is in part due to differences in Individual Set.

Cultural Set also influences the nature of the effective environment. Artistic conventions are cultural traits that cause members of a culture to interpret pictorial representations in similar ways. If the picture in Figure 4.2 were shown to members of some African groups, they would judge the elephant to be between the man and the antelope. However, most of our readers, whose background includes many presentations of pictures with implicit size-distance associations, will judge the antelope closer to the viewer and the elephant further away. It must be emphasized that neither judgment is correct in any absolute sense. An individual's only basis for making such a judgment is his or her cultural background and the artistic conventions of that culture. Different cultures also provide different objective environments, as will be seen in the next chapter.

Figure 4.2
Pictorial Representation of Depth
(From W. Hudson, "Pictorial Depth Perception in Subcultural Groups in Africa," Journal of Social Psychology, 52 *(1960), Fig. 1, p. 186. Reproduced by permission of the author and The Journal Press.)*

In summary, *Experiential Set* is defined as the influence of present and past effective environments on behavior. The effective environment consists of a selected sample of stimuli from the objective environment. Selection may be accomplished by means of the distinctive features of some stimuli. The organism may attend to less distinctive stimuli because of internal states and expectations. The internal or organismic bases of stimulus selection reflect Phylogenetic Set, Ontogenetic Set, and previous experience. Cultural Set may influence the perception of effective stimuli as well as determine in part what objective stimuli are present.

Specific
Environmental
Dependence

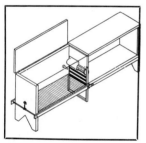

Figure 4.3
Miller-Mowrer Box
(From N. E. Miller,
"Studies of Fear as an
Acquirable Drive: I, Fear
as Motivation and Fear
Reduction as Reinforce-
ment in the Learning
of New Responses," Journal
of Experimental Psychology,
38, 1948, p. 90. Copyright
1948 by the American
Psychological Association.
Reprinted by permission.)

In Chapter 1, classical conditioning and instrumental learning were presented as two laboratory models for specific environmental dependence. In these procedures, some specific stimulus or situation is associated with a response or class of responses. Much research on this sort of acquisition of behavior is available. The stimulus-response view of learning is particularly relevant for aspects of Environmental Set that deal with the influence of particular experiences on specific response patterns.

In classical conditioning, a stimulus-response bond is developed by repeated temporal association of the stimulus and response. A stimulus is selected that does not produce the desired response. That stimulus is presented repeatedly just before the presentation of a second stimulus that is consistently followed by the desired response. After many pairings, the conditioning stimulus becomes a conditioned stimulus that will produce the response of interest.

In instrumental learning, some response is selected as correct. When that response is produced by the subject, a reward is made available. This pairing of response and reward increases the frequency with which the behavior occurs. The reward or *reinforcer* is somewhat circularly defined since anything associated with increased rates of responding is a reinforcer. Reinforcers include basic necessities of life such as food and water as well as social contact, opportunities for exploration, and, for humans, smiles and praise. The reinforcement used in instrumental learning may also be escape from unpleasant or painful stimuli. Rats, for example, will learn new responses in order to escape electric shock or bright light. Some situations have been devised so that animals may respond to avoid rather than to escape from unpleasant stimuli. In these situations, such as the Miller-Mowrer box (see Figure 4.3) the animal first learns to escape the shock. The animal will later anticipate shock by responding before it occurs. Once the rat begins to anticipate, it may continue to avoid punishment without experiencing punishment. When this pattern of anticipatory avoidance has been established, it is very difficult to extinguish. It may be that many learned fears follow this pattern. New responses may be learned to counter this.[2] The stimulus for the new learning is an internal state ultimately resulting from the original source of pain or unpleasantness. This state is labeled *anxiety* because it is a kind of expectation of punishment.

Phylogenetic Influences

From the 1920s many psychologists assumed that any response in an organism's repertoire could be utilized in any learning situation. Recent studies indicate that Phylogenetic Set influences learning.[3] In avoidance or escape situations, animals learn much more rapidly if the required behaviors are compatible with species typical escape reactions. Phylogenetically *prepared* stimulus-response associations may be learned under conditions that would not permit the organism to learn to associate phylogenetically irrelevant stimuli and responses. A good example is seen in the rat's development of an aversion to a new food. If a novel taste is followed by nausea, rats will tend to avoid food with that taste. This association is formed rapidly, even if the ingestion of the food occurs eight hours before the nausea.[4] Apparently, rats cannot associate taste with foot shock, that is, they are *contraprepared* for this association. When foot shock is paired with a previously learned instrumental response, it is effective in eliminating that response only when it occurs immediately after the response. This sort of immediate response-reinforcement temporal sequence is typically necessary for *unprepared* or phylogenetically irrelevant associations.

2. O. H. Mowrer, "A Stimulus-Response Analysis of Anxiety and its Role as a Reinforcing Agent," *Psychological Review*, 46 (1939), 553–565.

3. M. E. P. Seligman, "On the Generality of the Laws of Learning," *Psychological Review*, 77 (1970), 406–418.

4. J. Garcia, D. J. Kimeldorf, and R. A. Koelling, "Conditioned Aversion to Saccharin Resulting from Exposure to Gamma Radiation," *Science,* 122 (1955), 157–158.

Figure 4.4
Transformations in
Straight Curved Features
of a Letterlike Form
(Reprinted from The
Psychology of Reading, *by
E. J. Gibson and Harry
Levin, 1975, by
permission of MIT Press,
Cambridge, Ma.)*

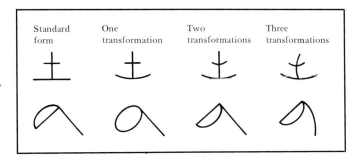

Standard form	One transformation	Two transformations	Three transformations

Ontogenetic Influences

Clear, specific environmental dependence is seen in the development of learned discriminations. For example, learning to name the letters of the printed alphabet requires the presence of a number of distinctive cues in the letters.[5] Some of these cues present the learner with relatively easy tasks. General shape, number of curves and lines, and horizontal, vertical, and oblique lines are among these readily evident cues. Figure 4.4 illustrates some cues used in letter discrimination. The Roman capital letters are easy for young children to name because of these cues and the absence of irrelevant cues. Some lower-case letters are almost impossible for very young children to discriminate. For example, *b, d, p,* and *q* in many type faces differ only in orientation. All other features are identical. Children below age seven or eight frequently misread these letters. If not disturbed by early failure, most children above eight use the orientational cue readily. Alphabetic identification requires specific experiences with the printed letters. If the child is not sufficiently mature he or she may incorrectly identify some letters, indicating the influence of Ontogenetic Set on learned discriminations.

Applications of Instrumental Learning

Parents and teachers are frequently concerned with matters relating to the control of behavior. Techniques employing instrumental learning are frequently recommended for achieving behavior control. A typical institutional program might be directed toward teaching mentally retarded children to dress themselves. The children would be reinforced with candy and praise for responses that approximate successful dressing. Thus, the response is shaped by reinforcement. As a child progresses in such a program, his or her

5. E. J. Gibson, "Learning to Read," *Science,* 148 (1965), 1066–1072.

responses must come closer and closer to the goals that have been set. Such programs have been very successful and in some cases have enabled the child to function on a limited basis outside the institution.

Other successful uses of behavior modification techniques include elimination of undesired behaviors. A frequent approach is to ignore the child when an unacceptable behavior is being exhibited and pay attention to the child when behavior is acceptable. Temper tantrums in three- or four-year-olds can often be brought under control in this way. Excessive talking without regard for the conversational rights of others in ten- to twelve-year-olds is also responsive to such an approach, particularly if peers control the reinforcement.

However, we believe that controlled social reinforcement is an inappropriate foundation for the total parent-child or teacher-pupil relationship. Some professional opinion would dispute this statement. We believe that unconditional affection and personal acceptance is important to developing children. A completely controlled child would have little opportunity to understand unconditional acceptance. Further, during adolescence the development of autonomy would be difficult for a person who had a consistent history of extrinsic control.

Nonspecific Environmental Dependence

Natural Settings

In most real world situations, the effective environment includes stimuli at moderate levels of magnitude and complexity. Flashing lights, horns, shouting, jackhammers, and the odors of spicy cooking are the familiar grist of the urban novelist. The peaceful rural setting also provides plentiful stimulation. A city dweller spending a vacation in the country is kept awake by the animal sounds, train whistles, bright moonlight, and olfactory side effects of fertilizer. The forests, mountains, prairies—all habitats—provide more than enough stimulation for their human and other inhabitants.

Moderate levels of stimulation appear to be necessary for adequate behavioral development. Maintenance of a coherent pattern of behavior in adult organisms also requires stimulation within a fairly wide acceptable range. The organism is usually not dependent on particular stimuli for adequate development and functioning, but it does require some set of sensory inputs. Past experiences may influence the amount of stimulation a particular organism can tolerate, and among individuals with similar personal histories there will be a range of acceptable stimulus levels.[6]

Extremely high levels of effective stimulation are found in nature only in catastrophic circumstances. Extremely high levels of auditory and visual stimulation are found during snowstorms, tornadoes, fires, and flooding. The paradoxical behaviors of immobility and panic are seen in humans and other animals under these circumstances. These responses are a product of excessive stimulation and consequent intense arousal. The effects of manmade stimulation excesses (such as punchpresses, jet airplanes, and bombing) are not easily assessed. An educated guess would be that prolonged exposure to these stimuli would disrupt organized behavior in many individuals.

At the other extreme, restrictive and monotonous environments disrupt the development of behavior in immature organisms.[7] At maturity, organisms reared in such environments may fail to display specific behaviors typical of their species. The behaviors that do develop are often misdirected by the adult raised in a restrictive environment. Exposing adults to settings providing restrictive stimulation produces fragmentation and disorganization in the patterning of behaviors.[8] The effect of restriction is something like breaking up a jigsaw puzzle: all the pieces of behavior are retained, but they do not fit together in a functional way.

Since extreme restriction of stimulation is disruptive, it is rarely found in existing groups of humans or animals. Most of the data from which the previous conclusions about restriction were made were collected in laboratory studies of animal behavior or in short-duration studies using volunteer human subjects. Reduced stimulation is frequently encountered by captive animals in laboratories and zoos. While light, sound, and some conspecific social stimulation are available in some of these settings, the patterns of stimulation are extremely different from those of the natural habitat. Moreover, the environment is constructed for human purposes. The physical and

6. W. N. Dember, "The New Look in Motivation," *American Scientist,* 53 (1965), 409–427; and G. P. Sackett, "Effects of Rearing Conditions upon the Behavior of Rhesus Monkeys *(Macaca mulatta),*" *Child Development,* 36 (1965), 855–868.

7. See Chapter 2, pp. 64 to 66.

8. W. Heron, G. K. Doane, and T. H. Scott, "Visual Disturbances after Prolonged Perceptual Isolation," *Canadian Journal of Psychology,* 10 (1956), 13–18.

social objects may be arranged in patterns for which the animals are unprepared or contraprepared.

Whatever the explanation, cage rearing of monkeys produces fairly bizarre behaviors seldom seen in the field.[9] Stereotyped pacing, constant self-stimulation by picking at the body, and aggressive attacks on themselves—or on the cage walls—are not typical of these animals in their natural environment. The adjustment of rats to their meager surroundings is more difficult to assess. Most domestic rat strains have been bred for laboratory use. It is difficult to tell when the behavior of a domesticated rat is bizarre, since the base line behavior would necessarily be that of other captive rats.

Institutional Environments

Human infants are sometimes cast out by their families or societies. Numerous cases have been reported of children raised in foundling homes or very restrictive orphanages. When the restriction in environment includes little attention from adults, the child's physical, intellectual, and emotional development is greatly impaired.[10] The development of children reared in these restrictive institutions reflects deficiencies of experience. Children do not require a particular and specific experiential history, but they do need a background similar to one of the many patterns of experiential history provided by most human families. Normal children who develop adequately do so within one of many family arrangements. While adequate effective environments have features in common, they are never identical, even for different children in the same family. It is evident in the studies described below that a number of alternative patterns of experience can support adequate development. The needs of the developing child may be categorized as environmentally nonspecific.

The timing of environmental restriction has a bearing on its consequences. In a foundling home in Lebanon, children were kept in covered cribs as long as possible, often for three or four years.[11]

9. H. F. Harlow and M. K. Harlow, "Learning to Love," *American Scientist,* 54 (1966), 244–272.

10. S. K. Escalona, *The Roots of Individuality,* Aldine, Chicago, 1968; and R. A. Spitz, "Hospitalism: An Inquiry into the Genesis of Psychiatric Conditions in Early Childhood," *Psychoanalytic Study of the Child,* 1 (1945), 53–74.

11. W. Dennis and Y. Sayegh, "The Effect of Supplementary Experiences upon the Behavioral Development of Infants in Institutions," *Child Development,* 36 (1965), 81–90.

Attention from adults was limited by a shortage of attendants, many of whom had themselves been raised in the foundling home. Children remaining in the foundling home were found to be retarded in perceptual-motor, intellectual, and emotional development. The older the children and the longer they remained in the home, the greater their retardation. Children who were adopted at age six or older stabilized in development, that is, they did not fall further behind, but they did not recover their losses. Children adopted when they were between ages two and six were able to recoup some of their losses. The closer the child was to age two at the time of adoption, the more nearly his or her development resembled that of typical family-raised Lebanese children. Children less than two years old at adoption were not different from family-reared children.

Another group of children in this foundling home was transferred to a different institution. This was a boarding school that provided books, toys, and a large staff of caretakers and teachers who had themselves been raised in typical family settings. As with adoption, the effects of transfer to the school depended on the age of the child. By age six much of the damage to development in the earlier years could not be overcome. In contrast, children younger than two showed patterns of development similar to family-reared children.

Another report of successful amelioration of the effects of restrictive institutional care involved foster mothers. The unique aspect of this program was that the foster mothers were themselves institutionalized retarded adolescent girls.[12] Children placed in their care as infants on a one-to-one basis were found to profit substantially from their foster care. The mothered children were more likely to be employed, married, and have families, and otherwise resemble the general population. Their peers who had no foster mother were likely to be institutionalized as adults and were unable to cope with the ordinary demands of society. An important and perhaps contributing factor was that children with foster mothers were selected for adoption in much greater proportion than were nonmothered children. The social responses of the mothered infants may have strongly influenced the decision to adopt them. This same social competence undoubtedly contributed to their eventual adjustment.

12. H. M. Skeels, "Adult Status of Children with Contrasting Early Life Experiences," *Monographs of the Society for Research in Child Development*, 31, No. 3 (1966).

These studies of institutionalized children show that early environments markedly affect adult behavior. This effect is similar in many respects to the effects of early social restriction on monkey behavior described in Chapter 2. In the human studies the salient experiences occurred prior to an age most adults can remember. Experiential Set, of course, includes the effect of experiences that cannot be recalled.

Specific Restrictions of Experience

In this section the effects of specific kinds of restriction on behavior will be described. The effects of deprivation of particular sensory modalities and certain kinds of motor responses will be included. It is intriguing to note that restriction of a single sensory modality such as vision or hearing generates a pattern of generally successful adaptation, in contrast to the effects of early restriction of the social environment. Sensory restriction demonstrates another kind of nonspecific environmental dependence. Organisms deprived of a sensory modality or a set of sensory experiences demonstrate individually variable patterns of adjustment. Even when the functional outcome is the same across individuals, the pattern of behavior underlying adjustment to sensory loss may be different.

In some classic research from the early days of experimental psychology, rats were systematically deprived of sensory input.[13] These rats were engaged in a maze-learning task. An attempt was made to determine the value of vision, olfaction, audition, feedback from the whiskers, and kinesthesis for maze learning. Each of these sensory systems was disabled for some group of rats. In every case the disabled animals were able to negotiate the maze using the undamaged senses. The inescapable conclusion from these studies was that "no single one of the senses is essential for maze learning."[14] This also implies that the process of maze learning differs for individual rats. Maintenance of maze-learning capacity may, of course, have little relevance for the effect of sensory loss in a less contrived environment.

The studies of maze learning in rats showed that no one sensory system could completely account for learning. The environment offers a variety of cues. The organism makes multiple responses and

13. J. B. Watson, "Kinesthetic and Organic Sensations: Their Role in the Reactions of the White Rat to the Maze," *Psychological Monographs,* No. 33 (1907).

14. R. S. Woodworth and H. Schlosberg, *Experimental Psychology,* Henry Holt, New York, 1954, p. 616.

stores the memory of the experience in several ways. This duplication of information about present and past experience is called "redundancy." However, each sensory system involved also makes a unique contribution to the reception and storage of experience.

One way to study the contribution of a single sensory system is to disable or restrict its usefulness to the organism. In a series of studies of visual development, the visual environment of young chimpanzees was subjected to varying degrees of restriction.[15] One group was raised in total darkness. A second group had diffuse lighting available. Other animals were exposed to a normal laboratory room that provided patterned light stimulation for an hour and a half each day. These animals were otherwise in a darkened room. All of the animals were reared in these conditions from birth to sixteen months of age. While a number of visual functions were not affected, striking disruptions of visual functioning were found in those reared in the dark and those reared in diffuse light. These chimps did not protrude the lips in anticipation of a baby bottle in their visual field. Their eye movements in following moving objects were jerky rather than smooth. The deprived chimps were also unable to learn simple visual discriminations such as horizontal versus vertical stripes. The contrast animals that had been exposed to one and one-half hours of patterned light per day showed none of these disturbances.

Children with cataracts apparently experience visual stimulation similar to the diffuse light group discussed above. These individuals can discern light and dark and can experience some sense of variations in brightness. Sharp contrasts and clearly defined shapes are not part of their visual world. When there is surgical removal of congenital cataracts, a long period of postoperative visual experience is required for normal visual functioning.[16] The major problems encountered by the patients included judging distance using visual cues and following moving objects. Visual detection of meaningful patterns was also difficult. One subject, for example, could see her pet cat running toward her but did not know what the object was until it jumped into her lap.

15. A. H. Riesen, "Stimulation as a Requirement for Growth and Function in Behavioral Development," in *Functions of Varied Experience*, eds. D. W. Fiske and S. R. Maddi, Dorsey Press, Homewood, Ill., 1961, pp. 57–80.

16. I. D. London, "A Russian Report on the Postoperative Newly Seeing," *American Journal of Psychology*, 73 (1960), 478–482.

When congenitally blind children or those with cataracts come to have visual capacity, they report visual experiences in terms of previously acquired tactile and kinesthetic meanings. The present visual environment is interpreted in terms of previous sensory experience. Experiential Set is necessarily a factor in much of what is called perception.

Visual experience alone does not necessarily provide the basis for adequate visual functioning. Kittens that experience patterned light but are unable to move their bodies become visually handicapped.[17] Contrast kittens with exactly the same visual experience that are able to move about in the patterned light environment show no deficits. Pairs of kittens were placed in the apparatus seen in Figure 4.5. One kitten could walk, while its partner was carried in the cart. Both kittens experienced moving visual patterns, but one kitten caused the movement. The kitten whose visual stimulation changed as a result of its own motor activity developed normal visual functioning. The kitten whose visual stimulation was unrelated to its motor activity was functionally similar in many respects to a dark-reared animal.

Auditory sensory input is particularly important for human social interaction and information exchange. Deafness interferes greatly with both receptive and productive language.[18] When deafness occurs after the age of six, special training is necessary for the individual to maintain speech and to learn alternative ways of understanding others, such as lip reading. Such training is fairly successful in many cases. Congenital deafness generally results in severely impaired comprehension and vocalization. However, the cognitive or thinking ability of the deaf individual is not impaired as long as verbal language is not required.

The effects of total deafness on communication demonstrate the influence of Ontogenetic Set on language development. If the individual becomes deaf after age six, as noted above, minimal disruption occurs. If deafness occurs between ages two and six, some impairment in language occurs, and special training procedures are even more important. These children are usually understood by the listener but have difficulty in controlling the pitch, vocal quality, and

17. R. Held and A. Hein, "Movement-Produced Stimulation in the Development of Visually-Guided Behavior," *Journal of Comparative and Physiological Psychology*, 56 (1963), 872–876.

18. E. H. Lenneberg, *Biological Foundations of Language*, John Wiley & Sons, New York, 1967.

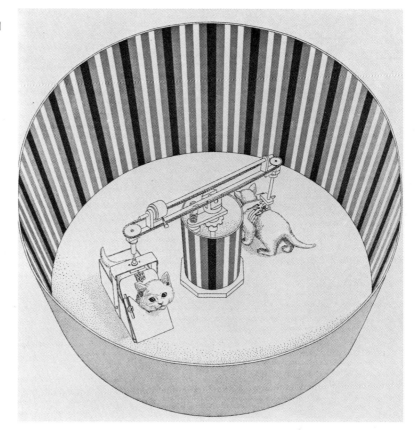

volume of their speech. Specific articulation problems may also be present. In contrast, if deafness is congenital or occurs before about age two, even intensive training does not usually result in comprehension or production of functional oral language.

Inexplicably, the actual production of sounds in infancy is not necessary for oral speech development. One author reported examining a fourteen-month-old who had been *tracheotomized* for six months. In this procedure a tube is inserted into the throat, making vocalization impossible. Within one day of removal of the tube, which prevented any speechlike sounds, the baby's babbling was typical for its age. Two-year-olds with long-term tracheal tubes also recover speech function within two or three weeks of removal of the tube. Many cases have been reported of children who were speechless due to emotional disturbance in their early years. In response to treatment, these children spoke fluently in short periods of time. It appears that experience in producing language is not an important prerequisite for oral fluency. However, auditory experience with speech is essential. This would suggest that speech production is an expression of Phylogenetic and Ontogenetic Set. Development of meaningful language performance requires hearing the language but not necessarily producing it. A moderate level of general stimulation and of activity are, of course, important for speech development, as well as for almost every aspect of behavioral development.

The Development of Language

Oral Language

The complex interaction of maturation and experience is illustrated well in the acquisition of language skills. Both specific and nonspecific environmental dependence are evident in language development. Oral speech develops in virtually all environments in which humans develop. Written language does not.

Oral language may be analyzed at several levels of complexity—from language sounds to meaning. The terms used by linguists in carrying out these analyses are phonemes, morphemes, syntax, and semantics.[19] *Phonemes* are the sounds actually used by speakers of a language. A *morpheme* is the basic unit of meaning. A word will have one or several morphemes, while a morpheme will contain one or several phonemes. *Syntax* refers to the grammar or the arrangement of morphemes in language. *Semantics* relates to the meaning of language in a broad sense. Discussions of semantics usually attempt to relate language to the characteristics of physical objects talked about and to the ideas of speakers.

The acquisition of language has been studied in some detail in the past decade. Languages in all parts of the world in diverse cultures have been analyzed carefully. It is clear that the human being is biologically wired to acquire hearing comprehension and spoken fluency of a language. This species-shared capability is an instance of Phylogenetic Set unique to humans. Other species communicate through other sensory systems. Nonauditory communication systems include olfactory and chemical transmission for some ants and the marking of territories in dogs and hyenas. For human beings, the communication system is laryngeal modulation of expired air. Reception is through the auditory sensory and perceptual systems.

The earliest aspect of language development is the production of

19. P. S. Dale, *Language Development,* Dryden Press, Hinsdale, Ill., 1972.

phonemes by young infants.[20] This *babbling* begins between three and six months. Sometime during the first year of life the child will make virtually all the approximately 150 sounds found in all human languages. After a specific language is acquired and utilized, unusual phonemes are formed with great difficulty. This phonemic constriction is evident after about six years of age. The college student taking a first course in a second language will be familiar with this problem. The student's two-year-old niece would have less difficulty with the French *r*. Babbling is a species typical trait of humans and occurs even in deaf children. These children, however, stop babbling; in fact, this is one early evidence of deafness. Hearing children engage in a great deal of phonemic play, which apparently requires auditory feedback in order to be maintained.

Translation of oral messages into coherent behavioral responses occurs at about one year of age. The initial transmission of oral messages interpretable by adults other than the parents begins at about eighteen months of age. The age of onset of oral language is similar across all human societies studied. Other skills are also initiated at the same age. From the age of two to six or seven there is rapid growth in vocabulary. By about age six, 2,500 different words are used in the oral vocabulary. Children of this age can understand many words they do not use and readily understand typical adult conversation. After this time additional words are added to the vocabulary more slowly, and environmental influences are increasingly powerful. Seniors in high school comprehend more than 40,000 different words, but of course they use a much smaller vocabulary in everyday conversation.[21]

Along with changes in vocabulary, there are progressive changes in language structure. These include the conventional use of parts of speech, increasing elaboration of morphemes by inflection, and the expression of subtle differences of meaning via word order. All of these elaborations tend to increase the length of utterances. At the same time, the functional range of a vocabulary of any given size increases dramatically with mature syntax. As the individual matures, he or she acquires more words and can use them in more ways.

20. D. McNeill, *The Acquisition of Language,* Harper & Row, New York, 1970.
21. D. McCarthy, "Language Development in Children," in *Manual of Child Psychology,* 2nd ed., ed. L. Carmichael, John Wiley and Sons, New York, 1954, pp. 492–630.

The form of oral language expressed by the child at the age of one year consists of one-word sentences.[22] These one-word utterances, called *holophrastic* by linguists, appear to be attempts by the child to express complex ideas. The utterances are closely linked to the child's own actions and to actions desired of others. For example, when the child says "milk" he or she is likely to be drinking milk or making a request for mother to refill the cup. Most of the recognizable utterances in the holophrastic phase are closely associated with sensory and motor experiences. This suggests that meaning or the semantic aspect of language already reflects the level of thinking typical of children at this age.

Sounds such as "mama" and "papa" are associated with specific stimulus configurations. Simple morphemes consisting of one or two phonemes, frequently repeated, constitute the first recognizable speech of the young child, as in "baba" or "dada." The appearance of one-word sentences is widely variable in normal children and ranges from about eight to eighteen months. These expressions of meaning may not be similar to and are rarely identical to the adult meaning of the same sound patterns. For one child, "doggie" may refer to a specific, well-loved pet. For another, "doggie" denotes all four-legged beasts.

At about one and one-half to two years of age the child utters two-word sentences.[23] These two-word sentences are not just random pairs of words. On the contrary, analysis of two-word sentences reveals elements of grammar. However, the grammar of eighteen- to twenty-four-month-old children contains parts of speech rather different from grammars describing adult language. Whereas adult grammars use nouns, pronouns, verbs, adjectives, and the like, the grammar of two-year-olds has only two parts of speech—called by linguists pivot words and open words. *Pivot words* are relatively few in number but are used frequently by the child. On the other hand, each of the large number of *open words* in the child's vocabulary is used infrequently. The two-word sentence of the two-year-old child consists of a single pivot word and one open word. Examples of pivot and open vocabularies are shown in Figure 4.6. Some pivot words usually precede an open word, while others typically follow. However, for a particular child, each pivot word will typically occur in a fixed position in all sentences in which it occurs.

22. Dale.
23. R. Brown, *A First Language*, Harvard University Press, Cambridge, Mass., 1973.

Figure 4.6
Pivot and Open
Vocabularies of Three
Children
*(Reprinted from
"Developmental
Psycholinguistics," by
David McNeill, in* The
Genesis of Language *by F.
Smith and G. A. Miller,
eds., 1966, by permission
of MIT Press, Cambridge,
Ma.)*

Child No. 1		*Child No. 2*		*Child No. 3*	
Pivot	*Open*	*Pivot*	*Open*	*Pivot*	*Open*
allgone byebye big more pretty my see night- night hi	boy sock boat fan milk plane shoe vitamins hot Mommy Daddy . . .	my that two a the big green poor wet dirty fresh pretty	Adam Becky boot coat coffee knee man Mommy nut sock stool tinker-toy . . .	this that the a here there	arm baby dolly's pretty yellow come doed . . other baby dolly's pretty yellow . . arm baby dolly's pretty yellow . . .

The order in which words appear in utterances is an important characteristic of grammar. Thus, the fixed order found in the two-word sentences suggests that these utterances should be regarded as grammatical although childhood and adult grammars differ. Inflection is another important grammatical cue. One example of inflection common in English is the addition of the *s* sound to a noun. This suffix is the usual transformation that changes a noun from singular to plural. Another common inflection changes the tense of verbs. The way children use inflections is an important feature of language development.

English-speaking children generally follow a particular developmental pattern in using the past tense of regular and irregular verbs.[24] Regular verbs are transformed from present to simple past tense by the addition of the suffix *ed* as in the verb "help," "helped." Irregular verbs, more frequent than regular verbs in everyday usage, follow no general rule. Examples of present and past tense usage of irregular verbs include "come," "came" and "fall," "fell."

The first verbs the child uses in the past tense are irregular, and he or she uses them correctly according to the adult language experienced. Examples would be: "Daddy came," or "Sister fell." At about the time the child expresses the past tense of regular verbs, as in the sentence, "Mommy helped," the usage of irregular past tense changes. The child overgeneralizes or overregularizes the past tense inflections of the regular verbs. The three-year-old is likely to say, "I comed," or "Jane falled." Sometime in the fifth year the child uses regular and irregular verbs in the past tense in accordance with adult usage.

The point is that the very young child first uses particular verbs as experienced. Shortly thereafter, the young child's usage suggests operation of a general rule, for example, adding the suffix *ed* at the end of all verbs. However, the child follows the rule more generally than the adult form of English permits. Only after years of experience are regular and irregular verbs differentiated.

In contrast to English nouns, Russian nouns are highly inflected. These nouns are changed in form by prefix, suffix, or internal transformations according to number and gender. Although the structure of the adult languages differ, the development of language for Russian children moves through similar stages of specific word usage, overgeneralization, and adultlike differentiation of forms.

Early stages of development in child grammar or syntax have been studied in children speaking about thirty different languages. The particular patterns of overgeneralization depend on the structure of the language studied. However, the same sequence of early stages involving first specific words, then overgeneralization, and finally differentiation has been found in all language groups. This universal progression appears to reflect the interaction of Ontogenetic Set with language experience.

This universal sequence of stages and the constancy of ages at which stages are mastered provide evidence that the developmental

24. D. I. Slobin, "On the Learning of Morphological Rules," in *The Ontogenesis of Language,* ed. D. I. Slobin, Academic Press, New York, 1971, pp. 215–223.

time table may be related to the human genetic code. The acquisition of oral language is an expression of Ontogenetic Set and Phylogenetic Set. As previously indicated, the environment must present patterned movements of objects and people, of sights and sounds. In a perfectly stable environment, not only would sensory and motor systems degenerate, but there would be nothing to talk about.

Language development reflects specific and nonspecific environmental dependence. As indicated previously, exposure to a social environment containing adult speakers ensures language development. The specific experiential history determines the mother tongue. It also influences dialect, the number of languages comprehended and spoken, and other variations in language. However, even rather divergent histories within a language community produce speakers who can communicate readily with each other.

Communication with Other Animals

There have been a number of attempts to teach human language to chimpanzees. Those attempts that focused on oral-aural language failed. Recently, a degree of success was achieved in teaching gestural language to one chimp and a pictorial communication system to another. In the first case a chimpanzee, Washoe, was taught a form of American Sign Language, which is commonly used by the deaf.[25] This animal was raised by human beings who always used this gestural language with her. Eventually, she developed a vocabulary of about eighty-five signs. She used about three hundred recognizable combinations of these signs, reflecting a rudimentary syntax. The order of these combinations was not related to meaning, as it is in early syntax in human gestural and oral language.

The pictorial system taught another chimp, Sarah, is not a natural language, but she can solve a number of problems using this system.[26] For example, she can classify objects according to their color, shape, or size. She can also state rudimentary causal relationships. Some of Sarah's symbols are shown in Figure 4.7. Sarah has learned a specific signal system that relates to the types of problems she has been assigned. While this procedure is similar to some accounts of

25. B. T. Gardner and R. A. Gardner, "Two-Way Communication with an Infant Chimpanzee," in *Behavior of Nonhuman Primates,* eds. A. Schrier and F. Stollnitz, Academic Press, New York, 1971, vol. IV, pp. 117–184.

26. D. Premack, "Language in Chimpanzees?" *Science,* 172 (1971), 808–822.

human language acquisition, we feel that it differs strikingly from the process by which human language is learned.

Attempts to train chimpanzees to communicate with human beings using human language are exceptional. Most communication between species requires that each species learn the signs or signals natural to the other. Many humans clearly understand many canine expressive movements, facial configurations, and postures. A few humans understand a similar repertoire produced by elephants. Dogs and Indian elephants, in turn, learn to understand a part of the human communication system. This kind of communication between species is dependent on specific experience. Such communication is usually limited to indications of emotion rather than specific informational content. On close examination, it appears that even highly trained dogs use tonal quality rather than phonemic configuration as cues to the correct response.

Reading

One of several special languages available to humans is a written form of language. In contrast to oral language, the acquisition of reading skills requires specific culturally designated experiences.

Reading skills are built on a foundation of oral language comprehension and production. However, mere exposure to reading during childhood does not ensure acquisition. Reading skills, then, show the powerful effects of Experiential Set, the effects of past and present experience on behavior. The ability to read is more exclusively dependent on specific kinds of experience than is the ability to speak. This does not indicate, however, that every reader develops this skill in exactly the same way. Nor is reading equally easy in every language, even when a phonetic alphabet is used. The following discussion will not deal with ideographic alphabets such as Chinese.

In general, some minimal level of spoken language is a prerequisite for reading. The written language is different from the spoken language, but its meaning derives from the spoken language. Background experiences relevant to reading begin in early childhood long before formal instruction is usually begun. In a literate society the child perceives that written information is utilized by adults. A child lacking that perception does not acquire that important motivation to learn to read. An early feat that is similar in some respects to reading is the identification of familiar trademarks and signs. Parental reaction to these feats may influence the child's desire to expand on them. However, the ability to recognize distinctive signs or even letter configurations is not reading. Reading is the ability to translate *graphemic* representations to semantic form. That is, reading is the ability to comprehend the meaning of written words. The ability to say the written words is usually, but not always, evidence of this interpretive skill. The fluent reader may understand words and phrases without being able to pronounce them.

There are a number of techniques for teaching reading.[27] In the *phonetic methods,* sound-letter correspondence is emphasized. Words are segmented for the child into phonemelike units. The oral-aural equivalence for each unit is presented. After initial presentation, the young reader is rewarded for correct responses and for correction of omissions or incorrect responses. The reader is particularly encouraged to sound out new words using sound-letter associations. An alternate set of methods emphasizes the written word-spoken word correspondence. That is, short words are learned as units rather than as sound combinations. Most middle-class American

27. J. Chall, *Learning to Read: The Great Debate,* McGraw-Hill, New York, 1967.

Figure 4.8
Eye Movements in Reading
(*From* Fundamental Reading Habits, *Supplementary Education Monographs No. 21 by G. T. Buswell, published by the University of Chicago, 1922. Copyright 1922 by the University of Chicago,. All rights reserved. Published June 1922.)*

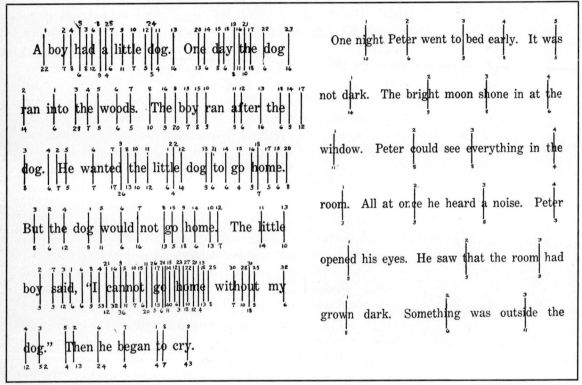

First grade reader   College senior reader

children learn to read with either method. Some children have difficulty whatever the method, while some children would learn readily by any method. Others would progress more rapidly with one method than with the other. It may be that controversies concerning methods for teaching reading have focused on a pseudo-problem. The problem may be to find the best method for a particular teacher working with a particular child. Individual Set influences both the teaching and the learning of reading.

It should be pointed out that fluent readers use neither the whole word nor the phonic process in reading. These methods are useful only to nonreaders who are learning to read and to beginning readers. As shown by the eye movements illustrated in Figure 4.8, fluent readers comprehend in units of three to five words, apparently interpreting that much material at a glance. In many cases, either method of initial teaching will result in this end product. It is interesting that many different experiential histories can lead to the same set of skills.

Experiential Set and Behavioral Development

The previous and present effective environment is a partial determinant of behavior. The behavioral repertoire of any organism reflects specific and nonspecific environmental dependence. The more pervasive the behavior is within a species, the less specific will be the environmental underpinning of that behavior. In Chapter 1, the sexual behavior of male rhesus monkeys was described as a behavior pattern demonstrating nonspecific environmental dependence. In this chapter, the wide range of problems exhibited by children reared in restrictive institutions was described. These children did not lack a specific prescriptive history but experienced an environment that was not one of the many situations that would support typical human social and cognitive development. Specific environmental dependence is seen in behavior patterns or capacities that occur as a consequence of a particular set of experiences. The ability to press a lever in a Skinner box, hold a tennis racket correctly, say "yes, ma'am" or "yes, sir" rather than "yes" to a teacher, or to discriminate among *b, d, p,* and *q* require some unique set of experiences and therefore reflect specific environmental dependence.

Most complex patterns of behavior reflect both specific and nonspecific environmental dependence. The acquisition of human language was used as an example. Oral-aural speech is a species typical trait for human beings. Many aspects of language develop in a way that indicates that Phylogenetic and Ontogenetic Set and the nonspecific aspects of Environmental Set control them. The development of a wide repertoire of phonemes and phonemic play or babbling is one of these patterns. The use of elementary syntax in two-word utterances is another. More specific environmental dependence is evident in the particular language spoken, although ready communication is possible among individuals whose personal histories vary considerably. When specific dialects or local accents are considered, the degree of specific environmental dependence for the pattern of speech is more evident. Figures of speech and verbal mannerisms may be used and understood by very small groups of people with very specific shared experiences.

Summary

Experiential Set is the influence of the effective environment on behavior. The effective environment is determined by the objective environment and the characteristics of the organism. The organism's species and level of maturity determine what stimuli will be recorded by its sensory systems and what patterns of stimulation will be noticed. In human beings, culture provides a particular range of stimuli and in some cases results in culturally specific interpretations of stimulus patterns. The individual's personal history and idiosyncratic sensory and perceptual abilities will also determine the stimuli that can become part of his or her effective environment.

The influence of Environmental Set on behavior is reflected in both specific and nonspecific environmental dependence. Specific environmental dependence is seen in the development of patterns that are simulated by laboratory models of learning. Classical conditioning and instrumental learning are models of behavioral acquisition based on specific environmental histories.

Nonspecific environmental dependence is seen in species typical behaviors that are developed in some but not all environments. Most behavior patterns determined by Phylogenetic Set exhibit a degree of nonspecific environmental dependence. A moderate level of early stimulation is necessary for adequate development. This form of nonspecific environmental dependence requires some amount of environmental input but not a specific prescriptive pattern of stimulation. The adaptation of organisms with loss or restriction of sensory modalities indicates that developing organisms compensate for particular deficits in stimulation. Such compensatory mechanisms, no doubt, explain why similar patterns of behavior develop from different experiential histories.

Many patterns of behavior in intact organisms in the real world exhibit both specific and nonspecific features of Experiential Set. Human language development has been presented as one example. Language development demonstrates both specific and nonspecific environmental dependence. Oral-aural language is less dependent on specific experience than is reading. However, reading may be acquired after exposure to any one of several sets of experience. The fluent, mature reader shows much the same pattern of behavior whether her or his early training was primarily phonetic or primarily oriented toward the whole word.

Experience determines behavior, but to understand the effects of experience on a particular organism, one must know more than the organism's personal history. As information about the species and the level of maturity of the organism is increased, understanding becomes clearer. Knowledge of the characteristics of human culture is also important to an understanding of human behavior. Even when the contributions of Phylogenetic Set, Ontogenetic Set, Experiential Set, and Cultural Set are known, understanding is still incomplete. Prediction of behavior will always be fallible. The individual characteristics of the organism, Individual Set, will increase and to some extent limit the possibility of our understanding behavior.

Defined Terms

Effective environment	Prepared	Babbling
Conspecific	Contraprepared	Holophrastic
Objective environment	Unprepared	Pivot words
Experiential Set	Tracheotomized	Open words
Reinforcer	Phoneme	Graphemic
Anxiety	Morpheme	Phonetic methods
	Syntax	
	Semantics	

Suggested Readings

D. W. Fiske and S. Maddi, eds., *The Functions of Varied Experience*, Dorsey Press, Homewood, Ill., 1961.

Reading this book is well worth the considerable work required to understand some of the complex and technical material. If time does not permit a complete reading, these two chapters are recommended: W. R. Thompson and T. Schaeffer, "Early Environmental Stimulation," pp. 81–105 and D. W. Fiske, "Effects of Monotonous and Restricted Stimulation," pp. 106–144.

F. A. Logan, *Fundamentals of Learning and Motivation*, William C. Brown, Dubuque, Iowa, 1970.

In this book, the interpretation of learning as the formation of associations between stimulus and response is explained in clear and concise language. Emphasis is on research studies of laboratory animals. The discussion of classical and instrumental conditioning is more enthusiastic and complete than in Chapter 4. Recommended chapters include the following: Chapter 1, "Introduction to Learning," pp. 1–7; Chapter 5, "The Scientific Theory of Classical Conditioning," pp. 59–73; Chapter 6, "Positive Reinforcement," pp. 74–101; Chapter 7, "Negative Reinforcement," pp. 102–112; and Chapter 10, "An Overview of Learning," pp. 146–148.

D. I. Slobin, *Psycholinguistics,* Scott Foresman, Glenview, Ill., 1971.

A short, nontechnical description of traditional and modern ideas and methods useful in understanding human language. Of special interest to our readers is the detailed discussion of language development in Chapter 3.

Chapter 5
Cultural Set

Human beings are born into and develop within a particular culture. Throughout life the traditions and expectations of the culture have an influence on behavior. Cultural influences are most evident at particular critical points in development such as early childhood, puberty, and mating. These periods will be considered in detail in this chapter, but cultural influence is not limited to specific points in development. In our species, Cultural Set influences the individual's behavior throughout his or her life.

So powerful is the influence of culture on human behavior that it is sometimes thought to be primary. When cultural variation is emphasized, human behavior appears to be infinitely plastic and capable of acquiring any pattern whatsoever. However, as explained in the discussion on Experiential Set, the influence of all experience on behavior is limited. As a specific type of Experiential Set, Cultural Set operates within the limits determined by Phylogenetic Set and Ontogenetic Set. That is, cultural demands vary within the limits of capacity and functional effectiveness characteristic of our species. Cultural demands on the individual are paced according to the maturity or age of the individual, reflecting the necessity for Cultural Set to function within the limits of Ontogenetic Set.

Cultural Set limits the experiences of individuals. Members of a society have unique individual experiential histories but they also have some similar experiences. These similar experiences enable members of a society to interact with and to understand others of their group. Human beings often assume that all people share their own experiential background. This is especially evident when scientists attempt to evaluate the intelligence of children from other cultures. A five-year-old Puerto Rican child who has never left the interior of the island may have some difficulty associating a ski with a ski pole or a football with a football helmet. Indeed, the child is likely to tell you that a football is a round ball about the size of a volleyball—and the child would be right! Soccer, not American football, is a part of this child's experiential world.

Tests of school aptitude assume that the experiences of the children to be tested are within a generally equivalent cultural context. The performance of the Puerto Rican child on a test designed to assess school readiness in the continental United States may, therefore, reflect Cultural Set and not school readiness. In this situation, assessment of school readiness would require sampling of behaviors that individuals typically acquire in their own culture and that are associated with performance in school.

The experiential component of Individual Set modifies the influence of culture. The characteristic attitudes and expectations of a culture are transmitted to an individual by particular people. In our own society, masculinity and femininity are culturally defined in terms of attitudes, preferences, speech patterns, gestures, and expected behaviors. But specific patterns are acquired by the developing child through contact with particular individuals, typically the parents. To some degree, then, masculinity and femininity are differently defined for each member of the society. The genetic component of Individual Set also influences the expression of Cultural Set. If an individual's appearance differs markedly from the cultural ideal of appearance for the appropriate sex, the expression of masculinity or femininity that person adopts may be altered.

Human cultures present a variety of patterns of living. In the following pages a few examples of child-rearing practices and marriage patterns in different societies will be described. While the patterns described do not exhaust the range of variation for these processes, they do provide an interesting set of contrasts.

Examples of Cultural Variation

Cultural variation influences a child from birth onward. Many authorities believe that both the kind and the amount of attention a child receives early in development have an important influence on her or his temperament and personality. In the examples given below a number of different patterns of child care will be summarized. As these patterns are described, the reader should consider their similarities and differences with memories of his or her own childhood experiences.

Early Child Care

Cheyenne In this plains Indian society of the mid-1800s, infants and young children were indulged, particularly by their grandparents.[1] The newborn was usually wrapped in soft robes and in cold weather was carried in the mother's arms for warmth. After a few weeks the baby was kept on a cradleboard placed near the mother. The cooperative nature of child care and responsibility for children is indicated by the number of caretakers given the same name. The mother, her sisters, and female first cousins were all addressed as

1. E. A. Hoebel, *The Cheyennes Indians of the Great Plains,* Holt, Rinehart and Winston, New York, 1960.

"mother." The father, his brothers, and male first cousins were addressed as "father." In line with the picture of indulgence and cuddling, infants were fed on demand. They were usually not permitted to cry for any length of time. If an infant was not readily comforted, the baby was taken to the edge of the village, and its cradleboard suspended from a tree until the crying stopped. (Dr. Spock recommends a similar procedure for sleeping problems at about eight months. He suggests leaving the baby in the crib to cry it out.) The good Cheyenne baby received much tender loving care from mother or grandmother. When the child was a little older, the mother often carried it in a blanket sling on her back rather than on a cradleboard.

Cheyenne children began to perform adult activities as soon as possible. By two or three years of age they rode with their mothers, and five- or six-year-old boys rode their own colts. Seven-year-old boys helped herd horses. Little girls gathered wood and carried water as soon as they could toddle. The boys hunted small game with miniature bows as soon as they could.

For Cheyenne children six to twelve years old, play was an elaborate simulation of adult life (see Figure 5.1). Mothers helped girls make small tepees within which toddlers served as babies. Boys brought in small game. In play buffalo hunting, boys took turns as buffalo and hunter. War games included girls, who dismantled tepees and fled with "babies" to safety. Even the ceremonial life of the group was duplicated in the children's elaborate miniature of adult society. For example, some of the boys pierced themselves with cactus thorns during Sun Dances.

Cheyenne discipline was physically mediated—by isolation—for totally unacceptable behavior, beginning with uncontrolled crying, and socially mediated—by shame and guilt—for lesser offenses. Cheyenne children were frequently given sermonettes by the indulgent adults around them.

Be brave, be honest, be virtuous, be industrious, be generous, do not quarrel! If you do not do these things people will talk about you in the camp; they will not respect you; you will be shamed. If you listen to this advice you will grow up to be a good man or woman and you will amount to something.[2]

Physical punishment was seldom used. Older girls are reported to have committed suicide after being struck by their mothers. In

2. Hoebel, p. 92.

Figure 5.1
Cheyenne Play

consequence, the mothers were guilty of homicide. The cultural response to homicide illustrates the importance of isolation as punishment. Homicide within the group was considered the most heinous of crimes; the punishment for homicide was banishment.

Gopalpur   This village in southern India provides an example of childhood in a contemporary agricultural society.[3] The Gopalpur infant is fortunate if born into a large "complete" family with older sisters, aunts, or grandmother available to help care for the baby. In relatively well-to-do extended families, the mother may be relieved of other duties to rest and care for the child for a short time after birth. In smaller, less affluent families the mother has little time for the infant. A male baby, particularly the first son, is most welcome. Females are not so welcome, particularly in upper caste families where large dowries are required. In most families, females are accepted as the means for widening economic and social contacts with other villages through marriage. Younger children of either sex born into large families are an economic burden. However, in this society a child of either sex is usually loved and wanted by both parents.

For the first year the child spends much of its time in a cradle suspended by ropes from the veranda ceiling. Babies are fed on demand, and if they continue to cry an older child rocks the cradle. Generally, this rocking is vigorous and continues until the baby goes to sleep or stops crying. If the baby continues to cry, the neighbors become involved, gathering around the veranda and shouting advice to the mother, usually ordering her to give the child the breast.

Older babies, no longer quieted by rocking, are sent out with older siblings to the courtyard in front of the house. The baby is carried on the hip of an older child who continues play activities. In Gopalpur, infants are carried by someone or remain in the cradle; they are given little opportunity to crawl and are not encouraged to walk. The baby is kept a baby as long as possible. Weaning is gradual and nursing is continued for as long as the mother can manage it.

3. A. R. Beals, *Gopalpur—A South Indian Village*, Holt, Rinehart and Winston, New York, 1962.

When the child does walk, infancy proper is over. The child is encouraged to join older children playing in the courtyard in front of the house, like those in Figure 5.2. Breast feeding continues, but after feeding the toddler is deposited outside. When the child comes in again, he or she is breast fed, but not before a mild scolding for interfering with the mother's work.

Groups of children two to eight years old play at household tasks such as pounding rice, using broken pots, stones, and discarded agricultural equipment. Younger boys become bullocks to pull imaginary plows. Older girls play mother, using their infant sibling rather than a doll. Children frequently carry peanuts or bits of bread in their shirt pockets, which they alternately share and squabble over. Physical aggression is rare and usually consists of slaps or pinches directed toward persistently whining two- or three-year-olds. Noisy crying, which generally brings adult intervention, is used

Figure 5.2
Typical South Indian
Village
(United Nations)

by younger children to control older children. For their part, older children control younger ones by threatening to desert them to play in another area out of the toddler's permissible range of wandering.

Interaction between the mother and weaned children centers around food. Both mothers and children are parties to food negotiations. Children refuse to rock infants unless paid in food. Mothers threaten not to feed children who fail to rock the baby or run errands. Mothers complain about the amount the child eats and its unwillingness to work. It appears that mothers make many threats to withhold food without actually doing so. This pattern of threatened denial followed by giving in is also seen with respect to other privileges. For example, a young child was told he could go with the family to the fair in a nearby village. After he had announced this to his play group, he was told that he was too young. Following extended negotiation, tears, and promises of good behavior, he was permitted to go. (There probably was no convenient place to leave the child anyway.)

Adults grumble and scold children a great deal. Physical punishment is not frequent, but is expected from time to time. Toddlers who insist on adult attention instead of playing in the courtyard are struck. Older girls who are irresponsible in their care of toddlers also receive blows. Apparently, physical punishment has no great emotional significance to these parents but is an ordinary parental response to persistent or annoying behavior in children.

Children control others by begging, crying, and working. They are threatened with "having to eat dirt" if they do not work. Withholding and giving food are central to play behavior with peers and to interaction with adults, especially the mother. Receiving food, so clearly associated with life itself by members of this society, is dependent on one's relations with the family. Children carry out family duties in order to get food and to avoid "having to eat dirt."

Ganda   Infants in this East African group were the subjects of an intensive study of infant-mother attachment.[4] Patterns of mother-infant interaction were quite variable in the group studied. To a great extent, these variations reflected the degree of westernization of the family in question. The Ganda were selected for study because

4. M. D. Ainsworth, *Infancy in Uganda*, Johns Hopkins Press, Baltimore, 1967.

they reputedly practiced abrupt weaning and frequent mother-infant separation, with the child sent to live with relatives shortly after weaning. These patterns turned out to be neither as generally practiced nor as rigid as was believed prior to the study.

Although some Ganda infants were bottle-fed, most were breast-fed. Many of these infants received supplemental feeding from an early age. Most babies were fed on demand, but a few mothers practiced scheduled feeding during the day. Breast-fed babies who slept with their mothers were fed on demand at night regardless of the daytime feeding regime. There appeared to be little play with young infants, and almost none of the face-to-face smile elicitation so typical of American adult-infant interaction. Ganda babies were typically held on the mother's lap facing away from the mother. Little cuddling of the babies was evident. Some mothers used the breast to comfort the baby when it cried, whether or not she judged the infant to be hungry, while others permitted suckling only when the baby was believed to be hungry. Babies were frequently carried on the back in a blanket sling.

Care of the infant was sometimes shared with other members of a household including the grandmother, older sister, cousin, or a second wife. Mothers were often the principal caretakers, and in such cases they took the baby to the garden and placed it on a nearby mat while they worked. Abrupt weaning was reported in early descriptions of this group, but is not confirmed by recent observations. All children were given supplementary feeding from an early age, and there was gradual reduction of daytime feeding. Night feedings were terminated when the last daytime feeding was dropped. Once discontinued, night feedings were rarely provided again.

In traditional practice, children were separated from their mothers for three days at weaning. This pattern was not typical for the contemporary sample studied, probably because in three generations the age of weaning had been reduced from three and one-half years to about one year. Traditionally, the three-and-one-half-year-old went to live with a grandmother after weaning. Children were sometimes raised by relatives in the more recent study, particularly if some advantage for the child was associated with the foster parents. A new husband might reject a child, who was then sent to his grandmother. An older child might live with relatives who were close to a school. Older children were sometimes sent to relatives at the birth of a new baby, although they returned later. Children were sent to relatives better able financially and socially to give them care and education.

Children living in a household were treated as members of that household. Their parentage outside the household was never mentioned in their presence. Not every child was sent to relatives, but the practice was not uncommon. Few children were sent away in the sample studied by Ainsworth, because of the availability of medical care for children included in the study. One couple repeatedly asked the investigator to take their toddler because of the advantages they perceived in his being raised in America by her.

In Ganda, physical punishment was common and thought to be necessary, at least by men, although not when the children were "too young to understand." The age of understanding came surprisingly early, as young as five months in one case, and many children were "beaten" (spanked once on the wrist or arm with cupped hand) before one year of age. Infants reportedly responded by attempting to hit the mothers.

A striking feature of development in Ganda infants was their early motor development. Ganda infants creep on all fours three and one-half months earlier than does the average American white child and they stand alone two months earlier. Other motor behaviors were similarly precocious. Ganda mothers encourage this motor precocity, in striking contrast to the women of Gopalpur described previously. The Ganda infant is "taught to sit," and a great deal of emphasis is placed on the ability to stay upright for even a few seconds. Acceptable sitting posture is required of toddlers.

Data from American blacks suggest that Ganda motor precocity is at least in part related to genetic factors.[5] The cultural stress on early motor skills probably also guarantees that these skills will appear as early as possible. Some authorities feel that attempts to teach the child to sit and the practice of holding the child in a standing position does, in fact, accelerate motor development. In any case, the outcome is a result of individual genetic variation and Cultural Set. Two alternative explanations could account for Gandian precocity. The cultural concern with early walking permits and emphasizes the

5. N. Bayley, "Comparisons of Mental and Motor Test Scores for Ages One-Fifteen Months by Sex, Birth Order, Race, Geographical Location, and Education of Parents," *Child Development,* 36 (1965), 379–411.

expression of a genetic disposition toward motor precocity. Alternately, genetic disposition toward motor precocity permits an effective result of early motor skill training. These alternatives are of course two sides of the same coin, but the first statement is more consistent with the ideas of the authors.

Modern Russia   According to reports provided by the American child psychologist Urie Bronfenbrenner, there is a great deal of physical contact between mother and infant in Russia as compared with typical American practice.[6] The baby, typically breast-fed, is cuddled and held much of the time, frequently while the mother is cooking or engaged in other household tasks. Children receive much contact and supervision throughout childhood. Even unfamiliar adults are addressed by the child as "uncle" or "aunt."

Supervisory responsibility and physical expression of affection also extends to unfamiliar children, as indicated by the following incidents. One day, an adolescent boy, walking along the street with a group of peers, picked up the investigator's four-year-old, greeted him enthusiastically, hugged and kissed him, and passed him to his friends, who repeated these actions. On a number of occasions when this child or his older sister wandered away from their parents, they were returned by adult strangers, even though they were still in sight of the parents. These helpful adults often indicated disapproval of the parents' lack of attention to the children.

There is an emphasis on obedience and self-discipline in the Russian home. Physical punishment is rare and is viewed as inappropriate. In contrast, many American and British families take some physical punishment for granted. The behavior of a Russian child is controlled by rare praise for outstanding performance and by withdrawal of love and attention for inappropriate behavior. It is important to realize that withdrawal of attention or refusal to talk to the child is particularly effective in the context of intimate conversation and contact typical of the Russian parent-child relationship.

Although large numbers of Russian mothers work outside the home, there appears to be more actual parent-child contact in

6. U. Bronfenbrenner, *Two Worlds of Childhood*, Simon and Schuster, New York, 1970.

Russian families than in American families. Russian day care nurseries also encourage a great deal of face-to-face contact between children and caretakers. Younger children are placed in large group playpens raised from the floor to encourage eye contact with adult caretakers, as seen in Figure 5.3. There is emphasis on sharing and appropriate social interaction. The caretaker points out approved behavior for group admiration. Of course, the time-honored nursery age technique of distracting the child is employed frequently to disrupt inappropriate behavior.

Russian children enter the elementary school at seven years of age, and this event is regarded as important and enjoyable for the children. The first day is a ceremonial event attended by the parents, older siblings, and family friends. The first day of school is on September 1 throughout the Soviet Union and receives much public attention via newspaper, radio, and television. There are short speeches, the teachers are presented with flowers by the children, and a "new, wonderful phase" of their lives begins.

In addition to content learning, the school program emphasizes character education including the value of work and the concepts of

Figure 5.3
Raised Playpen in Uzbekistan
(*From* Two Worlds of Childhood: U.S., and U.S.S.R. *by Urie Bronfenbrenner* © 1970 *by Russell Sage Foundation, New York.*)

duty and honor. The use of group approval introduced in nursery schools is continued through youth organizations. Sanctions and penalties for rule breaking and poor work are also administered by the youth organization. There is considerable group competition—row against row within classrooms, for example. Helping other group members and taking responsibility for doing one's best for the sake of the group effort are important aspects of this academic competition. Public statements of regret for shortcomings and vows for better work in the future are a common feature of youth meetings called to deal with problems. Repeated violators might be assigned peers to help with school work each day until acceptable competence had been achieved.

The major differences between Russian and American childhood as reported in this investigation are: (1) more physical contact and physical expression of affection in Russia; (2) more restriction, supervision, and control of Russian children, first by parents and later by peer groups guided by adults; (3) almost exclusive use of withdrawal of attention and loss of privileges as punishment in Russia as compared to physical punishment in America; (4) more overall interaction between parents and children in Russia; and (5) emphasis on character and morality in Russian schools in contrast to the content orientation of American public schools. This last difference may be particularly important if, as some authorities claim, neither parents nor religious organizations provide equivalent moral training in America.

A study of Chinese child-rearing practices similar to Bronfenbrenner's study of Russian children is now possible. The time and effort involved in such a study would certainly be well spent.

Marriage and the Attainment of Adult Status

Cultural variation is also evident in heterosexual interactions and in the way an individual acquires adult status in the society. Since these matters are frequently discussed together, we will follow this convention.

Cheyenne   Among the Cheyenne of the mid-1800s, premarital chastity was expected of females.[7] The girl donned a chastity belt at

7. Hoebel.

menarche and wore this device until marriage. After marriage the chastity belt was worn whenever the husband was absent for any prolonged period. Seduction had profound consequences for the unmarried girl in Cheyenne society. She would be publically taunted and unlikely to find a husband. After puberty there was relatively little casual interaction between boys and girls, and perhaps as a consequence, courtships were awkward. A suitor would station himself on the path between the lodge of the girl's family and the water supply. When she passed he tugged at her robe, whistled, or called to her. If she ignored him, all was lost. He was overjoyed if she deigned to stop for idle chit-chat. Should things go well at this initial interaction, casual conversations would take place near her lodge. If the romance really became serious, the young couple might exchange horn rings. This was more or less equivalent to engagement, but marriage involved consultation and cooperation between the two families.

Once the decision to marry was made, the prospective groom would seek approval and assistance from his close relatives. If they approved the match, they would contribute gifts, including horses, guns, bows and arrows, and blankets. Elderly relatives would lead the horses laden with the gifts to the girl's home. The boy's representative went in, chatted, smoked, formally proposed the marriage, and left. The father or brother of the bride sent for his male relatives, and they discussed the match. If the marriage was not approved, the horses and gifts were returned to the unlucky suitor's family. If approval was granted, the horses were unloaded and the gifts divided among the girl's relatives. These gifts were replaced the next day with gifts of equal value to be given to the groom. These were packed on horses selected to reciprocate for those contributed by the groom's family. The bride, painted and dressed in her finest, rode the best horse led by an old woman to her husband's lodge. There, she was repainted, her hair was redone, and she was dressed in new clothing by her husband's female relatives. The two mothers then set the young couple up for housekeeping in a tepee provided by the bride's mother. This new lodge was typically placed near the bride's mother's tepee. The young couple was then established as an independent household.

Cheyenne marriage was frequently unstable. Divorce was common and could be initiated by both men and women, although divorced women lost status. A woman who had been divorced four times was not considered marriageable and was fair sexual game for any man not related to her. When a woman left her husband for another man, the new husband gave the previous husband a pipe, horses, and other gifts. These petty matters were beneath the notice of a chief, who had to refuse the gifts or risk loss of status. He might dismiss the whole matter by casually saying, "A dog has pissed on my tent," to emphasize that he was far above such unimportant things. A chief who accepted such gifts or showed concern for the lost wife would be unlikely to be reappointed at the end of his five- or ten-year term of office.

Among the Cheyenne adult status was acquired gradually. The first accomplishments of the developing hunter or robe maker were formally recognized by the family. The first buffalo kill and the first war party of the twelve- to fifteen-year-old boy were recognized by celebration and gift distribution. Little girls of seven or eight who decorated a robe for a baby niece or nephew might be given a horse by their proud brother. A formal transition for the girl came at the first menstruation, which was announced by her father to all the camp and was recognized by gift distribution. Certain taboos were invoked to protect the virility and valor of the menfolk.

Young men received no such ceremonial recognition of their maturity. Their progress toward adult status was based on their accomplishments in war and the hunt. Actually, the major change for a male was not from child to adult but from nonleader to leader. The principal tribal chief was supposed to be "protector of the people" and father to every tribal member (see Figure 5.4). He was addressed as father by other tribal members. He was supposed to be even-tempered, wise, generous, kind, and brave. It was this model that the developing Cheyenne warrior, whether fourteen or twenty-five, tried to follow.

Gopalpur   While marriage among the Cheyenne was a family matter, it was frequently initiated by the bride and groom. In Gopalpur, the family predominates almost without involvement of the young couple.[8] When a child is born, the father is said to begin considering appropriate marriage partners in neighboring villages. The match is of concern to the whole village and requires the advice and consent

8. Beals.

Figure 5.4
Protector of the People
*(Smithsonian Institution,
National Anthropological
Archives)*

of the village's important men of all castes. The village reputation for
fulfilling marriage responsibilities is important for future marriages
and is everyone's concern. The village as a whole must approve and
support the marriage to insure the best economic and social relationships between Gopalpur and other villages. A man's prestige and
status are in part determined by the number of relatives he has in
other villages.

   When a young man is between fifteen and twenty-five years old,
his parents begin the search for a bride in earnest. They visit
neighboring villages and consult with relatives there concerning girls

of the right age and caste. Careful consideration is given to the reputation of the family of the bride, the number of relationships her family has with other villages, and its wealth and stability. Favored choices are the young man's sister's daughter or his mother's brother's daughter, but other relatives through mothers or sisters are also potential spouses. Relatives through the male parent are not potential mates.

When a suitable bride is located, her family is approached by a prominent relative of her mother, who acts as an intermediary. If they are interested in the union, the girl's parents visit the boy's village and inspect the family household and property. If these and the young man are satisfactory, they invite further negotiation. Formal negotiations of bride price between the two villages are held in the bride's village. A group, including the groom's family and officials from his village, come to the bride's village. Every household in the bride's village is asked to send one male to witness the proceeding, and every caste in the village must be represented. The bride price is negotiated, and if agreed upon, the nine- or ten-year-old bride and a younger sister or cousin receive ceremonial gifts. The bride receives a new sari and food, and her younger ceremonial sister receives a new blouse and a coin. Sugar is then distributed to everyone, and the bride's father feeds as many guests from both villages as he can. The number of guests largely determines his status in Gopalpur. More trips by the two families for negotiation and entertainment follow, with familial status demonstrated and reinforced by the family's provision of food for friends and relatives in the host village on each occasion. The wedding ceremony itself, seen in Figure 5.5, is similar to the betrothal ceremony except that both bride and groom participate.

The little girl then goes to live with her husband's family, but frequently visits her home. At her first menstruation she returns home for a nine-day ceremonial visit, after which the marriage is consummated. She is also likely to return home to have her first child, but will probably have subsequent children in her new home.

These carefully arranged family alliances are not always successful. Age differences between mates often induce stresses that upset the elder's careful planning. Wives are sometimes sent back to their parents, and sometimes they desert their husbands. In the latter case, the woman's father is frequently forced by social pressure to repay the bride price. After all, his village must retain its reputation

Figure 5.5   Hindu Wedding *(Porterfield-Chickering/Photo Researchers, Inc.)*

for fair dealing in marriage arrangements. Marital stability is partially reinforced by increased prices for divorced or widowed women, and also by a higher price (two or three times as great) for second wives than for first wives. About a year of work for wages would finance a first marriage; the three years of wage work necessary for a second marriage could spell financial ruin for a young man whose fields and home went untended for that period. All adults are expected to be married, and upon the divorce or death of a wife a man is required to arrange another marriage to a woman of equal status.

Adult male status in Gopalpur begins with marriage. Until then, regardless of age and contribution to the family's agricultural effort, the male is a dependent and is only someone's son. When a man becomes someone's son-in-law he begins to develop all-important economic ties outside his village. His status will later be increased by the birth of children and subsequent success in arranging marriages for his sons and daughters. Adult female status is dependent on producing children. Women with children share a degree of their husbands' status and are like them dependent on stable marriages of their children for continued status. Full status in the society is enjoyed by those men who "have made their name great" by careful marital arrangements and who head a multifamily household including their sons- and daughters-in-law.

United States   Mating behavior in the United States varies considerably across regions, social classes, and subcultures. The most typical pattern involves a legally sanctioned marriage based on mutual choice. The degree of advice and consent from parents varies but rarely extends either to blocking or arranging the marriage. While alternates to marriage are much discussed, it is predicted that 97 percent of American males and 96 percent of American females will marry sometime during their lives.[9] While romantic love is an expressed prerequisite for marriage in the United States, it is neither a necessary nor sufficient basis for every marriage. In our society, males are apparently somewhat less marriage-oriented than females and yet are somewhat more insistent on romantic love in a heterosexual relationship. Love at first sight—in the sense of a strong physical attraction soon after meeting—is reported by 8 percent of males and 5 percent of females in one sample of engaged couples.[10] Love, mutual respect, sexual satisfaction, and companionship are included in the ideal American marriage. Mate selection is based on the expectation that the selected person will satisfactorily fulfill a complex set of needs.

Most young adults have given thought to their selection of a mate. In a number of studies, college men and women have been asked to list characteristics of ideal mates. Their lists show little change from the 1930s through the 1960s.[11] Males express interest in attractive

9. J. Bernard, *The Future of Marriage,* Bantam Books, New York, 1972.

10. E. W. Burgess and P. Wallin, *Engagement and Marriage,* Lippincott, Philadelphia, 1953.

11. R. S. Cavin, *The American Family,* Crowell, New York, 1963.

personality, health, grooming, and affectionate disposition in a woman who is somewhat younger than themselves. The ideal woman does not exceed her prospective mate in intelligence and education, but this may be a primarily middle-class attitude. Females prefer males who are dependable, mature, in love, well-groomed, and well-mannered. The prospective groom should be more intelligent and have more formal education that his mate. He should also have good financial prospects and personality traits that suggest realization of this potential.

The desired-mate characteristics of college students summarized above may not be typical of those desired by other social classes. The future orientation of the females above is certainly middle-class, and male attitudes toward female academic performance may be quite different in lower-class younger males.[12] Lower-class adolescent males appear to see academic achievement as a feminine trait, something to be valued in girls. Middle-class boys see the same trait as threatening and competitive. These lists of traits may also be dated, changing with new expressed attitudes toward sex and women. One shift occurring between the 1930s and the 1960s was a reduction in the importance of chastity among the traits desired by college males for their prospective brides. One suspects that the importance of this trait and those suggesting male dominance or superior status will decrease in the future.

Actual mate choices deviate from the ideal and are determined by factors that young people may not list. Physical proximity is still an important determinant of mate selection. Physical separation is likely to reduce the probability of marriage, a fact that parents of young people frequently know and exploit. General similarity in social background, interests, and so forth appear to be important, and marriages across social class, religion, race, or culture appear to be somewhat more prone to stress than those between more similar individuals.

Divorce is relatively common in the United States. According to the United States Census Bureau, about one marriage in three ends in divorce.[13] A number of factors are associated with divorce in the

12. J. S. Coleman, "Scholastic Effects of the Social System," in *Adolescent Development: Readings in Research and Theory,* eds. M. Gold and E. Douvan, Allyn and Bacon, Boston, 1971, pp. 220–227.

13. J. C. Coleman and C. L. Hammen, *Contemporary Psychology and Effective Behavior,* Scott Foresman, Glenview, Ill., 1974.

United States. Low educational and occupational status, an unhappy home or divorced parents, lack of religious involvement, short courtship, and early marriage are all associated with higher divorce rates. Factors that appear unrelated to divorce rate include racial, religious, and age differences between spouses, and whether or not either or both members of the pair has premarital sexual experience.

In America, the bride and groom generally set up an independent household after a ceremony variable in pomp. Marriage ceremonies, as indicated in Figure 5.6, range from a few words exchanged before a bored civic official to elaborate and costly affairs in the presence of the extended family and friends. Divorce is somewhat less likely

Figure 5.6   American Weddings *(l. Ginger Chih from Peter Arnold; r. Christopher Morrow/Stock, Boston)*

after marriages conducted in a formal traditional manner than after those begun more informally.

Some Americans have opted for alternatives to traditional marriage between two individuals. Some maintain a primary marriage relationship but mutually agree to sexual encounters with others. The most common pattern of "swinging" appears to be two or more married couples who exchange mates for sexual interaction. While this practice has received much public attention, the actual level of participation is difficult to determine. One report indicates that most couples who engage in mate swapping drop out and return to a monogamous relationship after about two years.[14]

Another alternative that has received public notice is group marriage. Group marriages do not have an impressive track record. In one report such marriages are said to last from several months to several years, with the average duration being about fourteen months.[15] Community pressure is one source of difficulty for such unions. Other problems stem from the complexities of a number of adults trying to function as a social and emotional unit. Rogers lists the following sources of difficulty for group marriages and other communal living arrangements: (1) lack of means of handling interpersonal conflicts, hurts, and crosspurposes; (2) failure to provide support for the group; (3) jealousy; (4) individual needs for secure, one-to-one relationships; (5) the overall complexity of intragroup relationships; and (6) the need for individual privacy.[16]

It should be obvious to the reader that the United States does not consist of one monolithic culture but of a number of subcultural groups that live within a general cultural framework. Local, ethnic, religious, and social class differences are known to the reader and will influence marital choices and behavior. Some patterns discussed above, such as group marriage, may have functional difficulties due to the influence of Phylogenetic and/or Cultural Set. The problems that occur in communal living may be viewed in this light.

The attainment of adult status in the United States is not clearcut and absolute. A major problem faced by the young person maturing in our society is cultural ambiguity about when he or she is an adult.

14. C. Broderick, "Damn Those Gloomy Prophets—The Family's Here to Stay," *Los Angeles Times,* June 17, 1973. Cited in Coleman and Hammen.

15. D. Bremmer, "Bob and Barbara and Mike and . . . ?" *Los Angeles Times,* June 17, 1973. Cited in Coleman and Hammen.

16. C. R. Rogers, *Becoming Partners: Marriage and Its Alternatives,* Delacorte Press, New York, 1972.

Texts frequently provide a list of developmental problems whose solutions constitute becoming an adult, but few members of our society achieve stable solutions to all of these problems at any age. In short, economic independence is probably as important as any single factor in societally recognized adulthood, but such factors as marriage and parenthood are also obviously involved. It is generally recognized that limited opportunity for economic and social productivity provides many problems for those striving for adult status in the United States.

Culture and Thought

Within any particular culture, specific skills and attitudes toward the world are transmitted to children. Differences among cultures may be subtle or obvious. The most important differences may relate to fairly general attitudes rather than to specific information or skills. In the two subsistence cultures discussed, there were marked differences in the criteria of personal worth. The Cheyenne warrior was a worthy person to the extent that he became a protective father for all Cheyenne. That cultural ideal was not too different from the ideal specified for a good Boy Scout of today. A woman's status was also dependent on direct personal achievements, but to a lesser extent. In Gopalpur, a degree of status was determined by caste, designated at birth. Within the caste, status was achieved by marriage arrangements. The successful couple was one with sons who were married and living in the household. These successful marriages reflected considerable economic and social skill on the part of the family.

To a Cheyenne child, the adult world was made up of grandparents, mothers, fathers, uncles, and aunts. In an important sense the Cheyenne represent one family. The child of Gopalpur has relationships with many different adults, and these are associated with specific behaviors. Even within the caste, the status of adults with respect to a child show considerable formal variation. A thirteen- or fourteen-year-old in Gopalpur would address a well-dressed and affluent male stranger as "mother's brother." A less impressive man woud be called "father" or "grandfather." In Gopalpur society, "mother's brother" really means "potential bride giver." It is obvious that the way the child thinks about himself or herself and others is dependent on the values and practices of the culture.

The way an individual can symbolically manipulate the objective environment is highly influenced by the effective environments offered by the individual's culture. In one study, accuracy of estimating various volumes in different-shaped containers was studied.[17] In estimating the amount of colored water, American college students were far more accurate than were Kpelle adults from Liberia. However, when volumes of rice were used, the Kpelle farmers were more accurate than the American college students. The point is that we can think about and mentally manipulate those concepts that are culturally relevant.

As an adaptive response to our educational practices, American students may have developed some rather peculiar ways to think. Kpelle adults who were required to learn word lists did very poorly compared with American school children.[18] If the verbal material was placed in a culturally relevant context, such as a folk story, the Kpelle farmers performed well. Apparently, our school children are trained to learn words without context, as in spelling lists.

The particular characteristics of any language constitute a set of tools provided by the culture. As mentioned in Chapter 4, at the word and sentence level meaning in language is conveyed by lexicon and syntax. While some authorities believe a common structure to underlie all human languages, the surface characteristics such as vocabulary and permissible word orders vary from language to language. The patterns of language may shape the direction and range of thinking.[19] For example, it is easy for an English-speaking person to think of ten days: we can say, "They stayed ten days." A speaker of Hopi cannot use this concept; to express the same thing he or she must say (and think), "They stayed until the eleventh day." In Hopi a segment of time cannot be expressed as an object or collection. Durations are described as happenings in that language.

Cultural Set and Behavior

We have presented but a portion of the range of behavior and life style seen in different cultures. This presentation has had some of the characteristics of a slide show. It offered, in tantalizing and cursory flashes, glimpses of the behaviors of particular societies. One

17. J. Gay and M. Cole, *The New Mathematics and an Old Culture,* Holt, Rinehart and Winston, New York, 1967.

18. M. Cole, J. Gay, J. Glick, and D. W. Sharp, *The Cultural Context of Learning and Thinking,* Basic Books, New York, 1971.

19. B. L. Whorf, *Language, Thought, and Reality,* John Wiley and Sons, New York, 1956.

is impressed by the degree of cultural variation evident in just these few societies. No attempt has been made to associate particular features of the cultures described with specific characteristics of temperament or personality in the members of these societies.

It is usually of limited value to look at one particular aspect of a culture and attempt to evaluate its effect on members of that society. The results of such efforts are seen in the outcome of studies of children of the kibbutz of Israel.[20] It was once thought that communal rearing of children, as was supposed to occur in the kibbutz, would provide information relevant to a number of questions concerning mother-infant relationships. It was felt that the function of interactions with parents could be understood by noting the behavioral characteristics of these children reared with minimal parental contact. Communal rearing in the kibbutz was viewed as a natural experiment with predictable outcomes in terms of personality, temperament, and eventual adjustment of kibbutz-reared individuals.

Kibbutz children sleep and eat away from their parents. However, they also know their parents, interact with them frequently, and evidently develop a warm affectionate relationship with them. Thus, communal rearing in the Israeli kibbutz does not provide a natural experiment involving a lack of parent-child attachment. It is not a situation in which one or more professional caretakers serve as the exclusive social and affectional resource for many children. Cultures must be considered as total patterns, and the influence of child-rearing practices on the personality traits of children must be teased out by individuals completely familiar with the culture in question. A particular practice, such as communal rearing, must be considered in light of what else is going on in the society, and how this practice is viewed and valued by the society.

Different patterns of behavior are expected, approved, or required among different groups. In addition, the same behavior may have considerably different meaning across cultures. Consider the action of a parent striking a child who is misbehaving. The Ganda parent, and many American parents, would consider this behavior necessary for the child's development into an acceptable member of society. The mother in Gopalpur would look upon the action as an infrequent but typical form of parent-child interaction.

20. R. A. LeVine, "Cross Cultural Study in Child Psychology," in *Carmichael's Manual of Child Psychology*, ed. P. H. Mussen, John Wiley & Sons, New York, 1970, vol. II, pp. 559–612.

Russian parents using this technique would be viewed as unsuccessful, inept, and possibly cruel. For the Cheyenne parent, striking a child was considered totally unacceptable and un-Cheyenne. As noted earlier, older girls struck by their mothers are reported to have committed suicide. In such cases, the offending mother was banished from the group as a murderer.

It should be obvious that any attempt to superimpose the social practices of one culture onto another is unlikely to be productive. Imagine attempting to explain the "spare the rod and spoil the child" maxim to a Cheyenne mother or father. Similar discontinuities between cultures are evident when items identified as nonfood by the starving recipients are enthusiastically donated by members of another culture, to no avail. Any interaction with members of another culture should be made with the expectation that one will for a time make a fool of oneself and the hope that offended parties will be forgiving. Fortunately, individual contacts are frequently able to overcome culturally based difficulties. This is probably because most humans expect these problems.

Interactions between groups, or even between individuals acting as group representatives, may not go as smoothly. This may be due in part to the typical assumption by one or both groups that its attitudes and behaviors are correct and those of the other group are incorrect. These misconceptions are particularly troublesome if one cultural group within or between societies sees itself as dominant through right or customary practice. The destructive influence of helpful Westerners among many so-called primitives is an all-too-common example.

An attempt to perform a recognized social or educational function by a member of a self-designated dominant culture toward members of another group can be frustrating and nonfunctional. A midwestern physical education teacher reported the details of his attempts to organize a high school basketball team among members of the Red Lake band of the Ojibway (Chippewa) tribe. The teacher had a horrible experience and left the situation with considerable hostility toward his students. The assignment of specific roles in the game was not coherent with their culture, and these roles were not accepted by the boys. In addition, selection of good players was virtually impossible, since the students would not compete with each other in tryouts. It is likely that the hostility of the teacher was adequately reflected by the students. This somewhat minor incident provides a pattern for many unsuccessful intercultural interactions.

When individuals or societies elect to interact with members of another culture, they have a responsibility to attempt to understand that culture.

Culturally determined behavioral patterns are not necessarily conscious or consistent with attitudes and beliefs. One of the authors, raised in the rural South, believed himself to be relatively free from racial prejudice. As a student he experienced a minor revelation that caused him considerable concern. While lost in thought or terror concerning some aspect of graduate training, he attempted to walk through a door leading from a classroom building. To his surprise his passage was blocked by someone trying to pass through the same doorway in the opposite direction. Looking up from the broad chest directly in front of his eyes, he saw a very black face decorated with tribal scars down each cheek, wearing a slightly confused expression that matched his own. The "racially liberal" southerner had not thought about, considered, planned, or indeed even noticed, the black man approaching the doorway. He acted unconsciously on a culturally based expectation that his way through the door would not be blocked by a black man. The African black who blocked the way no doubt had his own expectations. Perhaps a princeling, or at least from a family of some consequence, he no doubt expected no one to block his passage through a doorway. Individually adapting to our foreign midwestern environment, we sidestepped each other and went on our way. The point is that cultural background may determine behavioral patterns that we are unaware of and that we might consciously reject should we ever notice them.

Animal Analogs of Culture

This discussion will not contribute to any debate as to whether animals demonstrate cultural traits. Some animal groups have behavioral patterns that are nongenetically transmitted across generations. These include food habits and preferences and perhaps methods of food acquisition. Whether these patterns are pre-, proto-, or noncultural depends on specific definitional characteristics of culture. These will be left to those social scientists with sufficient expertise to make such distinctions. For our purposes, it is sufficient to demonstrate that some social animals have behavioral patterns that reflect some of the characteristics of human cultural transmission. Transmission of behavioral patterns among animals within a group is necessarily different from analogous transmission in human beings. The most striking and important differences are related to human linguistic and communicative skills, which provide a mechanism for detailed and specific informational exchange across generations. Animal groups do have a recent history, and this history influences the behavioral repertoire of the group.

Food Habits in Monkeys

The Japanese macaque monkey is one of the few animal species for which longitudinal studies of different social groupings have been conducted.[21] The Japan Primate Center has conducted a research program for many years involving individual identification of members of many troops. The Japanese macaque is similar in behavior and social organization to other macaques and the savannah baboons of Africa. The most dominant members are adult males, who occupy a central position in the social organization of the troop. Females of all ages and infant and juvenile males may associate with these dominant males with discretion. The dominance status of a female determines in part her proximity to the most dominant males and in turn the proximity of her offspring to these males. Older juvenile males and nondominant adult males are usually found on the outskirts of the troop. They are clearly members of the group but are denied favored locations and interactions within the center of the troop. A few adult males exist as solitary animals and are rejected and attacked when they attempt interactions with troop members.

One aspect of the Japan Primate Center's research program has been to feed animals at fixed locations. The procedure is intended to reduce crop damage. The animals are therefore less mobile than they might otherwise be, and farmers are less likely to demand that something be done about them.

Different troops of Japanese macaques have different food habits even when they live in similar locales with apparently identical resources. One troop will ravage particular food crops, while a different troop in another area will ignore an equally acceptable field of the same food. Careful observation has provided two examples of how new food habits are acquired by these monkey troops. In one

21. J. Itani, "On the Acquisition and Propagation of a New Food Habit in the Troop of Japanese Monkeys at Takasakiyama," *Primates,* 1 (1958), 84–98; and M. Kawai, "Newly Acquired Pre-Cultural Behavior of the Natural Troop of Japanese Monkeys on Koshima Island," *Primates,* 6 (1965), 1–30.

case, a troop was introduced to raw wheat. Animals ignored this food at first. The first animal in the troop observed to eat the food was the most dominant male. The habit quickly spread to other troop members and was seen in virtually all troop members within a few weeks.

The second pattern may be somewhat more typical of behavior relating to new foods in these animals. A troop living near the ocean was introduced to raw sweet potatoes. One juvenile female, apparently through accident, learned that washing the potatoes in sea water removed grit effectively and perhaps improved their taste. She quickly began to carry her sweet potatoes into the water and wash them before eating. This practice was next observed in her mother and in members of her play group. After several months, about one-third of the troop showed this pattern, and eventually most members of the troop adopted it.

This slow acquisition of sweet potato washing was attributed to the youth of the initiator and the low dominance status of her mother. The rapid acquisition of wheat eating was attributed to the high dominance of the initiator. Differences in the complexity of the behaviors also may have been involved. Older monkeys are typically more conservative with respect to new foods than are juveniles. The adaptive value of juvenile initiation and slow spread of harmful new foods is obvious. Should a new food be poisonous, even if the harmful effect were delayed, the death of a relatively unimportant juvenile would halt further consumption of the food. It is unlikely that the more conservative and valuable active breeding members of the group would acquire the food habit until at least several juveniles had practiced the behavior for some time. It appears reasonable to expect that changes in food habits would be most rapid under conditions of limited food availability and least rapid when acceptable foods were plentiful.

Similar differences in food preferences are reported for other species. Spotted hyena clans vary in the degree to which scavenging and hunting contribute to diet as well as in the preferred prey when hunting.[22] One zebra-hunting pack is reported to keep to that prey species even when it is relatively rare and when the wildebeest, the other common hyena prey species, is plentiful. No data are available on the development of group differences in these animals.

22. H. Kruuk, *The Spotted Hyena. A Study of Predation and Social Behavior*, University of Chicago Press, Chicago, 1972.

Tool Use in
Chimpanzees

Jane Goodall has provided a number of reports concerning the behavior of chimpanzees in the wild.[23] One of her most striking findings concerns tool making and tool use in these apes. Chimpanzees have been observed to use sticks as weapons and as probes to investigate out-of-reach or potentially dangerous objects. They also use a stick or twig to get termites by poking the stick into a nest and fishing out termites that cling to it. Leaves are used as sponges to soak up water for drinking and for cleaning the body.

Even more impressive than the use of tools is the modification of objects for use, that is, tool making. The chimpanzees remove twigs from trees, strip the leaves, and break the twigs into suitable lengths for termite fishing. Individual chimpanzees are reported to acquire this pattern through observation and imitation of older animals. There is no report of variation in tool use among different chimpanzee groups, but further studies will probably find such variation. Certainly, learning from elders how to exploit the environment is a culturelike phenomenon.

Cultural Set influences the behavior of some social animals. This influence, however, appears to be neither as pervasive nor as important for animals as it is for human beings. Culturelike processes among animal groups provide examples of kinds of behavioral transmission that may have occurred among our own precultural ancestor species.

Summary

Cultural Set refers to the influence of membership in a particular culture on behavior. This influence is minimal, but not necessarily absent, at birth. From birth onward the experiences of the individual will be in part determined by the typical practices of his or her society. The attitudes and expectations of those around the individual will become increasingly important determinants of behavior as he or she grows older. These attitudes and expectations reflect the culture within which a human being must develop. The influence of culture on behavior may be dramatic and apparent, as when a Cheyenne brave tortures himself during the Sun Dance. The influence of culture may be subtle and unconscious, as when a "racially liberal" white southerner fails to hesitate when on a collision course with a black person passing through a doorway. Often, the ideals of

23. J. van Lawick-Goodall, *In the Shadow of Man,* Houghton Mifflin, Boston, 1971.

a culture are transmitted to the young by means of verbal admonitions. Less apparent and more pervasive cultural transmission involves repeated observation of the acts of other members of society and social interaction with them.

Cultural influences on behavior are seen throughout life in human beings. In this chapter a few patterns of child rearing and mate selection practices have been described. This glimpse into the variations in behavior across cultures gives some indication of the importance of Cultural Set as a determinant of human behavior. Variations among human groups are certainly not limited to child rearing and mate selection. Variations in these practices merely provide convenient examples.

Cultural differences, including differences in language, influence the patterns used in thinking by members of a society. The cognitive skills that develop fit into the life of a people. When problems that are not culturally relevant are presented to a competent person, she or he will often fail to solve them. If the same problems can be restated in a culturally relevant manner, solution is much more likely.

Differences in behavior among social groups of the same species are not limited to human beings. Differences between monkey troops or hyena clans are more subtle to the human observer than variations among human groups. Such differences attest to the capacity of these organisms to adapt to various environments. The influence of a group's past on current members of that group is seen in many social species. This influence is most evident and important for our own species.

Suggested Readings

Case Studies in Cultural Anthropology is a series of short descriptive books, each written by a different author. The books in this series, which is edited by George and Louise Spindler, are readable and informative. There are over forty volumes in the series. The following books are representative examples from that list:

A. R. Beals, *Gopalpur—A South Indian Village,* Holt, Rinehart and Winston, New York, 1962.

N. A. Chagnon, *Yanomamo, The Fierce People,* Holt, Rinehart and Winston, New York, 1968.

E. A. Hoebel, *The Cheyennes Indians of the Great Plains,* Holt, Rinehart and Winston, New York, 1960.

J. A. Hostetler and G. E. Huntington, *The Hutterites in North America,* Holt, Rinehart and Winston, New York, 1967.

W. A. Lessa, *Ulithi, A Micronesian Design for Living,* Holt, Rinehart and Winston, New York, 1966.

C. M. Hart and A. R. Pilling, *The Tiwi of North Australia,* Holt, Rinehart and Winston, New York, 1960.

L. Pospisil, *The Kapauku Papuans of West New Guinea,* Holt, Rinehart and Winston, New York, 1963.

U. Bronfenbrenner, *Two Worlds of Childhood,* Simon and Schuster, New York, 1972.
    This book presents an interesting comparison of the treatment of children in two contemporary societies. Although the findings have been summarized in this chapter, the interested student will find the volume rewarding.

Chapter 6
Individual Set

Every living organism is unique, and one basis for this uniqueness is genetic makeup. As noted in Chapter 2, genetic identity is improbable among siblings, and even identical twins have minor chromosomal variations. Genetic differences between individuals are directly and indirectly related to individual differences in behavior and development. The other basis for the individuality characteristic of behaving organisms is an idiosyncratic experiential history, which is almost necessarily different for different organisms. An understanding of these sources of individual differences will increase the reader's comprehension of the behavioral variability to be found in any group of organisms. These concepts also partially explain some of the limitations inherent in the prediction and control of behavior.

Individuality is easiest to recognize in those members of our own species we know well. Review the characteristics of the members of a club, team, class, or other group you know well. Consider physical characteristics, appearance, mannerisms, voice quality and accent, personal preferences, postures—all the personal characteristics you can recall. This exercise will generate an amazing range of traits even in a small group. Now consider adding to the group another individual you know well. The range of traits seen in the augmented group will be even greater. This procedure could be continued indefinitely, and each individual considered would be different in some respects from the other group members, for individual human beings are unique.

It is a little more difficult to conceptualize individuality among organisms, even human groups, when they are less familiar to you. Some writers with little experience with animals write as if different members of other animal species were more or less duplicates of one another, having few if any individual behavioral characteristics. The supervisor of a riding class for nine- and ten-year-old girls certainly would know better. Horses are carefully assigned to the children on the basis of the known personality of the horse and a quick estimate of the personality of the prospective rider. The task of matching horses and their young riders is simplified by previous selection of a group of horses having individual traits compatible with inexperienced nine- and ten-year-old riders.

Careful consideration of individual characteristics of animals is also required in breeding some animals. In a monkey colony, mating pairs are determined by the female's estrus, the male's record of baby production, and the pair's compatibility. Young, nervous, or aggressive males are not suitable mates for skittish, inexperienced, or peculiar females. Even with careful attention to such details, the animal's personal preference may require termination of an attempted mating, and another effort with a different partner. For very practical reasons one needs to be aware of individual differences in behavior in all organisms.

At this point, it may appear that individual differences are so powerful and pervasive that regularity in behavior and development does not exist. However, Individual Set is only one of several determinants of behavior. Nevertheless, Individual Set does limit the precision of predictions that are based on these other determinants.

Individual Set implies a regularity of its own. For any given individual organism there is an integrity of organization, a degree of continuity across time, in his or her constellation of personal traits. This consistency is important for a social organism since it provides a set of expectations for others. Individuals vary in the extent of their personal consistency across time, and the degree of intraindividual variability has an influence on each individual's social interactions. The most striking evidence of a stable constellation of personal attributes is found when one recognizes a person who has not been seen for many years. Almost every specific trait one might think of has changed, but the configuration of traits still identifies a unique and recognizable individual.

Genetic Mechanisms and Individuality

In Chapter 2, genetic processes were introduced in terms of population genetics and evolutionary processes. In this chapter the genetic bases of behavioral individuality will be described in more detail. The field of behavior genetics or behavior-genetic analysis provides the basic information used in the sections that follow.[1]

Early work in the field of behavior genetics sought to demonstrate genetic influences on behavior. *Selective breeding* studies were common. Tryon's classic work with maze-bright and maze-dull rats described in Chapter 1 is a familiar example. A similar study was conducted with fruit flies.[2] Fruit flies were selected for the tendency to fly up or down (positive or negative geotaxis) in a vertical maze. As

1. J. Hirsch, "Behavior-Genetic Analysis," in *Behavior-Genetic Analysis,* ed. J. Hirsch, McGraw Hill, New York, 1967, pp. 416–453.
2. L. Erlenmeyer-Kimling, J. Hirsch, and J. M. Weiss, "Studies in Experimental Genetics: Selection and Hybridization Analysis of Individual Differences in the Sign of Geotaxis," *Journal of Comparative and Physiological Psychology,* 55 (1962), 722–731.

Figure 6.1
Negative and Positive
Geotaxis
*(From L. Erlenmeyer-
Kimling, J. Hirsch, and J.
M. Weiss, "Studies in
Experimental Behavior
Genetics: III Selection and
Hybridization Analyses of
Individual Differences in
the Sign of Geotaxis,"*
Journal of Comparative
and Physiological
Psychology, *55, 1962, p.
725. Copyright 1962 by
the American Psychological
Association. Reprinted by
permission.)*

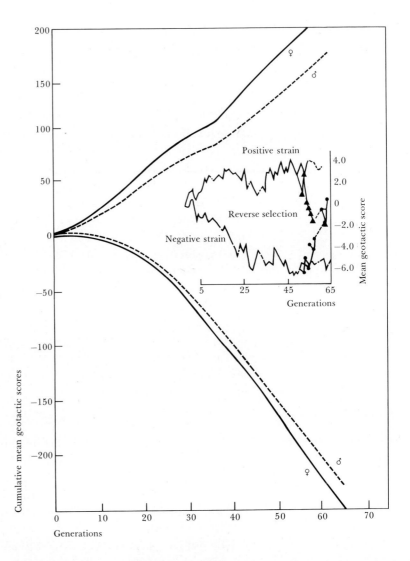

indicated by Figure 6.1, large differences in this tendency were
produced by selective breeding.

Genetic influences on behavior are also demonstrated by compar-
ing different inbred strains of laboratory animals on a number of
traits. An *inbred strain* is developed through within-litter breeding
across many generations. The usual result of comparisons between
strains is that every trait measured will be different.[3]

3. J. Hirsch, "Behavior Genetics and Individuality Understood," *Science,* 142
(1963), 1436–1442.

The pervasive influence of genetic makeup on behavior has been clearly demonstrated. While this general statement is well supported and generally accepted when applied to most species, there is much less agreement on the implications for human behavior.

Heritability

One way to understand genetic influences is to try to determine the heritability of a trait. It is thought that some part of the variability seen for any trait may be explained by genetic variability. In order to understand what heritability means in behavior genetics, we must understand some of the ground rules generally recognized in this field.

Robert M. Murphey, a behavior geneticist at the University of California, posits four fundamental principles of modern genetic theory:

1. Behavior is always a phenotype, never a genotype.
2. Genotypes are inherited but phenotypes are not inherited.
3. Phenotypic variation in a population is the sum of environmentally determined variation, genetically determined variation, and variation due to gene-environment interaction.
4. Phenotypic variation is always present for any population and any trait. (In other words, no two organisms are alike.)[4]

The first and second principles mean that behavior, like all other traits, cannot be inherited. These principles apply as well to physical characteristics such as eye color. What is inherited is the genetic code. This complex chemical structure is the *genotype* and is physically transmitted from parents to offspring. The *phenotype* refers to the expression of physical or behavioral traits. All grossly observable characteristics and behaviors are phenotypes. Behavioral activity level is a phenotypic trait that is determined in part by the genotype. One way to measure activity level is to place mice on a platform divided into 6-inch squares and record the number of squares entered in ten minutes. Mice from different strains will consistently differ in their activity scores. In addition, such factors as diet, illness, sex, age, room temperature, and time of day also influence activity level. Furthermore, the activity level of some strains will be more

4. R. M. Murphey, "Genetic Correlates of Behavior," in *Perspectives on Animal Behavior*, ed. G. Bermant, Scott Foresman, Glenview, Ill., 1973, pp. 72–101.

Figure 6.2
Normal and Bar-Eyed
Fruit Flies
(From Perspectives on
Animal Behavior: A First
Course, *edited by G.
Bermant. Copyright ©
1973 by Scott, Foresman
and Company. Reprinted
by permission of the
publisher.)*

susceptible than that of others to the influence of such factors as room temperature.

The third principle means that the total variability in any phenotypic trait can be attributed to inheritance, to the environment, and to interaction between inheritance and environment. Remember that this principle concerns variability and that variability implies a group of organisms. The statement says nothing about the relative influence of genetics and environment for a trait in a particular individual organism. This point is frequently misunderstood. When this principle is translated into a mathematical formula some rather complex manipulations are possible. One result of such manipulations is a heritability ratio. A *heritability ratio* expresses as a decimal fraction the proportion of variability for a specific trait that can be attributed to genetic inheritance. Because of the logic behind these manipulations, heritability ratios apply to a particular genetic population in a particular environment. If the same population were exposed to different environments, the ratio would change. If a different population were exposed to the same environment, the ratio would change. A heritability ratio established for a population and an environment does not apply to a particular individual.

Even when a trait is related to a single gene location on a chromosome, the environment may affect the expression of that trait. For example, the bar-eye condition in fruit flies is related to a single gene. When this gene is present, the number of eye facets is reduced from 740 to about 90 in males and from 780 to about 70 in females (see Figure 6.2). However, the expression of this trait is modified by the ambient temperature.[5] If the flies are raised at 30°C, the average number of eye facets is 57; at 25°, 101; at 20°, 141; at 15°, 242. Even this trait, which shows extremely high heritability under a single

5. J. Krafka, "The Effect of Temperature upon Facet Number in the Bar-Eyed Mutant of *Drosophila:* Part I," *Journal of General Physiology,* 2 (1920), 409–432.

environmental condition, shows considerable environmentally related variance across a range of conditions.

With this rather simple example in mind, let us briefly consider the application of the heritability concept to human intelligence. We are now considering a very complex trait, which is almost certainly influenced by many gene locations on many chromosomes. Further, human intelligence is partially determined by environmental influences, probably from the moment of conception. Finally, the authors are convinced that there exists no human breeding population and environment for which a heritability ratio might be calculated. Reports of estimated heritability ratios for human populations are based on data for which the necessary preconditions are not met. Even if this exercise were possible, the heritability ratio would apply only to the population and environment for which it was calculated. The heritability concept thus appears to have little to offer toward the solution of pressing social problems in the real world.[6]

Variations in Gene Expression

Single gene determination of a trait is an easily understood phenomenon. The power and simplicity of a modern presentation of Mendel's work on peas or the inheritance of attached and free ear lobes in humans may lead a reader to infer that genetic processes are straightforward and easily understood. This misconception fades quickly when more than one or two gene locations and more than one or two phenotypic traits are considered.

A gene may be *pleiotropic,* that is, one gene locus may affect many phenotypic traits. In mice, for example, a single gene is expressed by abnormalities in the whiskers, the eyelids, the shape of the pituitary gland, and the bones of the skull. This gene is also associated with cerebral hemorrhage immediately after birth.[7] This particular lethal gene appears to be associated with abnormal cartilage development, which is directly or indirectly causal in producing the other abnormal traits.

Another genetic phenomenon that complicates the picture is the existence of phenocopies. A *phenocopy* refers to two or more equivalent phenotypic traits with different genetic bases. For example, two

---

6. Hirsch, 1967.

7. C. L. Market and H. Ursprung, *Developmental Genetics,* Prentice-Hall, Englewood Cliffs, N. J., 1971.

boys might be exactly the same height yet have quite different genotypes for height. One boy might be the descendant of Japanese ancestors, with a genotype typically associated with small stature. In contrast, the other boy might be an Appalachian immigrant whose early nutrition left a lot to be desired. The identical phenotypes in this hypothetical case would be due to different genotypes expressed in interaction with different early environments.

Genes from different loci interact in producing phenotypic variation. Most readers notice that the dominance-recessive explanation of brown and blue eye color in humans does not exhaust variation in eye color. Variants, other than blue or gray and brown or black, are probably related to gene locations other than the specific location involved in the simple brown-blue relationship. Even for a simple trait such as eye color, one gene may modify or mask the expression of another gene.

Genotypic Variation

When the complete genetic makeup of an individual organism is considered, the potential genetic variation in a population is bewildering. Ignoring variation within chromosomes and considering them as indivisible genetic units, we find that any human being can produce 8,388,608 genetically different sperm or ova. Any two human beings could produce offspring from among about 70 trillion genetically different combinations available. This is a conservative estimate, since each chromosome contains hundreds or thousands of divisible genetic units.

It is easy to see that the potential genetic variability in a group of siblings is many times greater than the variability that is realized. What is not so easy to see is that the potential genetic variability in the germ plasm of any human couple is greater than the genetic variability that has ever existed in the entire human population! The current world population is estimated at about four billion individuals. This figure is supposed to be greater than the total number of human beings who lived before the present generation. We may take eight billion as an upper estimate of the total number of human beings previously or currently alive. These eight billion or so individuals represent less than .02 percent of the potential genetic variability possessed by each human couple. Remember that these numbers are the result of assumptions that underestimate genetic variation by assuming that chromosomes are indivisible units.

What does this amazing possible range imply for those of us interested in human behavior? It should be clear that every human being is truly unique. No two individuals have ever existed who were genetically identical. Individual uniqueness is a necessary attribute of sexually reproducing organisms. If each human being is genetically unique, and if behavior is under genetic influence, it follows that each human being is behaviorally unique, even if environmental influences on behavior are ignored. Of course, two individuals may share some behavioral traits, but when the total behavioral repertoire of any two individuals is considered, differences will be evident. These differences will be the joint outcome of genetic differences between the individuals, differences in the effective environments experienced by those individuals, and differences in the effect of specific environmental features on different genetic makeups.

Precise prediction of individual behavior is not a reasonable goal for a science of behavior. Individual differences limit the applicability of any behavioral prediction to most or many of the population of organisms under consideration. Even in the confines of a controlled laboratory, some subjects do not conform to predictions that apply to most of the subjects. This state of affairs may be discouraging to those who would like psychology to provide mechanisms for the control and prediction of the behavior of individual human beings. The pervasiveness of individual variability in human behavior is heartening to those who fear a "Brave New World" or a "1984." These nightmare worlds would be possible only if individual variability could be virtually eliminated. The uniqueness of the individual is a basic biological characteristic of our own and other sexually reproducing animal species.

As you read the next section, which considers the evidence for genetic influences on human behavior, keep in mind the basic concept of individual variability. And remember that statements about heritability apply to populations and not to the constellation of traits seen in an individual.

Stability and Change in Human Behavior

Since the genetic makeup of individual human beings is unique, equivalent behaviors in different individuals cannot have an identical basis in the fundamental genetic sense. Instead, identical behaviors represent a common behavioral outcome arising from different genetic patterns. In fact, no two behaviors are identical—even from the same individual. The correspondence between behaviors is functional. A bar is pressed; a verbal message is transmitted; a child is disciplined. The behavioral patterns may be similar in their effects but are uniquely patterned in detail.

Individual differences in behavior are in part a matter of genetic differences. In addition, behavioral differences result from individual experiential histories. Recall that the physical and social environment as objectively described is not the same as the effective environment. The effective environment consists of stimuli selected and filtered by the organism from the total environment. A unique genetic makeup expressed through a unique developmental history would account for some differences in the effective environments selected by individuals. Individual behaviors vary even more than could be attributed to genetic differences because the physical and social features of various habitats differ in both subtle and obvious ways. To account for individual human behavior we need to consider a unique genetic arrangement, an idiosyncratic history, and finally, the present environmental setting.

Intelligence

Human intelligence has been studied in attempts to get at genetic influences. One approach has been to compare intelligence test scores for a range of related and unrelated individuals. Figure 6.3 summarizes fifty-two studies of this kind.[8] A *correlation coefficient* is a

8. L. Erlenmeyer-Kimling and L. F. Jarvik, "Genetics and Intelligence: A Review," *Science,* 142 (1963), 1477–1479.

Figure 6.3
Familial Relationships and Intelligence
(From L. Erlenmeyer-Kimling and L. F. Jarvik, "Genetics and Intelligence: A Review," Science, 142, p. 1478, December 1963. Copyright 1963 by the American Association for the Advancement of Science.)

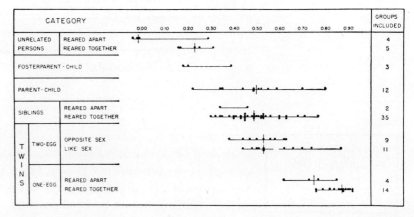

measure of relationship between two variables. The correlation coefficients given in this figure indicate the degree of relationship between intelligence test scores for the various family relatives. These correlation coefficients are *not* percentages.

As shown in the figure, individuals with common ancestry resemble each other behaviorally more than do those who are unrelated. Related individuals reared together resemble each other more on behavioral traits than those reared apart. The closer the genetic similarity, the higher the correspondence on IQ. Identical twins, even those reared apart, show a closer correspondence on IQ tests than nontwin siblings reared in the same family. Note, however, that identical twins reared apart show less similarity on IQ than those reared together.

Something should be said about the way the environments of separated individuals are assessed. We assume that individuals in different households are exposed to environments more divergent than those reared in the same household. However, in most of the studies reported, environmental assessments were made on the basis of very crude indices. Sociological variables such as family income, occupation, and education were the primary basis of evaluation. While these variables obviously affect the social environment, we lack the conceptual underpinnings to make anything much of this sort of analysis.

In one study of identical twins reared apart, an interesting contrast was shown between those raised in similar and dissimilar environments.[9] The families in which separated twins were placed were rated on educational, physical, and social advantages. The differences in IQ between individual members of the separated twin pairs showed correlations of .5 to .8 with these social and educational ratings. That is, the greater the differences in environment, the greater the difference in IQ score. Differences of ten points or more were typical between pair members placed in greatly different socio-educational environments, whereas twins placed in similar homes typically differed by less than ten points on IQ tests.

These studies of family relationships and intelligence support the notion that intelligence has some genetically related variability. However, the results suggest no more than that. They do not and cannot provide anything like a heritability ratio as described earlier in this chapter.

9. A. Anastasi, *Differential Psychology*, Macmillan, New York, 1958, pp. 298–299.

Another approach to the study of intelligence involves longitudinal studies of IQ scores. In *longitudinal studies* the same individual subjects are observed across a long time period. In such studies, constancy in intelligence might be interpreted as support for a genetic component in intelligence. In the author's opinion, this interpretation would be unwarranted. In the early history of mental testing, the constancy of the IQ was usually assumed. Psychology textbooks have frequently asserted individual constancy as a characteristic of intelligence scores. If this were true, a child's score at one age would point to the score at a later age. The test-retest correlations for several individual and group intelligence tests are given in Figure 6.4.[10] The figures show the correlation between tests given at the ages indicated in the figure and tests given at maturity. Note that the closer the tests are in time, the greater the agreement between

10. B. S. Bloom, *Stability and Change in Human Characteristics*, John Wiley, New York, 1964.

Figure 6.4
Age and the Predictability of Intelligence.   Each line represents a different study, as indicated by the investigator's name. Correlations are between tests at indicated ages and tests at maturity.
(From B. S. Bloom, Stability and Change in Human Characteristics, John Wiley, New York, 1964, p. 54. Copyright 1964 by John Wiley and Sons. Reprinted by permission of John Wiley and Sons, Inc.)

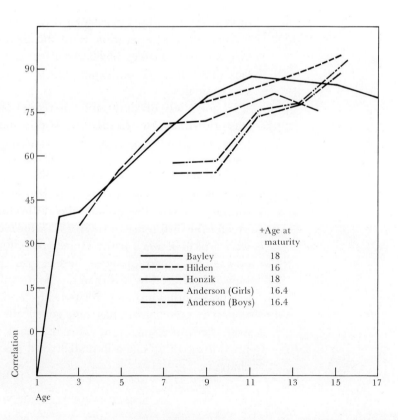

	+Age at maturity
——— Bayley	18
- - - - Hilden	16
——— Honzik	18
—·—· Anderson (Girls)	16.4
—··— Anderson (Boys)	16.4

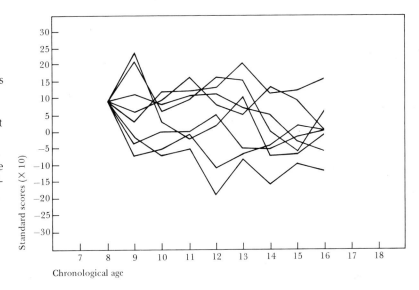

Figure 6.5
Individual Changes in Intelligence. Zero indicates average intelligence. Each line represents an individual child.
All children had the same intelligence score at age eight.
(W. F. Dearborn and J. W. M. Rothney, Predicting the Child's Development, *Sci-Art Publishers, Cambridge, Mass., 1941, Fig. 49, p. 182.)*

scores. Tests of children below age seven do not permit individual prediction of mature intelligence. Even when tests are given at about age ten, individual predictions involve many errors. This means that one cannot accurately predict test scores for individual children. This point is well illustrated in Figure 6.5, which shows intelligence test variability among eight girls.[11] In one major longitudinal study, half of the children showed changes of twenty or more IQ points between the ages of six and eighteen, and three-quarters of them changed ten points or more.[12]

The studies of intelligence summarized here represent a monumental attempt to understand genetic influences and developmental trends in a measurable human trait. We must conclude, however, that this effort has largely been in vain. The genetics question was poorly cast from the beginning. The limitations on heritability summarized earlier in this chapter were only recently recognized by geneticists. Questions concerning the developmental characteristics of intelligence remain unanswered and are still current. The reader may wish to refer to Chapter 3 for an alternate concept of intelligence.

11. W. F. Dearborn and J. W. M. Rothney, *Predicting the Child's Development,* Sci-Art Publishers, Cambridge, Mass., 1941.

12. M. P. Honzik, J. W. Macfarlane, and L. Allen, "The Stability of Mental Test Performance between 2 and 18," *Journal of Experimental Education,* 18 (1948), 309–324.

Personality

The general methods just reviewed for intelligence have been applied in studies of personality. This area is even more complex, because the measurement of personality is less standardized than is the measurement of intelligence. In one study, several personality measures were used to compare identical twins reared either together or apart. In general, intelligence tests gave higher correlations than did personality measures. Only one test produced data comparable to that obtained from intelligence tests.[13] It is generally believed, however, that personality is somewhat more similar in identical than in fraternal twins.

One major study of the developmental course of personality is

13. N. L. Munn, *The Evolution and Growth of Human Behavior*, Houghton Mifflin, Boston, 1965, p. 538.

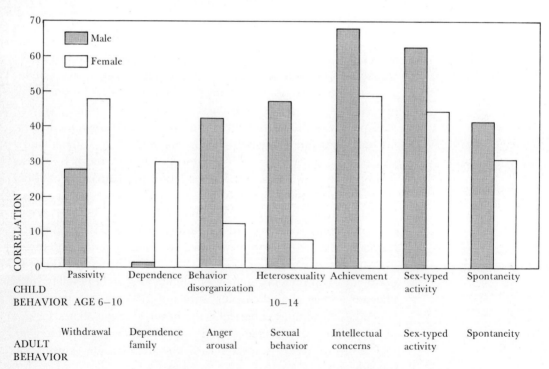

Figure 6.6
Correlations between Child Behaviors and Similar Adult Behaviors
(From J. Kagan and H. A. Moss, Birth to Maturity, *John Wiley, New York, 1962, p. 267. Copyright 1962 John Wiley and Sons, Inc. Reprinted by permission of John Wiley and Sons, Inc.)*

summarized in Figure 6.6.[14] Early data were based on observations of the child at home and at an experimental nursery school. Adult data were based on personality tests and interviews. One striking aspect of the data was the presence of clearcut sex differences. Only two characteristics show correlations above .50, and these were only for males. These data indicate a degree of consistency across time that is only slightly less than that seen in tested intelligence.

Our conclusions concerning personality are similar to those concerning intelligence. There is evidence for some genetic component in personality. There is no meaningful way to measure the degree of genetic determination of personality. There is some individual consistency across time in personality, but changes in specific traits are to be expected.

Environmental Bases of Individuality

In Chapter 4 the damaging effects of early experience in specific, obviously inadequate institutions were described. Behavioral deficits and disorganization in intellectual, emotional, and social development were found. In general, these effects could be overcome if an adequate environment was provided in early childhood, sometime before age four. Additional evidence for environmental influence on intelligence is found in several studies of populations living in culturally isolated environments. The populations studied include isolated mountain children in Appalachia, British children reared on canal boats and gypsy children in Great Britain, and rural blacks in the southern United States.[15] Most of the studies are not current.

In these studies, the effects of living in isolated, divergent environments were cumulative on the children's performance on intelligence tests. In general, the longer the child lived in the isolated, divergent subculture, the greater his or her deficit on behavioral tests. By the period of adolescence, the children's typical test performance suggested an inability to cope with the problems of living in

14. J. Kagan and H. A. Moss, *Birth to Maturity,* John Wiley, New York, 1962.

15. M. Sherman and C. B. Key, "The Intelligence of Isolated Mountain Children," *Child Development,* 3 (1932), 279–290; H. Gordon, "Mental and Scholastic Tests among Retarded Children," Pamphlet No. 44, London Board of Education, 1923. Cited in Anastasi, 1958, pp. 522–523; and W. A. Kennedy, V. Van De Riet, and J. C. White, "A Normative Sample of Intelligence and Achievement of Negro Elementary School Children in the Southeastern United States," *Monographs of the Society for Research in Child Development,* 28, No. 6 (1963).

the prevailing culture. These data emphasize the possibility of powerful and pervasive environmental effects. When individuals are placed in extremely divergent situations, differences in the course of their development are under primary environmental influence.

In these studies it is presumed that a normal range of genetic variability exists in each population. Early test scores support this assumption. As the children develop, their test scores drop, reflecting the influence of a limiting environment on a normal population. The environmental effect is so strong that not only does the average score drop but the variability of the scores also decreases with age.

This situation shows only one of the many possible relationships between genetic characteristics and the environment. A unique feature of these studies is that a large number of children shared a peculiar environmental history, permitting an evaluation of the environment's effect. Many environmental characteristics are idiosyncratic to a particular child in a particular family. Quantitative evaluation of such characteristics is not feasible. However, individual differences in environmental history do contribute to the ever present individual variability seen in all traits.

As explained in the first part of this chapter, the genetic makeup of each individual organism is a unique assortment of the genes common to the species of the organism. This fact, of course, holds for human beings as well as other species. A distinctive genetic arrangement means that the effective environments encountered by the individual in the course of development must be unique as well. The sensory, perceptual, and motor systems of individuals would differ as a function of different underlying genetic processes even if early environments were identical, thus ensuring variability among individuals whose objective environmental histories are absolutely identical. In reality, of course, the objective environments encountered by different individuals cannot be identical. Individuals differ at conception, and from that time onward each is exposed to an environment that is in some respects unique.

Summary

In this chapter, we have described two bases of individuality—the two components of Individual Set. The genetic basis of individuality was considered first. Each individual human being is genetically unique, that is, no two identical individuals have ever existed or ever will exist.

Some evidence for genetic influence on behavior was presented. Animal studies provide evidence from selective breeding experiments and strain difference investigations. The results of these studies suggest that every measurable trait is in part determined by genetic makeup, yet no trait is in a strict sense inherited. Traits such as intelligence are the phenotypic expression of a genotype interacting with an environment. The concept of heritability was introduced. A heritability ratio was seen to apply only to a defined population in a particular environment.

Evidence for genetic influences on human intelligence and personality was reviewed. In both of these areas, genetic influences were evident. The information and concepts available, however, do not permit a quantitative expression of these influences. What proportion of intellectual variation is due to genetic influences? We don't know. The question as posed proves to be unanswerable.

Finally, environmental influences on behavior were considered. In populations exposed to relatively peculiar environments, anomalies in behavioral development can be seen in the entire population. In other situations, idiosyncratic environmental histories contribute to individual differences in behavior.

Every living organism is unique.

Defined Terms	Selective breeding	Heritability ratio	Correlation
	Inbred strain	Pleiotropic	coefficient
	Genotype	Phenocopy	Longitudinal studies
	Phenotype		

Suggested Readings   I. Asimov, *The Genetic Code,* Orion Press, New York, 1962.

Basic genetic information is presented in a clear and interesting style. Although somewhat dated, this book is very helpful for students with a limited background in biology.

W. F. Bodmer and L. L. Cavalli-Sporza, "Intelligence and Race," *Scientific American,* 223 (1970), 19–29. Reprinted in W. T. Greenough, ed., *The Nature and Nurture of Behavior,* W. H. Freeman, San Francisco, 1973, pp. 125–135.

Two geneticists present a balanced discussion of the inheritance of intelligence with emphasis on the question of racial differences. The concept of heritability is further explained in this reading.

U. Bronfenbrenner, "Is 80% of Intelligence Genetically Determined?" in *Influences on Human Development,* ed. U. Bronfenbrenner, Dryden Press, Hinsdale, Ill., 1972, pp. 118–127.

Arthur Jensen concluded that 80 percent of the variation in intelligence is determined by heredity. He then applied this idea of hereditary differences to racial differences. Herrnstein applied the same conclusion to social class differences. (See the next suggested reading.) Bronfenbrenner analyzes the same studies as Herrnstein and Jensen but concludes that no percentage figure can be estimated for hereditary variation in intelligence. A careful analysis is presented. The student should read Herrnstein *and* Bronfenbrenner to understand the importance of this IQ issue.

R. Herrnstein, "IQ," *Atlantic Monthly,* 228 (1971), 43–64.

Drawing on a large number of studies, Herrnstein states that social status in the United States is gained largely on the basis of IQ. He argues also that marriage partners are selected mostly on the basis of social class similarity and thus on IQ similarity. Finally, Herrnstein concludes that individual IQ is largely "hereditary." Over a period of generations, social status and jobs will be given to individuals on the basis of inherited IQ. This is a provocative article in which the scientist delves into the social implications of his scientific premise.

J. Hirsch, "Behavior Genetics and Individuality Understood: Behaviorism's Counterfactual Dogma Blinded the Behavioral Sciences to the Significance of Meiosis," *Science,* 142 (1963), 1436–1442.

This is an extremely important paper that has been reprinted in a number of sources. Many of the ideas presented in the previous chapter are discussed. Any student majoring in psychology, biology, or education should expend the effort necessary to read it carefully.

F. W. Stahl, *The Mechanics of Inheritance,* Prentice-Hall, Englewood Cliffs, N.J., 1964.

This brief introduction to genetic processes is considerably more technical than the volume by Asimov. It is recommended for students with one or two courses in biology. Other students might choose to read the Asimov volume first, and then read Stahl's book.

Chapter 7
Summary and a
Look Ahead

In Part I we have presented a conceptual framework for thinking about behavioral development. Behavior has been considered as the product of multiple nonindependent determinants that we have called Sets. Each of the five Sets influences behavioral outcomes, but no Set alone determines any behavioral outcome.

The ideas developed in Part I will be used as a point of departure in Part II for considering several processes that are important in human development. These processes may be considered the modes of expression of the five Sets. Each behavioral process to be discussed develops as a result of dynamic interaction among the determinants of behavior.

<table>
<tr><td>The Determinants of Behavior</td></tr>
</table>

Behavioral development is species typical, which is another way of saying that Phylogenetic Set is one determinant of behavior. The evolutionary history of a species influences the current behavior of members of that species. For this reason, some knowledge of an organism's evolutionary history helps us understand its behavior.

Phylogenetic Set is the expression of genetic similarity within a species. As a result of Phylogenetic Set, there are strong tendencies for the development of species typical patterns of behavior. However, even the most basic biological behavior patterns are subject to the influence of other determinants. This fact was evident when the aberrant sexual and maternal behavior of isolate-reared monkeys was discussed. Even when behavior is quite variable within a species, Phylogenetic Set may place limits on that variability. Human languages are highly variable in many ways, but language may be considered a universal behavioral characteristic of *Homo sapiens*.

Ontogenetic Set is the influence of maturation on behavior. Within a species, behavior tends to be age typical. The influence of Ontogenetic Set on behavior is most evident at certain periods of development when change is rapid and dramatic. Infancy, adolescence, and old age are periods during which rapid physical and physiological changes accompany rapid changes in behavior. However, the influence of Ontogenetic Set is not limited to such periods. Maturational changes occur throughout development, and behavior is always determined in part by the organism's level of maturity. Some patterns of behavioral development are strongly related to Ontogenetic Set. The development of locomotor behavior is one example. Across most environments, locomotor skill develops in a species-typical sequence. Individual differences are expressed as differences in the rate of development, but the sequence is very similar in most members of a species.

Ontogenetic Set may be expressed as a limiting factor on the influence of experience. Some skills, such as learning to read, are obviously related to experience, but the experience is effective only if the learner is sufficiently mature. The term "readiness" is used to identify this particular kind of interaction between Ontogenetic Set and Experiential Set.

Behaviors influenced by Experiential Set may exhibit either specific environmental dependence or nonspecific environmental dependence. Classical conditioning and instrumental learning are laboratory models of learning that provide examples of specific environmental dependence. The behavior of a rat in a Skinner box or a dog in a conditioning apparatus is shaped by a particular series of experiences. Nonspecific environmental dependence is seen in behavior patterns that develop in some but not all environments. Sexual behavior in monkeys provided an example of a behavior pattern that develops adequately in many different environments but that does not develop in some environments. Many patterns of behavior that are important for species or individual survival exhibit nonspecific environmental dependence.

One evidence for the importance of experience as a determinant of behavior is that organisms with similar experiential histories tend to behave in similar ways. Human beings who develop within the same culture have a set of shared experiences. These shared experiences shape behavior and also help the individual understand the behavior of other group members. Cultural Set is a powerful influence on human behavior, and individuals with different cultural backgrounds may have difficulty understanding one another. The results of such misunderstanding range from irritation or hurt feelings to unnecessary violence and tragedy.

In our presentation of Cultural Set we emphasized areas of human behavior that showed dramatic contrasts in child-rearing practices or marriage customs. Cultural Set influences almost all human behavior, and these effects may neither be evident nor dramatic. In some cases our overt behavior is culturally shaped in ways we do not consciously recognize. Teachers and social scientists must be aware of subtle as well as dramatic cultural influences on behavior and behavioral development.

Even within a single culture we expect to find variability in behavior. Individual organisms are behaviorally unique, and we can never accurately predict the behavior of all organisms. Individual Set is expressed in the ever present variety exhibited in the behavior of individual organisms. Individual Set is based on two sources of uniqueness, one of which is the organism's genetic makeup. The probability that any two individuals will be genetically identical is essentially zero; each human being is truly unique from the moment of conception. The other source of uniqueness is the unique experiential history acquired by each individual. Every organism develops within an environment that is in some respect different from that experienced by any other organism. Even when the objective environment appears to be identical, there will be individual differences in the interaction between the organism and the environment.

An awareness of Individual Set helps us to recognize that perfect prediction of every individual's behavior is not possible. In a particular case, we may know something about the influence of the various Sets that determine behavior. We can make predictions based on this knowledge, and these can be of great practical significance. There will always be some individuals who do not behave as we predict. Some of this unpredictability in behavior is an expression of Individual Set.

In Part II we will discuss behavioral processes that result from interactions among the Sets. In every instance the determinants of behavior discussed in Chapters 1 through 6 jointly influence the process under consideration. The Sets will be mentioned occasionally. In other cases, the reader should now understand the pervasive influence of the Sets.

| The Development of Behavioral Processes |

We have selected four behavioral processes for presentation in Part II. Two of these, the orientation of behavior and the organization of behavior, are characteristic of all behaving organisms. All behavior is oriented and organized in some way. The orientation of behavior will be discussed in Chapter 8 and the organization of behavior in Chapter 9. The other two processes are particularly important aspects of human behavior and development and are also characteristic of some other species. The development of affection will be discussed in Chapter 10 and social organization will be considered in Chapter 11. The next few pages will provide a brief preview of our discussion of these topics.

The Orientation of
Behavior

An organism is always receiving information from the environment. Stimuli are selected from all of those available. Available stimuli are defined by the nature of the perceptual systems of an organism, and the selection process is attention. Initial attention may be a response to stimulus attributes, as when attention is externally focused by loud noises, bright lights, and so forth. Attention is sustained when the stimuli may be incorporated into coherent patterns with meaning for the organism. If a stimulus is not meaningful, attention is focused elsewhere. As used in Chapter 8, the term "meaningfulness of stimulation" refers to the formation of coherent cognitive structures in response to the energy patterns coming from the stimulus. In part, this coherence involves the incoming energy patterns, but the functioning of sensory systems and the experiences of the organism also influence perceptual organization.

The organism responds to information about its internal state as well as about the external world. Motivational systems are those that provide the internal information. The perceptual and motivational systems are interrelated. Perceptual information modifies the behavioral consequences of internally derived information, and conversely, motivational information moderates the behavioral effects of perception.

"Drives" or "motives" are terms used to describe states that direct or energize behavior. An aroused drive, such as intense hunger, clearly influences the orientation of an organism. Some drives, like hunger, are related to physiological tissue needs, while others may be directed toward gaining information from or control of the environment.

The Organization of
Behavior

Behavioral organization is basic to individual and species survival. As indicated in the previous section, information about the environment is interpreted by the organism. The ability to interpret information means that the responses of the organism's perceptual systems are organized. The behavior elicited by external stimuli as well as that initiated by the organism is also organized. The fundamental concept underlying organization is the schema. A schema is the internal organizer that permits incoming information, previous experience, and response feedback to be integrated. Several schemas of particular relevance for the development of organized behavior in human beings will be described.

The schemas presented in Chapter 9 will include those underlying the developing child's view of the self and the world around the self. The schemas are expressed and structured by the child's interactions with the environment. The schemas underlying problem-solving behavior will also be considered. Finally, the schema concept will be used to analyze food-getting behavior in two quite different adult organisms. The apparently simple series of responses found in the wood tick will provide a contrast for the evidently complex patterns of organized behavior seen in a grocery shopper in a supermarket.

Affectional Relationships

Social and emotional attachment is an important and pervasive behavioral pattern in social organisms. Affection will be presented in Chapter 10 as the emotional concomitant of attachment behavior. The first attachment objects of most birds and mammals is a parental figure, usually the mother. Attachment in precocial birds, such as ducks and chickens, is an almost immediate reaction to the first moving object seen after hatching. This process and other complex patterns of attachment in other birds and mammals, including human beings, will be considered in some detail.

In social species, affectional relationships do not necessarily terminate at weaning. Affectional relationships are certainly not limited to parent-offspring interactions in our own species. Other affectional relationships in human beings, including romantic love, will be discussed in the latter part of this chapter.

Social Organization

Group living requires social organization. The particular characteristics of social organization vary widely among species. Within our own species there is considerable variation in social organization across cultures. Ecological variables affect social structure in some species, including our own. Social organization is seasonally variable in some species. Annual shifts in group membership and structure will be described for three species. In all three cases, these shifts are associated with breeding cycles.

More permanent social organization is characteristic of a number of animal forms, including social carnivores and many primate species. Two carnivores, spotted hyenas and wolves, will be presented as examples. Among the primates, baboons show considerable variation in social structure between and within species. These animals will be presented as examples of primate social organization.

Human social organization will be discussed primarily in terms of development in Western society. A specific series of studies of group behavior in school age and adolescent boys will be the focus of this presentation. As will be seen, each group studied develops a coherent group structure. Individual roles are established within a patterned social organization. Once established, the roles are fairly stable. When the demands on a group change, individuals might shift roles. The studies to be reviewed are obviously culture specific. Cultural variation in social roles and social structure is to be expected, but some structure will exist in any human group.

| Variation in Adaptation |

The adaptability of any individual organism, culture, or species is the outcome of all behavioral influences. In Chapter 12, adequate and marginal adaptability of selected species and cultures will be discussed. Adaptability of behavior at various levels of development in human individuals will also be considered.

Adaptive success for species and cultures is indicated by a stable or increasing population. Judging the adaptiveness of individuals is more difficult than for groups. For individuals, adaptability is indicated by access to mates and resources. Even during childhood resources are allocated differentially to individuals. Some differences in individual adaptiveness are present throughout the life span. Other individual variations are specific to particular ages. Typical problems in individual adaptation will be described at various stages of the human life span.

Two primates will provide examples of species adaptation. The baboons, whose population is increasing, are an example of successful phylogenetic adaptation, while gorillas, whose population is rapidly decreasing, are an example of marginal adaptation. A similar comparison will be made for cultural groups, using the Hutterites of North America and the Bushmen of Africa as examples.

The adaptive success of groups depends on the fit between environmental resources and demands on one hand and the behaviors of individuals constituting the group on the other. Typical behaviors and the range of behavioral variability enter into this fit.

Adaptation for individuals and adaptation for groups of organisms provide the broadest concepts used in this text. For the species or for the culture, adaptive success is the mechanism underlying changes in typical behavior in successive generations. Adaptive success and failure provide information to reinforce behavioral change during individual development.

Looking Ahead

The behavioral processes described in subsequent chapters are modes of expression of the Sets described in Part I. Every pattern of behavior to be described is influenced by all of the Sets. The Sets and interactions among the Sets explain behavioral development. The processes are dynamic expressions of the Sets. We have now completed Part I, in which we classified the determinants of behavior. We now turn to a consideration of modes of behavioral expression.

Part II
The Development of Behavioral Processes

Chapter 8
The Orientation of Behavior

Typically, the behavior of organisms is directed or oriented in some way. The orientation of behavior is in part a response to the external environment. Some stimuli have an overriding and immediate influence on behavior. For example, a loud noise usually results in an interruption of ongoing behavior, a startle reflex, and a refocusing of the sensory-perceptual systems. Other external stimuli may not have a similar dramatic effect on the orientation of behavior, depending on the context and the organism's previous experience. A faint train whistle might focus attention in the same way—if it is recognized when the listener is walking on a railroad bridge.

The organism responds to some of the stimuli available to it. This selective response is accomplished by *attention,* which focuses the organism's perceptual systems. Attention increases the influence of some stimulus patterns and at the same time reduces the influence of other patterns. For example, a student sitting in a classroom will hear a lecture only if she or he is attending to it.

Behavioral orientation is in part determined by the internal state of the organism. Depending on the organism's blood sugar level, gut motility, and degree of stomach distention a stimulus such as the odor of food may be the focus of an organism's attention and behavior.

Typically, internal and external sources of information simultaneously determine the orientation of behavior. In the normal organism, the orientation of behavior is constantly shifting in response to the shifting pattern of internal and external stimulation.

The behavior of human beings and other organisms must fit the environment. This requires that the organism receive information from physical and social objects in the environment with some degree of accuracy. In addition to knowing something about the characteristics of its habitat, the organism must know something about its own internal state and needs. A harmonious fit between organism and environment means that these two kinds of information, characteristics of the environment and needs of the organism, are integrated and that this integration is expressed in the organism's overt behavior.

| Sources of Information |

Information about the external world is conveyed to living organisms through various forms of energy, including electromagnetic radiation, vibrations in air, gravitational forces, and energy stored in specific molecular structures.[1] These forms of energy are sensed through specialized detectors as light, sound, body equilibrium, tastes, and odors. The specialized detectors or receptor systems are not sensitive to all energy. For example, only a narrow range of the electromagnetic spectrum is seen as light. Different organisms have different visual spectra. Honeybees see light in the ultraviolet range, which is invisible to human beings.

Similarly, all air vibrations are not heard as sound, and the auditory system varies in different species. Dogs, cats, and bats hear sound at frequencies high above the human auditory range. Thus, the information available to organisms is restricted by the nature of their sensory systems. Figure 8.1 lists the human perceptual systems, their energy sources and functional capacities.

Even with the restrictions imposed by the sensory systems, the organism receives too much information from environmental energy. Throughout this book we have distinguished between objective and effective environments. The objective environment includes all physical and social sources of information that could influence behavior. The effective environment includes only those objects that actually influence the organism's present behavior.

Attentional processes are at work as you read this chapter. A number of potential sources of information have been ineffective. For example, the pressure of your clothing and the chair you sit in have stimulated touch receptors. Now you can feel the clothes or chair because you are attending to them. A number of sounds are probably present. Perhaps if you listen you can hear a bird singing, the buzz of fluorescent lights, or the noise of a ventilating system. Sensory information that was unavailable just a moment ago has become effective stimulation through attentional focusing.

So far we have discussed only input from external sources. An organism also detects information relevant to its internal state. Some of this information is more or less directly sensed. Bladder pressure, stomach motility, and the location of body parts may be directly sensed. Other internal information is evaluated more globally. Some combination of low blood sugar level, stomach distention, typical feeding schedule, and perhaps blood temperature is sensed as hunger. Other states such as thirst and anxiety similarly involve many sources of internally produced information.

1. J. J. Gibson, *The Senses Considered as Perceptual Systems,* Houghton Mifflin, Boston, 1966, pp. 31–58.

Figure 8.1
The Perceptual Systems *(From J. J. Gibson,* The Senses Considered
as Perceptual Systems, *Houghton Mifflin, Boston, 1966, Table 1, p. 50. Reprinted by permission of the author and the publisher.)*

Name	Mode of Attention	Receptive Units	Anatomy of the Organ
The Basic Orienting System	General orientation	Mechano-receptors	Vestibular organs
The Auditory System	Listening	Mechano-receptors	Cochlear organs with middle ear and auricle
The Haptic System	Touching	Mechano-receptors and possibly thermo-receptors	Skin (including attachments and openings) Joints (including ligaments) Muscles (including tendons)
The Taste-Smell System	Smelling	Chemo-receptors	Nasal cavity (nose)
	Tasting	Chemo- and mechano-receptors	Oral cavity (mouth)
The Visual System	Looking	Photo-receptors	Ocular mechanism (eyes, with intrinsic and extrinsic eye muscles, as related to the vestibular organs, the head and the whole body)

For purposes of analysis we can now treat separately the several aspects of this complex information interchange between the organism and the physical and social environment. We will first consider the functioning of attention. Next we will discuss *perception,* the interpretation of information available through attentional processes. Subsequently, we will present detailed information about internal states. In this presentation, drives and motives will be considered to be expressions of internal information. Finally, we will attempt to put the picture together, preparing the reader for the next chapter on the organization of behavior.

Figure 8.1 (cont.)

Activity of the Organ	Stimuli Available	External Information Obtained
Body Equilibrium	Forces of gravity and acceleration	Direction of gravity, being pushed
Orienting to sounds	Vibration in the air	Nature and location of vibratory events
Exploration of many kinds	Deformations of tissues Configuration of joints Stretching of muscle fibers	Contact with the earth Mechanical encounters Object shapes Material states solidity or viscosity
Sniffing	Composition of the medium	Nature of volatile sources
Savoring	Composition of ingested objects	Nutritive and biochemical values
Accommodation Pupillary adjustment Fixation Convergence Exploration	The variables of structure in ambient light	Everything that can be specified by the variables of optical structure (information about objects, animals, motions, events, and places)

Attention

Orienting Response

The initial direction of attention to some features in the environment is called the *orienting response.*[2] This response, called the "orienting reflex" by the eminent Russian physiologist I. Pavlov has received a great deal of attention from Russian physiologists and psychologists working in the classical conditioning tradition. Their term, "reflex," should not be interpreted narrowly. It is clear that the psychologists studying the "orienting reflex" use the word "reflex" to mean a complex response system. We will use the term "orienting

2. G. H. S. Razran, "The Observable Unconscious and Inferable Conscious in Current Soviet Psychology," *Psychological Review,* 54 (1961), 81–147.

response" here to be sure the reader understands that the initial reactions to stimulation involve a response pattern. Gregory Razran, an American psychologist who has followed the Russian work closely, describes the orienting response (OR) as follows:

The OR is in no sense a single reflex but is in all respects a centrally organized, holistic system of a variety of specifically distinguishable visceral, somatic, cognitive, neural, and neuromotor reactions.[3]

The OR is, then, a complicated pattern of responses that accomplishes the initial tuning of receptor systems. In many cases, external behaviors can be used as indicators of orienting responses. Changes occur in head and body orientation, motor activity, and eye movement. Less obvious indicators of the OR include changes in pupillary size, vascular activity, and respiratory and cardiac rates. In young children, pupillary orientation is an especially valuable indicator because it can be observed easily.

Two types of orienting responses may be considered: stimulus-controlled and interactional. The stimulus-controlled OR occurs in the presence of stimuli for which the organism is highly prepared phylogenetically. The visual response of a newborn duckling to a moving adult in imprinting is one example of stimulus-controlled OR. The visual following of a moving light by a human being is also an example of stimulus-controlled OR, as is the temporary cessation of respiration in a neonate on exposure to light. Phyletic differences in the effectiveness of various stimuli in producing ORs have apparent ecological significance. Rustling sounds produce weak orienting responses in dogs but powerful reactions in hares. Other powerful species typical ORs include the owl's response to the sight of a cat and the beaver's response to the sound of splintering wood.

The role of the OR in the course of exploratory behavior is explained by the interaction between the stimulus and the internal state of the organism. In a classic study of pupil size changes, subjects were shown pictures of a baby, a mother and baby, a male pinup, a female pinup, and a landscape.[4] The changes in pupillary size shown in Figure 8.2 are an indication of interest in the pictures. These changes are indicators of the orienting response and demonstrate sex differences in human adults. These sex differences indicate

3. Ibid, p.112.
4. E. Hess, "Attitude and Pupil Size," *Scientific American,* 212 (1965), 46–54.

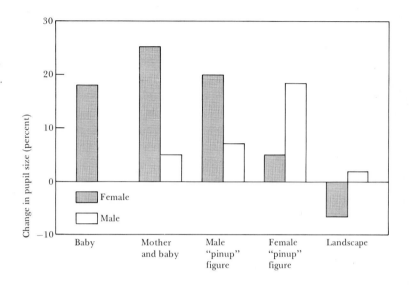

differences in motivation. Babies are compelling stimuli for female
subjects, and female pinups are compelling stimuli for male subjects.

Habituation

The orienting response just described is an indicator of an organism's initial engagement with selective features of the environment. This initial tuning process is an essential preparation for obtaining an adequate sample of stimulation on which to base judgment and action. Of equal importance in these decision processes is the ability to ignore otherwise informative features when the stimulus information is already known to the organism. *Habituation* is the process that is manifested when a stimulus ordinarily eliciting attentional responses is ignored. Habituation occurs when a familiar object that previously attracted attention fails to do so. Many regularly occurring stimuli in your environment are no longer a source of stimulation for you. The ticking of a clock is one familiar example of an habituated stimulus. Familiarity with a particular stimulus pattern may produce inhibition of the OR. This inhibition is called habituation.

While habituation is a general phenomenon, it is not universal. Phylogenetic Set and Ontogenetic Set partially determine the occurrence of ORs and habituation of the OR. For example, the leaf-rustling sound pattern that elicits weak ORs in dogs and powerful

ORs in hares is quickly habituated in the dog but is highly resistant to habituation in the hare. The differential adaptive significance of this sound should be clear to the reader.

Orientation and
Habituation

The twin phenomena of orientation and habituation constitute the basic unit of the organism's initial engagement with features of the environment. Orientation channels stimulation into the organism. Habituation to a stimulus pattern indicates that the organism has shifted orientation to other stimulus patterns. The only behavioral systems involved in orienting are those required for the maintenance of orientation. In effect, an organism whose behavioral repertoire consists entirely of orienting and habituating responses would be passive to the environment, a nonparticipatory observer of events. Such a nonparticipant would deserve Sherlock Holmes's comment to his colleague, "You see, Watson, but you do not observe." Effective behavioral responses require more than tuning. Some information must be selected from the stimulus pattern for behavior to be influenced. Some information is selected for further processing. Other information is ignored.

The orienting response tunes the organism's perceptual systems. For effective behavior to occur, incoming stimulus patterns must also be interpreted. Interpretation may involve further attentional shifts that could be considered to be fine tuning of the perceptual systems. The perceptual processes combine incoming information from the external environment and the internal state of the organism with information from previous experience. The perceptual systems interpret the external environment using these three sources of information. In the next section perception will be discussed.

Perception

The identification and interpretation of environmental features is called perception. Perception gives meaning to objects and events. The stimulus patterns associated with objects, transformed by sensory systems, and tuned to a sharp focus through orienting responses are the raw material of perceptual processing. Many levels of meaning can be attached to the available information.

At a simple level, objects and events are detected, that is, selected features of the environment are formed into a unit and differentiated from other features of the environment. This bundle of features is called the *figure*, the focus of perception. The rest of the pattern of stimulation from the environment is considered to be the *ground*. While perhaps suggesting objects in the visual world, the terms figure and ground are in fact used to describe detection in all perceptual systems. One interesting feature of figure-ground relationships is demonstrated in Figure 8.3, in which either the two profiles or the goblet can be seen as the figure, but not both at the same time. Perceptual experiences are typically organized into figure-ground configurations.

One determinant of perceptual organization is the structure of the patterns of energy that come to the organism from the environment. About fifty years ago, a group of German physicists and psychologists calling themselves gestalt psychologists studied the objective characteristics of objects that were important determinants of the organization of visual perception. Some principles of visual organization discovered by these psychologists include nearness, similarity, good continuation, and good form. These characteristics were features that, when present in the stimulus pattern, provided an adequate informational foundation for the organism to identify and remember visual stimulation.

The diagrams in Figure 8.4 display these organizational characteristics. *Nearness* means that things close together are seen as a unit. *Similarity* refers to like objects that are grouped together as a unit. Unlike objects are separated into separate units or figures. *Good*

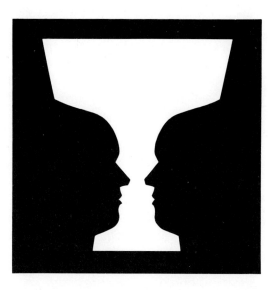

Figure 8.3
Reversible Goblet

Figure 8.4
Gestalt Perceptual
Principles
(From Fundamentals of
Child Development *by
Harry Munsinger.
Copyright © 1971 by
Holt, Rinehart, and
Winston. Adapted by
permission of Holt,
Rinehart, and Winston.)*

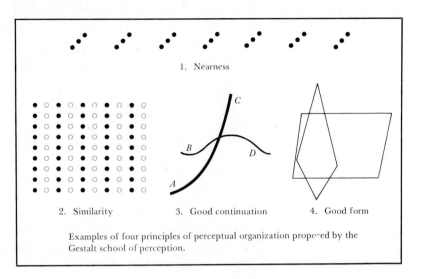

Examples of four principles of perceptual organization proposed by the Gestalt school of perception.

continuation means that lines that continue as straight or as curved are viewed as a unit. Finally, *good form* is illustrated by certain regularities such as squareness, triangularity, and circularity. Figures with these characteristics are seen as units, while irregular figures are more often fragmented or distorted.

Interpretation

A human being sees a square as a square, a circle as a circle, and a tree-shaped object as tree-shaped. Perception deals with environmental features and not with sensory events. This is not to say that the information derived from the energy conveyed by objects is presented in the form of a copy. In fact, extensive energy transformations occur both in the transmission media and in the sensory and perceptual systems of animals. In normal organisms, the informational content of perception correlates with the objective world; that is, the organism selects and organizes the informational content so that the interaction with the environment is adaptive.

The variables that determine the perception of depth are a convenient example. These variables are size of the image on the retina, differences between images in the two eyes, textural quality, interposition, and apparent movement. These cues are not perceived directly. When the head is moved, the objects that appear to move rapidly are seen as further away than those that have little movement. Fine textures are associated with distance, while coarse textures are associated with nearness. Objects that occlude other objects are seen as being the closest. For close objects, the different locations of images on the retina are distance indicators. Finally, the distance of objects whose size is known can be estimated from size of the retinal image. All of these cues are integrated into a single distance perception.

A number of perceptual processes are usually functioning at a given time. A familiar sequence of perceptual activity occurs when a student sits in a classroom like the one in Figure 8.5 while a teacher is lecturing and writing on the blackboard. As already indicated, the stimuli provided by the instructor will not be effective if the student is not attending to them. Once attention is directed toward the instructor, additional tuning of the perceptual systems will be necessary. The visual system will fluctuate between fine focusing on the blackboard and scanning for other cues, such as the teacher's facial

Figure 8.5 A Perceptual Field *(Ellis Herwig/Stock, Boston)*

expressions. The auditory system will be tuned to the lecturer's voice. In both visual and auditory modalities, context and previous experience augment incoming information. In addition, the two systems interact: the lecture may make the scrawled diagram meaningful, or the diagram may provide a useful context for the words that are said.

In this example, the student's engagement with the classroom situation demonstrates a number of features of perceptual activity. Some of the stimulation available to the student's sensory systems was selected for processing. Other stimuli were ignored. The information from different sensory systems was processed and integrated. Finally, experience and context were important sources of the meaning associated with the sensory input.

The activity of the student in this example is in part the result of a lifelong process of perceptual development. Certain aspects of perceptual abilities are specifically learned. The student's comprehension of the technical vocabulary used by the instructor is an obvious example. Other features of perception are more universal and can be seen from early infancy. We now turn to a consideration of the early development of visual perception.

Early Perception

The general view of infant perceptual competence has changed markedly over the past twenty years. It had been thought that the newborn infant had little capacity for organizing stimulation from the outside world. Twenty-five years ago, many psychologists believed that virtually all perceptual discrimination was acquired through experience, through maturation, or through a combination of experience and maturation.

Recent advances in methods of studying infant perception have produced data indicating the infant to be a great deal more competent at organizing stimulation than was formerly believed.[5] Most of these studies have examined the visual perception of infants during the first two months of life. In these studies visual stimuli, including facelike drawings and nonsense figures, are presented in the infant's visual field. The amount of time that the infant looks at the objects is recorded. These studies indicate that the infant will gaze at stationary targets if they are constructed of highly contrasting contours.[6]

5. B. L. White, *Human Infants,* Prentice-Hall, Englewood Cliffs, N.J., 1971.

6. W. Kessen, "Sucking and Looking," in *Early Behavior,* eds. H. W. Stevenson, E. H. Hess, and H. L. Rheingold, John Wiley, New York, 1967, pp. 147–179.

Figure 8.6
Early Perception
(Erika Stone from Peter
Arnold)

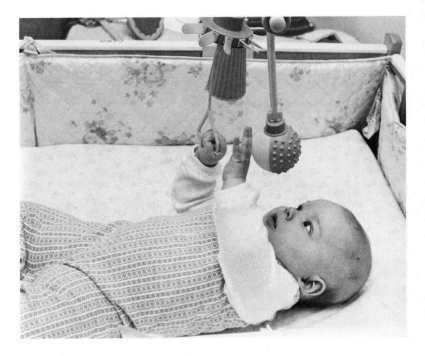

Infants also show some capacity for visual pusuit of a moving target. By six weeks of age they show flexible visual focusing.

An example of a study of size constancy in newborns gives some appreciation of the elegance characterizing many of the studies.[7] Size constancy is present when the perceived size of objects remains constant over varying distances. The stimulus patterns present at the retina, of course, vary with changes in distance between the organism and the object. In this study, two-month-old infants were conditioned to turn their heads in response to a 12-inch cube presented at a distance of 3 feet. These infants also turned their heads to the same 12-inch cube presented at 9 feet. They were less likely to respond to a 36-inch cube presented at a distance of 9 feet, which would produce the same retinal image as the original 12-inch stimulus at the 3-foot distance. The study shows not only perceptual size constancy but also compensation for depth. Evidence from this study and others shows that by the time of birth and in the weeks following, the infant has the perceptual capacity for size constancy and depth perception. Of course, there is considerable improvement in these perceptual capacities during the first six to ten years of life.

7. T. G. R. Bower, "Discrimination of Depth in Premotor Infants," *Psychonomic Science,* 1 (1964), 368.

Figure 8.7
Visual Cliff Apparatus
(William Vandivert)

A classic series of studies has shown early ability to perceive depth in many species.[8] The visual cliff studies of Gibson and Walk used the ingenious apparatus shown in Figure 8.7. This apparatus consists of two glass-covered sections, one on either side of a center platform. The opaque surface on one side is immediately beneath the glass. In contrast, the opaque surface on the other side of the central platform is approximately 3 feet below the glass, thus making for a "visual cliff." The visual cliff studies have investigated the response of infants of various species to this apparatus. These studies show that infants of most species avoid the cliff side of the apparatus, remaining on the central platform or moving over the shallow, noncliff side. More than 90 percent of the children tested between the ages of six and fifteen months avoided the deep side. Infant rats, guinea pigs, dogs, monkeys, and goats also avoid the deep side. However, ducks do not. The differential adaptive significance of cliff avoidance for this aquatic bird should be obvious.

8. E. J. Gibson, *Principles of Perceptual Learning and Development,* Appleton-Century-Crofts, New York, 1969.

These studies of cliff avoidance show not only the capacity for depth perception, but also a contextually relevant response.

The adaptiveness of early behavior is illustrated in studies of responses to "looming" objects. In these studies, an object is projected on a screen so that its image increases in size. An adult viewing this size increase judges the object to be approaching. The infant apparently makes the same judgment, and the typical infant response is to turn the head aside as if protecting the face from being struck by the apparently approaching object. The looming studies illustrate that the motor responses of very young infants are not random but are responsive to some aspects of the environment. Both the visual cliff and looming studies show organized patterns of motor behavior related to available perceptual information. Even the newborn uses perceptual systems adaptively.

The perceptual systems enable organisms to interpret the physical characteristics of the external environment. While the energy coming to the organism is transformed in many ways, the message must be clear. That is, the information must be correlated with the objective features of objects and events. Not every characteristic of the environment is conveyed to the organism: some characteristics are filtered out; others are tuned out. Also, the information received varies from time to time. However, information received must provide a representative sample of the important features of the physical and social environment.

Motivation

Perceptual systems are those that provide information about the state of the external world. Motivational systems are those that provide similar information about the internal state of the organism. These systems are interrelated, that is, the perceptual and motivational systems are in a reciprocal relationship. Perceptual information modifies the behavioral outcomes of information derived from motives. Motivational information alters the behavioral consequences of perception. Motivational systems also influence the focus of attention and perception.

As was indicated in the beginning of the chapter, behavior with respect to salient features of the environment tends to be directed. One source of this direction is the internal state of the organism, which has a more or less constant influence on the organism's perceptual processes as well as the organism's overt behavior. Particular kinds of internal states are associated with particular drives or motives. The labels "drive" and "motive" are used by psychologists for states that appear to direct or energize behavior.

Drives are, of course, inferred from the behavior of organisms and cannot be measured directly. A drive is presumed to exist when an organism responds to deprivation of a class of objects or a class of behaviors. For example, if a rat is deprived of food, a number of changes in its behavior may be observed. Among the changes that occur are increased activity (at least for a time), increased work output on tasks previously associated with food reward, increased sensitivity to food-related stimuli, and increased willingness to withstand noxious stimuli such as electric shock in order to obtain food. These behavior changes are characteristic of motivated behavior. It may be said that food deprivation is associated with a drive state called hunger. When hunger is aroused, the organism's behavioral orientation is focused on food, food-related behaviors, and food-related sources of stimulation.

Drives are also inferred when subjects will work or learn in order to perform acts or to have access to objects. Monkeys that are kept in a completely enclosed cage will learn to press a lever in order to see through a small window.[9] They will work harder to see a moving electric train than a bowl of fruit, and even harder to see another monkey. Their behavior in this situation is clearly motivated, but it is difficult to find a completely satisfactory label for the drive reflected by this behavior.

Homeostasis

Homeostasis is a general principle frequently used in discussing motivation.[10] *Homeostasis* is the orientation of organisms toward a state of internal equilibrium. Whenever internal conditions deviate from a steady state the body attempts to effect a return to equilibrium. When physiological reflex actions are not sufficient to retain the steady state, internal tensions result that, according to this view, are the bases for drives.

The homeostatic model applies rather well to the behavior of a hungry rat. For a long time, many psychologists accepted the model as a basis for all motivated behavior. One idea was that all motives were directly or indirectly related to homeostatic tissue needs. While homeostatic mechanisms are obviously involved in many kinds of

9. R. A. Butler, "Curiosity in Monkeys," *Scientific American,* 180 (1954), 70–76.
10. W. B. Cannon, *The Wisdom of the Body,* W. W. Norton, New York, 1932.

drive-related behavior, the physiological homeostasis model does not apply as generally as was once hoped.

The homeostatic model is clearly applicable to some drives. These are drive states that are directly related to the survival or well-being of the individual or species. Since there are well-known internal concomitants of these drives, they are sometimes known as *physiological drives* or *primary drives*. Drives with recognized physiological bases include hunger, thirst, pain avoidance, fatigue, suffocation avoidance, eliminative needs, thermal regulation, and sexual motivation. Two of these drives, hunger and sexual motivation, will serve as examples of physiological drives.

Hunger

Instigation   In the laboratory, hunger is usually defined in terms of hours of food deprivation. A common procedure is to reduce an animal's diet in order to reduce the animal's weight. The animal is first maintained on an unlimited diet. Its weight is determined, and then its diet is reduced until its weight is 70 percent of its previous weight. The subject is then fed enough in a one-hour period each day to maintain the 70 percent body weight. This procedure provides for testing each day an animal deprived of food for twenty-two and one-half hours. The behavior of rats tested on this kind of schedule indicates that they are strongly oriented toward food.

The experience that humans subjectively identify as hunger is influenced by factors other than deprivation. The schedule of eating varies considerably in different human societies. In our society, most people experience hunger as a result of learned schedules of eating; that is, they tend to experience hunger when it is near time to eat, more or less independently of basic tissue needs. The relationship between hunger as it is operationally defined in the laboratory and the personal experience of hunger by most individuals in our society is complicated. Few people reading this text have experienced food deprivation similar to that of a rat reduced to 70 percent body weight on a twenty-three-hour deprivation schedule.

Feeding behavior is also related to stimulus characteristics. Some food objects are more likely than others to stimulate eating. Food deprivation or hunger increases the probability of eating, but some foods will be eaten if the organism can eat, while others will be ingested only if the organism must eat. Taste and odor are important characteristics of food objects, and studies with rats show that sweet solutions are consumed whether or not they satisfy any nutritional need.[11] In fact, saccharine solutions, which have no nutritive value, are more effective reinforcers than dextrose solutions, which satisfy nutritive needs but are less sweet. Similar incentive-related behavior factors are seen when starving people reject unfamiliar or culturally unacceptable food despite their critical need for nourishment. In these situations, objectively defined food is not perceived as food and is therefore irrelevant to the organism's need for nourishment.

Satiation   In the normal intact organism, hunger is satisfied by ingesting food. The consummatory responses of taking food into the mouth, chewing, and swallowing are sometimes viewed as the goal of food-directed behavior. This point of view is reasonable and may be adequate for many real world situations. Consummatory responses are not, however, necessary for satisfying hunger. Rats will learn when a food reward is injected directly into the stomach although not as rapidly as they will learn when food is ingested normally. Consummatory responses are satiated, at least temporarily, when food is not permitted to enter the stomach but leaves the body immediately after swallowing. Animals with the esophagus surgically diverted outside the body eat larger amounts of food than intact animals but they do stop eating, at least for a time.[12] We must assume, then, that the intact organism limits intake amounts via sensory input from the mouth, throat, esophagus, and stomach and that frequency of eating is related to learned habits, blood sugar levels, and incentive variables.

Sex

Sexual motivation is unique among the physiological drives in that it is not related to individual survival.[13] Individual organisms, particularly human beings, show wide variation in motive strength, behavior patterns leading to satiation, and incentive choices. This variation

11. F. D. Sheffield and T. B. Roby, "Reward Value of a Non-Nutritive Sweet Taste," *Journal of Comparative and Physiological Psychology*, 43 (1950), 471–481.

12. H. D. Janowitz and M. T. Grossman, "Some Factors Affecting the Food Intake of Normal Dogs and Dogs with Esophagostomy and Gastric Fistula," *American Journal of Physiology*, 159 (1949), 143–148.

13. W. H. Masters and V. E. Johnson, *Human Sexual Response*, Little, Brown, Boston, 1966; and R. Brecher and E. Brecher, eds., *An Analysis of Human Sexual Response*, Little, Brown, Boston, 1966.

has led some writers to conclude that sexual motivation in human beings is a learned appetite rather than a physiological drive. In any case, the influence of learning and experience, including cultural factors, is clearly evident in the sexual behavior of human beings. As noted in Chapter 3, the relationship between sexual motivation and hormones is quite variable among species and among individuals within a given species.

Recent data on human sexual behavior suggest that male and female sexual responses and motivation are more similar than was once believed. Developmental differences are found between the sexes in the frequency of sexual behavior, but these may be strongly related to differential cultural pressures. In terms of ejaculation frequency, males show a peak of sexual activity at about eighteen years of age and a subsequent slow but steady decline in sexual activity (as measured by ejaculation frequency). Females in Western society show a gradual increase in reported sexual interest up to about thirty years of age, and then maintain a fairly consistent interest with gradual decline occurring well after the menopause. Some females show a sharp fluctuation in sexual interest at the time of the menopause, with declines in interest being interpreted in terms of the attitude of the individual and increases in interest explained in terms of previous fear of pregnancy.

Instigation   The arousal of sexual motivation is related to period of deprivation, internal hormonal environment, presence of an adequate sexual stimulus, presence of stimuli previously associated with sexual arousal, previous sexual experience, direct physical stimulation of sensitive portions of the body, and cognitive images related to sexual behavior. Any one or a combination of these factors may induce at least the first stage of sexual arousal in humans. Appetitive behavior related to sexual behavior may precede clear physical evidence of arousal. However, physical arousal is related to only one aspect of sexual motivation and behavior.

Sexual arousal in the male is accompanied by erection of the penis, elevation of the testes, increased heart rate, increased blood pressure, and in some light-skinned individuals, a widespread rashlike flush. Sexually aroused females produce a lubricating fluid that moistens the vagina and experience blood pressure and heart rate changes similar to those seen in the male. The shaft and glans of the clitoris also increase in size with sexual arousal. At the same time the vagina responds to sexual arousal by an increase in the length and diameter of the inner two-thirds of the vaginal barrel. During arousal the female breasts increase in size and the nipples become erect, and women are more likely than men to show a sex flush over large portions of the body.

As sexual excitement increases in males, the coronal ridge at the base of the glans penis increases in diameter, the testes increase in diameter by about 50 percent, the nipples may or may not become erect, and a sex flush may develop if it has not previously. Breathing rate increases at this time, and there are further increases in heart rate and blood pressure. In a similar state of increased excitement, a number of changes occur in the female. The tissues surrounding the outer third of the vagina swell and reduce the size of the vaginal opening by as much as 50 percent. At the same time, the inner two-thirds of the vagina continue to increase in volume.

Satiation   Sexual satiation is associated with orgasm. In males, orgasm is associated with a series of rhythmic contractions of the penis and related structures, resulting in the ejaculation of semen. Orgasm in females is associated with rhythmic contractions of the outer third of the vaginal barrel and the engorged tissues surrounding the vagina. It is interesting that the interval between orgasmic contractions, four-fifths of a second, is identical for males and females. Orgasm is not universal in sexually active females, and women who do not experience orgasm report pleasant and satisfactory reactions to copulation. Previous scientific belief in two types of female orgasm, vaginal and clitoral, are not supported by recent data. Engorgement of vaginal and related tissues provides for clitoral stimulation during copulation, and female orgasm appears to be a single physiological event, regardless of the source and location of stimulation.

Other Basic Drives   The idea that all drives are directly or indirectly based on homeostatic tissue needs is not generally accepted at this time. Organisms do not cease behavior when all known tissue needs are satisfied, and motivated behavior is frequently directed toward goals that appear unrelated to basic survival needs. When a monkey works to see a toy train or another monkey, its behavior is motivated but is not clearly related to any homeostatic process. Similarly, young children and

Figure 8.8 Play *(Ellis Herwig/Stock Boston)*

many adults expend a great deal of energy in various activities that are called play. The children in Figure 8.8 are expending much energy. They can be rewarded by access to the playground or punished by not being permitted to play. Research scientists may spend years pursuing an unclear answer to an obscure question. An amateur golfer may work long hours to improve his or her game, with full knowledge that she or he cannot become a competitive professional. A fisherman will select tackle that makes it quite possible that a fish might escape once hooked, expend great effort and expense to go to an appropriate place to fish, and then either release the catch or give the fish away. All of these behaviors are clearly motivated. Psychologists have somewhat reluctantly recognized that basic human motivation includes a number of motivational tendencies not typically included in the physiological drives. At this time the physiological bases of drives underlying play, sports, and similar activities are unclear.

One unsatisfactory solution to the problem presented by the kinds of activities and orientations described above is to postulate a drive for any otherwise unexplained activity. Thus, we could talk about a play drive, a curiosity drive, a golf drive, and so forth. The difficulty with this approach is that we would end up with a list of names and no real idea of the basis of motivated behavior. A more satisfactory approach is to postulate as few basic motivational tendencies as possible and still account for motivated behavior in a fairly simple way. In the following section we will attempt to understand a motive that elicits a great deal of behavioral orientation and activity that is not directly related to tissue needs or immediate individual survival.

Competence

Human beings and other animals alike show motivated behavior in the absence of homeostatic crisis.[14] A caged monkey will manipulate a chain-and-hasp puzzle until it has solved it and will return to work as soon as a human reassembles the puzzle. Likewise, some readers of *Scientific American* eagerly turn to the puzzle page and attempt to solve intricate mathematical problems. Given a new toy, young children work to see what it will do. Once they have mastered it, they spend some time using it as it was intended and then proceed to discover how many parts it contains. If a preschool child is playing in a park where a low hill or mound of earth is located, the child will climb it, run down it, climb it, run down it, and so forth for a considerable period of time, exhausting any adult foolhardy enough to try to keep up. The child is also likely to exhaust the psychologist who tries to account for behavior in terms of basic tissue needs.

A recurrent pattern may sometimes be seen in a developing organism's acquisition of new skills. Learning to ride a bicycle is a good example. A child spends a period of time acquiring the skill necessary to easily ride and control the bicycle. During the initial period the child works very hard and endures falls, scraped knees, and frustration in order to acquire the new skill. If skill level increases at a satisfactory rate, the child will continue to make efforts until she or he is a competent rider. Then for a time the child will enjoy riding the bicycle as an end in itself; that is, he or she will ride up and down a familiar street simply for the sake of riding. As skill and experience with the bicycle continue to increase, riding for the

14. R. W. White, "Motivation Reconsidered: The Concept of Competence," *Psychological Review,* 66 (1959), 297–333.

Figure 8.9
Acquiring Competence
(Bohdan Hrynewych)

sake of riding may decline, but the skill of bicycle riding becomes incorporated into other activities such as going to a friend's house to play, riding to school, or terrifying automobile drivers. Bicycle riding has then passed through three stages: a difficult and challenging task, a pleasant pastime, and finally an accepted technique for interacting with the environment. With the skill of bicycle riding mastered, the child may turn to other tasks and, like the boy in Figure 8.9, enlarge his repertoire of skills.

Another aspect of competence motivation is directed toward the acquisition of information. Exploratory behavior is seen in many different species. Examples include rats' exploration of mazes without food boxes, monkeys' pervasive manipulation of objects, and the most valuable educational experiences of human beings.

A drive toward competence, called effectance, has been postulated to account for much of the motivated behavior, like the child's bicycle riding, that occurs without homeostatic crisis. Effectance motivation insures that the organism will continually interact with the environment, acquiring information and skills that can subsequently be used in the service of homeostatic drives. The idea is that homeostatic crises override the drive toward competence, and that once homeostatic needs are met, competence motivation is again in force.

Characteristics of Behavioral Orientation

The perceptual and motivational systems function together to permit a fit between the organism and its environment. Through perceptual processes, behavior is brought to terms with the objective characteristics of the environment. Through motivational processes, behaviors serve the internal needs of the organism. The vehicle that serves to bring the internal and external worlds into harmony is the organization of information from internal and external sources. As conceptualized here, motivational and perceptual systems are regarded as information sources that, when organized into a single structure, permit coherent behavior on the part of the organism.

Summary

The orientation of behavior has been presented in this chapter in terms of three interrelated processes. Attention permits the selection of a part of the available patterns of stimulation. This selective process reduces confusion by limiting the input to the perceptual systems of the organism. Attentional processing begins with an orienting response that brings part of the environment into broad focus. Subsequent tuning of sensory systems involves both attentional and perceptual processes. In addition to the information provided by the sensory systems, the perceptual process uses previous experience and context to give meaning to stimulus input.

In this chapter, motivation has been viewed as information concerning the internal state of the organism. One aspect of motivation is related to the balance of internal systems, which is called homeostasis. Hunger is one homeostatic drive. Other features of motivation include activities directed toward gaining control of or information from the environment.

Motivational and perceptual mechanisms are in constant interaction. These processes permit the effective orientation of the organism's behavior.

Defined Terms

Attention	Ground	Good form
Perception	Nearness	Homeostasis
Orienting response	Similarity	Physiological drive
Habituation	Good continuation	Primary drive
Figure		

Suggested Readings

T. G. R. Bower, *Development in Infancy,* W. H. Freeman, San Francisco, 1974.

This paperback by a leading scientist in the field is a summary of research done on infant perception. The application of the experimental method to the behavior of infants is particularly interesting.

C. N. Cofer, *Motivation and Emotion,* Scott Foresman, Glenview, Ill., 1972.

This traditional introduction to motivation and emotion will supplement the material just presented. The book is especially recommended for psychology majors. It will also be particularly useful to students who have not had a recent general psychology course.

R. L. Gregory, *Eye and Brain, the Psychology of Seeing,* McGraw Hill, New York, 1966.

This readable account of the physiological bases of visual perception will supplement the nonphysiological treatment of perception we have employed. It assumes no particular background in zoology and physiology.

W. Wickler, *The Sexual Code,* trans. F. Garvie, Anchor Press/Doubleday, Garden City, New York, 1973.

This book is written for the general reader and contains many examples of social and sexual behavior in a number of animal forms. The material is relevant to the discussion of sexual motivation in the previous chapter and to the topic of affectional relationships that will be presented in Chapter 10.

Chapter 9
The Organization
of Behavior

One feature of the behavior of organisms is organization. That is, an animal behaves in a coherent manner most of the time. Disorganized behavior is seen, but it is usually maladaptive. Maladaptive behavior will be considered in some detail in Chapter 12. In this chapter, the development of behavioral organization will be considered. Two basic categories of organized behavior will be described; these are goal-directed behaviors and information-seeking behaviors.

Goal-directed behaviors range from rooting and sucking in the hungry infant to designing and constructing an Apollo spacecraft. Information-seeking patterns of behavior overlap with goal-directed patterns in that information is obtained during goal-oriented activity. However, some patterns of responses do not have a specific goal or goal object. For example, early manipulatory activity of the infant constitutes an information-gathering pattern. Self-manipulation, illustrated in Figure 9.1, is an important kind of information seeking. At a different level of intellectual organization, an adult visitor like the one in Figure 9.2 to the Smithsonian Museums in Washington is usually engaging in information-gathering behavior. A combination of goal-directed and information-gathering behavior may be seen in the typical college student who takes a course to meet specific requirements and as a consequence increases his store of knowledge.

In previous chapters, the determinants of behavior were described in terms of various Sets. This required a description of each defined determinant in a somewhat artificial way. Now we will examine the development of behavioral organization as it occurs in the real world, with all Sets simultaneously influencing the organism. This section will involve discussion of underlying intellectual processes, which include necessary skills for obtaining information from the environment and for interacting with it.

Food-getting behavior in adult human beings and wood ticks provides an example of an organized behavior pattern in mature animals. The concepts of intellectual organization introduced in the next section will be used in an analysis of food getting in these two very different animals.

The Development of
Organization

The concept of the *schema* derives from Piaget's theory and was introduced in Chapter 3. Schemas are the internal structures that are basic to organized behavior. A schema is said to be an internal organizer mediating: (1) incoming information from the environment, (2) the organism's previous experience, and (3) feed-

Figure 9.2
Adult Exploration in the
Museum of Science
*(Museum of Science,
Boston.)*

Figure 9.3
A Schema

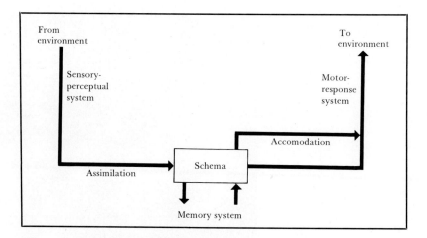

Schemas

back from its responses. A schema is shown in Figure 9.3. Incoming information is shaped to fit existing schemas. A good fit between the patterns of incoming information and the existing schemas results in the *assimilation* of the environment into the schemas. Thereby, an *equilibrium,* a set of balanced relationships between the environment and the organism's mental structure of it, is developed. When the fit between incoming information and the schema is poor, the organism's responses lead to changes in the schemas. These response-related changes are called *accommodation.* Together, accommodation and assimilation are the mechanisms that establish a correspondence between schemas and the environment. These two operations maintain organismic equilibrium with changing environments.[1]

Smiling

In Chapter 1 the development of smiling in human infants was discussed. As indicated previously, the first releaser for smiling is an auditory stimulus, the sound of a human voice. Later on, visual stimulus patterns that elicit smiling behavior include a dot configuration somewhat similar to human eyes. As the infant develops, the visual stimulus patterns include more and more elements of the entire human face. Finally, components such as head movement and changes in facial expressions are important. The schema for smiling

1. J. H. Flavell, *The Developmental Psychology of Jean Piaget,* Van Nostrand, Princeton, N.J., 1963.

thus develops in a species typical sequence toward the knowledge of social communication seen at maturity.[2]

When the child requires the presence of a human face to elicit smiling, a familiar face comes also to be required. It is not surprising, therefore, that differentiation among faces is also typical. Along with differentiation, the development of the schema for face involves the integration of many distinctive features of faces.

Self-Schemas

The discrimination among various faces is an example of early social behavior. Of equal importance to social behavior is the development of schemas of the self. These schemas begin with the infant's visual and tactile exploration of its own body, an example of information seeking. The schemas for self are structured from the sensory information from visual and tactile channels and from the motor feedback obtained from the movements involved in touching various body parts. Since the visual and tactile stimulation obtained from one's body differs from that obtained when touching and looking at another person, separate schemas are constructed for one's self and others.

The differentiation of self and nonself through construction of the self-schemas is a critical landmark in human development. Mature individuals who cannot clearly distinguish between themselves and other things usually exhibit psychotic symptoms. In the growing awareness of physical reality, too, these schemas of self underlie the ability to look at things from several points of view. Even the simplest idea of the physical characteristics of objects requires some general idea of inside and outside. The schemas of self are fundamental to knowledge of the physical and social world.

The development of many schemas relating to ordinary objects, persons, and events is the major intellectual accomplishment of the first two years of life in human beings. In Piaget's theory this is the period of sensory-motor development.

Schemas for Geometric Form

The development of behavioral organization is illustrated well by the acquisition of schemas for geometric forms, which can be precisely

2. P. H. Wolff, "Observations on the Early Development of Smiling," in *Determinants of Infant Behavior,* ed. B. M. Foss, John Wiley & Sons, New York, 1963, Vol. II, pp. 113–138.

defined.[3] However, the individual's actual ideas of geometric form may not conform to these precise definitions. Acquisition of the idea of a circle involves several forms of behavioral organization. These include the ability to recognize a circle as different from a square, a triangle, or some other form. One who understands circles may be able to copy a circle from a model or to name or make other symbols that represent the idea of a circle. There are a number of ways of knowing about objects and relationships between objects, and this knowledge can be expressed in many ways.

The development of knowledge of geometric forms reflects schemas formed during the sensory-motor, preoperational, and concrete operational periods of development. The complexity of these schemas can be gauged from the development of responses available to the child. Within weeks of birth, the infant can make visual discriminations between various shapes found in the natural world. For example, the baby will attend longer to pictures of human faces than to other pictures and longer to a black and white checkerboard pattern than to a simple square. By about six months of age, the infant can visually discriminate a circle from other geometric forms.

Visual discrimination among shapes requires assimilation of the stimulus to existing schemas that code the distinctive features of these shapes. The stability of these visual perception codes is maintained over various stimulus locations and head and eye positions and movements. These schemas, then, are accommodated to the feedback information associated with relative position and movement.

These early discriminations of shape assimilate environmental objects to schemas present at or shortly after birth. Thus, after minimal early experience with faces, the distinctive features of face are "recognized." Motor accommodations permit locating these objects in space by orienting movements of the eyes and head and later on of the whole body.

By about six months, the infant recognizes the differences between circles, squares, and triangles if objects having these shapes are available in the environment. The infant's grasping of objects with different shapes and placing these objects side by side and inside one another provide kinesthetic feedback and tactile information that form additional schemas for shapes. The original recogni-

3. J. Piaget and B. Inhelder, *The Child's Conception of Space*, Humanities Press, New York, 1956.

Figure 9.4
Three-Hole Formboard

tion schema, primarily visual in origin, is now accommodated to a *superschema* that combines schemas for visual, tactile, and kinesthetic information. This superschema ties together a number of existing schemas at the same level of development.

The next milestone of knowledge of geometric form requires the assessment of two sets of form discriminations and the establishment of a concept of *form equivalence* that ties together separate superschemas acquired in responding to particular objects. A task illustrating this form equivalence is the formboard used by psychologists in the assessment of intellectual growth. A commonly used formboard is seen in Figure 9.4. The formboard consists of a board containing wells of various shapes. Blocks are provided, each of which conforms to the shape of one of the wells. The human infant is well prepared for this task, since its information-seeking behavioral repertoire includes placing objects in every position including inside another object.

At about age two, a child will pick up a block and try to place it in every well. When the block fits into a well, the child goes on to the next block. The two-year-old child's behavior indicates that sensory-motor equilibrium is reached when the block fits the hole and the child terminates the relationship with that particular block.

A child less than two years of age will choose a well for the block in hand. If the block doesn't fit, force is used. Often he or she persists in trying to force the square block into the round hole until the whole endeavor is given up. The two-year-old child shows a different approach. On encountering a misfit, the two-year-old child rotates the block, stares at the block and the well, and after a short time moves on to the next hole. At this stage of development, a superschema subsumes schemas for object and for well.

The block-fitting behaviors also involve a number of specific sensory and motor schemas and may be thought of as ensembles of these schemas. This visual, tactile, orientation, locomotion superschema guides the initiation, redirection, and termination of action. Even at two years of age, the child is capable of complex behavior, showing sensitivity to the environment and the effects of her or his actions on it. A detailed account of behavioral development seen in the acquisition of knowledge about geometric forms could fill a book. The contrast between the early schemas required for visual discrimination of shapes and the later superschemas underlying complex behavior patterns gives some idea of the extent of early intellectual development.

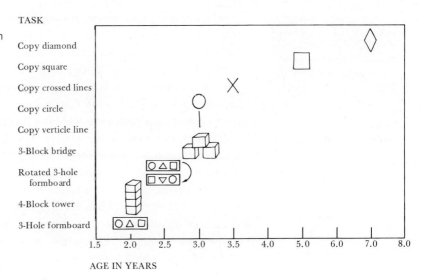

Figure 9.5
Typical Age of Acquisition
of Knowledge of
Geometric Forms

AGE IN YEARS

In Figure 9.5, data from a number of studies of geometric form acquisition are summarized.[4] As seen in this figure, the knowledge of geometric form required for copying regular figures is typically acquired by age seven. The child learns these behaviors, from simple matching to copying, during the years covered by Piaget's sensory-motor and concrete operations periods. While the complexity of the child's behavior increases markedly during these periods, the child still requires tangible, concrete referents in order to use available schemas. From age seven on, the child's superschemas for geometry become increasingly tied to definitions. The manipulations that can be performed involve symbols and logical conventions. When concrete referents are required, the child is said to be functioning in Piaget's stage of concrete operations. When manipulations of symbolic and logical definitions are involved, the stage of formal operations has been achieved. During all stages of intellectual development, the organism actively seeks coherent patterns of stimulation. Schemas that organize the outside environment encompass progressively larger units and show more differentiations between parts of the environment.

The eighteen-month-old child will typically pick up a block in each

4. P. Cattell, *The Measurement of the Intelligence of Infants and Young Children,* The Psychological Corporation, New York, 1940; A. L. Gesell, H. Thompson, and C. S. Amatruda, *Infant Behavior: Its Genesis and Growth,* McGraw-Hill, New York, 1934; and Q. McNemar, *The Revision of the Stanford Binet Scale,* Houghton Mifflin, Boston, 1942.

hand and clap them together.[5] The four-year-old child will clap the blocks together also. However, the older child will also build block towers and match blocks of the same color. These behaviors indicate that the four-year-old, while retaining earlier schemas, has acquired schemas not available to the eighteen-month-old.

Another aspect of tower building is a running verbal commentary that includes description and self-instruction. Building a block tower is a behavioral expression of the simultaneous and sequential operation of perceptual, motor, and self-schemas. Several features of this performance are clear indications of cognitive or conceptual development. To the child, the towers take on attributes such as tall, good, and pretty. To the behavioral scientist, these towers indicate the integration of visual, tactile, and motor activity under the guidance of a plan that changes in the course of performance.

By the time the child has begun to build towers he or she has already developed a concept of equivalence and difference. At first, these concepts are applied to specific attributes of objects present in the environment. That is the meaning of concrete operations. For example, the child might get the idea of differences between blocks of different colors but not shapes. Even within an attribute, the concept might apply to a limited range. The child can tell the difference between two blocks and three blocks but not between four and five blocks.

Counting

By about age seven, the child has developed strategies for determining quantitative equivalence or difference. Let us describe the strategies involved in determining whether the number of objects in two sets of blocks is the same or different. The schemas necessary to accomplish this operation are forerunners of counting.

The first schema developed is that of matching one object with another. The child matches by placing one block next to one and only one other block. This matching is done for every block in both sets, as shown in Figure 9.6. This procedure of matching is called by Piaget one-to-one correspondence. The schema for one-to-one correspondence is developed at about age five.

The second stage in developing the idea of quantitative difference or equivalence involves a "test" for the results of the one-to-one correspondence outcome. This test involves the idea of "coming out

5. J. Piaget, *The Child's Conception of Number,* Humanities Press, New York, 1952.

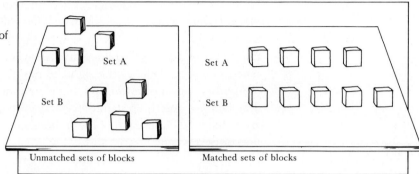

Figure 9.6
One-to-One
Correspondence in Sets of
Blocks

Set A

Set B

Set A

Set B

Unmatched sets of blocks   Matched sets of blocks

even." When objects are matched and there is nothing left over, the child who has mastered this test judges the sets to be of the same number. When one set has blocks for which there are no matching blocks in the other, the test tells the child that the number of objects is different. Later on, the child attributes "greater than" to the set with the surplus blocks. Finally, the child places concrete objects in one-to-one correspondence with a set of names previously learned (one, two, three). This is counting.

Schemas for Naming

We have mentioned the lack of correspondence between the child's use of labels and that of the adult. Children both overgeneralize and undergeneralize the meaning of particular names. The word "daddy" may refer to all adult males, and "cat" may refer only to a particular loved pet. One of the accomplishments of typical intellectual development is the acquisition of conventional schemas associated with names.

The child goes from a very specific schema for "cat" to the conventional meaning of the word, which denotes a class of animals. This development reflects the formation of a superschema that ties together previously developed separate schemas for each discriminably different cat. The child will develop a functional code for such superschemas. The code may not take the form of a conventional spoken language, but usually does.

In the case of overgeneralization just mentioned, a schema for adult males exists, but the label is not conventional. Here the child's task is to develop a vocabulary that permits conventional labeling of schemas. In addition, the label "daddy" must be attached to the appropriate person. We have seen how a name first applied to a single object is generalized to a class. Another word, applied more broadly than adults permit, is eventually limited to its conventional restricted meaning. As the child develops, the organization of rules for naming begins to correspond to the general system of logic permitted in her or his culture.

Problem-Solving Schemas

Learning Sets   The accomplishment of some tasks requires the use of problem-solving schemas that are tested for appropriateness in a particular setting.[6] These schemas are called hypotheses or expectancies.

In the classic work of Harlow, a monkey was presented with two objects that covered the two food wells of a tray in the apparatus shown in Figure 9.7. One object was arbitrarily identified by the experimenter as correct. Between trials the location of the object was randomly changed or not changed, so that position was not related to the solution. If the monkey pushed the correct object it got the

6. H. F. Harlow, "Learning Set and Error Factor Theory," in *Psychology: A Study of a Science*, ed. S. Koch, McGraw Hill, New York, 1959, Vol. II, pp. 492–537.

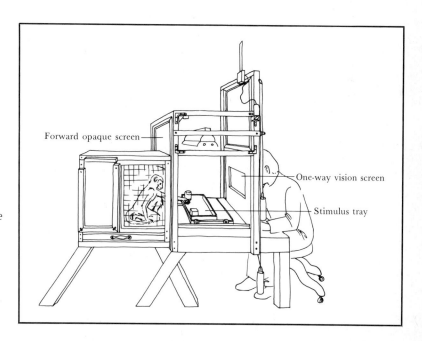

Figure 9.7
The Wisconsin Test Apparatus Used with Monkeys
(From H. F. Harlow, "The Formation of Learning Sets," Psychological Review, *56, 1949, p. 52. Copyright 1949 by the American Psychological Association. Reprinted by permission.)*

Forward opaque screen

One-way vision screen

Stimulus tray

raisin or peanut under the object. If it pushed the incorrect object it got nothing on that trial.

Monkeys that were new to the game required about twenty or thirty trials to correctly identify the correct one of two new objects. Experienced monkeys with two hundred or more problems behind them chose the correct one of two new objects on the second trial.

This feat can be understood in terms of the problem-solving schemas or hypotheses underlying the monkey's behavior. At first, the monkey tends to stick to one side of the tray. This position preference appears to reflect a pervasive schema in animals. Other problem-solving schemas that are ineffective in this situation include simple object preferences, that is, the monkey pushes the most attractive object and stays with it regardless of reinforcement.

Eventually, the animal learns that only one of any new pair of objects is correct. According to Harlow, the elimination of ineffective problem-solving schemas is central to the formation of learning set. When the animal has eliminated schemas for position preference, object attractiveness, and other sources of error, it responds according to a schema organized around the fact that one of any two new objects covers a reward. This schema is a *learning set*.

Adaptation   An interesting feature that occurs in studies of learning sets is the period of pretraining, or *adaptation training*, that precedes actual data collection. In the animal work, the purpose of adaptation training is to have the animal learn how the apparatus works. A stimulus tray with a single food well is used. At first, food is placed on the flat surface of the tray. When the monkey readily takes the food from the tray, the food is placed in an open well. Next, an object such as a block is placed behind the food well. The object is gradually moved over the well, covering more of it on each presentation. The pace of this gradual process is set by the animal. Finally, the block occludes the piece of food in the recessed well.

This procedure involving a series of small changes from a situation to which the animal can already respond more or less appropriately to a situation calling forth a desired pattern of behavior is called *shaping*. What the animal learns in shaping is the code used by the experimenter. In the present case, it learns that getting the food indicates a correct response. It also learns that information as to correctness of response can be obtained by moving an object on the tray. When the monkey consistently pushes the object and takes the food, adaptation is complete.

Some psychologists and physiologists believe that the food reward for animals is a psychological reflection of pleasure and satisfaction, related to the nutritive value of the food. In our opinion, the food is an informative token in the same way as verbal communication can be informative for humans. The fact that the adaptation training is necessary before the specific studies can be undertaken shows the importance of communicating general information to the animal before specific problem strategies can be assimilated. In short, these objects and events define a lawful environment as determined by the experiment. The importance of these rules to the animals is most clearly seen when an experienced old monkey is used to train a new human tester. When the novice puts the reward under the wrong object by mistake, the old monkey responds with rage and righteous indignation. Adaptive behavior consists of response patterns within this lawful environment.

These problem-solving schemas are the internal codes for relationships between objects in the environment and the available set of responses. External feedback in the form of informative tokens tells the animal about the adequacy of its schemas, that is, the suitability of the fit between the environment and its behavior. When action results in a misfit, processes of accommodation change the schemas. When a good fit is obtained, the objects and responses will be assimilated into preexisting schemas.

Reversal Learning   Another kind of problem-solving schema is seen when the correct object is changed during the experiment.[7] Typically, an object is correct for a specific number of reinforced trials. For example, if the problem objects are a square block and a circular block, the circle might be correct for ten trials, and then the square would be correct for the next ten trials. The adaptation for reversal learning is discrimination training; that is, the subject must form schemas for object discrimination before reversal training is possible. The subject must make consistent correct responses before reversal is meaningful.

7. G. A. Kimble, *Hilgard and Marquis' Conditioning and Learning*, 2nd ed., Appleton-Century-Crofts, New York, 1961, p. 388.

In simple reversal learning, two discriminable objects are presented on each trial. When the subject has learned to choose one of
these objects, the rules change. Now the other object is correct, and
the previously correct object is not reinforced. A reversal learning
set or problem-solving schema is achieved when the subject shifts
after one error.

Reversal and Nonreversal Shifts   A more complex kind of schema
is necessary for the solution of problems in which relevant attributes
of stimuli are learned and then changed.[8] In these problems, performance differs between humans and other animals, and between
adult humans and young children. In this type of problem four
objects are presented to the subject. A set of objects might consist of
a white square, a black square, a white circle, and a black circle, as
shown in Figure 9.8. Either color or shape might be selected by the
experimenter as the relevant attribute. If color is relevant, the

8. T. S. Kendler and H. H. Kendler, "An Ontogeny of Optional Shift Behavior,"
Child Development, 41 (1970), 1–27.

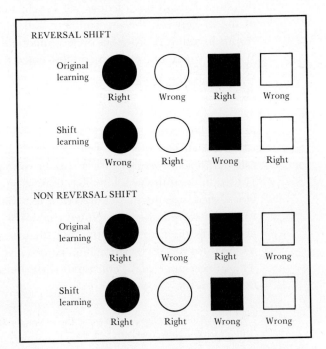

Figure 9.8
Reversal and Nonreversal
Shift Problem

subject first learns that black is correct. That is, both the black circle and the black square are reinforced, and the white objects are not reinforced. When the subject consistently makes correct responses, the rules are changed.

There are two ways that new rules are made. In a reversal shift, the incorrect attribute becomes correct. Now the white objects are reinforced and the black objects are not reinforced. This kind of rule change, called a reversal shift, is easier for adults and children more than about seven years of age than is the other kind of rule change, the nonreversal shift.

Nonreversal shifts are made when the relevant attributes for problem solution are changed. Let us assume again that black was initially rewarded. A nonreversal shift would now define circle as correct and square as incorrect. This kind of shift is quite difficult for adults and children more than seven. However, younger children and rats find nonreversal shifts to be easier than reversal shifts.

This difference in the ease with which rule changes are accommodated relates to the way objects are viewed by the subjects. Older human subjects organize the environment in larger units and respond in terms of superschemas for form or color. Once a particular superschema has been associated with a problem setting, a shift relevant to that superschema is relatively easy. If black has been correct, the other color is easily assimilated. Black and white are specific elements in a superschema for a class of attributes called color. However, once the superschema for color is a part of the problem-solving schema, a shift to a superschema for form is quite difficult.

Younger children do not appear to use superschemas for form or color in initial discriminations. Instead, they respond to the specific characteristics of correct stimuli. Since the nonreversal shift leaves one previously correct stimulus still correct, the new problem is half solved when the shift occurs. The rat's problem-solving behavior is associated with very specific schemas too, although probably coded in a different way.

Problem-solving schemas have been presented here as examples of behavioral organization. Some general organizational schemas must be available before focused problem-solving behavior is possible. In the experiments discussed here, the adaptation phase of each study provided the subject with these general schemas. In the real world, many general schemas are available to the organism through previous experience. If a new problem is definable in terms of existing schemas, the organism will solve it. If a new problem does not fit existing schemas, exploratory behavior will constitute the organism's initial response. Problem definition is recognized as essential to problem solution. "Define the problem" is another way of saying "Find the effective problem-solving schema."

Behavioral
Organization at
Maturity

The Wood Tick

Food-getting behavior is seen in all animals. The behaviors involved in locating, obtaining, and consuming food are varied. The functional outcome is to bring food from outside the organism to the inside. One consumer whose food-related behaviors are different from those of human beings is the wood tick.[9] The wood tick shown in Figure 9.9 is widely distributed in foliated areas throughout the world. Many readers may have found ticks on their household pets or perhaps on themselves. The tick is hatched in an immature state and lacks sex organs and one pair of legs. Before sexual maturity, it perches on blades of grass and preys on cold-blooded animals such as lizards. At maturity the tick mates, but the sperm is stored in the female until after her first, and last, adult meal.

After mating, the female tick stations herself on a twig of a tree or bush until a potential host comes near. The wait may be up to eighteen years. Its host is any mammal. After gorging on the mammal's blood, the tick swells to the size of a pea. The stored sperm are

9. J. von Uexkull, "A Stroll through the Worlds of Animals and Men," in *Instinctive Behavior,* ed. and trans. C. H. Schiller, International Universities Press, New York, 1957, pp. 5–80.

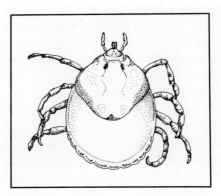

Figure 9.9
Wood Tick

released to fertilize the eggs. Finally, the eggs are discharged and the animal dies.

The food-getting behavior of the tick involves three functional patterns. The animal climbs onto a twig. The best height is one suitable for dropping onto a small mammal or being brushed onto the body of a large mammal. The tick tests for the presence of warm blood on the landing site. The tick inserts its snout between hairs on the animal's hide where blood is available.

Three receptor systems and three effector systems constitute the tick's food-getting behavior system. Photosensitive sensors on the skin provide information about the height of the perch. An olfactory system sensitive to the chemical, butyric acid, triggers release from the twig. This chemical also serves to maintain exploratory behavior on the host. If the chemical is absent on the landing site, the tick goes to another twig. If the odor of butyric acid persists, location on an animal having the temperature of mammalian blood releases stabbing and sucking behavior in the tick.

The Human Adult

Our second example will focus on human food getting in a complex physical and social setting constructed by other human beings. An adult member of a family is shopping for the week's groceries in a supermarket like that seen in Figure 9.10. This simple expedition is an extremely complex game in which the shopper and the grocery management are contestants. The purpose of the game is simple and old. The manager intends to structure a physical and social environment where the buyer will purchase items yielding to the seller maximum profit. The buyer intends to buy necessary items.

Both the manager and the customer share the same set of human abilities, but they employ different strategies in the game. Each will organize behavior around desired goals. This organization will call into play perceptual systems that detect information from the external and internal environment. A learning retention system permits retrieval and reconstruction of the effects of previous experience. The motivational systems for evaluating the present needs and states of the organism itself are also available. Finally, in the case of interacting human beings, an elaborate symbol system and the general rules for its use are sure to be used by the manager and customer.

Before the customer comes to the store, both the grocer and the

Figure 9.10
Supermarket
(James Karales from Peter Arnold)

customer have made a number of moves. The grocer has arranged the merchandise so that some items are placed close to eye level. Packages for these items are bright and colorful. The displays are large and are located close to heavily traveled paths in the store. These high profit products are set apart, distinctive boundaries separating them from goods less favored by the management. Soft, familiar, bland music emanates from a number of ceiling loudspeakers. The structure of the music and the diffusion of sound ensure nonrecognition either of its character or its location in the environment. The general features of the store setting are meant to inhibit problem-solving schemas.

The customer has also prepared for the match. Before leaving home, the shopper took note of the items present and absent in the family larder. Members of the family were asked what grocery items were needed. Memories were searched for the previous few days to construct the list. Family members queried each other as to this item or that. The designated shopper made mental or written notes recording this information. The adult family members discussed the food budget and agreed on the allowance to be made.

On arrival, the shopper encounters a prepared environment. Store temperature is 68°F, selected to produce a high level of activity in the shopper. On his way to the produce section, he sees large colorful signs displaying goods not on the list. The shopper can react in several ways. A hibachi is handled carefully and placed in the grocery cart. A sausage display is located beside a photograph of a smiling young matron whose decorous sports attire leads to an inference of certain culturally valued physical features. Since our shopper is male, this display attracts his attention. He places two packages of sausage in the cart, momentarily forgetting his wife's reminder that the family refrigerator is overstocked with that commodity.

An observer at the cash register would be surprised to find that the game between manager and customer ended in a draw. The customer purchased most but not all of the items on his list. He couldn't find the prunes and somehow skipped over the onions. He bought one or two unneeded items of high profit, including the hibachi and the sausage.

The environments and behaviors described in this shopping trip illustrate the organized features of behavior. The reader will notice that, by and large, the behaviors of both shopper and manager are purposeful and have functional meaning to the individuals. The interplay of physical and social features characterizes every phase of the behavioral display. The episode is more orderly than random and more functional than mystical.

Let us review the shopping behaviors seen. The shopper engaged in preparatory behavior prior to the shopping trip. Human beings and individuals of other species typically prepare for anticipated events. This preparation involves the processing of information from sources within the individual and from external sources. In most cases, even initial preparation for action involves both inside and outside sources. Mature human beings can and do identify the locus of these sources of stimulation, although imprecisely. Our shopper may have gone shopping because he felt hungry. In some but not all species food-searching behavior is often triggered by hunger. However, in our example, the shopper probably had a regular weekly shopping schedule. Much ordinary human behavior is ritualized. It is also possible that the bare refrigerator or a long shopping list on the kitchen wall initiated the trip. Individuals acquire information from many sources and use every efficient detector available. The information from all sources is integrated to guide behavior.

The mature human being can use both direct and indirect sources of information. Empty pantry shelves provide direct information about the need for shopping and the specific items needed. Symbolic and indirect sources of information, including the conversation of the family or the words on a shopping list, may provide equivalent information. These indirect sources of information do not need to have any physical resemblance to food objects to be effective. Direct and indirect cues reflect the same objective situation for the adult shopper.

Inside the store, the environment is constructed to impose information on the shopper. The manager's intention is to camouflage some items into the background and highlight other items, thus capturing the shopper's attention. As was pointed out in the last chapter, the "natural" world provides patterns of stimulation that animals, including human beings, interpret to reflect the objective shapes of things. In this case, the art of display exploited this tendency.

Analysis of Behavioral Organization

The Wood Tick

Let us return to the wood tick and then the grocery buyer in an attempt to conceptualize the organization of behavior. For many years, psychologists began their studies of behavior at a neurobiological level. In the case of the wood tick, three reflex arcs, each composed of a receptor component and motor unit, might suffice. However, some of the behaviors of the tick are not well explained in these terms. A major problem exists in the sequence of actions. When does one system switch to another? A second problem concerns the correction of errors and the termination of misdirected activity.

These problems have led behavioral scientists to propose the idea of central controlling processes. These controlling processes are said to monitor the external and internal environments. Central processes control the initiation and termination of behavior. Central controlling processes are not welcome concepts for the scientist because they seem to imply a little human inside a human and a little tick inside a tick to interpret events. However, recent developments in the computer sciences suggest that guidance systems of this sort do not require the mystery of little beings within a being. For example, computers have been built that repair defective internal circuits, decide which customers to serve first, and select the most efficient computer language for a particular problem.[10]

One interesting feature of these computers is the structure of their component parts. Pre-1960 computers were composed of vacuum tubes, capacitors, and resistors whose behaviors were well understood. When first used, machines using solid state chips were not so well understood. Circuits using such chips are illustrated in Figure 9.11. The computer scientists knew what information went into and what came out of each module. They knew that each chip

10. D. C. Evans, "Computer Logic and Memory," in *Information, A Scientific American Book,* W. H. Freeman, San Francisco, 1966, pp. 17–39.

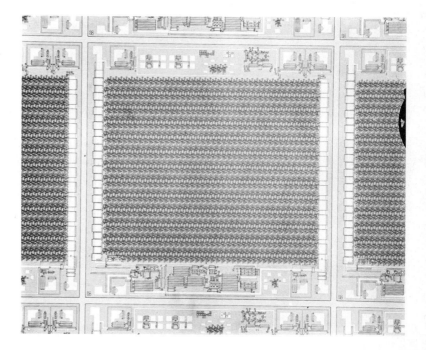

Figure 9.11
Microelectronic Circuits
Used in Computers
(magnified)
*(Fairchild Camera and
Instrument Co.)*

did the work of many transistors, capacitors, and resistors. They did not know exactly how or why this occurred. The scientists who designed these computers were able to do so in spite of a limited understanding of the behavior of these component parts.

Similarly, we can conceptualize the intellectual structure of organisms. Our concept can account for the way organisms use information without giving a detailed description of the underlying internal processes involved. The name we have given to each central information-gathering and organizing process is the schema. The definition of schema and the relationship of schemas to learning and development were described earlier. Taking that description, we now interpret the food-getting behaviors of the wood tick and human shopper in Piaget's terms. Our interpretation will go beyond Piaget, for we will extend the schemas to account for animal behavior.

The food getting behavior of the tick requires three receptor and three response-producing units. However, these units operate in close harmony with each other and in harmony with changes in environmental stimulation.

In terms of a Piagetian conceptual framework, the tick's food-getting behaviors occur in three sequential episodes. First, the animal climbs to the twig. Next, the host is located and the tick lands on it. Finally, the site where blood is accessible is selected and sucking begins. Three sensory-motor schemas are required: climbing to a specific height; jumping or releasing to a mammal; and stabbing and sucking to blood. The three drawings in Figure 9.12 show these schemas.[11] Each drawing represents a schema, and the perceptual, motor, and internal guidance systems that permit the tick to maintain equilibrium for that schema. In Figure 9.12A, a perceptual phase (primarily visual) signifies the "real event." A perceptual pattern fitting the location schema will terminate climbing. When the pattern obtained from the "real event" does not fit, climbing is initiated or continued.

The second phase in food getting involves the fit between the schema for mammal and the olfactory cues provided by butyric acid, emitted exclusively by mammals. This odor-based system is shown in Figure 9.12B. Finally, a blood source is located by the match between temperature points on the mammal's surface and the schema of

11. H. G. Furth, *Piaget and Knowledge,* Prentice-Hall, Englewood Cliffs, N.J., 1969.

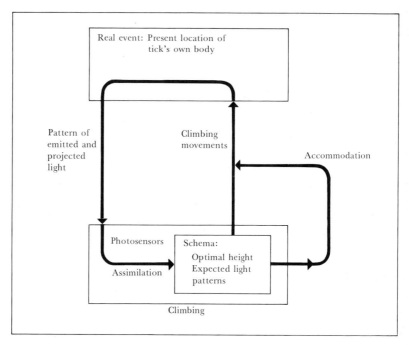

Figure 9.12
Sensory-Motor Systems for
Food Getting in the Tick

a. Climbing

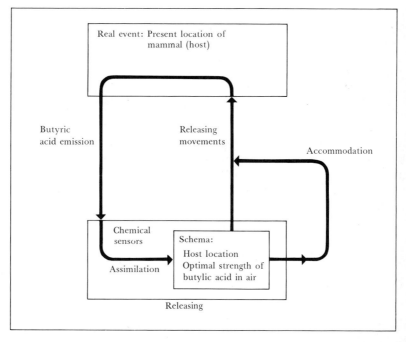

b. Releasing

Figure 9.12 (cont.)

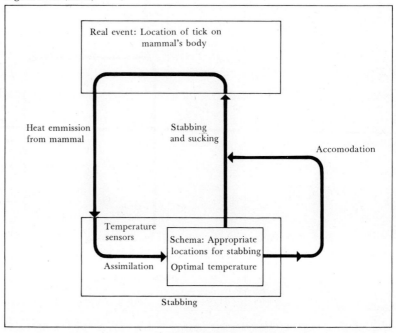

c. Stabbing

optimal temperature, as shown in Figure 9.12C. These three schemas, in sequence, constitute the organized behavior system for food
getting in the tick.

The term *system* is applied to indicate that each component
response contributes to the functioning of the whole set of behaviors
involved in getting food. Climbing up, noticing a potential host,
releasing from the perch, stabbing, and pumping blood must be
accomplished in that order. The term *organization* indicates that at
one time particular responses coordinate with previous, concurrent,
and subsequent responses. Organization also implies that some components of stimulation must be selected by the organism and related
to other components of stimulation.

The active behaviors of the tick are essential if it is to obtain food.
Of equal importance are the guidance of these behaviors and the
continuous monitoring of information. One source of stimulus
information is the energy from the external environment. Another
source comes from the organism itself, its own behavior. The organized behavior system integrates all stimuli and modifies all
responses in the context of the information available.

This explanation of the relationship between behavior and the environment has been complex. Taken together, the behavioral system, the perceptual system, and the internal guiding system represent what Piaget calls the *circle of knowing*, that is, the internal pyschological structure of the organism.

The Human Adult

We will now turn to an analysis of the behavior of the grocery shopper, describing central processes that guide and monitor behavior. While the general approach will be similar to the one used in analyzing the wood tick's behavior, the level of analysis will be different. With the wood tick, three very specific schemas at the sensory-motor level were sufficient to analytically describe food-getting behavior. The more complicated behavioral pattern of the grocery shopper might be described at this level, but several volumes would be required to get through the grocery store. This sort of molecular analysis of human behavior would be rather difficult to translate back into real world human behavior.

The behavior of the grocery shopper will be analyzed in terms of superschemas that subsume many different sensory-motor, preoperational, concrete, and formal schemas. These superschemas orient and organize the shopper's behavior in a way that permits more effective utilization of environmental resources than would be possible in a simple system of the sort seen in the wood tick.

Four situations have been selected for discussion. In the first example, the shopper finds a listed item that is in its usual location. In the second example, a listed item is in a new package. In the third, a listed item is relocated. Finally, the shopper purchases an unlisted, unneeded item. In each of these examples, an adaptation of Piaget's circle of knowing concept will be used. However, the level of analysis is much more general than in the case of the wood tick.

In his search for sugar, a listed item, the shopper establishes his initial schema as he reacts to the word sugar on his list. His sugar schema is functional for the situation; that is, it presents to the shopper the distinctive visual features of the sugar package. Meanwhile, immediate spatial schemas deal with visual features of objects in the near environment. As the shopper proceeds, temporal-spatial superschemas come into play. These superschemas combine the sugar schema, the store map schema, and the present location schema. The resulting behavior is a steady course through the store directing the shopper to the general area of the sugar. Near the sugar site, the shopper's locomotion is slowed markedly. Visual behavior changes to close range rather than distant scanning. When a match is found between the sugar package schema and a sack of sugar, the search pattern is complete. This "matching" behavior is an example of almost pure assimilation. Probably, the entire searching behavior sequence is a series of assimilations to existing schemas based on previous shopping experience. At this point, more or less automated routines take over and the sugar is deposited in the shopping basket.

The next item on the list is coffee of a particular brand. The coffee company has done our shopper a disservice and changed its packaging. To locate an item in a new package, the shopper passes through initial stages identical to those in the previous example. If the coffee can is now a different color and the trademark has been changed, the shopper will be confused when he initiates near environment visual searching. At this point, the visual input will be discordant with the schema. The shopper will change his behavior, terminating his visual search of near environment. A new super-schema might go into operation. Perhaps a social help-seeking superschema would be used. The shopper might ask a store employee for help in finding the coffee. A second possibility would be initiation of an intensive visual examination schema. These switches in strategy are made smoothly and almost without conscious planning. In any case, a response to a mismatch between existing schemas and the external situation is an example of accommodation.

Accommodative behavior results in changes in schemas. The next time the shopper needs coffee he will not look for the old package. Recognizing the new package as equivalent to the old, the shopper would proceed just as he had in the first example. It is possible, however, that even after solving the problem of a new package, the shopper would wonder why the package was changed. This curiosity might lead him into exploratory behavior. He might ask the grocery clerk about the package, mention the change to a friend, or pay attention to coffee advertising in an attempt to resolve this small environmental instability. This curiosity-inspired exploration is typical of human behavior and is seen in other species as well. Curiosity is an example of almost pure accommodation.

In the next example, a familiar package has been placed in a new location. Again, the shopper proceeds to the old location. Again, signs of confusion appear. The strategies already described are instituted, but in this case only the social-helping schema is effective. The shopper may become somewhat aggressive in response to frustration caused by his inability to manipulate the environment.

All of the examples given so far have dealt with items on the shopper's list. A shopper's decision to purchase an unlisted item is an example of stimulus-initiated accommodation. In this case, the superschema resulting in the purchase of sausage is activated by the display rather than by the list. It is interesting to note that the superschema that led to the creation of the grocery list balanced needs against cost quite effectively. Purchase of an unlisted item disturbs this balance. In the store, the location of the sausage display elminated the need for search routines. These routines provide a time delay between schema elicitation and action. Such delays have been found to assist in the achievement of balanced behavioral outcomes.

The schemas described for the shopper help us understand his food-getting behavior. However, two aspects of this behavior are not encompassed by the schemas we presented. First, specific sensory-motor schemas are not detailed. Second, the human being's ability to carry out routine activities and simultaneously engage in other activities is not addressed. For example, some mathematicians have reported problem solutions coming to them while they were engaged in nonintellectual, often routine, activity. Common activities that coincide with shopping include social interactions with friends, control of young children, and evaluation of the appearance and orderliness of the store.

Different levels of analysis were required for food-getting activity in human beings and wood ticks. In both cases, an organizational framework was necessary. Our framework, derived from Piaget, is not the only one possible. But whatever framework is adopted, the behavioral scientist attempts to account for the complexity of the behavior of even the simplest species.

Summary

The theme of this chapter has been the organized nature of behavior in all species. Behavioral equilibrium is achieved when both goal-directed and information-seeking behaviors are in a harmonious relationship with the environment. This equilibrium is maintained in changing environments through central processes in the organism.

These processes, called schemas by Piaget, initiate, guide, and terminate behaviors in each episode in the life stream. The ontogenetic development of schemas was presented in terms of differentiation of a single schema into numerous schemas.

The term superschema was used to describe schemas that chunk other schemas together. The following specific examples of superschemas that develop during childhood were presented: those for learning sets (including reversal learning) and those for sets for reversal and nonreversal shifts.

The functions of schemas in mature organisms were described and analyzed for the wood tick and human adult in food-seeking situations. Schemas and superschemas at sensory-motor, concrete operational, and formal operational levels reflect the ability of organisms to adapt to an orderly environment. The internalization of some version of this external order permits the organism to maintain equilibrium by anticipating environmental changes and the consequences of its behavior on that environment.

Defined Terms		
Schema	Superschema	Shaping
Assimilation	Form equivalence	System
Equilibrium	Learning set	Organization
Accommodation	Adaptation training	Circle of knowing

Suggested Readings

J. Bruner, *Toward a Theory of Instruction,* Belknap Press, Cambridge, Mass., 1964.

Many of the concepts found in this chapter are used in building this elegant theory of development and learning. Bruner uses the concept of "cognitive mediating process" in a sense similar to the way superschema was used in this chapter. The discussion of the functional value of language and symbols for the child is excellent. The book will require some work from the reader, but the ideas are rewarding and the writing style spritely and pleasant.

John Dewey, *How We Think,* D. C. Heath, Boston, 1910.

An eminent American philosopher and early psychologist presents a speculative account of the processes of thinking and the behaviors associated with thought. This readable, somewhat introspective, work integrates philosophical and psychological approaches. The ideas in this book will help the reader understand recent empirical work in cognitive psychology and human problem solving. Part II (pages 68–156) on "Logical Considerations" is especially valuable.

Donald Hebb, *The Organization of Behavior,* John Wiley & Sons, New York, 1949.

A physiological model of behavioral development, learning, and memory. This model attempts to deal with the questions of behavioral organization discussed in this chapter. Hebb approaches these problems in terms of underlying neural mechanisms. This approach would supplement the explanation in terms of psychological mechanisms presented in the previous chapter.

G. Katona, *Organizing and Memorizing,* Hafner Publishing, New York, 1967.

A classic book that emphasizes insight in problem solving. The importance of meaning is a main theme. The problems in geometry used as examples are a challenge. The reader may find himself pondering about his own thoughts as he attempts to solve these fifth grade exercises.

K. S. Lashley, "The Problem of Serial Order in Behavior," in *Cerebral Mechanisms in Behavior,* ed. L. A. Jeffress, John Wiley & Sons, New York, 1951.

A pioneering researcher in neuropsychology argues for the need of a concept to account for the onset, regulation, and termination of behavior. This article is clearly written but will require some concentrated effort. The student will be amply rewarded by the pleasure of sharing the ideas of a brilliant scientist.

J. L. Phillips, *The Origins of Intellect: Piaget's Theory,* W. H. Freeman, San Francisco, 1975.

A highly readable description of Piaget's theory designed for the undergraduate student. The student without background in psychology will gain some understanding of this complex theory. The student with some previous background will find that this small book pulls together the ideas he has previously seen in a fragmented way.

Michael I. Posner, *Cognition: An Introduction,* Scott Foresman, Glenview, Ill., 1973.

Posner reviews studies in experimental psychology in the areas of thinking, memory, concept formation, and problem solving. Detailed theories on each of these topics are described. This book takes a traditional psychological approach using laboratory data and presents specific concepts describing particular behaviors elicited in the laboratory.

Chapter 10
Affectional
Relationships

Attachment to other members of one's species is integral to the development of social organisms. In many species, attachment to a parental figure is essential for survival. If a social animal is raised to maturity without forming attachments to others of its kind, it may never be able to function effectively as a member of a social group. The ability to interact effectively with conspecifics is usually important for reproductive functioning. Typically, attachment is necessary for the evolutionary and individual adaptation of a social animal.

Affection is the emotional concomitant of attachment. Both the feelings and the motivational states accompanying social attachment are implied in the use of the term affection in this chapter. Affection is indicated when one organism strives to gain or maintain social or physical contact with another and is reinforced by that contact. Emotional disturbance or behavioral disorganization as a response to separation from another organism also indicates an affectionate bond. Affection is, of course, an internal characteristic of organisms that must be inferred from their behavior. We cannot know that nonhuman animals have feelings similar to our own, but in this chapter similar behavioral patterns will be assumed to reflect similar internal states.

For most organisms, initial attachments are to the mother or to a mother substitute. In Chapter 3, the phylogenetically determined fit between the neonate and the species typical social environment was discussed. A newborn organism has a set of behavioral capacities that are suited to the immediate postnatal environment. In addition, the newborn presents a stimulus configuration that elicits maternal responsiveness from normal adult female members of the species. A fairly wide range of acceptable infant characteristics has obvious survival value for a species. A certain amount of .overlap is sometimes evident in the stimulus characteristics that release parental behavior in different species. Cross species adoption is not uncommon, particularly in domestic animals. An example of cross species attachment is illustrated in Figure 10.2. Certainly, some human behaviors directed toward pets have many characteristics in common with behaviors directed toward children.

As already indicated, initial attachments are important in later development. In turkeys and some ducks, *sexual imprinting* is said to occur in the young; that is, the species of the initial mother figure will determine the species of the preferred sexual choice in the adult bird. This effect is seen in male birds but not females and varies

Figure 10.1
Attachment to the Mother is Seen in Many Species
*(a. Wayne Miller/Magnum Photos, Inc.; b. David Thompson/Editorial
Photocolor Archives; c. Australian News and Information Bureau; d. Judy
Campbell/Black Star)*

Figure 10.2
A Common Example of
Cross Fostering: Domestic
Fowl
(J. C. Allen and Son)

somewhat among species. Some ducks will court only the foster mother's species. Other ducks and turkeys will court their own species if the preferred species is not available. Early attachment and the associated social interaction have been shown to have important effects on social and sexual behavior in monkeys, as described in Chapter 2.[1] Likewise, a sheep or goat that is separated from the group and hand-reared has slight chance of later integration into a herd.

People who have difficulty developing and maintaining affectionate relationships are likely to have serious adjustment problems. While it is dangerous to generalize concerning such cases, many such individuals have had early histories that suggest difficult or inadequate early emotional attachment.

In this chapter, patterns of emotional attachment in a number of different animals and birds will be considered. Immediate early attachment in *precocial* organisms will be described first. Precocial birds are hatched with down and locomotor capacity. The term precocial will be used also to describe mammals such as goats and horses with early locomotor capacity. Next, we will consider analogous patterns in more *altricial* birds, that is, birds that are naked at hatching and must be brooded and fed by their parents. Animals

1. Chapter 2, pp. 60 to 64.

such as dogs, cats, and rats, which are relatively helpless at birth, will also be referred to as altricial animals. Finally, human early attachment will be considered.

Social attachment and affection are lifetime concerns for social organisms. One kind of relationship of particular interest is pair formation. *Pair formation* is the development of a more or less exclusive long-term relationship with a conspecific of the opposite sex. A number of social species do not form mated pairs, and pair formation is the exception in most primates. Since pair formation is common in our own species, it will be discussed in some detail later in this chapter.

In almost all mammals and birds there is a period of close association between mothers and their offspring. During this period, early affectional bonds are formed. In the following sections, several patterns of early attachment will be described.

| Early Attachment in Precocial Birds and Mammals |

Imprinting is the rapid development of an attachment for a mother or mother substitute. Imprinting is indicated when the infant follows the maternal object. This process has received a great deal of attention in the research literature on animal behavior. While the term imprinting has been used to describe almost all filial attachments, the term will be limited in this discussion to attachment that is evident soon after birth or hatching. The behavioral patterns that indicate such attachment include following, and the mammals and birds discussed here include precocial birds and grazing mammals that are able to walk soon after birth. Attachment in many of these organisms is necessarily rapid, since the young animal's locomotor skill is potentially dangerous unless its movement is limited and directed. Early attachment, which is evidenced by following, provides the necessary limitation of range and direction of movement for some species. In other precocial animals, the mother herds the baby and prevents it from following other females or strange objects.

Precocial Birds

Soon after hatching, birds such as ducks, geese, and chickens show an attachment to moving objects.[2] Their tendency to follow the first moving object seen and to show distress when separated from that object is evidence of imprinting. Imprinting was described by several

2. W. Sluckin, *Imprinting and Early Learning,* Aldine, Chicago, 1965.

Figure 10.3
Konrad Lorenz *(Yves de Braine/Black Star)*

early students of animal behavior but was brought to the attention of behavioral scientists largely by Lorenz.[3] Lorenz, pictured in Figure 10.3, observed that when he was the first moving object seen by greylag geese, they followed him as if he were their mother. A gosling that had followed a person would not later follow its own natural parents. According to Lorenz's early description, imprinting was immediate and limited to a narrow time span or *critical period.* Once a bird had imprinted on an object, imprinting to other objects was difficult. Imprinting appeared to be independent of reinforcement and was viewed as a special kind of influence of experience on behavior.

Of special interest is the finding that the imprinting object sometimes determines adult mate preferences. Birds imprinted on human beings may, as adults, treat humans as conspecifics. Turkey cocks handled after hatching exhibit their entire repertoire of courting to human hands.[4] In the absence of human beings they will begin to court turkey hens, however.

3. K. Lorenz, "The Companion in the Birds' World," *Auk,* 54 (1937), 245–273.

4. M. Schein and E. Hale, "Stimuli Eliciting Sexual Behavior," in *Sex and Behavior,* ed. F. A. Beach, John Wiley & Sons, New York, 1965, pp. 440–482.

Sexual imprinting is usually seen in male but not female birds, and this is sometimes attributed to the more obvious markings on the male.[5] It is thought that, because of their distinctive coloration, appropriate male mates can be identified more easily by the females' genetic coding. Thus, mate identification for the female is resistant to experience. Another possibility is that correct identification is more important for females than for males and is therefore not left to the variation of experience. That is, if a female that mates only once during a breeding season makes an error in mate selection, she may not reproduce that year. In contrast, males of many species may mate with several females, and an error in species identification may not be so costly in terms of their contribution to the gene pool. In many species of birds and mammals, females are more selective in their choice of sexual partners than are males.

Precocial Mammals

Many grazing animals share with precocial birds the ability to loco-mote at an early age. Newborn goats struggle to their feet within fifteen minutes of birth and begin to nuzzle the mother's body. In most cases, the mother has already licked the baby vigorously for most of this period, and she continues this response as the baby pushes against her. The kid mouths its mother and sucks clumps of her hair, portions of the afterbirth hanging from the mother, and finally the teat.

The initial feeding may be fairly brief and is usually followed by a nap. By the second day of life, kids follow the mother and efficiently nurse from her. To an observer familiar with animals that develop more slowly, the kids are truly amazing. Many mammals with early locomotor ability show following responses that appear to resemble the behavior of an imprinted duckling. The immediate attachment that occurs in goats, however, is the mother's attachment for the infant rather than the infant's attachment for the mother.[6]

Mother goats are quite infant specific, in that they permit only their own infants to nurse. Rejection of presumptuous neighbors, as indicated in Figure 10.4, may be quite violent and is usually unam-biguous. Identification and acceptance of an infant is based on the

5. F. Schutz, "Sexuelle Pragung bei Anatiden," *Zeitschrift fur Tierpsychologie,* 22 (1965), pp. 5–103 as cited in A. Manning, "Evolution of Behavior," in *Psychobiology,* ed. J. L. McGaugh, Academic Press, New York, 1971, pp. 1–52.

6. P. H. Klopfer, "Mother Love: What Turns It On?" *American Scientist,* 59 (1971), 404–407.

Figure 10.4
Portrait of Rejecting Mother
(Peter H. Klopfer)

mother's interaction with the infant during the first five minutes
after birth. If kids are removed as they are born and the mother is
not permitted to contact them or the birth fluids, she will reject the
kids. If she is permitted to lick a kid for five minutes, she will accept
it. Twins and triplets are common in the strain studied by Klopfer,
and if one kid were licked, its twin would also be accepted. Mothers
that have the vital five-minute experience accept their own kids and
reject others. Mothers that do not have this experience of licking
reject all kids.

If alien kids are presented to the mother during the critical five
minutes, they will be accepted and so will the mother's own kids,
even if they were removed at birth. Goats prevented from smelling
their own babies by having cocaine sprayed in their nostrils tend to
accept all babies if they have had any experience with any kid during
the first five minutes after birth. If they do not smell, they do not
discriminate. This very brief period of infant acceptance is probably
related to blood chemicals released during the birth process.

Kids quickly learn to identify their mother. Errors are quickly
punished by other mothers and the correct choice is rewarded by
nuzzling from the mother and an opportunity to nurse.

A similar pattern of exclusiveness is seen among American bison.[7]
Bison cows permit only their own calves to nurse. Bison calves
attempt to follow any large brown object, including men on horse-

7. D. F. Lott, "Parental Behavior," in *Perspectives in Animal Behavior,* ed. G. Bermant,
Scott Foresman, Glenview, Ill., 1973, pp. 239–279.

back. Birth usually occurs away from the herd, and the cow stays close to her calf. She licks, nuzzles, and follows it. The cow also calls when the calf wanders away from her.

In goats and bison, the offspring appear be be attracted to any stimulus resembling an adult member of the species, while mothers develop specific identification of their own babies and reject all others. At least among goats, babies learn to identify their own mothers through differential reinforcement—it is easy for the kid to tell the difference between the female that butts it and the one that lets it nurse.

The moose calf is typically isolated by the mother and does not discriminate well between her and other objects her size.[8] A young moose calf will approach and follow a man on horseback or a passing bull moose. The mother responds by vigorously attacking the intruder and performing a cutting maneuver to separate her calf from its prospective foster mother. In one case, a passing horse was pursued into the water, beaten, and chased to another island. Moose cows vigorously defend their young. One cow is reported to have rescued her calf from a bear with neither cow nor calf sustaining an injury. In this solitary grazing mammal the following response does not indicate that the infant is specifically attached to anything, but the mother is very strongly attached to and protective of her infant.

Precocial mammals appear to develop recognition of the mother more slowly than precocial birds. Mothers of the mammalian species discussed above appear to be quite infant specific, but their babies discriminate their own mothers only after some unfortunate errors. Following (or heeling) patterns in the species described above and also in elk produce behavior similar to that found in imprinted ducklings. Compared with imprinting in ducklings, the development of heeling appears to be much slower in elk and somewhat slower in moose. Heeling is probably much less stimulus specific and much more reversible than is following in birds.[9]

Early Attachment in Altricial Birds and Mammals

Many birds, including songbirds, crows, ravens, and other birds of prey, are hatched without down and cannot locomote for some time. These birds have no equivalent to the following response seen in

8. M. Altman, "Naturalistic Studies of Maternal Care in Moose and Elk," in *Maternal Behavior in Mammals*, ed. H. L. Rheingold, John Wiley & Sons, New York, 1963, pp. 223–253.

9. Ibid.

Altricial Birds

ducks and geese.[10] For periods of time that vary among species, parents brood, protect, and feed their altricial young. This period of dependency provides a more leisurely opportunity for the development of social bonds than is available to precocial birds. It is possible that social learning may be more important in altricial than in precocial birds.

Crows, ravens, and jackdaws have been hand-reared by a number of people. All these birds appear to identify their caretakers quite readily as appropriate objects for species typical social behavior. Many hand-tamed altricial birds of this group direct courtship behavior to familiar humans as well as to members of their own species. Inappropriate mate choices are made by both males and females. Shifts from human to conspecific mates and simultaneous courting of humans and conspecifics are more common in altricial than in precocial birds. Parrots, owls, falcons, and storks are also reported to direct sexual and social behavior toward human caretakers. In one case, a female sparrowhawk who courted her caretaker was caged with a male of her own species for breeding purposes. After she killed and ate her conspecific suitor, she resumed her courtship of her human keeper.

Several species of pigeons may be successfully reared by foster parents of a different species. These birds subsequently tend to mate with members of the foster parent species. This situation has been exploited in a number of successful attempts to produce hybrid pigeons. The mate choice of pigeons is also influenced by the species they contact after leaving the nest; that is, the sensitive period for developing a tendency to mate with a different pigeon species extends beyond the period of total dependency on the parents.

The conseqeunces of social attachment to another species are not limited to mating and courtship. One male homing pigeon preferred picazuro pigeons to his own species. When he was released ten miles from his home loft with other homing pigeons, he flew home by himself rather than with the group, keeping a distance of 50 to 100 feet from them. In the loft he roosted by himself when picazuros were not available. This bird eventually mated with another homing pigeon but only after a season of fruitless courting of picazuros that did not respond to him. After this he was housed in

10. E. Klinghammer, "Factors Influencing Choice of Mate in Altricial Birds," in *Early Behavior, Comparative and Developmental Approaches,* ed. H. W. Stevenson, E. H. Hess, and H. L. Rheingold, John Wiley & Sons, New York, 1967, pp. 6–42.

a loft containing only homing pigeons for four months before forming a pair with a homing pigeon.

After reviewing mate choices in many altricial species, one may conclude that many factors influence such choices.[11] The influence of very early and somewhat later exposure to future mate choices varies among species. Whenever mating or courtship behavior toward humans is shown, taming, defined as the lack of any tendency to flee from humans, also occurs. In general, it appears that events throughout the bird's life can affect adult mate choices, but taming requires very early exposure to human caretakers.

Altricial Mammals

Many mammals, including rodents and carnivores, are born in a relatively helpless state with little initial locomotor ability. As in altricial birds, social attachment in these mammals can proceed in a relatively leisurely manner with many opportunities for the influence of experience. The apparent helplessness of altricial birds and mammals is somewhat deceptive. Their behavioral repertoire is efficient as a means of exploiting the environment they encounter upon hatching or at birth. These organisms must get parental care and must respond to it appropriately. Individual members of altricial species born without these abilities simply do not survive.

Recently, social carnivores have been the focus of considerable attention because of the suggestion that modern *Homo sapiens* may be descended from a social carnivore.[12] If the primitive ecological niche of human beings were similar to that of dogs and wolves, the behavior of these animals could provide important insights into human behavior. This idea is based on a number of assumptions that we will not challenge here. However, much is known about social attachment in dogs. As we review this information, we might think about implications for attachment in human beings.

Dogs are born at a relatively immature stage of development. The newborn pup is blind and deaf and has a limited olfactory capacity. The puppy squirms, throwing its head from side to side, and accomplishes slow forward movement. The puppy has a repertoire of

11. Ibid.
12. J. P. Scott, "Comparative Social Psychology," in *Comparative Psychology: A Modern Survey*, ed. D. A. Dewsbury and D. A. Rethlingshafer, McGraw-Hill, New York, 1973, pp. 124–160; R. Ardrey, *African Genesis*, Dell Publishing, New York, 1967; and D. Morris, *The Naked Ape*, Dell Publishing, New York, 1969.

feeding behavior similar in many respects to the behavior of a human neonate. Like the human infant, the puppy's behavior is suited to the species typical postnatal environment. By the fourth week, a number of changes have occurred in the puppy's behavior and sensory capacity. This rapid development is illustrated in Figure 10.5. The animal's eyes and ears have opened, it is able to walk, and most important to the human master, it has begun to wag its tail.

From about three to twelve weeks, puppies can form attachments for human beings. It is suggested that they can form attachments to any animate being living with them during this period. They appear to form attachments most readily at five to eight weeks of age. Later, attachment to novel kinds of animals is increasingly difficult. If puppies are reared by their mothers in an open field for fourteen weeks, having no interaction with human beings, they become almost impossible to tame. One week of interaction with humans, particularly at five to eight weeks of age, makes it much easier to tame the dogs. There is, then, some sort of sensitive period during which dogs form affectionate bonds that partly determine later social behavior.

If a puppy is removed from its litter mates at three weeks of age and is hand-reared, it will be attached to humans, but it will have difficulty interacting with other dogs. The puppy interacting with both dogs and people during the period from four weeks to fourteen weeks will typically respond to both dogs and people as social

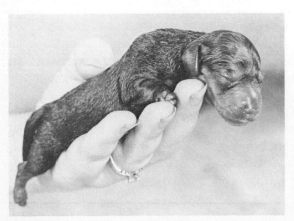 

Figure 10.5
Two Stages of Development in Puppies
(a. Jerome Wexler/Photo Researchers, Inc.; b. Walter Chandoha)

objects. In general, the domestic dog directs its behavior toward its human master as if the human were a socially acceptable canine companion.

Early Attachment in Primates

Monkeys

Rhesus monkeys are somewhat more mature at birth than are dogs. The newborn monkey can see and hear and is capable of limited locomotion. Its most evident motor behavior is clinging to the mother, which it does well indeed. The rhesus infant also has the usual mammalian repertoire of feeding behaviors. Rhesus monkeys spend the first days of life clinging to the mother. The mother in the wild moves with her troop from the day of birth; although she occasionally supports the infant with one arm, her usually quadrupedal gait requires the infant to maintain contact with her. The infant nurses soon after birth and will nurse intermittently during the day for several months thereafter. At night the infant sleeps clinging to the mother's ventral surface, often with the nipple in its mouth.[13]

At one time, psychologists believed that affectional attachments were derived from the satisfaction of more basic needs. The general idea was that infants came to love their mothers as a result of the mother's association with feeding, relief from discomfort, and so forth. At the University of Wisconsin Primate Laboratory, studies were conducted designed to identify the bases of infant-mother attachment in monkeys.[14] Young monkeys separated from their mothers appeared to become attached to diapers left in their cages. For this reason, the investigators suspected that soft objects that could be clung to might become a kind of substitute mother. They thought that another possible determinant of attachment was feeding.

Infant rhesus monkeys separated from their mothers were provided with two artificial surrogate mothers. One surrogate consisted of a wire cylinder mounted on a U-shaped platform. The other surrogate was an identical wire cylinder, but had a terrycloth cover.

13. H. F. Harlow, M. K. Harlow, and E. W. Hansen, "The Maternal Affectional System in Monkeys," in *Maternal Behavior in Mammals*, ed. H. L. Rheingold, John Wiley & Sons, New York, 1963, pp. 254–281.

14. H. F. Harlow, "Love in Infant Monkeys," *Scientific American*, 200 (1959), 68–74; and H. F. Harlow and R. R. Zimmerman, "Affectional Responses in the Infant Monkey," *Science*, 130 (1959), 421–432.

A cloth-covered mother surrogate is shown in Figure 10.6. In the original study, only one of the two surrogates provided food, via a bottle inserted through the artificial mother's body. Time spent on the surrogate mother was recorded automatically. In Figure 10.7 the hours per day infants spent on their wire and cloth surrogate mothers are plotted. Regardless of whether the infant was fed by the wire or cloth mother, it spent much more time on the cloth mother.

The fact that the monkeys spent more time on a relatively comfortable object than on an uncomfortable one might not be convincing evidence for attachment, if that were the extent of the finding. However, surrogate mothers also served as sources of security and as bases for exploring strange environments. This is compelling evidence for attachment. Frightened baby monkeys fled to a cloth

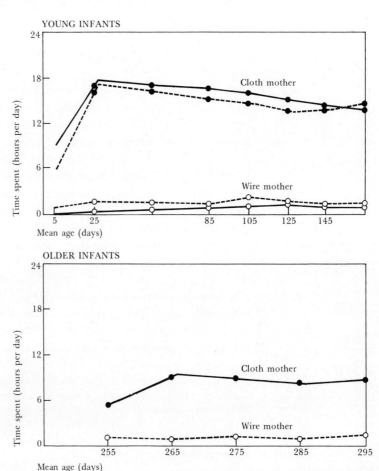

Figure 10.7
Strong Preference for Cloth Mother
(Modified from "Love in Infant Monkeys," by H. F. Harlow. Copyright © 1959 by Scientific American, Inc. All rights reserved.)

mother but not to a wire mother. They would even go to the cloth mother rather than to a hiding place further away from the feared object. On the other hand, frightened babies did not go to the wire mother.

When a surrogate-reared infant is placed in a strange environment alone, it will scream, roll up in a ball, and stay relatively immobile. If the cloth surrogate is present, infants that have formed an attachment to it will cling to it for a time and then proceed to explore the environment. The behavior seen in these monkeys is remarkably similar to the behavior of an outgoing eighteen-month-old child in a strange home. The toddler will use the mother as a base of operations. The child will wander away from the mother, manipulate a new object, return to her for a moment, then return to his or her fascinating new world. The value to the developing organism of a secure base for environmental exploration is clear.

This research seriously challenges the idea that food and feeding form the basis of emotional attachment to the mother. What then does form the basis of early emotional attachment? Ducklings become attached to moving objects that they can follow. Kids and buffalo calves appear to be attached to anything roughly resembling a mother of their species that does not violently punish them. Puppies become attached to any animate object with which they interact between four and twelve weeks of age. Altricial birds show evidence of social attachment to birds or animals in their environment during their development. Rhesus monkeys become attached to soft objects to which they can cling. Is there some general principle that explains these diverse patterns of early social attachment? Before trying to answer this question, let us consider early social attachment in our own species.

Human Beings

Human babies are difficult to classify in terms of their relative maturity at birth.[15] Their locomotor response systems are certainly immature, and in this sense they are similar to altricial birds and mammals. However, their sensory development is much more rapid than their motor development for some months. It is not unreasonable to say that human infants are motorially altricial and sensorially precocial. This permits attachment formation before the baby is capable of following or going to the mother.

By four months of age infants respond differentially to their

15. J. Bowlby, *Attachment and Loss,* Basic Books, New York, 1969, vol. I.

mothers and to other adults. They smile and vocalize in response to their mother and visually follow her movements. These responses are directed toward other family members as well, but the principal caretaker elicits the strongest and most sustained patterns of response. If attachment is defined by attempts to gain or maintain physical proximity or contact, many infants display attachment behavior to the mother or principal caretaker by six months of age and most do so by nine months of age. Differential responding to the mother by vocalization and focusing attention on her rather than on another person is evident at one month in about 20 percent of one sample of one-month-old children. By three months of age about 80 percent clearly recognized their mothers, and by five months all of the babies differentially responded to their mothers.[16]

The developing human infant becomes attached to other members of the family and even to inanimate objects, but its principal attachment is to one person. As she or he grows older the child will show characteristic symptoms of emotional upset when separated from the mother. Emotional reactions to short-term separation from the mother peak for most children at about two to two and one-half years of age. By four or four and one-half, many children can happily leave the mother for nursery school with no indication of upset. The older child is probably not less attached to the mother but is able to comprehend something about the duration of her absence and has had a chance to develop absolute certainty concerning her return.

Long-term mother-infant separation is a more serious matter. This may be associated with considerable disturbance in preschool children. Bowlby has described a child's reaction to relatively long-term maternal separation in terms of three stages, which he calls protest, despair, and detachment.[17] The protest stage occurs immediately after separation and is characterized by crying, throwing the body about, and other overt indications of emotional upset. The despair stage, during which the separated child becomes morose and relatively inactive, follows the protest stage. Detachment is indicated by aggression directed toward the mother when the mother and child are reunited and by difficulty in reestablishing a good, affectionate relationship with her.

16. L. J. Yarrow, "The Development of Focused Relationships during Infancy," in *The Exceptional Infant*, ed. J. Hellmuth, Brunner/Mazel, Inc., 1967, vol. I, pp. 427–442.

17. J. Bowlby, "Separation Anxiety: A Critical Review of the Literature," *Journal of Child Psychology and Psychiatry*, 1 (1961), 251–269.

According to Bowlby, maternal attachment consists of a number of specific responses, which include for humans visual following, manipulating, clinging, embracing, directed vocalization, smiling, touching, following, and sensory-motor reactions to physical contact and cuddling. These behaviors are associated with the maintenance of proximity or physical contact with the maternal figure. Emotional attachment is the internalized counterpart of this system of behavior. The specific responses important for forming attachments will vary for different babies. No particular response mode is essential for attachment. In fact, babies with sensory or motor deficits do form clear, essentially normal, emotional attachments. Emotional attachment is so essential for individual and species adaptive survival that it has multiple forms of expression. Many responses can and do form the behavioral basis for human affection.

In every species previously discussed, infant animals became attached to objects eliciting particular behaviors. Ducklings follow moving objects and later show distress when separated from these objects. Baby monkeys cling to diapers or cloth surrogates and are disturbed when these objects for clinging are taken from them. The monkey infants derive security from the presence of their bizarre foster mothers. For a number of species, sexual object preferences are related to early affectional bonds. The objects of early affectional bonds have a continuing influence on the developing organism.

For some animals, it is somewhat difficult to specify the responses underlying social attachment. Dogs form attachments readily to almost any animate object. The attachment behavior in this species includes approach, mouthing, and licking, but sometimes attachment is reported with no record of behavior directed toward the object of attachment. If dogs develop attachment without clearcut responses to the loved object, the species is somewhat unique. It is possible that long-term genetic selection for attachment of dogs to human beings has reduced the necessary response component in the dog to an almost imperceptible point. The authors suspect that passive contact, however, cannot be a sufficient basis for emotional attachment.

Other Attachments in Developing Organisms

The previous material has focused on the attachment of infants to mothers or to mother substitutes. Even in the case of the dog's attachment to humans, we are dealing with attachment to a surrogate parent. Attachment to the mother is a basic and necessary part of the development of mammals and some birds. Yet other affectional bonds are basic to the development of social organisms. The multiple affectional bonds found in social organisms can be studied in terms of multiple affectional systems.[18] Harry Harlow, the foremost American primatologist, has described five affectional systems. These systems are maternal affection, infant-mother affection, paternal affection, peer affection, and heterosexual affection. These systems are not independent. In the course of normal development, adequate functioning in one system will foster adequate functioning in a subsequent system. Harlow is particularly impressed by the importance of peer affection in young monkeys as a precursor of adequate sexual and maternal functioning.

It has been assumed that human social development and personality are dependent on the infant-mother relationship. This is certainly true in the sense that inadequate patterns of early attachment to a maternal figure may be associated with later emotional or behavioral problems. In human beings, the development of affection for peers has been largely ignored or has been assumed to be secondary. This assumption is more or less accurate, in the sense that peer affection appears later in development and to a certain extent derives from love for the mother. Peer affection is probably not secondary, however, in terms of importance for normal emotional and social development. The secondary nature of peer affection is emphasized in the notion that affection for peers is generalized from affection for adults.

In one study of emotional development, a child's affection for other children was said to be evident at about eighteen months of age.[19] If the notion of generalization were accurate, we would have to believe that children were sufficiently similar to mothers as stimulus patterns to cause similar emotional responses. It is impossible to see the world as an eighteen-month-old sees it, but it does not seem reasonable to assume that children and adults are similar stimuli to such young children. But if generalization is not the answer, what is the basis of peer affection?

The reader will recall that affection for the mother was seen as the emotional concomitant of some set of behavioral responses directed

18. H. F. Harlow, J. L. McGaugh, and R. F. Thompson, *Psychology*, Albion, San Francisco, 1971, pp. 42–105.
19. K. Bridges, "Emotional Development in Early Infancy," *Child Development*, 3 (1935), 324–341.

Figure 10.8 Children at Play *(Kunsthistoresches Museum)*

to the mother. The same line of reasoning would lead us to say that peer affection is the emotional concomitant of some set of responses directed toward peers.

In human beings, there is considerable overlap in the response systems underlying peer and filial affection. Both systems include smiling, touching, following responses, and directed vocalization. The human peer affection system also includes chasing, manipulating, rough and tumble play, and joint or contiguous manipulation of the environment.[20] Figure 10.8 provides examples of possible peer-directed behaviors. All of these behavior patterns may be directed to a maternal figure, of course, but a peer is more satisfactorily and

20. N. G. B. Jones, "An Ethological Study of some Aspects of Social Behavior of Children in Nursery School," in *Primate Ethology*, ed. D. Morris, Aldine, Chicago, 1967, pp. 347–368.

consistently receptive and available to many of these patterns. In macaque monkeys, the response systems underlying filial and peer affection may be more sharply different than those in humans, since macaque mothers are rather intolerant of manipulation and rough and tumble play directed toward them by their infants.[21]

Normal peer affection does not usually represent an extension of filial responses to conspecific age mates, although such extension does occur when immature organisms are housed together without adult caretakers. Turkeys and other precocial birds imprint on other newly hatched birds if housed with them.[22] Monkeys reared together from birth form close attachments and spend a great deal of time clinging to one another.[23] Orphaned children may develop filial-like attachments to each other if kept in a group with little adult attention.[24] These filial attachments to peers constitute a redirection of filial affection due to the absence of an appropriate maternal object. Such attachments may be an adequate foundation for ensuring a degree of normality in adult social behavior, and clearly they do serve this purpose in monkeys. However, this kind of attachment is not what is meant here by peer attachment or affection.

Affection for peers typically develops while the organism still has a strong emotional attachment to the mother. The developing human infant shows orientation to and interest in peers at a very early age, if the child is able to control access to the mother at the same time.[25] In the apparatus illustrated in Figure 10.9, young children were given access to an area outside the mother's visual field. When they were in the toy and peer area they could not see the mother and the mother could not see them. Babies as young as seven months of age left the sight of the mother in order to interact with same-age human infants for a short period of time. In the study referred to, a baby occasionally became disturbed and went through the door to its mother. The baby's new-found friend went away from its own mother and accompanied the retreating infant to this strange adult. If no peer were available, these infants would stay with the mother rather than play

21. B. Seay, R. Schlottmann, and R. Gandolfo, "Early Social Interaction in Two Monkey Species," *Journal of General Psychology,* 87 (1972), 37–42.

22. M. W. Schein and E. B. Hale, "The Effect of Early Social Experience on Male Sexual Behavior of Androgen Injected Turkeys," *Animal Behavior,* 7 (1959), 189–200.

23. Harlow, McGaugh, and Thompson.

24. A. Freud and S. Dann, "An Experiment in Group Upbringing," *Psychoanalytic Study of the Child,* 6 (1951), 127–168.

25. B. M. Barnes, "Mothers, Peers, and Toys as Stimuli for Locomoting Infants under Two Years of Age" Ph.D. diss., Louisiana State University, 1973.

Figure 10.9
LSU Mobile Research Facility—Infant, Toy, Peer Study
(From unpublished doctoral dissertation by B. M. Barnes. Reproduced by permission of the author.)

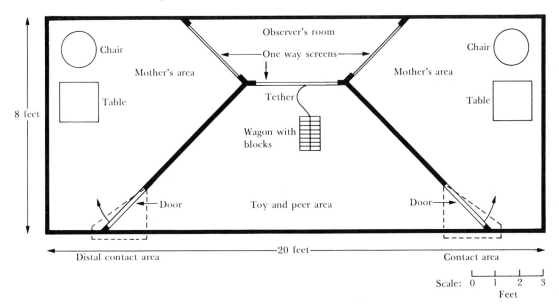

with available toys outside the mother's visual field. Older children interact with other children more frequently, and they are likely to evidence strong peer social attraction. When the door was closed to give only one eighteen-month-old access to the toys, the separated children made every effort to tear the door down, despite maternal restraint.

As children grow older, interaction with peers becomes increasingly capable of satisfying the child's affectional needs. Two-year-olds play most happily with peers when the mother is near. By age five, the child can spend long periods of time with peers if any familiar adult is nearby. It is probably not coincidental that kindergarten attendance usually begins at four or five. For younger children in a nursery school, the close proximity of a familiar adult is quite important.

School-age children require brief contact with parental figures. Most mothers are familiar with a pattern of behavior that consists of five to fifteen minutes in the home after school followed by intensive efforts to return to the peer group. In American society, adolescent contact with the parents and other adults is often limited to formal situations like school and to periods of distress or financial need. Adolescents frequently view adult-initiated contacts as unwelcome intrusions, but they do need adults available for crisis periods. They also need to believe that parents are available to them. During the adolescent period, peer social relationships are even more important than during earlier periods, at least in the view of the adolescent.

Heterosexual Love

Poets, novelists, and other reasonable people rarely doubt the reality of love as an important aspect of human heterosexual behavior. One of the functions of a science is to question accepted assumptions. The general assumption that love is an essential part of heterosexual interaction has been questioned from several points of view. It has been said that romantic love was created by medieval troubadours and that courtly love is the sole ancestor of romantic love. While there is some support for this view, recognition of love as one aspect of heterosexual interaction predates the medieval troubadour. The Old Testament contains repeated references to domestic problems in polygamous households due to the husband loving one wife but not the other. The career of King David of Israel recorded in I and II Samuel includes a number of references to sexual love. The Song of Solomon clearly indicates a relationship between love and sexuality. The basic motivation for the Trojan War was not platonic. The culturally accepted working definition of heterosexual love changes across time, but sexual relationships are frequently assumed by many cultures to be associated with love and affection.

Behaviorist psychology has attacked the validity of love as an important aspect of sexual interaction.[26] Here the idea is that if love is derived from sex, security, and dependency, then love may be unnecessary if these more basic needs are met. Love may be an emotional expression of unfulfilled needs and may in fact reflect inadequate adjustment with respect to these needs. A fully mature individual who is well adjusted should not need love or need to love, since adjustment would include satisfaction of needs for sex and security and consequent independence.

The position just stated is based on the hypothesis that love is secondary to more basic needs. In previous sections, we described love as a primary emotion in developing organisms. Heterosexual

26. L. Casler, "This Thing Called Love Is Pathological," *Psychology Today*, 3 (1969), 184+.

Figure 10.10
Lovers
(Ed Keren)

love is probably best understood as the emotional concomitant of behaviors directed toward a potential or actual mate. In some instances, the early stages of a developing love relationship are characterized by intense preoccupation with the other party. This intense early aspect of love relationships is labeled infatuation. Characteristics of this state include a felt need to be near the other party, considerable fantasy concerning that person, and considerable lack of objectivity concerning the other person. Another term used to describe infatuation is "falling in love." Some ethologists feel that the relatively irrational behavior of lovers is an indication of instinctive behavior in human beings.

The behavior of lovers provides some clues about the behaviors underlying affectional bonds in mated pairs of human beings. Lovers touch each other a great deal, walking arm in arm, holding hands, or occupying remarkably little of an automobile seat. Another frequent interaction between lovers is talking. In the developing stage of the love relationship, many couples talk interminably. Frequently, the subject of these verbal exchanges is the personality of the other. Another topic may be the couple's future plans. It may be that the topic is rather irrelevant and that conversation is in fact an important behavior pattern manifesting affection. Lovers also eat together. The importance of eating as one means of sealing social relationships in many cultures would suggest that this communal behavior may have a part in supporting affection. Communal eating may be more important in situations where food is in short supply than in our own society.

Lovers also engage in precopulatory behavior, with participation in sexual intercourse dependent upon local custom and the stage of development of their relationship. Human precopulatory behavior includes kissing, fondling the partner's body, making copulatory movement against the partner's body, orally manipulating parts of the partner's body, and a vast number of fairly idiosyncratic alternate behaviors. Almost all of these behavior patterns are also seen in infant-mother and other affectional relationships, but their relative frequency is fairly low and the obviously sexual patterns are eventually prohibited. When an eight-month-old directs pelvic thrusts toward the mother, they are usually quietly misinterpreted. The same pattern in a five- or six-year-old would not be tolerated.

Copulation is neither necessary nor sufficient for intense heterosexual love. In Western society at least, there appears to be a sex difference in the relationship between copulatory behavior and affection. In general, sex and affection are more likely to be dissociated for males than for females. Adolescent females are more likely than males to assume that sex is a mutual expression of affection.[27] These differences in attitude sometimes lead to unfortunate misunderstandings. Freud interpreted the dissociation of love and sex in males as a result of the Oedipus complex and saw reuniting of sex and affection as one aspect of mature sexuality.

Love relationships do not necessarily begin with infatuation. In many societies, marriages are arranged and the young couple may not see each other until the marriage ceremony. Westerners sometimes assume that such relationships are therefore without love. In many societies, love is assumed to be the result of a successfully arranged marriage. Whether a relationship begins with mutual infatuation or the careful arrangements of parents, successful continuation of that relationship is in part dependent on a continuing pattern of affectional behavior.

Those who doubt that romantic or heterosexual love is characteristic of human beings point to some cultures in which love is not

27. J. J. Conger, "A New Morality: Sexual Attitudes and Behavior of Contemporary Adolescents," in *Basic and Contemporary Issues in Developmental Psychology,* ed. P. H. Mussen, J. J. Conger, and J. Kagan, Harper and Row, New York, 1975, pp. 453–460.

associated with sex or marriage. The anthropologist Margaret Mead reports that the Manus do not associate love with sex.[28] Men in this group heap affection and attention on their young sons. Another form of affectionate relationship in this group is seen among cross cousins. Rough precopulatory play, including breast fondling, may be directed by a man toward his female cross cousin. These behaviors are not supposed to lead to copulation. The behavior appears to be associated with a form of joking affection. When Mead asked a woman if her husband touched her breasts, the woman indignantly replied, "Of course not; that [privilege] belongs to my cross cousin only."[29] Familiarity and affection between cross cousins extends at least into middle age in this group.

There is no question that love and sex can be dissociated by both males and females. It is also true that multiple love relationships are possible. Sequential pair formation appears to be increasingly frequent in Western society. Monogamous pair formation is certainly not the only way for the human organism to handle sexual behavior. It does appear that human beings need sex and love. To have these needs satisfied as a member of a successfully mated pair is a common goal for members of our species.

If we assume that a need to love and be loved is a characteristic of members of our species, we might speculate on the adaptive value of that phenomenon. It appears the affectionate bonds serve as one support for the maintenance of adult associations that provide an effective child-rearing situation. Members of our species need a relatively long period of protection and support before reaching reproductive maturity. This protection and support requires some adult grouping.

The human capacity for affection is based on many possible social responses. When sexual behavior or motivation is included in the response systems underlying an affectionate relationship, we define that kind of affection as romantic or heterosexual love. If a capacity and need for heterosexual love evolved in the service of child rearing, that capacity will be present even in individuals who do not wish to reproduce. Organisms do not eat because they need food but because they are hungry.

Pair formation in other species is often associated with parental behavior in both males and females. This is most typically seen in

28. M. Mead, *Growing up in New Guinea*, Mentor Books, New York, 1953.
29. Ibid, p. 103.

altricial birds, in which brooding and feeding the offspring is attended to by both parents. Other birds, such as mallard ducks, form pairs during the breeding season even though parental behavior is seen only in females. Pair formation is relatively rare in mammals, and this is accounted for by the relative unimportance of male parents among mammals. However, there are many examples of pair formation among nonhuman species. The following example has been chosen because of its uniqueness.

Emperor penguins form long-term pairs.[30] At the beginning of the breeding season males arrive on the breeding grounds as a group. A few days later the females begin to arrive. Each female seeks out her particular mate. When the birds meet there is a ritual greeting, followed by a couple of weeks of close association, including much caressing and beak rubbing. If the mate is too late, a new relationship may begin to develop. When the previous mate arrives, developing relationships are abruptly terminated. After courtship, a two- to three-minute copulation takes place. Copulation occurs once in each breeding season. After copulation the pair stays together for about twenty-five days, after which the female lays her egg. She holds the egg on her feet in an egg pouch for about twelve hours. The egg is then transferred to her mate, who shows some reluctance to take it. His apparent reluctance is understandable, since his mate leaves for a good feeding area for the next two months. The male does not eat during this period, apparently living on stored fat. The fattened female then returns for her own two-month stint at brooding. At around the time of hatching the male returns and both parents feed the chick until it is able to feed on its own.

In this example, the function of pair formation is to care for the young. Sexual reproduction requires only brief periods of interaction between organisms, and in species in which the male parent is not important to infant survival pair formation is not typical. The assumption that human beings are pair-forming animals does not appear to be unrealistic. If pair formation is characteristic of our species, male parents should be of some value to their offspring. Fathers or adequate father substitutes may serve many functions in the personality and social development of children. In Chapter 3 the father's influence on sex-role development in male and female children was discussed. Research that may uncover other paternal functions is being pursued.

30. J. Johns, *The Mating Game,* St. Martin's Press, New York, 1970, pp. 40–45.

Affection and Development

In social organisms, including human beings, social attachments are important throughout life. Early attachments are necessary for normal development, and the object of early attachment may determine later social behavior. As the human child develops beyond infancy, the number of objects of affection increases. Social attachment behavior is directed toward siblings, peers, and nonfamilial adult caretakers and teachers. In the authors' view, attachment to other children is central to normal emotional and social development. In societies where heterosexual social interaction is permitted during adolescence, attachment behaviors begin to be directed toward specific members of the opposite sex. If human beings cannot be classified as a pair-forming species, it can be said that there is certainly a strong tendency in our species to form heterosexual pairs. Pair bonds in our species are not necessarily permanent, and an individual can maintain multiple pair bonds, but pair formation does appear to be a common characteristic of heterosexual behavior among human beings.

Figure 10.11
Affection
*(Raimondo Borea/Editorial
Photocolor Archives)*

One frequent concomitant of heterosexual affection is the birth of children. Human parents normally form affectionate bonds toward their children, although this process may not be immediate. Occasionally young mothers who have been separated from their babies for three or four days following birth are disturbed by a lack of felt affection for their new baby. These concerns are usually short-lived and the endless routine of infant care becomes a more or less pleasant interaction with a much loved person. Parental affection fulfills the emotional needs of the child and of the parent. Human beings need to love as well as to be loved. This is obvious in our own society when the developing child seeks to loosen the tie to the parents in late childhood and adolescence. Many parents find it difficult to relinquish the close emotional ties that they had with the child in its early years, and considerable conflict may occur at this stage of the child's emotional development.

The parent-child bond changes as both parties mature. In the most fortunate cases, adult children come to be younger friends of their parents. This relationship may be complicated by increasing economic or social dependence as the parents approach old age.

One important set of emotional and social attachments for members of our species is that between grandchildren and grandparents. In many cases, the grandparents can provide a form of parental love not tempered by responsibilities for socialization or behavior control. Interaction between grandparents and grandchildren may be an important basis for cultural continuity. A sense of belonging to some social group may be diminished in children with no contacts beyond their parents' generation.

Social organisms are dependent on other members of their species. This dependence is a central aspect of a social species's ability to get along in the world. Adaptive dependence within a species is mutual; it is interdependence. Our species consists of individual organisms who must form social attachments to others.

Summary

Affection is the emotional concomitant of attachment. Attachment to the mother or some mother substitute is characteristic of most mammals and of many bird species.

Initial attachment in precocial species is frequently indicated by a tendency to follow the mother. The term imprinting is used to describe an immediate attachment to the first moving object the organism encounters. Imprinting is most clearly identified in various species of precocial birds. Precocial mammals exhibit similar patterns of following but appear to be much less specific in their choice of maternal objects than are birds. Bison calves, for example, will follow a man on horseback if not restrained by their mothers.

Altricial birds and mammals develop attachment at a more leisurely pace. When altricial birds are hand-reared by humans they frequently direct adult social and sexual behavior toward humans. Among the altricial mammals, early attachments of dogs to humans have been extensively studied. There appears to be a sensitive period in the puppy's development that ranges from about three to about fourteen weeks. If a puppy interacts with people during this period, it is likely to develop a capacity for attachment to human beings.

Research studies of attachment in monkeys fail to support the view that affection is based on more basic drives. Affection appears to be associated with attachment behavior. In monkeys, clinging is the most evident attachment behavior and is most clearly associated with the development of filial affection.

Human infants may be classified as sensorially precocial and motorially altricial. Attachment in our species precedes the development of whole body attachment behaviors, such as following. Infants typically develop a strong attachment for their principal caretaker, and this preference is particularly evident at six or eight months of age. Responses associated with the development of attachment to a mother figure include visual following, clinging, embracing, directed vocalization, smiling, touching, following, and sensory-motor reactions to physical contact and cuddling.

The development of affection for peers is an important aspect of human social behavior. It appears reasonable to assume that, like affection for the mother, peer affection is based on some set of responses directed toward the object of affection. Peer attachment behavior in humans includes many of the responses underlying filial attachment as well as chasing, manipulating, rough and tumble play, and joint or contiguous manipulation of the environment. Peers become increasingly important affectional objects as the individual grows older.

Heterosexual affection or romantic love is frequently a concomitant of prospective or actual mating in our society. While some healthy skepticism concerning this phenomenon exists within the literary and scientific communities, cross-cultural and historical evidence supports the notion that love is an expected part of long-term sexual relationships in many societies. Behaviors associated with this kind of affection include talking, touching, precopulatory behavior, and copulation. Sex and affection can be dissociated, of course, but needs for both can be fulfilled in the same relationship.

Human beings need to love and to be loved throughout development. The expressions of love appropriate for different ages are of course different. The early adolescent may be made uncomfortable by the same expressions of parental affection that were essential only a couple of years ago. However, changes in the expressions or in the objects of affection do not imply a change in the human being's need for affection. We need to love and be loved throughout life.

Defined Terms

Attachment	Precocial	Imprinting
Affection	Altricial	Critical period
Sexual imprinting	Pair formation	

Suggested Readings

J. Bowlby, *Attachment and Loss: Attachment,* Basic Books, New York, 1969.

This is a somewhat lengthy presentation of the British psychoanalyst's ideas about affectional ties between mother and child. A student might choose to read only Chapters 11, 12, 14, and 15 to get the gist of Bowlby's position.

L. Casler, "This Thing Called Love Is Pathological," *Psychology Today,* 3 (1969), 184+.

A behaviorist approach critical of the notion that adults need to love and be loved is presented in this brief article. Since the previous chapter took an opposing position, Casler's article would provide the student with a more convincing presentation of his ideas.

H. F. Harlow, *Learning to Love,* Albion Publishing, San Francisco, 1971.

In this short book the author presents the five affectional systems described in the previous chapter and reviews some of the research that is based on his concept of love. The book is written in a casual, frequently amusing style and will provide the student with an impression of a prominent American psychologist as well as a review of his work.

H. L. Rheingold, *Maternal Behavior in Mammals,* John Wiley, New York, 1963.

Each chapter in this book except the summary by the editor is a review of research on maternal patterns in some particular species. It is recommended for students majoring in psychology or the biological sciences.

"The Song of Solomon," *Holy Bible, Authorized King James Version* (various editions available), or "The Song of Songs," *The New English Bible,* Oxford University Press, 1970, pp. 797–807.

This ancient love poem might prove enlightening to students not familiar with biblical literature. The New English translation is probably the most poetic version in modern English. The King James version provides an equally poetic translation in seventeenth century English.

Chapter 11
Social
Organization

Organisms that spend a large part of their adult life in groups of their own kind are termed *social animals*. One characteristic of social groups is that they are organized in some way. In this chapter, social organization in several species will be described. The particular organizational structure exhibited by a given social group will be seen as a function of the interaction of Phylogenetic Set, Cultural Set, and ecological pressures on the group. The specific roles that individuals take within social groups are determined by Ontogenetic Set, Experiential Set, and Individual Set.

An Example of
Social Organization

Japanese *macaque* monkeys live year round in troops called "oikia" that consist of animals of all ages and both sexes.[1] The organization of these troops when at rest or in movement is an expression of Phylogenetic Set. Figure 11.1 is a schematic representation of the distribution of animals at a feeding location. The size of the group is in part dependent on the amount of food and the ease of obtaining

1. K. Imanishi, "Social Behavior in Japanese Monkeys, *Macaca fuscata*," in *Primate Social Behavior*, ed. C. H. Southwick, Van Nostrand, Princeton, N.J., 1963, pp. 68–81.

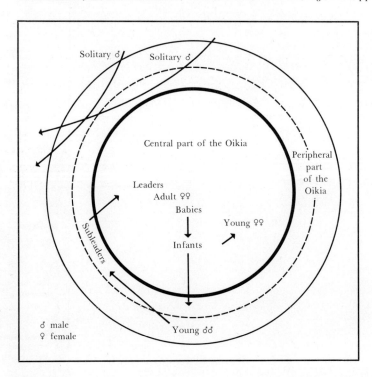

Figure 11.1
Social Organization in Japanese Macaque Monkeys
(From Primate Social Behavior, edited by C. Southwick © 1963 by Litton Educational Publishing, Inc. Reprinted by permission of Van Nostrand Reinhold Company.)

it. Some adult males are identified as the *dominant* members of the group and function in troop defense, control of aggression within the troop, and effective reproduction. Other males, including most young adults or late adolescents, are ordinarily peripheral members of the group but are capable of assuming the dominant male role in the absence of dominant males. Becoming a dominant, or alpha, male does not necessarily require apprenticeship as a peripheral male. The male infant of a dominant female that regularly associates with alpha males may become one of the dominant males at maturity. It appears that association with dominant males prepares this youngster to act like an alpha male. As a result of his behavior he is accepted as an alpha male. Thus, one could say that the combined effects of Ontogenetic and Experiential Set determine, at least for some individuals, dominance in the troop.

The most stable social unit among many troop-living primates is an old female, her daughters, and her granddaughters. These adult females and their immature offspring usually stay close together within the troop. Social behaviors, such as grooming, are more frequently directed toward other members of this closely knit unit than to outsiders. As they mature, Japanese macaque males usually leave the family unit to become either peripheral or alpha males in the troop. Some permanent association between adult males and their juvenile matriarchal family unit is seen in persistent grooming behavior and an apparent mother-son incest taboo.

For Japanese macaque monkeys and other species, some sort of social contract permits the animals to live together, to reproduce, and to nurture their offspring. While the organisms involved may or may not recognize a social contract, they behave in a manner consistent with a contract.

In the following section, the social organizations of several animal species will be described. For different species, the social group serves different functions. Perhaps some of the groups and group functions are analogous to those seen in human societies.

Temporary Organizations

Some organisms demonstrate a seasonal cycle of social organization that is frequently tied to the species's reproductive cycle. Aggregations of animals change during the year. An individual animal may change group membership several times, joining and rejoining particular groupings. This sort of shifting group organization is typical of a number of birds and grazing mammals. Some of these systems of organization will be described.

Bison

Social organization in American bison is sex-segregated during most of the year. As many as twelve bulls move and graze together. Cow herds, including immature animals of both sexes, reach as many as twenty-four animals. Both bull and cow herds are loosely organized and relatively open. Dominance behavior is seen in individuals in herds of either sex, particularly at locations where hay or other food is found.[2]

During the breeding season, cow herds coalesce into larger units and bull herds break up. Some but not all bulls join the enlarged group of cows and immature animals. Dominance fights among bulls are frequent at this time, with the victor gaining the right to tend the female. Following the *rut,* the period of intensive breeding activity, smaller groups of mature bulls re-form. Group membership may not be the same after rut as before. Cow herds also break up into the smaller units after rut.

Mallard Ducks

This pair-forming bird[3] usually lives with a large group of *conspecifics.* Courtship behavior and pair formation are communal activities. Male mallards congregate in late summer or early fall and begin communal courtship displays. The responses that comprise courtship displays are performed by groups of males in the presence of females. These communal displays continue for four or five months, although many pairs will form within the first month or two. Paired birds continue to take part in communal displays. The pairs live in large flocks on ponds or the sea. Within these flocks mates stay near one another, and a male is sometimes observed driving other males away from his mate.

The pair leaves the flock to copulate. The duck and drake withdraw from the group, engage in a mutual display, and mate. After copulation the females go off by themselves to build nests and rear the young. Males congregate nearby and at this time respond to any approaching female by chasing her and attempting to mate. The

2. T. McHugh, "Social Behavior of the American Buffalo *(Bison bison bison),"* *Zoologica,* 43 (1958), 1–40.

3. M. Bastock, *Courtship and Ethological Study,* Aldine, Chicago, 1967, pp. 40–45.

attempted rapes are communal activities of the males that are thought to ensure dispersal of breeding females.

Seals

Male seals come onto the breeding grounds about a month before the females arrive.[4] Each male appears to try to hold a territory on the beach. New male arrivals are challenged, and within a couple of weeks no male may gain a place on the beach without a fight. Late arriving bulls form territories from parts of territories previously established by the early birds. Bulls that have previously held territories return to the same beach, acquiring new territories in the same general areas as the old. The territories are established by active fighting, but after a couple of weeks they are maintained by threat displays along the boundaries. These displays are illustrated in Figure 11.2.

After the worst of the fighting, pregnant females come onto the breeding grounds. Females appear to come to particular locations rather than to particular males. Males attempt to herd them to the middle of their territories. Each male tries to get as many females on

4. R. S. Peterson, "Social Behavior in Pinnipeds," in *The Behavior and Physiology of Pinnipeds,* eds. R. J. Harrison, R. C. Hubbard, R. S. Peterson, C. E. Rice, R. J. Schusterman, Appleton-Century-Crofts, New York, 1968, pp. 3–53.

Figure 11.2
Threatening Bull Seals at a
Territorial Boundary
(Dr. Cathleen R. Cox)

his territory as possible. Since the females are attracted to groups of females, success builds on success.

Within thirty-six hours of arrival the pregnant seal gives birth. For about five days she is a protective and intense mother. She then goes into *estrus,* a period of sexual receptivity usually associated with ovulation. The single copulation by females during the breeding season occurs within eight days of their arrival on the beach. The female copulates with a proprietory male in his territory. Since bulls hold territories that are occupied by several females, they are said to have *harems*—that is, a number of females are the mates of one male. The term harem is given a specific meaning to describe the social organization for mating in seals. The female seal copulates with the holder of the territory she occupies. If before copulating with him she crosses over to another territory, she mates with the bull that claims the territory she has entered. After copulation, the female leaves the beach and her pup for seven or eight days, presumably to feed. The pups are typically found in groups called pods near the beach. The females return about ten times over the next four months for two-day nursing visits to their pups. Female fur seals find their own pups and refuse to nurse alien young.

The bulls leave the breeding grounds in August much the worse for wear. Pups stay on the grounds for two or three more months. After the bulls leave, the groupings of females and young disperse and move inland. From August until late October, females return to suckle the pups about every ten days. About the first of November, pups and their mothers leave the breeding grounds.

These three examples of seasonal social organizations are in striking contrast to the more stable year round social organizations to be described below. In the groups just described, membership changes with the reproductive cycle of the species. In the animals to be described, the activities of the group are influenced by the birth of the young or the sexual cycle of the females, but group membership is relatively stable.

Permanent
Organizations

Many social species live in relatively permanent year round groups. Two classes of mammals, primates and carnivores, are of particular interest to students of human behavior. The social behavior of other primates provides examples from phylogenetically close animal forms that help us to understand possible phyletic influences on human social organization. The behavior of social carnivores provides other examples important to an understanding of human beings. Because human beings may be considered social hunter-scavengers, solutions to the problems of survival in a similar ecological niche may provide useful perspectives for human social organization.

Spotted Hyenas

Hyenas are popularly considered to be more or less solitary scavengers. Recent studies indicate that spotted hyenas frequently act as social hunters.[5] Figure 11.3 shows a group of hyenas pulling down a wildebeest bull. In areas with stable populations of prey animals, such as the Ngorongoro crater, hyenas live in groups called clans and establish and defend group territories. Within the hyena clan, females are dominant over males. Within the same sex, larger animals are dominant over smaller animals. Females, which are larger than males, have an enlarged erectile clitoris, a false scrotum, and are distinguished from males only by their enlarged nipples. Even experienced observers find it impossible to distinguish between immature male and female hyenas.

Animals older than three or four weeks engage in ritual greeting of other clan members. This greeting is initiated when the subordinate hyena approaches the dominant animal. In this case, dominant means older, larger, or female. The animals sniff each other's mouth and head. In a full greeting response the animals next stand head to tail with erect clitoris or penis, lift the leg nearest the other animal,

5. H. Kruuk, *The Spotted Hyena,* University of Chicago Press, Chicago, 1972.

Figure 11.3
Social Hunting in Hyenas
(From The Spotted Hyena, *by H. Kruuk, published by the University of Chicago, 1972. Copyright 1972 by the University of Chicago. All rights reserved. Published 1972. Photograph courtesy of Hans Kruuk.)*

and sniff and lick the genitals. Even in young pups the ritual is fairly complete, including erection. Erection of the clitoris is seen only in the greeting ritual, while erection of the penis occurs in both greeting and sexual contexts. The greeting ritual may be associated with the hyena's tendency to break away from the group alone or in pairs for a time and then return to it. The elaborate ritual provides a means of welcoming returning individuals.

Clans generally maintain communal dens where several litters of pups are left together. A single female may guard several litters at a den site but will not nurse pups other than her own. Hyenas, unlike dogs and wolves, never regurgitate meat for pups. They do regurgitate hair balls and splintered bone, but no nutrient value remains and these are not eaten by other hyenas. Male hyenas are not permitted close to very young pups and appear to have no role in caring for them. Adult males play with older pups and sometimes initiate chasing bouts with pups.

In the stable clans of the Ngorongoro crater, groups of hyenas from a clan visit latrine areas near territorial boundaries and defecate communally. Other points near territorial boundaries are scent-marked by the secretions of the anal scent glands of these patrols. These boundaries are so clearly marked that a hunting hyena may abandon a prey animal that crosses the boundary into another clan's territory.

Hyenas frequently hunt in packs, particularly in areas where there are stable territories. Hunting packs and border patrols are small mixed-sex groups composed of animals belonging to a single clan. These groups rarely consist of all adult clan members. After a kill, other members of the clan join in eating the animal. The carcass usually disappears in a very brief time. In one report, four hyenas killed a 185-kilogram wildebeest bull. Within forty-five minutes fourteen hyenas had eaten or carried away everything except the head and spine.

When a hunting pack fails to respect a territorial boundary, conflict between clans over the kill is likely. Feeding hyenas are very noisy, and resident clan members are drawn to the kill site by the growling, grunting, giggling gluttons. Lions, vultures, wild dogs, and jackals are also attracted by the racket. Even when outnumbered, resident hyenas chase off nonresident hunters with little direct interaction. A hyena surrounded by members of another clan may be badly mauled or killed and eaten after the preferred wildebeest or zebra has been consumed.

Male hyenas do change clans, but acceptance into a new group is slow and dangerous. On recognition, which is apparently visual, resident hyenas threaten and attack intruders. A frequent form of threat to an outsider is a parallel walk, with two or more hyenas advancing as a unit directly toward the intruder. Most intruders find urgent business elsewhere at this point. As in hunting and marking, females and males are equally likely to engage in territorial defense of this sort. One persistent male managed to change from one clan to another in Ngorongoro within one year. At the end of a year he was able to stay on the den site of his new clan without being chased. It is interesting to note that he was tolerated during a hunt before he was permitted to be near the group at other times.

Hyena social organization is different in areas such as the Serengeti, where prey animals are migratory and less plentiful than in Ngorongoro. Group membership is more open, and clearcut territories are not formed. The den site is defended against other hyenas, but a defined hunting preserve does not exist. Groups of hyenas fight in clan units over kills, but the outcome depends more on the number of animals in each group than on the location of the kill. Scent-marking and communal defecation is sometimes seen as a response to another group of hyenas. Latrine and scent-marking areas in the Serengeti are near hyena paths or automobile roads and have no apparent territorial boundary functions.

In one area, the social organization of hyenas is a closed system tied to territorial boundaries. A stable supply of prey and a hyena population of high density occupy this area. However, where prey animals are migratory and hyenas more dispersed, only rudiments of territorial behavior are seen. In this type of habitat, clans are more open and are likely to have a shifting membership. The den area is defended, but no clearcut group hunting territory is evident. The specific social organization of hyena groups is thus dependent in part on the ecological features of the immediate environment.

Wolves

Another social carnivore that has always held a peculiar fascination for human beings is the wolf.[6] Wolf packs are smaller units than are hyena clans. A wolf pack consists of a mated pair of adult wolves and their offspring. A large pack of twelve to fourteen animals probably includes two successive litters of about a half dozen pups each. Sometimes the litters of more than one bitch are found in a single

6. L. D. Mech, *The Wolf,* Natural History Press, Garden City, New York, 1970.

Figure 11.4
A Group Ceremony in
Wolves
(Patricia Caulfield)

pack. In one recorded case two bitches were found denning their pups together. The conditions for formation of new packs are not completely understood. Some authorities believe that packs are based on the separate dens established by two-year-old wolves at the time of pair formation.

Wolves have a repertoire of social signals involving facial expressions and tail positions. These expressions are generally similar to those found in domestic dogs. Wolf greetings are roughly similar to those of hyenas. Subordinate wolves nuzzle the head and mouth in the same way that wolf pups beg for regurgitated food. Figure 11.4 shows a pack attempting to nuzzle the pack leader. This group ceremony is seen just after the pack wakes up, when the leader returns to the group after being separated, and just after prey is scented on a hunt.

Care of pups appears to be the exclusive responsibility of the hyena mother. The only exception is seen when a female guards but does not feed pups in a communal den. In contrast, all adult members of a wolf pack appear to have an intense interest in pups. Males and females other than the mother regurgitate meat for the pups. Babysitting involving contact and nuzzling is common in yearling females and is sometimes seen also in males. In one case, a young female stayed with a litter in the den while the mother joined the regular night hunt. More typically the mother stays with her young pups during the hunt. The area around the den is a focal point for the group. Hunts begin here, and all members of the pack rest near the den.

While hyena mothers feed only at the site of a kill, wolf mothers have no such requirement. Pack members bring meat near the den and cache it. Meat is transported in the stomach of the providers as far as eighteen to twenty miles from a kill. Hyenas carry animal parts away from a kill, but apparently only for their own use.

Hyena social organization appears to function most clearly in hunting. Communal dens are maintained by hyenas, but there is minimal communal care of infants. Wolf social organization is functional in hunting, but communal care of pups may be an equally important aspect of social organization in this species. Hyena mothers usually have two or three pups that are their almost exclusive responsibility. Wolf mothers have six to eight pups that are the responsibility of the pack. These alternate strategies are the result of different phylogenetic histories interacting with similar (but still different) ecological pressures.

When wolf pups are eight to ten weeks old they leave the den area for a series of *rendezvous sites*. A rendezvous site is an area where older pups are left while the mature members of the pack hunt. When the pups are young, a particular rendezvous site will be occupied for about twenty days. However, when the pups are about seven months old, occupation lasts for approximately seven days. Rendezvous sites are usually near a bog, but well drained. They are crisscrossed by trails and show evidence of a great deal of activity by pups and adults. The rendezvous site is a focal point for the pack's activity.

When the pups reach seven or eight months of age, they are no longer left by the pack. They now run with the pack, and this permits greater pack mobility.

The wolf pack is organized as a structured dominance hierarchy for both sexes. There are actually two hierarchies, one for males and one for females. The most dominant male and female are usually a mated pair forming the pack nucleus. The alpha, or most dominant, male is the pack leader that initiates and directs movement. Other pack members may influence the pack's activity by hanging back in difficult terrain or by restless movement when the leader delays initiation of the daily hunt. In a hunt the pack leader apparently makes first contact with the prey. Wolves typically chase prey only short distances before giving up. The leader ends a chase by halting, and the rest of the pack follows suit.

Both wolves and hyenas typically kill prey much larger than

themselves. In general, only social predators kill larger prey, while solitary predators take animals no larger than themselves.

Wolves scent-mark areas within their range. They also show hostility to some but not all strange wolves. There is no clear evidence of anything like the clearcut group territories of the hyena clans in the Ngorongoro crater. The wolves' marking and pack defense appear much closer to the behaviors of the hyenas in the Serengeti. The prey of the wolves described here are primarily migratory. If the two species, wolves and Serengeti hyenas, had developed similar capacities for group territory, we would expect wolves with a stable prey supply to show more clearcut territoriality.

An intuitive grasp of the behavior of other organisms is difficult to come by and is frequently inaccurate. A characteristic shared by hyenas and wolves may help us to understand this point. The evidence indicates that hunting and killing in these species are not particularly related to hunger. Both wolves and hyenas hunt and kill whenever possible. Once a kill has been made, feeding and concomitant social behavior appear to inhibit immediate further hunting. However, wolves will hunt and kill with a partially devoured kill nearby. Hyenas will kill many animals without eating if the opportunity presents itself. For adult social carnivores there is no direct analogue of hunger as human beings experience that state, although these animals are almost always willing to eat with gusto. Hunting and killing are not instrumental responses in the service of aroused hunger; instead, they are relatively autonomous behaviors that happen to provide food.

Baboons

Savannah Baboons   The several species of baboon that live on the African savannah have a troop social organization similar to that of the Japanese macaque described earlier.[7] These troops are mixed age and sex groupings. The dominant males within the troop direct troop movement and defend the troop against predators and other baboons. Like the Japanese macaques, a structured dominance hierarchy exists among adult males. There is also evidence of matrilineal primary social groupings among savannah baboons. The most attractive and important members of the troop are the dominant males and the infants. Females crowd around mothers with infants, and adult males are remarkably tolerant of infants.

7. S. L. Washburn and I. Devore, "The Social Life of Baboons," *Scientific American,* 204 (1961), 62–71.

Savannah baboons exhibit orderly and coordinated troop movement. When moving across the savannah, a vanguard of juvenile
and low status males is followed by the main body of dominant
males, infants, and females of all ages. A rear guard of juvenile and
low status males follows. Dominant males lag behind the troop only
when accompanying mothers that have just given birth. Only the
mother with a very young infant can slow down these males, and
thereby the main body of the troop. Other animals that fall behind
are abandoned.

When a predator is encountered a member of the vanguard stops,
stands on his hind legs, and calls. A dominant male comes forward
and looks the situation over. The dominant male's behavior following this situational assessment appears to cue the troop. If a pride of
lions is seen, the troop may flee rapidly. If a hunting cheetah is seen,
the other adult males may come forward and help chase the predator away.

Baboons frequently forage and flee with herds of ungulates. A
mixed herd of baboons and impala is said to be very difficult to
sneak up on, due to the baboons' visual ability coupled with the
impala's olfactory sensitivity.

Dominant males in these troops are not the only sexually active
males. As a female goes into estrus she might copulate with juvenile
or subordinate males from the troop's periphery. At the peak of
estrus, which corresponds with ovulation, dominant males are most
likely to copulate with the females. There appeared to be no permanent pair bond between males and females, leading Washburn and
Devore to discount earlier descriptions of harems in the desert-living
Hamadryas baboon.

Forest Baboons   Some baboon species occupy both savannah and
forest environments.[8] Baboons occupying forested areas demonstrate a number of differences from those occupying the more open
savannah. These differences are accounted for in part by a more
lush environment in the forest with a plentiful food supply and
adequate protection from predators. Forest baboons appear to be
more relaxed and friendly in their social relations, with less evidence
of an enforced male dominance hierarchy. Baboon troops in the
forest are more open than are those on the savannah. Males change

8. T. E. Rowell, "Forest Living Baboons in Uganda," *Journal of Zoology,* 149 (1966),
344–364.

troops in both environments, but there appears to be less antagonis-
tic behavior toward newcomers in the forest. Movement through the
forest is less orderly, with little evidence of age-sex groupings. Any
member of the troop may delay or slow down movement, and even
injured or ill animals can keep up with the troop. If an individual
falls behind, other members appear upset and the troop stops until
the laggard catches up.

Male baboons in the forest show little tendency toward troop
defense. Occasionally, males are seen between some fearful object
and the rest of the troop; however, this seems to occur only when the
object frightens juveniles but not adult males. Serious danger initiates a free-for-all rout, with adult males quickly outdistancing
younger animals and females burdened with infants.

Desert Baboons   The first field studies of savannah baboons by
Washburn and Devore led these investigators to discount reports of
harems among any baboons. More recent studies of a different
species, *Papio hamadryas,* the Hamadryas baboon, clarified this question of harems. The Hamadryas baboon lives in areas even more
barren than the savannah. Hamadryas baboons do have harems.
Their basic social unit consists of an adult male, his females and
young, and subadult male followers.[9] A one-male unit with two
females, an infant, and a subadult follower is seen in Figure 11.5.
The sparse food supply in the desert probably has something to do
with the adaptive value of foraging units comprised of four to ten
animals as opposed to the forty- to eighty-animal units observed in
the savannah.

The social organization of desert Hamadryas baboons is somewhat
more complex than that of other baboons. There are three levels of
social organization in Hamadryas baboons. The largest unit is a
sleeping troop of up to seven hundred animals. During the night,
these animals occupy a communal protected site. Favored locations
are mounds of rock or cliffs with ledges. The sleeping troop appears
to be made up of a number of bands. These bands roughly correspond in number and composition to the savannah troop. Such
bands of six to ten males and their harems are difficult to identify
when the troop has formed at night. They are most apparent when

9. H. Kummer, *Social Organization of Hamadryas Baboons,* University of Chicago
Press, Chicago, 1968.

Figure 11.5
A One-Male Unit of
Hamadryas Baboons
(From Hans Kummer,
Social Organization of
Hamadryas Baboons,
University of Chicago
Press, 1968, p. 53.
Copyright 1968 S. Karger
AG, Basel. Reprinted by
permission of S. Kargar
AG, Basel.)

the sleeping troop breaks up and goes out foraging or when fights break out within the troop. Bands tend to leave the sleeping area together and travel as a unit for a short period of time. When fighting breaks out within a troop, bands fight each other as units. This is true even when the fight is begun by an incompatible troop's attempt to occupy the site. Regardless of the cause of a fight, each band fights together as a unit against all other bands. Kummer believes that one characteristic of a band is that males within it will not compete for or even accept the females of their band mates.

Within a sleeping troop, males do not actively compete for females from allied bands but will apparently accept such females into their harems. When males and their harems are released into strange sleeping troops the males are attacked and the females are immediately incorporated into existing harems.

The one-male units of a band sometimes join into two-male foraging teams. When such teams move, each female must stay close to her own male to avoid threat or aggression from him. In the two-male foraging team, the usual order of movement is a rough single file headed by the younger male and his females and juveniles, which are followed by the females and juveniles of the older male. The older male usually brings up the rear of this small procession. The interposition of any adult male between a harem master and his female will result in an attack or threat directed toward the offending female. Her offense is determined by her location regardless of how she got there. A female frequently responds to the proximity of any adult male by screaming and rushing to embrace her mate.

While copulation does occur between the adult males and their females, sexual motivation does not appear to be the primary basis for the harem. When juvenile males copulate with adult females, the harem master does not show undue disturbance. In fact, most copulation among Hamadryas baboons is between postpubescent males and adult females. However, copulation during peak estrus usually involves only the harem master, so he sires most infants.

The manner of harem formation also causes one to doubt the primacy of sexual motivation as a basis for the harem. Young adult males adopt prepubescent females as their initial harem members. Interaction with these child brides involves a great deal of parental behavior and little or no sex. The adult males appear to be concerned that their females be close to them and not close to other adult males. Juvenile males are tolerated as hangers-on in the group, moving freely among the females. Adult males with established harems pay little attention to juvenile females, confining their attention to herding and isolating their own adult females.

Small foraging units and gigantic sleeping units are basic aspects of the Hamadryas baboon's adaptation to a relatively hostile environment. Scarcity of food and shortage of protected sleeping sites would make the moderate-sized closed groups of the savannah baboons maladaptive. Kummer sees Hamadryas social organization as an evolutionary adaptation developing from the simpler troop organization of the savannah baboons. Baboon social organization in the savannah appears to function primarily to protect members against predation. Within the troop, the behavior of dominant males serves to reduce aggression and to protect babies from rougher juveniles. In the lush forest environment, social structure and male dominance are lax. In the harsh desert, the adaptive range of the species occupying forest and savannah has apparently been exceeded. The evolutionary adaptation of the Hamadryas baboon is expressed in a modified social organization that permits the formation of larger sleeping groups and smaller foraging groups than in the savannah.

As we review these descriptions of social organization in many different species, a few general themes are detectable. First, the behavior of social organisms does reflect organization. Organization is a necessary part of the Phylogenetic Set of adaptive social animals. Second, social organization is influenced by environmental factors.

Hyenas have closed clans and clearcut group territories in an area with stable nonmigratory prey. In an area with dispersed migratory prey this tight organization breaks down, although many behavior patterns relevant to territory are maintained. Savannah and forest baboons of the same species have different social structures. Savannah troops are more closed and more highly organized than forest troops, with more emphasis on dominance hierarchies. Phylogenetic social adaptations are seen in the Hamadryas baboons, which are able to exploit the desert environment via a unique combination of large sleeping groups and small foraging groups.

Another point that should be emphasized is that no other single species can be an adequate model for human social organization. It is tempting to take a particular pattern seen in some other species and assume that it is basic in our own. The maternally related primary social groups in some macaques and baboons are an example. One might assume that since these animals are social primates as we are, and since the maternal parent is the easiest parent to know, the matriarchal group is the basic primate social unit. This unit is the basic unit in some but not all social primates. The one-male unit of the Hamadryas baboon is no less a basic social unit. Neither the matriarchal nor the one-male organizational unit is an adequate model for human social organization. The study of social organization in other species provides many hypotheses or perspectives about human social organization. However, studies of social organization in other species cannot reveal the basic nature of human social organization. Comparative studies of social organization, like those of other aspects of animal behavior, are only one of many approaches necessary for a reasonable understanding of human behavior.

There are several academic disciplines devoted to the study of human social organization, and a complete coverage of the area would require considerations of anthropology, sociology, and economics beyond the scope of this book. Human beings live in organized societies. They live under many different sets of ecological and environmental restraints. These account only in part for the variety evident in human social systems. Cultural elaborations of social structure also produce some of this variety. In this chapter, we will limit our discussion to the developing child and the groups the child encounters in the course of development in Western society.

Human Social Organization

Human children, like wolf pups, hyena cubs, and baboon babies, are members of an organized social unit at birth. The rare exceptions to this statement are unlikely to survive to maturity in an unimpaired state. A child becomes a part of a particular social organization that varies with culture and social class. Among middle-class Americans the child is a member of a nuclear family that has ties with other families. In some societies the child is a member of an extended family, and like the aboriginal Cheyenne, may address a number of individuals as "mother" and "father." In some segments of American society the child may be born into a matriarchal unit and be the joint responsibility of its mother, grandmother, aunts, and uncles. The particular characteristics of the group the child joins at birth have a persistent and continuing influence over its subsequent development.

Early in the child's life, social contacts with others are usually related to family activities. If two or more reproducing females are members of the family unit, their children will of course interact with each other a great deal. When families socialize, the interaction of their children is an unemphasized correlate of adult activities.

As children grow older, their social groupings are less influenced by parental activities. Preschool children play with close neighbors, even when adult relationships are slight. The membership of children's spontaneous groups is determined primarily by availability.

Figure 11.6
Social Organization in
Children
(Terry McCoy)

When children enter nursery school, kindergarten, or first grade their social groups develop within the constraints set by adult-imposed, age-segregated units. Even then, spontaneous groups continue to form that cut across age and grade lines.

Adult interpretations of children's group activities are usually cast in terms of play. That is, anything a group of children are doing is seen as play. If it is not too noisy, quiet, destructive, dangerous, or sexual, it is not examined in any detail. There has been, in fact, relatively little research on social behavior and organization in spontaneous groups of children.

Studies of play groups in nursery schools have found them to possess a degree of social organization. Children's tendency to cluster in small groups, as seen in Figure 11.6, is one indication of social organization. In one study, groups of children in day nurseries were observed to establish traditions such as who sat where, what toys "belonged" to subgroups, and so forth.[10] Hartup interprets this finding as an indication that three- to six-year-old children in small groups establish norms and subgroup identifications.[11] Children attribute particular typical activities and particular roles in those activities to the group and parts of the group. From the children's point of view, certain toys belong to the group and are associated with certain roles in the group. That is, a group of children may identify themselves as the ones who play Star Trek, and specific members of the group are identified as the captain, Mr. Spock, or space monsters. Crew members would, of course, get the phasers.

The Robbers
Cave Study

Social organization in older children was one focal point of a famous series of studies culminating in the Robbers Cave study.[12] In three studies, groups of eleven- and twelve-year-old boys were observed at summer camp. In all cases, the groups were formed or reconstituted

10. F. Merei, "Group Leadership and Institutionalization," *Human Relations*, 2 (1949), 23–39.

11. W. R. Hartup, "Peer Interaction and Social Organization," in *Carmichael's Manual of Child Psychology*, ed. P. H. Mussen, John Wiley & Sons, New York, 1970, vol. II, pp. 361–456.

12. M. Sherif, *In Common Predicament*, Houghton Mifflin, Boston, 1966; and M. Sherif, O. J. Harvey, B. J. White, W. R. Hood, and C. W. Sherif, *Intergroup Conflict and Cooperation: The Robbers Cave Experiment*, University Book Exchange, Norman, Oklahoma, 1961.

so that members were unfamiliar with one another. Experimenters served as camp personnel and the boys were unaware of the study or the observations. The following account will concentrate on the Robbers Cave study, with some references to the earlier investigations.

In the Robbers Cave study boys who had not previously known each other were formed into two random groups. The groups were brought together as they were picked up by separate buses to go to camp. The camp area was near Robbers Cave, which is supposed to have been a hideout for the James brothers and Belle Star. The layout of the camp and the two group areas is illustrated in Figure 11.7a. Figure 11.7b gives a good idea of the terrain.

A status hierarchy with identifiable leaders emerged quickly in both groups. The groups developed accepted norms for their group, such as cursing among the Rattlers and nude swimming among the Eagles. The Rattlers spontaneously adopted their group name after an interaction with a rattlesnake. The Eagles adopted their name after finding out about the other group and learning of possible athletic competition with them.

In one group, leadership was not stable across the period of the study. In the Rattler group, the leader retained his position throughout the period studied. In both groups, the leader designated another boy to act as baseball captain. In the Eagle group the baseball captain gradually assumed other leadership activities, eventually displacing the original leader. This shift occurred under intense competitive hostility between the two groups. A series of athletic encounters between the groups was arranged with very attractive prizes, including a large trophy for the winning group and four-bladed pocket knives for each boy in it. During the competitive phase of the study, group identification was intensified, as was hostility toward the other group.

In both groups, different boys assumed leadership and responsibility for specific activities such as removing rocks from the swimming pool. This temporary sort of task direction was almost always assumed with the approval of the accepted group leader. Activities such as raids on the other group's cabin might be initiated by any group member, but unless the leader picked up on the suggestion, the activity was usually rejected by the group. Rejection of the leader's suggestions was rare but did occur when strong opposition was apparent among a clear majority.

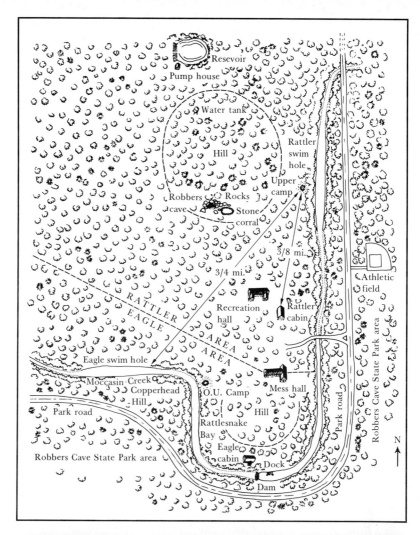

Resevoir
Pump house
Water tank
Rattler swim hole
Hill
Upper camp
Robbers cave
Rocks
Stone corral
3/8 mi.
3/4 mi.
RATTLER AREA
EAGLE AREA
Recreation hall
Rattler cabin
Eagle swim hole
Moccasin Creek
Copperhead Hill
O.U. Camp
Mess hall
Park road
Rattlesnake Bay
Hill
Park road
Robbers Cave State Park area
Eagle cabin
Dock
Robbers Cave State Park area
Dam
N

Figure 11.7
The Camp Area Near Robbers Cave
(From Muzafer Sherif and Carolyn W. Sherif, Social Psychology, Harper & Row, 1969, figs. 11.1c, 11.1d, 1969.)

The competition between the groups was rigged so that the least stable group won. At this point, hostility between the groups reached nearly unmanagable proportions. The losing Rattlers raided the Eagles' camp, messed the area up, and swiped the knives and medals awarded to the winners. Fortunately, the Eagles had entrusted the trophy to adult camp personnel. In the aftermath of the raid, camp personnel eventually had to separate the boys, although very little actual fighting occurred. A high level of intergroup hostility was evident thereafter. Meals in a communal dining hall ended in garbage fights between the two groups, and loud insults were exchanged when the groups made contact. Complaints were heard whenever interaction was required by the camp personnel.

At this point a series of crises was created by the experimenters. In the first crisis, when the water supply was interrupted, both groups were involved in searching for the problem and attempting to restore the supply. During this combined activity hostility was reduced, but a garbage fight began again at the next meal. The second crisis involved insufficient camp funds to rent a movie. The groups finally decided to contribute equal amounts, although the individuals in the smaller group had to contribute more money. The leader of the Rattlers took the joint vote on this proposition, giving it his support after it was suggested by a high status Eagle.

The third crisis was a stalled truck that was needed to bring food to both groups at a remote campout site. The solution required that the two groups cooperate to pull the truck with a tug-of-war rope. Again, the Rattler leader initiated the combined group activity and determined that they would pull rather than push the truck. When the truck was pulled forward a little, the experimenter-driver turned on the ignition and the joint effort was therefore successful. The stalled truck crisis was staged a second time, and the groups again joined to pull it. This time the members of the groups were interspersed along the rope, rather than with their own group as they had been the first time.

During the course of these necessarily cooperative problem solutions, intergroup hostility diminished. It is interesting to note that the joint leader was the leader of the losing but more stable group. The Rattler leader appeared to have more reservations about the Eagles than other members of his group, but went along with the group's inclinations to get along. He retained leadership throughout the study.

Leadership in the Eagles changed again with the reduction of hostilities. The Eagle leader who had come to power during the hostilities was strongly opposed to friendly interaction and did not shift with his group. The original leader of the Eagles did not return to power. He had been a reluctant and somewhat timid participant in competitive and hostile encounters with the Rattlers, and this had resulted in a marked drop in his status in the group. The Eagles' third leader was a close friend of the athletic combat leader but was somewhat more peaceful than his predecessor. However, the "war leader" retained high status in the group.

These children developed clearcut group structures in a very short period of time. The structures of the groups were dynamic, and status in the group shifted across the period of study. The more stable group retained the same leader throughout the study. This leader neither initiated nor physically led all group activities. Low status members did suggest activities and sometimes led the group into raids. The leader mediated suggestions, selected alternatives, supported his or some other point of view, and verbally expressed group decisions. On a couple of occasions, leaders lectured their groups on specific aspects of their competitive activities. The leader had certain prerogatives, such as designating the ball team captain and naming his own position on the ball club. There were limits to these rights, and the group would resist abuse of power. Examples of resistance included group rejection of an attempt to override an umpire's ruling and an attempt by one leader to act as an umpire. The boys insisted that umpires must be from the adult staff.

It is somewhat difficult to identify any specific trait associated with leadership in these groups. The very effective leader of the Rattlers was smaller than most of the boys and not particularly gifted athletically. As one reads the reports of group activities, it appears that he was able to focus on one alternative of those available to the group and to persuade others that that alternative was the appropriate choice for the group.

Adolescent Social Groups

In another series of studies, the same investigators observed the behavior of intact groups of adolescents.[13] These boys, ranging from fourteen to eighteen years of age, were studied in natural groups in urban areas of the southwest.

13. M. Sherif and C. W. Sherif, *Reference Groups,* Harper & Row, New York, 1964.

Figure 11.8
An Adolescent Social
Group
*(Owen Franken/Stock,
Boston)*

These groups of older boys were selected from lower-, middle-, and upper-class neighborhoods and were drawn from Anglo, black, and Spanish-speaking populations. The groups varied in size, preferred activities (except talking about sex, which was pervasive in all groups), degree of openness to new members, and the expected behaviors for group members. Every group reflected a status-popularity hierarchy and contained an identifiable leader. A position as group leader was maintained by successful leadership. The leader initiated, organized, and coordinated group activities. If these activities consistently failed to lead to success, pleasure, or other group goals, leadership shifted or the group disintegrated. As among the younger boys, the leader was not necessarily the best at whatever the group valued. In a *machismo*-oriented Spanish-speaking group, the best fighter and lover was too impulsive and too belligerent. He had high status, but he was held in check by the group leader and other group members.

Leaders frequently appeared to wait until discussions were about to run down, and then set a course of action for the group. In one case, financing a party was being discussed. During the course of the discussion, needs and available resources became apparent. At this point the leader assigned contributions, arranged necessary loans, and made specific arrangements for procuring the needed supplies. Discussion abruptly terminated and the activity was on.

The observers were struck by the fact that some decisions were made with no verbal input from the leader. If seating arrangements in a stadium containing hostile groups became a group concern, the problem would be voiced to the leader, who responded by walking to an area of seats and sitting down.

It is an error to divide groups into leaders and followers, some directing group activity and others passively taking whatever direction is indicated. All members of the natural groups of male adolescents had input into group activities. Members did not necessarily conform to all group norms but did have some functional role in the group. In one upper-class group, a low status member did not drink and was more socially conservative than the other boys. He was the president of the student council at the high school that all group members attended. This boy's role in the group was based on two functions. He was well regarded by adults and gave the group an appearance of respectability. Within the group, he acted as a stabilizing force, limiting the degree and openness of unacceptable group activities. He could also be depended on to see that everyone got home after a party.

Some idea of how leadership functions in these groups can be seen in the following example of a change in leaders. A Spanish-speaking group in a lower-class neighborhood was called Los Apaches. Their leader, while not the toughest member of the group, carried group and cultural norms of tough masculinity very well. He also happened to be the younger brother of the former leader, called the Apache, who was now a young adult. During the course of observation of this group, competitive basketball became an important activity for Los Apaches. The original leader was not a good player and knew it. In tight games he would take the bench and sometimes apparently feign illness to cover this necessary withdrawal from action. Gradually, leadership of the group shifted to a better athlete who handled team strategy very well. The original leader retained high status in the group and was usually but not always consulted when the new leader announced a decision.

In these studies of boys' groups there is striking similarity across the range from eleven to eighteen years of age. Individuals acquire specific roles and have particular functions within the group. Some group member assumes a leadership function and retains that role as long as he is successful. Leadership changes occur when the group's activities, interests, or goals shift and the original leader cannot or will not shift with the group. Group members are supported by the group and defended against outsiders. Hostility toward other groups is typical in these social units. In urban areas with many recognized gangs, other groups will be recognized as allies or enemies. The enemies and allies of Los Apaches were younger relatives of the enemies and allies of Los Apaches' older brothers.

Comparable observations of groups of girls are not available. However, high school populations are made up of a number of small groups of girls and boys called *cliques* as well as a number of diads and triads of outsiders.[14] Girls' groups are believed to be somewhat less hierarchal and somewhat less open to newcomers than are boys' groups. Some cliques contain both boys and girls, but strong heterosexual ties frequently break up cliques or are associated with dropping out of a clique.

Adult Social Organization

In American society, informal social organization among adults—that is, among those who have completed their formal education—is extremely complex. An individual may have one set of social contacts associated with work, another associated with religious organizations, still another associated with the home and neighborhood, and a group of friends who have little or no association with any of these enterprises. A unique feature of modern Western society is that an adult's associates are frequently people who were not childhood friends. This discontinuity between the important and familiar individuals of childhood and those of adult life is probably one basis for the lack of a sense of community in modern America.

In less mobile societies and in the less mobile parts of our society, relationships within and between groups are slowly established and well understood. In animal species with complex social organization, such as baboons, the developing organism acquires specific expectations with respect to the behavior of other individuals in the group. In stable human communities, an individual's place in the group is defined in part by his or her familial relationship with other members. In Gopalpur, a man is so-and-so's son, then so-and-so's son-in-law, and finally so-and-so's father-in-law. Among the nineteenth-century Cheyenne, a person's identity was with a family, a band, and the tribe as a whole. In rural Arkansas, one of the authors is permitted to fish in many private ponds because he is Carl Dees's

14. J. S. Coleman, *The Adolescent Society,* The Free Press, New York, 1961.

son-in-law. In these examples, the individual's place in the informal social organization of the adult world is based on a familial or marital relationship with some known member of the group.

Adults in a mobile society lack the security and restrictions that accompany membership in a transgenerational informal social structure. In an American city, if one sees another human being in distress one must decide whether to get involved. If the person in distress is a recognized member of an existing social unit, the question is moot. Even if the person in distress is low status and not particularly popular, those who know him as a member of a social community are necessarily involved. One unsolved problem facing urban America is how to replace the natural tendency to support and protect group members, with a norm requiring aid for *all* members of the species.

The structure of formal units like army companies, academic departments, and city, state, and national governments reflects the human tendency to organize social units. Military organizations reflect a particularly tight and explicit structure (see Figure 11.9). Even when formal structures are abhorred, some minimal structure proves necessary for effective group functioning. The Soviet army's early experiment with elimination of rank was quickly abandoned under combat. The structure of government takes many forms. Usually, however, there are a number of differences between the stated structure of a formal social unit and the actual organization of the unit.

Figure 11.9
Structured Social Organization
(Frank Siteman/Stock, Boston)

Summary

In this chapter, social groups in several species have been described. In every instance, groups of animals were seen to behave in an organized way. The behavior of groups of any species is partially determined by Phylogenetic Set. Even under similar ecological pressures, different species develop species typical social organizations. Social organization is determined in part by the environment. Serengeti hyenas had a looser and less territorial social system than Ngorongoro hyenas. Forest baboons had a more relaxed structure with less emphasis on dominance than savannah baboons. Experiential Set does play some role in social organization.

The Hamadryas baboon provides an example of adaptation—or change in Phylogenetic Set—that permits exploitation of a new environment. The social structure of troop-living savannah baboons requires that all members of the troop forage together. An evolutionary adaptation present in Hamadryas baboons permits foraging in small units coupled with sleeping in very large units. This pattern fits the desert environment beautifully, since forage is sparse and sleeping areas scarce. This expression of Phylogenetic Set in social organization is reminiscent of the fit between the neonate's behavioral capacities and the species typical postnatal environment.

Cultural Set is an important determinant of human social organization. In this chapter, the development of social organization in Western society was considered. From their first contacts with age mates, young children tend to behave in a way that reflects rudimentary social organization. The best descriptions of social organization in children were from the Robbers Cave studies and the studies of adolescent groups conducted by Sherif and his colleagues. In these studies, a status hierarchy and a leadership structure existed in school age and adolescent groups. It is most interesting that leadership in these groups was not usually associated with outstanding skill or perfect conformity with group ideals. The leader often turned out to be the one who made a choice among several alternatives available to the group. In both series of studies it was pointed out that nonleaders could and did initiate activities, make suggestions, or lead group activities.

Some sort of social contract, some set of organizational rules, must exist for any adaptive group of organisms. To understand the behavior of any social organisms, including human beings, we must consider the influence of the typical social organization upon the species and culture in question.

Defined Terms

Social animal	Rut	Harem
Macaque	Conspecific	Rendezvous site
Dominant	Estrus	Cliques

Suggested Readings

P. E. Ellis, "Social Organization of Animal Communities," *Symposia of the Zoological Society of London,* No. 14, 1965.

  A series of fairly technical descriptions of social organization in specific animal species or groups. A student with strong biological interests would find this selection rewarding.

H. Kummer, *Social Organization of Hamadryas Baboons,* University of Chicago Press, Chicago, 1968.

  This short book is an excellent example of field research at its best. There are many fine photographs of baboons in their natural habitat.

G. Park, *The Idea of Social Structure,* Anchor Press/Doubleday, Garden City, New York, 1974.

  This book discusses human social organization from an anthropological perspective. Many interesting examples from a number of cultures are used to illustrate the author's presentation.

J. P. Scott, "Social Behavior and Social Organization," in *Animal Behavior,* 2nd Ed., Revised, University of Chicago Press, Chicago, 1972, pp. 174–212.

  This chapter discusses social organization from the perspective of traditional comparative psychology. Some of the material presented by Scott is also relevant to Chapter 10, "Affectional Relationships."

S. L. Washburn and I. Devore, "The Social Life of Baboons," *Scientific American,* 204 (1961), 62–71.

  This article provides an interesting brief summary of the field studies conducted by the authors.

Chapter 12
Variation in
Adaptation

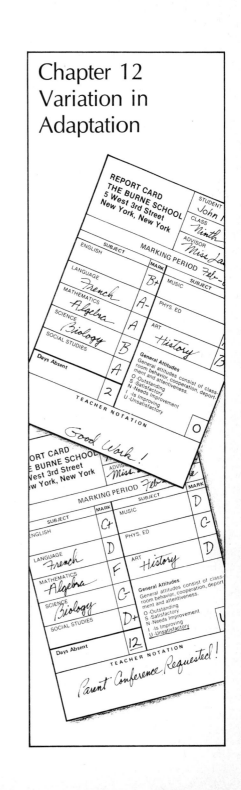

Organisms differ in their adaptability. In this chapter we will focus on two kinds of adaptive variability: population variability and individual variability. *Population adaptability* refers to adaptive success among a group of organisms. Adequate adaptation for a group is indicated by a stable or increasing population across a reasonable time span and a high probability that this trend will continue. Marginal adaptation for a group of organisms is indicated by reducing numbers, low birth rates, low viability of individuals, and a high probability of continuation of this trend. *Individual adaptability* refers to a group member's access to mates and to the resources of the group.

Population adaptability is an attribute of both species and cultures. Phylogenetic variation in adaptability is the expression of the evolutionary process at work. Species that demonstrate marginal adaptability are becoming extinct. Species with adequate adaptability will continue to reproduce. Cultures that show marginal adaptability are also becoming extinct. It is important to recognize that adequate population adaptability does not imply constancy in the adaptive species or culture. Adaptive species continuously respond to evolutionary pressures by changes in the species gene pool. In response to similar pressures, adaptive cultures change. The analogy between processes that influence changes in cultures and species have so impressed anthropologists that they use the term *cultural evolution* to refer to adaptive changes in cultures. A culture or species that does not change to accommodate changes in the environment is marginally adaptive and will probably become extinct. A discussion of the many factors that determine population adaptability is beyond the scope of this book. Instead, examples of species and cultures demonstrating marginal and adequate adaptability will be presented and briefly discussed.

The discussion of individual adaptability will proceed somewhat differently. As stated previously, individual adaptability is evidenced by access to mates and to the resources available to the group. In our own species, there are many traits that serve as determinants of adaptability. The adaptive human being possesses technical and social skills. Technical skills vary considerably across and within cultures. Social skills may be culturally specific in detail but are more similar across cultures than are technical skills.

Task-related skills include accurate spear throwing, riding a bicycle, making a clay pot, passing a test, and writing a book. The physical objects and social contexts involved in these tasks vary from one culture to another, as indicated in Figure 12.1. However, each culture defines the skills expected of adults in rather precise ways. In addition, most cultures provide norms of skillful behavior for children at different levels of development. Both mature and immature individuals are also expected to attain adequate competence in dealing with other individuals. Maintaining a proper distance from another person, knowing when to listen and when to talk, and knowing when to gaze and when to avert gaze are examples of social skills. Societies set norms for social skills similar to those set for task-related skills. Children, young adults, and older adults are expected to know the norms and to produce behavior within the acceptable range.

Social judgments as to the adequacy of performance are communicated to the individual. In subsistence cultures, this social feedback is often explicit and tangible. Adults are given information by means of the allocation of economic and social resources. The successful male hunter, warrior, or farmer may receive more food, more desirable housing, more and better land for his use. He may have more wives or a greater choice of mates, or his relatives may be allowed a larger selection of mates.

A competent individual may be accorded higher status by members of the group. The competent person's opinions may count more heavily than those less successful. Often, a high status individual is given explicit tokens of rank. Custom may dictate medals, titles, and baubles as the material representation of status bestowed on successful individuals and their relatives. In human societies, adaptability is both a cause and a result of social status. That is, the status accorded to a human being is one sign of the individual's adaptability. On the other hand, high or moderate status may help the individual attain some of the characteristics of adaptability; for example, in our society access to certain kinds of technical and professional training is more or less restricted to those who can afford it. High status individuals may have control of as well as access to resources and goods. In some cultures, control of resources may be more clearly related to status than use of these resources.

For the very young and the very old, adequate and inadequate levels of competence have social consequences that are grossly similar to those described for middle adults. There are of course differences in form for the various ages. Compared with a child whose

Figure 12.1
Variation in Work Roles
*(a. Western Electric; b.
U.S.D.A. Photo by Murray
Lemmon; c. Care Photo;
d. Care Photo)*

behavior is within the expected range, the child with defective development may receive considerably less physical and social nurturance. Nurturance may be denied to children whose physical or behavioral development is manifestly poor. In many cultures, older individuals are rewarded for their longevity. Their experience is often used in teaching the young and in preserving religious and artistic traditions. In other societies, including our own, the enfeebled older individual may experience withdrawal of emotional and social contacts with younger members of society.

Another characteristic of individual adaptability is the ability to tolerate stress.[1] The adaptive individual is probably subject to less stress than the marginally adaptive person. At the same time, the adaptive individual deals with stress more effectively than the marginally adaptive person. It is obvious that the person who has adequate social and technical skills avoids many potential sources of stress. There is evidence that one of the effects of intense stress is to reduce subsequent resistance to stress. Thus the individual who handles the routine demands of existence with little stress is better able to withstand nonroutine stressful events.

Stress reactions are a series of physiological and psychological adaptations to extreme conditions in the environment. Extremely

1. H. Selye, *The Stress of Life*, McGraw-Hill, New York, 1956.

intense light levels and rapid changes in sound levels are events in the physical environment that produce stress reactions. Psychological events may also produce stress. Confronting an angry friend or remembering cheating on an exam are stress-producing events.

The sources of stress are both physical and psychological, and the responses to stress are physiological and behavioral. Physiological reactions to stress include cardiac, vascular, digestive, and hormonal changes (see Figure 12.2). Behavioral reactions involve the perceptual and motor systems. Under high stress, perception is narrowed and motor performance inaccurate. These perceptual and motor components of the stress response are frequently accompanied by

Figure 12.2
Physiological Reactions to Stress

Stress Reaction, or General Adaptation Syndrome		
Stage 1	*Stage 2*	*Stage 3*
Adrenalin discharge	Adrenalin reduction	Breakdown of adaptation
Changes in heart rate, blood pressure, muscle tone	Normalization of heart rate, blood pressure, muscle tone	Adrenalin deficiency Cardiac disorders Hypertensive disorders

changes in the emotional state. The phrase "blind with rage," describes a curious combination of changes in perception and emotion. Finally, prolonged high levels of stress may produce physical illness, including stomach ulcers and high blood pressure.

Individuals vary in their vulnerability to stress. Most people withstand exposure to fluctuations in typical environments without significant levels of stress. Some few tolerate wider ranges of environmental variation with less difficulty. Others experience more stress than is species typical within the expected range of environments. Very few individuals resist stress in every environment. A slightly larger number experience stress under ordinary environmental conditions.

The susceptibility of an individual to stress is called vulnerability. The concept of vulnerability to stress integrates many specific types of physical illness and psychological disturbance. Many of these specific problems may be considered individual responses to internal and external sources of stress. Some individuals show a remarkable degree of invulnerability and adapt well despite adversity. Norman Garmezy has recently brought invulnerable children to the attention of psychologists.[2]

Some individuals express reactions to stress-producing situations largely through symptoms of physical illness. In others, stress reactions are expressed through behavioral changes. All individuals experience and react to stress, and indeed some stress is probably essential for the maintenance of psychological and physiological health. In one view, orderly growth consists of cumulative reactions to changes in the internal and external environments. Some of these changes doubtless produce stress reactions. Without stress, there would be no mechanisms for internal change. Without a history of intermittent stress reactions, there would be no adequate physical and psychological defense against assault. Complete protection from stress may produce organisms unable to withstand stress. A troop of baboons was housed for more than five years in an air-conditioned building in which temperatures were maintained at 72°F, plus or minus 4°. Subsequently, the troop was placed in outdoor cages. When the temperature dropped to 50°F (well within the normal

2. N. Garmezy, "Children at Risk: The Search for Antecedents of Schizophrenia. Part II: Ongoing Research Programs, Issues, and Intervention," *Schizophrenia Bulletin,* No. 9 (Summer, 1974), 55–125.

range for these animals) most of the troop died. One suspects that complete protection from psychological stress would have similarly debilitating effects.

Some stress from the social and nonsocial environment can be predicted for all, no matter what their level of individual adaptability. Job crises, financial difficulties, personal disappointments, and tragedies are certain to occur. Illness and disability bring further stress. Maturational changes may also contribute stress, especially during infancy, adolescence, and old age. The adaptive individual is able to cope with a considerable amount of stress. Such an individual is adaptive in some situations and not in others. There is probably some level of stress that would produce maladaptive behavior in any individual.

Variation in individual adaptability is characteristic of all species, but in this chapter we will focus on individual adaptability in our own species. A few of the many sources of individual variation in adaptation have been selected for discussion later in this chapter. Ontogenetically related variation in adaptability will be discussed in some detail.

Phylogenetic Variation in Adaptation

Adequate Adaptation: Baboons

The savannah baboons of Africa are an example of several related species that appear to meet the criteria for population adaptability.[3] Baboons are so successful that, according to some estimates, their numbers are increasing faster than the human population. Even if this is an overestimate, there is no question that these semiterrestrial social primates are an adequately adaptive species.

In an evolutionary sense, baboons and their close relatives have been successful for a very long time. One indication of the adaptability of these species is the vast geographic range they occupy. Since the early Pleistocene epoch, baboons have inhabited much of sub-Saharan Africa. Any consideration of the bases of adaptive success is necessarily speculative and somewhat circular. Baboons have been and are adaptive animals. In one sense, when we describe the traits of these animals, we also describe the basis of their adaptability. We do not know which traits are most important in determining their adaptability.

3. S. A. Altmann and J. Altmann, *Baboon Ecology,* University of Chicago Press, Chicago, 1970.

The primatologists Stuart and Jeanne Altmann discuss several characteristics of baboons that may be related to evolutionary adaptability. Baboons eat a variety of foods and are able to utilize the food resources of both the savannah and the more densely forested areas. An important difference between baboons and vervet monkeys is that the baboons are strong enough to pull up grass roots in the savannah. The baboons are also less dependent on trees for protection than the vervet monkeys, and move further from trees in their search for food. Independence from trees during daylight is thought to be related to the large size of the baboon males and the social organization of the troop. In some baboon troops, males defend other troop members from predators. Aggressive tendencies enable baboons to defend themselves from predators and may also displace other monkey species from shared parts of the habitat.

The food habits, physical characteristics, and social behaviors of African baboons enable them to utilize resources over a wide area of the African continent. These species are adaptable in the sense that their numbers are increasing and probably will not decline in the near future. These species are able to use effectively the environments available to them.

Marginal Adaptation: Gorillas

Gorillas are included on most lists of endangered species. These large primates have only recently been subjected to intensive study.[4] The mountain gorilla appears to be a rather placid, phlegmatic creature, with few enemies other than man. In response to human beings as well as to strange gorillas, adult male gorillas perform a complex display that apparently is rather successful in intimidating the intruder. Gorillas look and act fierce, although they are apparently unlikely to attack. The animals become very excited during a display and will hit anything in their path, including other gorillas or human beings. Attacks, however, are more or less incidental to the display.

Gorillas live in groups that consist of one or more mature males, a larger number of mature females, and juveniles of various ages.

4. G. B. Schaller, "The Behavior of the Mountain Gorilla," in *Primate Behavior: Field Studies of Monkeys and Apes*, ed. I. DeVore, Holt, Rinehart and Winston, N.Y., 1965, pp. 324–367.

Figure 12.4
Gorillas
(George B. Schaller)

Group movement appears to be centered on the movements of the dominant male in the group. Gorillas are markedly dependent on a narrow range of temperature and humidity and are not capable of utilizing a wide range of food objects, as are baboons.

The gorilla's marginal adaptability appears to be associated with adaptation to a rather specific ecological niche that is disappearing. In both gorillas and baboons, adaptability is determined by species-environment interaction. Baboons have species typical characteristics that fit the current environment. Gorillas are well suited to a particular environment, but man is destroying that environment. Baboons appear to profit, at least temporarily, from agriculture and garbage dumps. Gorillas adapt poorly to human-induced environmental change, and the species may become extinct in the next hundred years.

Cultural Variation in Adaptation

Adequate Adaptation: The Hutterian Brethren

The Hutterites, or Hutterian Brethren, provide an example of adequate cultural adaptability.[5] This communal society is unique among other superficially similar groups on the North American continent. In 1874 there were eight non-Hutterite communal societies with seventy-two separate groups in the United States. At about this time three Hutterite colonies came to the United States. Since that time, all eight of the communal societies preceding the Hutterites in the United States have ceased to exist as viable societies. The Hutterites, in contrast, have increased from 3 to more than 225 colonies in this period.

The Hutterites are a religious society and regard living apart from the world in communal groups as an essential aspect of Christianity. Property is held in common by the members of a colony. All major decisions concerning the colony are made by the colony as a whole and are implemented by the colony council. The council consists of five to seven men selected as the executives of the colony. The preacher, the assistant preacher, the steward, and the field manager are always on the council. The preacher is also responsible for all aspects of community life. The steward is responsible for the economic well-being of the colony. The preacher mediates between the outside world and the colony and is called "elder." The steward represents the colony to the outside world in economic matters and is called "boss."

Modern Hutterite colonies are exclusively agricultural. Each colony consists of 60 to 150 people occupying from about 3,000 to 20,000 acres of land. (In Alberta, colonies are limited by law to 6,400 acres.) When a colony reaches maximum size, a new colony is founded. A new colony of sixty persons will include people of all ages, with about half of its members less than fifteen years of age. At least fifteen adult men will be included in a new colony. Five of these men will be baptized, married males more than twenty-five years old

5. J. A. Hostetler, *Hutterite Society*, Johns Hopkins University Press, Baltimore, 1974.

Figure 12.5
Hutterite Colony
(From H. A. Hostetler,
Hutterite Society,
published by The Johns
Hopkins University Press.
Copyright 1974 by The
Johns Hopkins University
Press.)

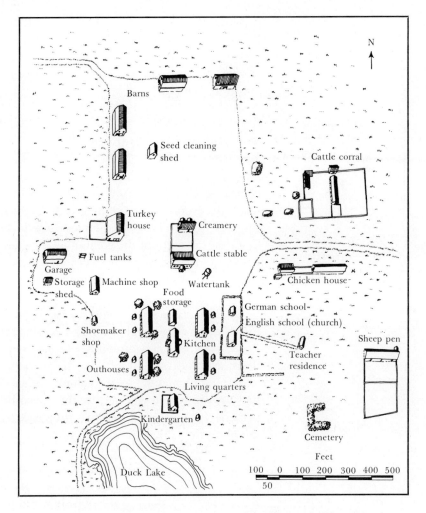

who can serve as foremen. At first there will be more positions of authority than eligible males. Double work assignments will be common, and the preacher may serve as steward in the early years of a new colony.

A new colony is initially financed by the parent colony. In 1970 this required savings of about $200,000. The average length of time between founding and branching is fourteen years, with some colonies branching in as little as twelve years.

In the mature colony, just prior to branching there are more qualified adult males than there are administrative roles. A twenty-five-year-old, baptized, married man expects some assignment of importance. Colony branching permits this expectation to be ful-filled. Delayed branching may cause serious problems in a colony, since most foremen are in office permanently.

Members of Hutterite colonies work long and hard. The attitude toward work is indicated by the fact that no adult is ever deprived of an opportunity to do meaningful work, even if he or she may no longer be allowed to eat with the brethren or to talk to anyone except the preacher. Work assignments are never used as punishment and no work is construed to be inherently unpleasant.

Goods are distributed to individual Hutterites on the basis of age and sex. The number of yards of material for clothing is specified to the inch and distributed on schedule. Specific allowances up to nine inches of fabric are made for the overweight individual. Hutterites eat in two communal dining halls in each colony. One hall is for children, the other for adults. Only the preacher and assistant preacher eat apart from the group.

Purchases of goods are made by the steward with the advice of the appropriate group members. The head seamstress knows how much cloth should be purchased. The preacher must approve the color and pattern of the cloth, and the steward approves the price before a salesman takes the order.

The Hutterite child is trained to be obedient to the colony and identifies with the colony rather than the family. Hutterite adults will use the pronoun "I" to refer to members of the colony. Hutterite children receive a great deal of warm affection coupled with firm, almost rigid, discipline. The assumption is that children naturally disobey and these tendencies must be curbed. The children do not appear to develop a strong sense of personal guilt, however, since misbehavior is an expected characteristic of the young.

The child's education begins with kindergarten at three years of age. The kindergarten child is trained to sit still and to be quiet and learns several prayers and hymns. At age six or seven the child begins to attend three schools: the English school, which meets state or provincial educational requirements; the German school, which teaches reading and writing in medieval German as well as Hutterite religion and philosophy; and the Sunday school, which is an exten-sion of the German school focusing on the sermon selected for a particular Sunday. Hutterite sermons are read by the preacher from books of sermons originating in the 1600s.

At age fifteen the child leaves school—except Sunday school, which is continued until baptism. The young person is assigned work as needed by the colony or neighboring colonies. After age fifteen the young person must make a commitment to the colony. Some young men leave the colony for a time during adolescence but almost all return. Few young women leave the colony. Young people select their own mates, usually from other colonies, but with complete veto control by the family and the colony. Since 1875 there have been four Hutterite desertions and only one divorce.

Hutterites have an average of ten children per family. The Hutterite birth rate resembles that of so-called underdeveloped countries, but the death rate is like that of industrialized countries. The population is, therefore, very young. There is no question that the Hutterian Brethren in North America meet our criteria of population adaptability. While a number of internal factors are basic to this adaptability, the importance of an appropriate environment must be emphasized. The Hutterian Brethren require a market for agricultural products, a supply of manufactured goods, and the opportunity for colony branching. Cultures, like species, are adaptable in particular environmental circumstances. When the environment changes, the culture will change or cease to exist.

Marginal Adaptation: Bushmen

The Bushmen of the desert areas of southern Africa provide an example of marginal cultural adaptability.[6] This Stone Age culture will probably cease to exist unless reserves are established where the Bushmen will be able to hunt and not be molested. Bushmen are hunters and gatherers living in small nomadic bands. They use poisoned arrows and spears to kill large game. Bushmen are especially skilled in finding food and water in the dry part of the year when large game is unavailable.

The Bushman way of life has been endangered by the effects of other human cultures. Bantu and European agriculture and cattle raising have gradually taken up the best land formerly available to the Bushmen and their large animal food supply. At the same time, laws and regulations protecting game animals have identified these hunters as criminals. When Bushmen took domestic cattle for food, they were in turn hunted by the enraged ranchers.

Bushmen are gradually beginning to seek employment in agriculture and mining. These dropouts from Bushman society are said to

6. J. Bjerre, *Kalahari,* Hill and Wang, New York, 1960.

Figure 12.6
Bushmen
(Wide World Photos)

gradually lose their ability to survive in the harsh surroundings of the present Bushman habitat.

It seems clear that Bushman society is remarkably well-adapted to the African environment—as long as there is little or no competition from other human cultures. The marginal adaptability of Bushman culture is caused by the fact that other human cultures are preempting or destroying the available resources.

In the case of both adequate and marginal cultural adaptability, the influence of other human groups is paramount. The Hutterites, who nearly ceased to exist in Europe, flourish in an environment where they are tolerated by other social groups. They are able to sell their agricultural products and buy needed goods from their neighbors. To be sure, they are superb farmers. However, to be a successful society, they must have land to farm and some sort of tolerable relationship with other groups in their area. The Bushmen are no less technically competent in the near-desert and desert areas they occupy. They are fine hunters and efficient foragers, finding food and water where a European would quickly die of exposure and starvation. The lack of adaptability seen in Bushman society is due to the influence of two more or less hostile competing societies. African and European agriculturists and cattle raisers have taken the Bushmen's livelihood from them.

| Ontogenetic Variability in Adaptiveness |

The preadult period is a long one in human beings compared with other species. This lengthy period permits, in fact, insures, a wide range of individual variability in behavior in our species. The adaptive significance of this broad range of typical human behaviors has been explained in previous chapters. However, variability implies maladaptive as well as adaptive development. In the next section of this chapter we will discuss the effects of variation in expected maturational patterns in our society.

Only in a broad sense is the development of behaviors and traits similar for virtually all human beings. The general plan is species wide, but specific behaviors and traits are expressed individually within this general plan. If we take a cross sectional measurement of some trait in a human population of individuals of the same age, a distribution of individual differences is obtained. In most individuals the trait is close to the average or middle range. In a few individuals the trait is extreme. While a trait may be extreme in individuals, behavioral trait differences are continuous in a population. That is, there are no gaps separating one group of individuals from the rest. The distribution of intelligence, as shown in Figure 12.7, is a familiar example.

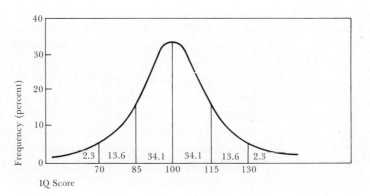

Figure 12.7
The Distribution of Intelligence

Complex interactions between genetic structures and experience result in these individual variations. In fact, the behaviors of two individuals could be identical only if their respective genetic structures and environments corresponded exactly. The actual pattern of genetic and environmental determination of individual differences is so complex that behavioral scientists typically start with behavioral differences and work backward to understand relevant genetic and environmental contributions.[7]

In the material to follow, common problems of development will be described. These are the problems which parents and teachers frequently see in children. Of course, at every age quite ordinary problems are of utmost concern to the individual having the problem.

Infancy

To a casual observer, infants may show very similar behaviors. However, parents with more than one child, physicians, and others who are experienced with infants report significant differences among individual infants. Physical differences are obvious. For example, the typical range of weights of newborn infants extends from approximately 5 to 10 pounds. One infant may weigh twice as much as another and yet both may be healthy.

Differences in temperament or personality are also seen at birth.[8] The child psychiatrists Alexander Thomas, Stella Chess, and their associates have followed a large sample of newborns from birth into middle childhood. By means of parental interviews and direct observation, they found a number of relatively persistent traits in infant behavior. Clusters of behavioral traits, such as activity level, social approach, intensity of reaction, and responsiveness to the behavior of others were studied. Thomas and Chess have identified three patterns of infant behavior as "the easy child," the "slow to warm up child," and the "difficult child." A summary of the traits attributed to each pattern is presented in Figure 12.9.

These traits are relatively persistent, but the child's adjustment

Figure 12.8
Infancy
(Erika Stone from Peter Arnold)

7. N. Garmezy, "Models of Etiology for the Study of Children at Risk for Schizophrenia," in *Life History Research in Psychopathology*, eds. M. Roff, L. N. Robins, and M. Pollock, University of Minnesota Press, Minneapolis, 1972, vol. II, pp. 9–34.

8. A. Thomas, S. Chess, and H. G. Birch, *Temperament and Behavior Disorders in Children*, New York University Press, New York, 1968.

Figure 12.9

Categories of Infant Temperament *(Modified from "The Origin of Personality," by Alexander Thomas, Stella Chess and Herbert G. Birch. Copyright © 1970 by Scientific American, Inc. All rights reserved.)*

Type of Child	Activity Level (The Proportion of Active Periods to Inactive Ones.)	Rhythmicity (Regularity of Hunger, Excretion, Sleep and Wakefulness.)	Distractibility (The Degree to Which Extraneous Stimuli Alter Behavior.)	Approach Withdrawal (The Response to a New Object or Person.)
"Easy"	Varies	Very regular	Varies	Positive approach
"Slow to warm up"	Low to moderate	Varies	Varies	Initial withdrawal
"Difficult"	Varies	Irregular	Varies	Withdrawal

depends on the relationships that develop between the child and his or her parents. That is, the difficult child whose behavior is more or less unpredictable thrives with parents who respond well to this pattern. On the other hand, the easy child whose behavior is usually predictable might have parents who expect and value more variability in their children. The studies described here focus on the tolerance patterns of typical parents. The point is that adequate adjustment in childhood requires some degree of correspondence between parental expectations and the child's behavior.[9]

The complexity of infant adjustment is illustrated by the course of maturation of an infant whose birth weight is extremely low. The causes of low birth weight are associated with prematurity, but many other factors are also involved. In fact, some low-birth-weight infants are full term. Poor general health of the mother, inadequate prenatal care, drug use, and poor maternal nutrition before and during pregnancy are just a few of the variables correlated with low birth weight in full term and premature infants.

The consequences of low birth weight are also diverse and gener-

9. L. J. Yarrow, J. L. Rubenstein, and F. A. Pedersen, *Infant and Environment*, John Wiley & Sons, New York, 1975.

Adaptability (The Ease with Which a Child Adapts to Changes in His Environment.)	Attention Span and Persistence (The Amount of Time Devoted to an Activity, and the Effect of Distraction on the Activity.)	Intensity of Reaction (The Energy of Response, Regardless of Its Quality or Direction.)	Threshold of Responsiveness (The Intensity of Stimulation Required to Evoke a Discernible Response.)	Quality of Mood (The Amount of Friendly, Pleasant, Joyful Behavior as Contrasted with Unpleasant, Unfriendly Behavior.)
Very adaptable	High or low	Low or mild	High or low	Positive
Slowly adaptable	High or low	Mild	High or low	Slightly negative
Slowly adaptable	High or low	Intense	High or low	Negative

ally negative.[10] Some effects, like respiratory problems, generally occur soon after birth. Some effects are seen later in childhood and are not predictable from earlier physical and psychological examinations. By school age, some 30 percent of children weighing less than 5 pounds at birth have been referred for problems in school learning, social adjustment, emotional adjustment, retardation, and the like. In contrast, only about 10 percent of the children weighing more than 5 pounds at birth are referred for the same sorts of problems. It should be remembered, however, that most children in both groups are *not* referred for professional help.

The diversity of problems associated with low birth weight illustrates the principle that vulnerability to stress is expressed uniquely in each individual. Furthermore, this vulnerability is displayed both physiologically and behaviorally. Note that most ordinary problems related to low birth weight are not identified until much later. Adequate adaptability in infancy is pervasive among all successful species, including our own. Within very wide limits, the age of

10. L. Wright, "The Theoretical and Research Base for a Program of Early Stimulation, Care and Training of Premature Infants," in *Exceptional Infant Studies in Abnormality*, ed. J. Hellmuth, Brunner/Mazel, New York, 1971, vol. II, pp. 277–304.

attaining traditional developmental milestones such as first word, first step, and so forth cannot serve to predict later development. A large degree of individual variation in these behaviors is to be expected in normal infants.

The Preschool Period

One pattern frequently found in the development of stuttering in preschool children shows the intimate relationship between the behavior of the individual child and the interpretation of that behavior by caretakers.[11] Some time between age two and five virtually all children show speech blocking; that is, the flow of speech is interrupted by short periods of silence. Listening to this pattern, one thinks the child knows more than he or she has words to express. The child's behavior suggests that during these hesitations she or he is searching for the appropriate words to say what is meant.

Most parents accept the hesitations without much concern, and within a few years, the child's speech is fluent. A few parents are concerned about the pauses and reflect their distress in their behavior toward the child. These negative parental reactions focus the child's attention on his or her speech. If one attends carefully to one's own speech, slight flaws and pauses become prominent. The stuttering cycle is established. Every time the child pauses, stress is increased. One effect of increased stress is to further disorganize motor activities, including those involved in speech. This reaction exaggerates the stuttering. This example of an ordinary imperfection becoming a major concern for adults and children extends to many, but not all, problems of early and middle childhood.

A number of behavior patterns are identified as problems by adults responsible for preschool children. These include bed wetting, nail biting, temper tantrums, aggression, and social immaturity. In most cases, these problems moderate with increasing age. Parents and teachers concerned about children's problems often find it helpful to discuss the situation with some professional person or an experienced teacher. In unusual cases, the problems listed above may reflect some serious psychological disturbance. It should be recognized that labeling a child as having a serious problem may in itself produce undesirable consequences.

11. W. Johnson, ed., *The Onset of Stuttering,* University of Minnesota Press, Minneapolis, 1959.

Figure 12.11
School Problems
(Bodhan Hrynewyck)

School Problems

When the child begins formal schooling he or she faces a series of adaptive demands. In current American practice, schooling may begin at any age from three to seven. The child is supposed to conform to expected school behaviors, such as remaining seated, attending to the teacher, and using materials in prescribed ways. Demands of this sort are more strongly emphasized from age six onward, whether or not the child has had kindergarten or nursery school experience. Another set of tasks that are emphasized for three- to six-year-old children relates to conventional social skills such as sharing and taking turns. A third set of academic tasks includes traditional activities in reading and arithmetic. Adequate adaptability implies minimal competency in all three areas.

Children who fail to reach age-appropriate minimal levels constitute problems for elementary school teachers. Often, special help for these children is associated with the assignment of diagnostic labels. These labels are necessarily tentative, and should be easy to change or remove from the child's records and reputation.[12] The most popular labels include hyperkinesis, MBD, and special learning disability.

MBD is the most general diagnostic classification. The acronym

12. N. Hobbs, *The Futures of Children,* Jossey-Bass, San Francisco, 1975.

Figure 12.10
Nursery School
(Inapert Gruttner)

stands for minimal brain damage or minimal brain dysfunction, but there is only weak evidence of verified brain damage among children so labeled.[13] The MBD child presents some pattern of problems in one or more of the three areas: expected school behavior, conventional social behavior, and academic behavior. Some of the test evidence used to classify MBD children is ambiguous and might also be used to indicate immaturity or individual differences within the range of normality. The difficulty of early diagnosis is demonstrated by the fact that 30 percent of all seven-year-olds and 10 percent of eight-year-olds fail to copy a diamond figure correctly. This is one test item used to classify MBD children.

Another frequent label is hyperkinesis, although this is sometimes included as part of the MBD syndrome. *Hyperkinesis* is characterized by restlessness, noisiness, and disobedience.[14] In the school setting the child is easily distracted, talks out of turn, and rarely finishes assigned work. Children labeled hyperkinetic are frequently given so-called paradoxical drugs such as amphetamines, which reduce the activity and alertness of immature organisms. These powerful drugs have undesirable side effects, some of which are known.[15] Medical opinion on the use of these drugs for children is divided, and the evidence on the long-term effects of these drugs is incomplete.

Special learning disabilities are also sometimes included in the MBD classification. The designation *Special Learning Disability* is given to children who have major problems in learning to read or do arithmetic but who have normal intelligence. Reading and arithmetic skills for such children are below the level predicted by their intelligence test performance. True alexia, an inability to learn to read associated with specific neurological damage, is a rare condition and does not apply to most nonreading seven-year-olds. It is the authors' opinion that most learning problems encountered by children in school should be amenable to educational rather than therapeutic procedures. Pseudomedical jargon and faddish treatment frequently result in harm rather than good.

13. M. Hertzig, M. Bortner, and H. G. Birch, "Neurologic Findings in Children Educationally Designated as Brain Damaged," *American Journal of Orthopsychiatry,* 39 (1969), 437–446.

14. M. A. Stewart, F. N. Pitts, Jr., A. G. Craig, and W. Dieruf, "The Hyperactive Child Syndrome," *American Journal of Orthopsychiatry,* 36 (1966), 861–867.

15. B. Fish, "The 'One Child, One Drug' Myth of Stimulants in Hyperkinesis," *Archives of General Psychiatry,* 25 (1971), 193–203.

Adolescence

Many problems persisting into adulthood originate during the adolescent period.[16] The primary adaptive task of the adolescent is to achieve full adult status. A persistent source of difficulty for American middle-class youth is the absence of clearcut criteria for adult status. Although adult status is not clearly defined, a number of the characteristics of adulthood can be listed. These include financial independence, stable sexual-social relationships, and satisfactory work roles. Crises occur during adolescence when the individual is totally dependent on the external social structure for personal identity. Our society provides little coherent information or structure for the adolescent's development of clear ideas of self. By early adolescence the adequately adaptive individual has some idea of his or her strengths and weaknesses. He or she can also evaluate the way he or she is judged by others without undue emotion.

Adolescents who differ markedly from their peers will have more stress than is typical. The most straightforward example of out-of-step development relates to the age of sexual maturity. Late- and early-maturing individuals experience different adjustive demands.

16. B. R. McCandless, *Adolescents: Behavior and Development*, Dryden Press, Hinsdale, Ill., 1970.

The late-maturing male lags behind all of his peers in physical and social maturity. He is childlike in appearance and behavior when most other children look and sometimes act much like adults. He is likely to have social problems with adults and peers. Late-maturing girls have less difficulty than boys. Early-maturing girls are subjected to some social stress, because they are treated as older than they are. Early-maturing males appear to profit from out-of-step development. They are generally more skillful socially with both peers and adults than are other boys.

Adolescence is a period of psychological integration. Emotions, values, and thinking are brought into some degree of harmony in the adaptive individual. When this harmony is not achieved to an acceptable degree, psychological disturbance is indicated in the person's behavior. One must realize that the degree of harmony indicated by behavior is usually greater than what actually exists. No one is quite as well adjusted as his or her public mask indicates. However, the behavior of disturbed individuals does reflect fundamental problems. It is during adolescence that adult psychological problems emerge.

Senescence

The intimate relationship between physiological and psychological functioning is clearly seen in old age.[17] At different points beyond sixty years of age, human beings experience a marked deterioration in various physiological functions. At the same time, some psychological functions show similar patterns of loss. The wide variation in age-related psychological loss must be emphasized. Some individuals make creative contributions to literature when they are well past eighty. Many people past seventy are quite capable of conducting their own affairs. A persistent societal problem relates to the need to support independence among the elderly. Nevertheless, adequate support should be provided for old people *as it is needed.*

One special psychological challenge of old age is to realistically face the changes that occur in one's own behavior and physical state. These changes include loss of stamina, sensory acuity, motor efficiency, and memory. Our own youth-oriented culture does a poor job of helping the elderly adapt. Isolation of the elderly from other age groups is clearly not in their best interest or in the best interest of

17. H. Geist, *The Psychological Aspects of the Aging Process,* Warren H. Green, St. Louis, Mo., 1968.

Figure 12.13 Old Age
(Burk Uzzle/Magnum
Photos, Inc.)

the other groups. Our society makes little or no provision for using the skills and wisdom of older people. Retirement usually means separation from the working world. In many cases the retiree could still contribute if allowed to do so.

| Adaptive Failure |

In this chapter we have not discussed a large number of profound problems in adaptability. Individuals with profound problems are generally isolated from society in either institutional or community settings. Such problems include chronic psychosis, severe mental retardation, and a number of congenital conditions. The student interested in these problems may consult the suggested readings at the end of the chapter. These problems are to some extent uniquely human. Among other species individuals having profound problems would not survive. The ability and desire to sustain these individuals is a human characteristic.

| Summary |

Variations in adaptability have been the focus of this chapter. Population adaptability is a characteristic of species and cultures. Adequate population adaptability is demonstrated when a species or culture is maintaining or increasing population size in a stable situation. Marginal population adaptability is demonstrated when a species or culture appears to be headed for extinction. Baboons and gorillas were presented as examples of adequate and marginal adaptability, respectively, for species. Hutterites and Bushmen were presented as examples of adequate and marginal adaptability, respectively, for human cultures. For both cultures and species, the fit of the groups' characteristics to the demands of the present environment determines adaptability. Any contemporary culture or species is descended from successful predecessors and would probably be successful in some, but not all, environmental situations. The species or culture that is unable to cope with its current environment is marginally adaptive and is likely to disappear.

Individual adaptability is certainly related to reproductive adaptability. However, adaptability in human beings is defined in more complex terms. While the adaptive human being has characteristics that would probably be associated with reproductive adaptability in a subsistence culture, adequate individual adaptability is also demonstrated when an individual has culturally acceptable competence in social and technical skills. The adequately adaptive human being acquires status among peers, has a good selection of mates, and uses and controls a reasonable share of the resources of the group. The adaptive individual is less stressed than marginally adaptive peers and at the same time is more capable of handling stress.

In ontogenetic development there are stages during which adaptive variability is particularly evident. In this chapter adaptive variability in infancy, early childhood, adolescence, and senescence was discussed. Common problems at each of these stages were briefly described.

Defined Terms	Population adaptability	Cultural evolution	Hyperkinesis
		MBD	Special learning
	Individual		disabilities
	adaptability		

Suggested Readings   N. Hobbs, *The Futures of Children,* Jossey-Bass, San Francisco, 1975.
This book is the report of the chairman of the Project on Classification of Exceptional Children of the U.S. Department of Health, Education, and Welfare. Hobbs argues that labeling and classifying exceptional children are necessary for both scientific and practical reasons. Careless and misapplied labels have resulted in harmful

placement and treatment programs. Specific suggestions are made for flexible diagnostic procedures to benefit individual children.

J. A. Hostetler and G. E. Huntington, *The Hutterites in North America,* Holt, Rinehart and Winston, New York, 1967.

This short paperback will supplement the discussion of Hutterite society presented in chapter 12. The book is especially recommended for students majoring in psychology, anthropology, or other social sciences.

I. L. Phillips, *Human Adaptation and Its Failures,* Academic Press, New York, 1968.

In this book, Phillips brings together research studies done over a fifteen-year period. His views on adaptive failure in individuals is similar to that advanced in Chapter 12. Specific and conceptual problems in research are pursued more fully than was possible in Chapter 12.

G. B. Schaller, *The Year of the Gorilla,* University of Chicago Press, Chicago, 1964.

This book is an entertaining account of the author's field study of gorillas. Any student interested in behavior will enjoy this nontechnical description of these fascinating animals.

P. J. Schoeman, *Hunters of the Desert Land,* H. Timmins, Cape Town, 1961.

This book is written for the general reader. It contains a number of Bushman folk tales as well as descriptions of hunting techniques, food sharing patterns, and courtship. It provides a sympathetic view of contemporary Bushmen from a European perspective.

L. L. Schwartz, *The Exceptional Child: A Primer,* Wadsworth, Belmont, Cal., 1975.

A brief introduction to the traditional categories of exceptionality in children. Intellectual, physical, emotional, and social differences are described. This book is written for the college student or layman who wishes to become familiar with this field.

Chapter 13
The Meaning of Development

Developmental change is a characteristic of life. In this book we have been concerned with the development of behavior. Our concern with behavior necessarily includes other aspects of development, such as physical growth. The behavior of developing organisms has been viewed as the outcome of interaction among five predisposing influences: Phylogenetic Set, Ontogenetic Set, Experiential Set, Cultural Set, and Individual Set. These nonindependent determinants provide a framework for understanding development. No behavior is the outcome of any one of these Sets alone, for no Set is ever expressed in isolation. Instead, each Set is expressed in interaction with the other Sets. In each organism, the pattern of interactions among Sets is unique. Thus, behavioral variability among organisms is ever present.

The interaction of Sets insures variability, but this variability has limits. Phylogenetic Set determines the boundaries of variability for a species. At any given time in its life, an organism will express only part of the range of behavior to be shown throughout life. Such age-related boundaries on variability are an expression of Ontogenetic Set. Experiential Set determines the degree to which potential Ontogenetic and Phylogenetic variability is expressed. For example, organisms with similar histories may develop similar behavioral repertoires. Cultural Set functions in much the same way and may be considered as a special kind of Experiential Set. For each organism, Individual Set determines the limits of possible behavior.

Development may be considered as a series of experiments in adaptability. When the limits imposed by Phylogenetic Set no longer permit adaptive success in a particular environmental situation, the species must change or cease to exist. The developing organism is more or less adaptive as a result of the rhythm and pattern of behavior. If individual development is far outside typical developmental patterns for the species, the organism may not survive or may be unlikely to reproduce. Certain environments eliminate the potential for adaptability. Vision does not develop in the dark; social behavior does not develop in isolation.

Cultural Set limits the range of environments; members of a particular culture are better adapted to some environments than others. An urban American would be unlikely to survive in the Kalahari desert. A Bushman would be unlikely to survive in Manhattan. Each individual is a miniature experiment in adaptability. This is the meaning of development.

The Human Species

Homo sapiens, like other species, has some unique characteristics and some traits in common with other organisms. This common heritage should be kept in mind as we discuss human characteristics.

One of the most striking characteristics of *Homo sapiens* is adaptive success. Every continent except Antarctica has been occupied by humans. Our species successfully exploits different ecological niches. We are carnivores, omnivores, and herbivores. We are hunters, gatherers, herdsmen, and farmers. In our most complex industrialized societies, our agriculture and animal husbandry are efficient. Many members of industrialized societies are freed from basic subsistence activities. The freed individual may engage in routine tasks such as working on an assembly line to produce luxury automobiles. On the other hand, freedom from subsistence activities permits people to function as artists and scientists. Success in meeting subsistence needs has permitted great variability in human behavior.

What are the characteristics of this adaptive animal? The following traits are not discussed in order of importance, since the order cannot be determined. The list is not exhaustive but is intended to help us describe ourselves.

Homo sapiens is a social animal. Human beings live in organized groups in which individuals are mutually dependent. One aspect of this dependence is related to basic economic needs, yet many of us are much more conscious of our emotional dependence on others.

Even when physical needs are met, humans suffer greatly in social isolation. Should an isolation-reared human being survive, his or her behavior would at best only approximate typical human behavior. Some workable social structure is found in every successful human group.

Social organization is one of three species typical characteristics that underlie human culture. Technology and language are the other basic components of human culture. Our species has always been a tool maker. It is probable that our species has always had language. The evolution of social organization and language is the history of culture. Culture is the mechanism by which man transmits information across generations and thereby effects long-term adaptive change. Adaptive change not based on biological evolution is one of the special achievements of *Homo sapiens.*

The transmission of culture to successive generations is facilitated by a long period of dependence in infancy and childhood in our species. Under primitive conditions the period of dependence is shorter than in technologically proficient societies. In some societies, adult status comes at or soon after sexual maturity. In the United States, the period of dependence and education may span an additional ten years or so. An extended period of education is necessary for human culture. However, the greatly extended period in which a young person has preadult status in our society is associated with special problems. An unclear definition of adult status is central to many of these problems. Failure to meet young people's needs for productive activity is another source of problems in industrial societies.

Two human traits that have caught the imagination and interest of modern Americans are altruism and aggression. Altruism is seen in behavior that helps someone else and offers no apparent reward to the actor. Aggressive behavior is frequently defined as behavior intended to harm another person. One function of culture is to control aggression and altruism. Untrammeled aggression is obviously maladaptive. Uncontrolled altruism is probably also maladaptive. Both aggression and altruism contribute to adaptive success when channeled to appropriate objects and situations. Cultures, like individuals and species, represent a series of experiments. The optimal level and most productive organization of aggressive and altruistic behavior is presently beyond our wisdom.

Our species may have reached a point in development at which population increase is no longer an indication of adaptability. Our numbers may become so great that the planet cannot support us. Technological progress places additional demands on available resources. The byproducts of technological progress change the environment. Pessimistic predictions are often based on these aspects of modern industrial society. On the other hand, *Homo sapiens* has been and is a superb problem solver. Men and women will no doubt achieve solutions to some current problems that we cannot now foresee. The ability to recognize and describe problems is the first step toward solving them.

The development of a species, like the development of an individual, is a continuous process. Each human generation must face difficult problems to initiate adaptive change. We cannot know which current cultures will give rise to adaptive successors. Western civilization has been a dominant influence in recent history. The next phase of human history may be dominated by cultures developed from other roots. Most readers will share the authors' hope that the best features of Western culture and thought will continue to be a strong, positive influence on human cultural development. However, from the species point of view, the origin of successful cultures is relatively unimportant. Adaptive continuity in our species is protected by the availability of cultural diversity.

<table><tr><td>

The Individual
Organism

</td><td>

Individual variability has been emphasized throughout this book. The enormous range of developmental outcomes is probably about the same for all human groups. Each society and situation favors particular kinds of individuals and is less favorable for others. Many believe that the arrangements used by cultures for educating developing individuals are intended to narrow the range of adult behavior patterns. In fact, the result of education is a widening of that range. Virtually everyone is illiterate if reading is not taught. When reading is taught, reading levels vary widely among individuals. The surest way for a society to promote conformity among its members is to restrict opportunities to learn. This course of action would, of course, limit the adaptability of the entire population.

</td></tr></table>

The same individual characteristics that provide maximal adaptability in one situation may limit adaptability in others. For example, Viking berserkers were valued members of raiding parties. These men were fierce and relatively uncontrolled warriors. Individuals with the same traits might find routine employment in a modern society hard to tolerate. Furthermore, they would be unlikely to conform successfully to the discipline of a modern army. They would be men out of their time and place. A central European peasant of the fifteenth century who was competitive and strongly motivated to better his social position probably led a short and unhappy life. Those same traits are valued and rewarded in contemporary American society.

At any period, individuals may be in specific situations that do not permit realization of their adaptive potential. We can all think of individuals whose temperament and skills are not suited to their vocational role. Had these individuals made other choices, they might well have been successful. Individual adaptability is dependent on a fit between the environment and individual characteristics.

Most individuals could adapt well to a number of situations. As mentioned earlier, the prolonged period of immaturity in our species gives members the opportunity to acquire an adequate experiential background for adult functioning in a variety of settings. One advantage of an extended period of adolescence is the opportunity to defer vocational choices. Particular features of the experiential history of the individual may support or limit adaptive development.

Benign Environments

For our species, a benign environment provides both order and variability. This is true for the physical features of the environment. The orderly arrangement of energy patterns in the environment is essential for animal survival. The benign physical environment is reasonably predictable. On the other hand, variation even in the physical environment is also essential. A static physical environment would soon produce a chaotic psychological state. If an organism develops in such an environment, it encounters extreme difficulty with any subsequent environmental change.

A benign social environment, while more difficult to describe, is also ordered and variable. Developing children clearly need a degree of structure in their social environment. At the same time, some flexibility in the social environment of children is essential. Social order and variability are provided by every human society. The particular balance between order and variability differs among cultures, but the range is somewhat narrow. The fact that many individuals have successfully adapted to cultures not their own is evidence for similarity among cultures and flexibility among individuals. Since culture is a human characteristic, cultural similarity could be an expected expression of Phylogenetic Set.

In the last few pages we have concluded our effort to present a framework for understanding development. We now turn to the implications of the point of view developed in this book for comparative psychology, developmental psychology, and education. We are considerably more confident of our ground in the first two areas than in the third. Our ideas about education are, therefore, more tentative than are our thoughts about our own disciplines. However, views from outside education are frequently helpful to education.

Implications for Comparative Psychology

The most important contribution this book can make to comparative psychology is to join others in stressing that *Homo sapiens* is an animal species that should be studied from that point of view.[1] Of course, no

1. U. Bronfenbrenner, "Early Deprivation in Mammals: Across-Species Analysis," in *Early Experience and Behavior, The Psychobiology of Development*, eds. G. Newton and S. Levine, Charles C. Thomas, Springfield, Ill., 1971, pp. 627–764; G. Mitchell, "Com-

comparative psychologist would deny this statement in the abstract. Many students of animal behavior frequently ignore *Homo sapiens* or else use some specific animal as a model for *Homo sapiens.* Either of these approaches may yield valuable data. In the authors' opinion, the results of investigation increase in value when a broader perspective is taken in interpreting these results.

Naturally, human beings have a strong interest in their own species. One concern many readers share may be stated as a question: "What does study of another species have to do with understanding human behavior?" If *Homo sapiens* is viewed as an animal species, answers to this question are suggested. Study might determine the degree of phylogenetic relationship between our species and others. When several species have a close phyletic relationship, hypotheses about the behavior of one species may be developed from studies of the others with more confidence. Another source of support for generalization from one species to another may be drawn from ecological similarities among several species. The interest in social carnivores seen in the studies of wolves and hyenas discussed in earlier chapters is based on ecological similarities between these animals and one view of early man.

Phylogenetic and ecological considerations suggest that study of certain species is particularly apt to produce hypotheses about human behavior, yet there is no good basis for eliminating any species as a possible source of principles that would aid in understanding human development. Because all life on this planet is related, information about the behavior of any species is potentially helpful for understanding others.

Animals are frequently used as models for human-oriented research. This is particularly likely if the procedures to be employed cannot ethically be applied to humans, as in the study of pain or of harmful drugs. In evaluating such studies, a view of *Homo sapiens* as an animal species will help to emphasize the tentative nature of the results. Any animal model for humans can provide only suggestive information about humans. Results must be interpreted in terms of known similarities and differences between the two species in question. We are not suggesting that generalizations should not be made.

parative Development of Social and Emotional Behavior," in *Perspecttives in Animal Behavior,* ed. G. Bermant, Scott Foresman, Glenview, Ill., 1973, pp. 102–128; and H. L. Rheingold, "A Comparative Psychology of Development," in *Early Behavior Comparative and Developmental Approaches,* eds. H. W. Stevenson, E. H. Hess, and H. L. Rheingold, John Wiley, New York, 1967, pp. 279–293.

They should and must. But they should be made carefully and tentatively, and when these generalizations result in applications to educational, medical, or child care procedures, the effects of such procedures must continue to be carefully evaluated.

Animal behavior studies cited throughout this book have come from many disciplines. The contributions of physiologists, zoologists, anthropologists, and psychologists have been included. Laboratory experiments, field experiments, animal case studies, and observational studies in the laboratory and field were discussed. This catholic acceptance of many different approaches to the study of animal behavior is an essential characteristic of a modern comparative psychology.

Implications for Developmental Psychology

Traditionally, developmental psychology has focused almost exclusively on human development, although there is no logical or scientific basis for this specialization. Certain areas of interest, such as the study of vocabulary growth, have been emphasized in the developmental literature. These interests have led to age norms for various attributes of children and to descriptions of individual differences for these attributes. Another area of interest in developmental work is the study of marginal individuals and marginal environments. Investigations concerning the effects of rearing in restricted institutional environments and studies of the behavior of retarded children fit into this category. Only recently has research been directed toward understanding developmental processes at more than a descriptive level.

When human beings are viewed as members of a species, as they are in this book, the directions most appropriate for developmental psychology become clear. The study of individual differences can come to be viewed as the study of individual experiments in adaptation, and some traditional areas mentioned above can be reevaluated from this perspective.

Much of the research literature on individual differences has emphasized variables correlated with IQ differences. These IQ measures reflect abilities that may be quite culture specific. These measures are fairly good predictors of the performance of middle-class children in middle-class schools, but cognitive and intellectual development might more profitably be studied from a wider perspective. The public schools are not the only context for cognitive adaptability, and therefore behaviors that correlate with school performance should not be the only focus of studies of intellectual development. Studies of cognitive functioning and development in nonacademic contexts present an exciting possible area of study. The role of culturally differing environments for intellectual development has only recently received some attention.

The study of marginal environments could be improved by a clearer concept of human needs. Sometimes any environment that differs from the cultural ideal of the observer is judged to be deficient. Early environments for children can vary widely and still provide an adequate basis for subsequent development. Cross-cultural studies of typical early environments would provide a data base from which to conceptualize. A focus on the human species reduces the probability of cultural provincialism.

Developmental psychology is dependent on information from many sources, and comparative psychology is one of these. No single specific method is adequate for the scientific study of development. Clinical reports, anthropological studies, field observations of typical behavior, and observational and experimental laboratory investigations are some of the useful sources of information for this field. It must be obvious to the reader that the authors believe that data must be interpreted. Interpretation is made not only by the investigator but also by the scientific and lay public. In this book we have offered a conceptual framework for the reader's consideration. Like all scientific endeavors, this conceptualization is based on available evidence but is carried beyond that evidence. The reader should feel free to impose his or her own structure on the body of knowledge presented in this book. We will likewise feel free to change our ideas as time goes by.

Implications for Education

Individual variation has been repeatedly emphasized in our presentation so far. The experienced teacher will recognize that this emphasis is indeed appropriate. In a typical sixth grade class, the tested reading levels will range from third through ninth grade. Children also vary considerably in their profile of abilities. A child may score at the third grade in mathematics and the tenth grade in reading. This striking inter- and intraindividual variability poses problems for the classroom teacher but at the same time provides a source of stimulation and challenge. Sometimes the teacher is advised to tutor each child individually. This is neither practical nor necessarily effective. Good teachers develop techniques that enable them to teach most of the children in their classes.

Individual children may prove refractory to the best efforts of most teachers. However, in our opinion, the education of children is not exclusively the province of the professional teacher. Other individuals who know the child are also potential teachers. Parents, siblings, and peers are teachers in many cultures. Older persons, actual and adoptive grandparents, often serve as educators. Earlier in our society, teaching functions were assumed by family and friends. The teacher can and should call on these lay teachers. This use of family, friends, and peers may be especially helpful where the teacher and students are from different subcultures and may not share attitudes about education, teaching styles, or personal goals.

As a system, the educational enterprise has been engaged in a proliferation of classifications for individual children. The Educable Mentally Retarded label was the earliest, coming into wide use with the development of intelligence tests. Wide use of other labels such as Emotionally Disturbed, Learning Disability, Minimal Brain Dysfunction, and so forth are more recent. These classifications generally have led to segregation of questionable value for the child and have not substantially eased the teacher's burden. Some children must be removed from the regular classroom. In some cases the child may profit from such special treatment, while in others, special classes are for the benefit of the children who remain in the regular classroom.

From the point of view of species typical development, the criteria for special designations and treatments must be regarded as arbitrary and sometimes even cavalier. The norms from which these specially labeled children deviate are too often based on large populations. The particular school and classroom population characteristics are seldom adequately reflected in the diagnostic procedures used in these cases. For example, it is not uncommon for the average IQ in a public school to be 80 or below. Such situations call for reconsideration of standards for special educational placement.

A child with special problems might be considered by the teacher to be a challenging individual experiment in teaching. In this light, most children could be taught by a regular teacher with available professional assistance.

Over the past twenty-five years the American educational system has been exposed to upheavals as have other institutions in the society. One type of response has been the widespread advocacy of new academic content and methods. Classroom observations and conversation with teachers suggest that these innovations are not carried out as fully as the educational literature would have us believe. The teacher must still apply his or her understanding of principles and experience to particular situations and particular students. Like other professionals, the teacher selects what is useful and discards the rest. The most important contribution made by new ideas, techniques, or content is to permit the professional teacher to rethink the problems presented. For example, some of the methods and content of modern mathematics fit poorly into the concepts of teachers, students, and parents. The initial efforts to incorporate modern mathematics into the teaching of the 1960s generally harmed the mathematical development of elementary school students. Fortunately, some teachers tempered the new materials with more traditional approaches. Some elements of these programs are found in contemporary elementary and secondary teaching. The resulting programs are stronger for having these ideas.

Teachers have also been bombarded with recommendations for specific novel approaches for classroom management. The authors believe that classroom management is an individual art. Techniques for classroom management must fit the personal traits of the teacher. General recommendations on how to maintain class discipline are about as helpful as specific instructions on how to be a good parent. The classroom is not a therapeutic community, and teachers cannot perform the functions of social workers or other mental health workers. The effectiveness of formal psychotherapeutic settings provides little evidence that more settings of this kind should be provided.

The authors believe that teachers should have knowledge and understanding of a wide range of individual children. Children will vary in their response to any teacher. The teacher should feel neither unduly guilty about the ones who have trouble nor unduly proud of those who do unusually well. The teacher should be supported in attempting to meet the needs of many different children. This is a complex and frustrating task. The teacher who recognizes some failure as well as some success has no basis for guilt.

Conclusion

This concludes our presentation of the development of behavior. Our intention has been to present a coherent framework for understanding development. We have drawn material from studies of human and animal behavior. We are psychologists, and our interpretations are colored by our point of view. However, we have gathered information from many disciplines. We feel the breadth made possible by this approach is valuable for both student and teacher.

The student should realize that many aspects of development and different theoretical orientations that are covered elsewhere were not included in this book. We hope the interested student will find this perspective useful as he or she pursues other studies in behavioral science.

Throughout, we have considered all contemporary species as evolving. Our species has a history and a future. We have attempted to view behavior from this point of view. The history of the species, the culture, and the individual always are to be seen in present behavior. The universals and particulars always interact. As much as we study present behavior and its foundations, the future behavior of the species and the individual cannot be predicted with certainty.

Glossary

Accommodation   Changes in psychological structure or schemas resulting from a poor fit between schemas and environmental information.

Adaptation Training   A period of training preceding data collection during which the animal is made familiar with the apparatus.

Affection   Feelings and motivation associated with social attachments.

Allele   Variation at a gene location in a particular type of chromosome.

Allopatric   Refers to different related species that occupy different geographical areas.

Altricial   Refers to birds naked at hatching that are brooded and fed by their parents; also refers to animals relatively helpless at birth.

Amblystoma   A salamander, a lizardlike amphibian.

Androgens   Male hormones that have an important role in sexual development and functioning.

Anxiety   An internal state representing anticipated punishment or discomfort.

Assimilation   Incorporation of environmental information into currently organized schemas.

Attachment   A tendency to strive to gain or maintain social or physical contact with an individual of the same or a different species.

Attention   An internal state in which the organism is alerted so that the influence of some stimuli are increased and that of other stimuli decreased.

Babbling   Sounds made by an infant that are not understood by adults.

Chromosomes   Long, complex DNA molecules that carry genetic information.

Circle of Knowing   Piaget's version of a superschema in which various schemas are integrated.

Clique   A small, informally organized group of same-sex adolescents.

Concrete Operations   The state of intellectual development in which manipulation of symbols only takes place when the objects and operations are more or less related to known referents.

Conditioned Response   A response that occurs after training upon presentation of the conditioned stimulus. This response is similar but not equivalent to the unconditioned response.

Conditioned Stimulus   A stimulus that produces the desired response after training. Before training this stimulus is called the conditioning stimulus.

Conditioning Stimulus   A stimulus that does not produce the desired response before training that is selected as the training stimulus. After training this stimulus is called the conditioned stimulus.

Conspecific   Refers to members of the same species.

Consummatory   Refers to a response that terminates a behavioral sequence and changes the motivational state.

Contraprepared   A relationship between stimulation and response pattern that cannot be learned or can be learned only with great difficulty after long periods of exposure.

Correlation Coefficient   A statistical term that represents the degree of association between two variables. Although this coefficient may have values between 0 and 1.00, it is *not* a percentage.

Critical Period   A narrow age span during which a behavioral pattern or characteristic develops if it is to develop at all.

Cultural Evolution   Sequential adaptive change in cultures.

Cultural Set   Influence of a culture on the behavior of members of that culture.

Demes   Relatively small, partially isolated breeding groups of a species.

Differential Reinforcement   With reference to sex-role development, encouragement of behavior that conforms to appropriate sex-role standards and discouragement of behavior that does not conform to those standards.

Diploid   Refers to a cell that has a pair of chromosomes of each type characteristic of the species. In contrast, haploid cells have a single chromosome of each type.

Dipper Training   A shaping procedure that results in a rat consistently drinking sugar-water presented by a retractable dipper mechanism.

Dominant   Refers to members of a group who control resources and direct the behavior of others.

Effective Environment   Those parts of the environment that influence the behavior of an individual.

Equilibration   The ultimate balance of all internal and external forces operating on an individual. This ultimate balance is not attainable in living organisms.

Equilibrium   A specific set of balanced relationships between the environment and the organism's psychological structure or schemas.

Estrogens   Female hormones that have an important role in sexual development and functioning.

Estrus   A period of sexual receptivity associated with ovulation in many species.

Experiential Set   The influence of past and present environments on behavior.

Extinction   Repeated presentation of the conditioned stimulus without the unconditioned stimulus. This normally results in a decrease and finally in disappearance of the conditioned response.

Figure   Those features of a stimulus pattern that are the focus of perception.

Fixed Action Pattern   Relatively stereotyped behavior patterns in which an organized sequence of responses is made to a particular stimulus.

Form Equivalence   A concept in which two or more geometric forms are considered as being the same.

Formal Operations   The last stage of intellectual development. In this stage, symbolic manipulations may be performed that do not directly refer to actual objects or events in the physical world.

Functional Invariants   According to Piaget, the intellectual processes of organization and adaptation that do not change with maturation.

Gene   Location on a chromosome related to some specific trait.

Genetic Drift   Changes in a population gene pool associated with factors other than selective pressures.

Genotype   The genetic material inherited from the parents, from which physical and behavioral traits develop.

Good Continuation   The tendency to see as a unit lines that continue at a regular rate of curvature, including straight lines. In contrast, irregular or broken lines are not perceived as a unit.

Good Form   A tendency to see regular geometric figures as units.

Graphemic   Refers to written or printed representation of spoken language.

Ground   Those features of a stimulus pattern outside the focus of attention.

Habituation   A process in which a stimulus pattern ordinarily eliciting attention is ignored.

Haploid   Refers to a cell that has a single chromosome of each type characteristic of the species. In contrast, diploid cells have a pair of chromosomes representing each type.

Harem   A group of females who are the mates of one male.

Heritability Ratio   A mathematical term that represents the proportion of trait variation in a population attributed to genetic inheritance.

Heterozygous   An individual is heterozygous for a trait if he or she may pass more than one kind of gene for that trait on to offspring.

Holophrastic   Refers to one-word utterances by a young child.

Homeostasis   The orientation of an organism toward a state of internal equilibrium.

Homozygous   An individual is homozygous for a trait if he or she can pass only one kind of gene for that trait on to offspring.

Hormones   Chemical products released directly into the blood stream that regulate or modify cellular activity.

Hyperkinesis   A label applied to children reported to be restless, noisy, and disobedient.

Identification   A process in the development of personality in which an individual assumes as his own the characteristics or behavior of another person.

Imprinting   A process of early social or object attachment found in precocial birds. Imprinting usually involves a following response.

Inbred Strains   Groups sharing genetic characteristics as a result of breeding organisms from the same litters.

Individual Adaptability   Adaptive success of an individual organism is evidenced by access to mates and to the resources available to the group.

Individual Set   The influence on behavior of unique individual characteristics. This Set means that even when all other variables influencing behavior are uniform there is individual variability in behavior.

Instrumental Learning   Learning in which reinforcement or reward is obtained after a desired response is made. In this text operant conditioning and instrumental learning are considered roughly equivalent.

Kineses   Changes in movement in response to a specific stimulus pattern.

Learning   Changes in behavior associated with experience or practice.

Learning Disposition   An organism's tendency easily to attain behaviors associated with survival or reproductive success for members of its species.

Learning Set   Problem-solving schemas that permit the organism to master problems of a general type.

Longitudinal Studies   Studies in which the same individuals are observed over a long period of time.

Macaque   A member of an old world monkey genus. Species of this genus occupy areas in Asia and the north coast of Africa.

MBD   Minimal Brain Damage, or Minimal Brain Dysfunction. A diagnostic label applied to a variety of children who have problems in school learning, school behavior, and social behavior. There may or may not be indications of neurological or physiological problems.

Morpheme   A basic unit of meaning in language at the word level.

Mutation   Changes in the molecular structure of the chromosome.

Nearness   A tendency for elements in a stimulus pattern that are close together to be seen as a unit.

Objective Environment   The environment as described from an outsider's point of view.

Observational Learning   In reference to sex role development, a process underlying a child's imitation of behavior of same-sex adults.

Ontogenetic Set   Influence of time-dependent processes on behavior. These time-dependent processes involve the interaction of genetic makeup and the environmental history of the organism.

Open Words   In grammar describing the language of two-year-olds, a relatively large number of words used infrequently in two-word sentences.

Operant Conditioning   A procedure in which the organism is rewarded only after making the desired response.

Organization   Refers to behavioral organization in which each aspect of behavior is integrated and coordinated with other aspects.

Orienting Response   An integrated pattern of behavior indicating attention. This pattern may include head and body orientation, changes in motor activity, and eye movements.

Ova   The primary female reproductive cells (eggs).

Pair Formation   A more or less exclusive long-term relationship between heterosexual mates.

Perception   The identification and interpretation of environmental features.

Phenocopy   Several phenotypic or expressed traits that are equivalent but have different genetic bases.

Phenotype   The physical and behavioral traits exhibited by an organism.

Phonemes   Categories of the sounds of a language.

Phonetic Methods   Techniques for teaching reading emphasizing sound-letter correspondence.

Phylogenetic Set   A predisposing influence on behavior that increases the probability that the behavior of an organism will be typical for members of its species.

Physiological Drive (Primary Drive)   A motive that has a recognizable physiological basis such as hunger, thirst, or pain avoidance.

Pivot Words   In the grammar describing the language of a two-year-old, a small number of words that occur in two-word sentences in combination with many other words.

Pleiotropic   Refers to a gene locus that may affect many phenotypic traits.

Polygenetic   A system in which several gene sites interact to influence a trait.

Population   An interbreeding group of animals, all members of the same species.

Population Adaptability   Adaptive success of a group of organisms is indicated by a stable or increasing population.

Precocial   Originally used to describe birds hatched with down that show early locomotor patterns; also used to designate mammals born at a relatively mature stage of development that show early locomotor patterns.

PreOperational Stage   The stage of intellectual development during which the cognitive structures necessary for concrete operations develop.

Prepared   A relationship between stimulation and response patterns that is easily learned by the organism.

Primary Drive (Physiological Drive)   A motive that has a recognizable physiological basis such as hunger, thirst, or pain avoidance.

Pseudohermaphrodites   Animals with both male and female genital traits who are members of a normally bisexual species.

Readiness   A level of physical and/or psychological maturity before which particular behavior patterns can be acquired with great difficulty or not at all.

Reflex   A more or less automatic response to a specific stimulus.

Reinforcer   Anything that increases rates of responding.

Releaser   A pattern of stimulation that initiates a Fixed Action Pattern.

Rendezvous Site   In the social behavior of wolves, an area where older pups are left during the hunt.

Rut   The period of intensive breeding in bison and other ungulates.

Schema   An internal organizer mediating information from the environment, from previous experience, and from responses.

Selection   Selective adaptive change in a population gene pool.

Selective Breeding   Refers to studies in which the scientist selects organisms with particular physical or behavioral traits to reproduce.

Semantics   The analysis of meaning in a language at the level of sentences and connected discourse.

Sensitive Period   An age span that is an optimal period for the development of specific behavioral or physical characteristics.

Sensory-Motor Stage   In Piaget's theory, the earliest period of intellectual development focusing on the basic behaviors involved in looking at objects, grasping objects, and the like.

Set   A predisposing influence on behavior that either increases or decreases the probability of a developmental or behavioral event.

Sexual Imprinting   In some bird species, preference for sex partners of the same species as the mother figure first encountered after hatching.

Shaping   A procedure in which reward is selectively presented for behavior approaching the desired pattern. As the training proceeds, the rewarded behavior begins to approximate the desired outcome.

Sign Stimulus   A stimulus associated with a Fixed Action Pattern. The term is roughly equivalent to releaser.

Similarity   A tendency for objects that appear to be alike to be perceived as a unit.

Social Animals   Animals who live in groups in their natural habitat.

Special Learning Disability   A label given children whose tested IQ is average or above average but who have major problems in reading or less often in arithmetic.

Species Typical   Behavior and development characteristic of most members of a species.

Sperm   The primary male reproductive cells.

Subspecies   A relatively isolated breeding group within a species, which has developed distinguishable characteristics.

Superschema   A level of psychological organization that combines or ties together the specific schemas for information from sensory and motor systems.

Sympatric   Refers to several related species that occupy the same general locale.

Syntax   The grammar or arrangement of morphemes in a language.

System   Behavioral system, wherein each response contributes to a whole set of behavior involved in goal-directed activity.

Target Organs   Organs that have specific sensitivity to particular hormones.

Taxes   Directional orientations toward or away from a source of stimulation.

Tracheotomized   Refers to a surgical procedure in which the windpipe is opened and a tube inserted.

Unconditioned Response   A response pattern of interest consistently produced by a particular stimulus prior to training.

Unconditioned Stimulus   A stimulus that consistently produces a response pattern before training is begun.

Unprepared   A relationship between stimulation and response patterns that can be learned slowly through extensive experience.

Bibliography

Ainsworth, M. D. *Infancy in Uganda.* Johns Hopkins Press, Baltimore, 1967.

Altman, M. "Naturalistic Studies of Maternal Care in Moose and Elk." In *Maternal Behavior in Mammals,* H. L. Rheingold. John Wiley and Sons, New York, 1963, pp. 223–253.

Altmann, S. A., and J. Altmann. *Baboon Ecology.* University of Chicago Press, Chicago, 1970.

Anastasi, A. *Differential Psychology.* MacMillan, New York, 1958. pp. 298–299.

Ardrey, R. *African Genesis.* Dell Publishing, New York, 1967.

Aronson, L. A. "Hormones and Reproductive Behavior." In *Comparative Endocrinology,* A. Gorbman. John Wiley, New York, 1959, pp. 98–120.

Barnes, B. M. *Mothers, Peers, and Toys as Stimuli for Locomoting Infants under Two Years of Age.* Ph.D. Dissertation, Louisiana State University, 1973.

Bastock, M. *Courtship and Ethological Study.* Aldine, Chicago, 1967, pp. 40–45.

Bayley, N. "Comparisons of Mental and Motor Test Scores for Ages One-Fifteen Months by Sex, Birth Order, Race, Geographical Location, and Education of Parents." *Child Development,* 36 (1965), 379–411.

Beach, F. A. *Hormones and Behavior.* Harper, New York, 1948.

Beals, A. R. *Gopalpur — A South Indian Village.* Holt, Rinehart and Winston, New York, 1962.

Bernard, J. *The Future of Marriage.* Bantam Books, New York, 1972.

Bjerre, J. *Kalahari.* Hill and Wang, New York, 1960.

Bloom, B. S. *Stability and Change in Human Characteristics.* John Wiley, New York, 1964.

Bower, T. G. R. *Development in Infancy.* W. H. Freeman, San Francisco, 1974, pp. 83–84.

Bower, T. G. R. "Discrimination of Depth in Premotor Infants." *Psychonomic Science,* 1 (1964), 368.

Bowlby, J. *Attachment and Loss: Attachment.* Basic Books, New York, 1969, vol. I.

Bowlby, J. "The Nature of the Child's Tie to the Mother." *International Journal of Psychoanalysis,* 39 (1958), 350–373.

Bowlby, J. "Separation Anxiety: A Critical Review of the Literature." *Journal of Child Psychology and Psychiatry,* 1 (1961), 251–269.

Brecher, R., and E. Brecher, eds. *An Analysis of Human Sexual Response.* Little, Brown, Boston, 1966.

Bremmer, D. "Bob and Barbara and Mike and . . .?" *Los Angeles Times,* June 17, 1973. Cited in Coleman and Hammen.

Bridges, K. "Emotional Development in Early Infancy." *Child Development,* 3 (1935), 324–341.

Broderick, C. "Damn Those Gloomy Prophets — The Family's Here to Stay." *Los Angeles Times,* June 17, 1973, Cited in Coleman and Hammen.

Bronfenbrenner, U. *Two Worlds of Childhood.* Simon and Schuster, New York, 1970.

Brown, J. H. N. *Basic Endocrinology for Students of Biology and Medicine.* F. A. Davis, Philadelphia, 1966.

Brown, R. *A First Language.* Harvard University Press, Cambridge, Mass., 1973.

Burgess, E. W., and P. Wallin. *Engagement and Marriage.* Lippincott, Philadelphia, 1953.

Butler, R. A. "Curiosity in Monkeys." *Scientific American,* 180 (1954), 70–76.

Cannon, W. B. *The Wisdom of the Body.* W. W. Norton, New York, 1932.

Carmichael, L. "The Development of Behavior in Vertebrates Experimentally Removed from the Influence of External Stimulation." *Psychological Review,* 33 (1926), 51–58.

Carmichael, L. "Onset and Early Development of Behavior." In *Carmichael's Manual of Child Psychology,* ed. P. H. Mussen. John Wiley and Sons, New York, 1970, vol I, pp. 447–563.

Casler, L. "This Thing Called Love Is Pathological." *Psychology Today,* 3 (1969), 184+.

Cattell, P. *The Measurement of the Intelligence of Infants and Young Children.* Psychological Corporation, New York, 1940.

Cavin, R. S. *The American Family.* Crowell, New York, 1963.

Chall, J. S. *Learning to Read: The Great Debate.* McGraw-Hill, New York, 1967.

Cole, M., J. Gay, J. Glick, and D. W. Sharp. *The Cultural Context of Learning and Thinking.* Basic Books, New York, 1971.

Coleman, J. S. *The Adolescent Society.* Free Press, New York, 1961.

Coleman, J. C., and C. L. Hammen. *Contemporary Psychology and Effective Behavior.* Scott Foresman, Glenview, Ill., 1974.

Coleman, J. S. "Scholastic Effects of the Social System." In *Adolescent Development: Readings in Research and Theory,* ed. M. Gold and E. Douvan. Allyn & Bacon, Boston, 1971.

Conger, J. J. "A New Morality: Sexual Attitudes and Behavior of Contemporary Adolescents." In *Basic and Contemporary Issues in Developmental Psychology,* ed. P. H. Mussen, J. J. Conger, and J. Kagan. Harper and Row, New York, 1975.

Dale, P. S. *Language Development.* Dryden Press, Hinsdale, Ill., 1972.

Dane, B., and W. G. Van der Kloot. "Analysis of the Display of the Goldeneye Duck." *Behaviour,* 22 (1964), 282–328.

Dearborn, W. F., and J. W. M. Rothney. *Predicting the Child's Development.* Sci-Art Publishers, Cambridge, Mass., 1941.

Dember, W. N. "The New Look in Motivation." *American Scientist,* 53 (1965), 409–427.

Dennis, W. *The Hopi Child.* John Wiley, New York, 1940.

Dennis, W., and Y. Sayegh. "The Effect of Supplementary Experiences upon the Behavioral Development of Infants in Institutions." *Child Development,* 36 (1965), 81–90.

Dethier, V. G., and E. Stellar. *Animal Behavior,* 3d ed. Prentice-Hall, Englewood Cliffs, N.J., 1970.

Dilger, W. C. "The Behavior of LoveBirds." *Scientific American,* 206 (1962), 89–99.

Dobzhansky, T. *Genetics and the Origin of Species.* Columbia University Press, New York, 1941.

Douvan, E., and J. Adelson, *The Adolescent Experience.* John Wiley, New York, 1966.

Ehrhardt, A. A., R. Epstein, and J. Money, "Fetal Androgens and Female Gender Identity in the Early Treated Andrenogenital Syndrome." *John Hopkins Medical Journal,* 122 (1968), 160–167.

Ehrhardt, A. A., and J. Money. "Progestin-induced Hermaphroditism: IQ and Psychosexual Identity in a Study of Ten Girls." *Journal of Sex Research,* 3 (1967), 83–100.

Eibl-Eibesfeldt, I. *Ethology.* Tran. E. Klinghammer. Holt, Rinehart and Winston, New York, 1970.

Erlenmeyer-Kimling, L., J. Hirsch, and J. M. Weiss. "Studies in Experimental Genetics: Selection and Hybridization Analysis of Individual Differences in the Sign of Geotaxis." *Journal of Comparative and Physiological Psychology,* 55 (1962), 722–731.

Erlenmeyer-Kimling, L., and L. F. Jarvik. "Genetics and Intelligence: A Review." *Science,* 142 (1963), 1477–1479.

Escalona, S. K. *The Roots of Individuality.* Aldine, Chicago, 1968.

Espenschade, A. S., and M. M. Eckert. *Motor Development.* Charles Merrill, Columbus, Ohio, 1967.

Evans, D. C. "Computer Logic and Memory." In *Information, A Scientific American Book.* W. H. Freeman, San Francisco, 1966, pp. 17–39.

Fish, B. "The 'One Child, One Drug' Myth of Stimulants in Hyperkinesis." *Archives of General Psychiatry,* 25 (1971), 193–203.

Fisher, A. E., and E. B. Hale. "Stimulus Determinants of Sexual and Aggressive Behavior in Male Domestic Fowl." *Behaviour,* 10 (1957), 309–323.

Flavell, J. H. *The Developmental Psychology of Jean Piaget.* Van Nostrand, Princeton, N. J., 1963.

Fraenkel, G., and D. Gunn. *The Orientation of Animals.* Dover, New York, 1940.

Freud, A., and S. Dann. "An Experiment in Group Upbringing." *Psychoanalytic Study of the Child,* 6 (1951), 127–168.

Fromme, A. "An Experimental Study of the Factors of Maturation and Practice in the Behavioral Development of the Embryo of the Frog *Rana pipiens.*" *Genetic Psychology Monographs,* 24 (1941), 219–256.

Furth, H. G. *Piaget and Knowledge.* Prentice-Hall, Englewood Cliffs, N.J., 1969.

Garai, J. E., and A. Scheinfeld. "Sex Differences in Mental and Behavioral Traits." *Genetic Psychology Monographs,* 77 (1968), pp. 169–299.

Garcia, J., D. J. Kimeldorf, and R. A. Koelling. "Conditioned Aversion to Saccharin Resulting from Exposure to Gamma Radiation." *Science,* 122 (1955), 157–158.

Garcia, J., D. J. Kimeldorf, and R. A. Koelling. "The Use of Ionizing Radiation as a Motivating Stimulus." *Psychological Review,* 68 (1961), 383–395.

Gardner, B. T., and R. A. Gardner. "Two-Way Communication with an Infant Chimpanzee." In *Behavior of Nonhuman Primates*, ed. A. Schrier and F. Stollnitz. Academic Press, New York, 1971, vol. IV, pp. 117–184.

Gardner, R. A., and B. T. Gardner. "Teaching Sign Language to a Chimpanzee." *Science,* 165 (1969), 664–672.

Garmezy, N. "Children at Risk: The Search for Antecedents of Schizophrenia. Part II: Ongoing Research Programs, Issues, and Intervention." *Schizophrenia Bulletin,* No. 9 (Summer, 1974), 55–125.

Garmezy, N. "Models of Etiology for the Study of Children at Risk for Schizophrenia." In *Life History Research in Psychopathology,* ed. M. Roff, L. N. Robins, and M. Pollock. University of Minnesota Press, Minneapolis, 1972, vol. II, pp. 9–34.

Gates, R. R. *Human Genetics.* Macmillan, New York, 1946.

Gay, J., and M. Cole. *The New Mathematics and an Old Culture.* Holt, Rinehart and Winston, New York, 1967.

Geist, H. *The Psychological Aspects of the Aging Process.* Warren H. Green, St. Louis, Mo., 1968.

Gesell, A. L., H. Thompson, and C. S. Amatruda. *Infant Behavior: Its Genesis and Growth.* McGraw-Hill, New York, 1934.

Gibson, E. J. "Learning to Read." *Science,* 148 (1965), 1066–1072.

Gibson, E. J. *Principles of Perceptual Learning and Development.* Appleton-Century-Crofts, New York, 1969.

Gibson, J. J. *The Senses Considered as Perceptual Systems.* Houghton Mifflin, Boston, 1966, pp. 31–58.

Gordon, H. "Mental and Scholastic Tests among Retarded Children." Pamphlet No. 44, London Board of Education, 1923. Cited in Anastasi, 1958, pp. 522–523.

Gottlieb, G. "Ontogenesis of Sensory Function in Birds and Mammals." In *The Biopsychology of Development,* ed. E. Tobach, L. R. Aronson, and E. Shaw. Academic Press, New York, 1971, pp. 67–128.

Hackett, C. F. *A Course in Modern Linguistics.* University of Chicago Press, Chicago, 1958.

Harlow, H. F. "Learning Set and Error Factor Theory." In *Psychology: A Study of a Science,* ed. S. Koch. McGraw-Hill, New York, 1959, vol. II, pp. 492–537.

Harlow, H. F. "Love in Infant Monkeys." *Scientific American,* 200 (1959), 68–74.

Harlow, H. F., and M. K. Harlow. "The Affectional Systems." In *Behavior of Nonhuman Primates,* ed. A. M. Schrier, H. F. Harlow, and F. Stollnitz. Academic Press, New York, 1965, vol. II, pp. 287–334.

Harlow, H. F. and M. K. Harlow. "Learning to Love." *American Scientist,* 54 (1966), 244–272.

Harlow, H. F., M. K. Harlow, and E. W. Hansen. "The Maternal Affectional System in Monkeys." In *Maternal Behavior in Mammals,* ed. H. L. Rheingold. John Wiley and Sons, New York, 1963, pp. 254–281.

Harlow, H. F., M. K. Harlow, and S. J. Soumi. "From Thought to Therapy: Lessons from a Primate Laboratory." *American Scientist,* 59 (1971), 538–549.

Harlow, H. F., J. L. McGaugh, and R. F. Thompson. *Psychology.* Albion, San Francisco, 1971, pp. 42–105.

Harlow, H. F., and R. R. Zimmerman. "Affectional Responses in the Infant Monkey." *Science,* 130 (1959), 421–432.

Hartup, W. R. "Peer Interaction and Social Organization." In *Carmichael's Manual of Child Psychology,* ed. P. H. Mussen. John Wiley and Sons, New York, 1970, vol. II, pp. 361–456.

Hass, H. *The Human Animal.* Trans. J. M. Brownjohn. Delta, New York, 1970.

Hayes, C. *The Ape in our House.* Harper, New York, 1951.

Held, R., and A. Hein. "Movement-Produced Stimulation in the Development of Visually-Guided Behavior." *Journal of Comparative and Physiological Psychology,* 56 (1963), 872–876.

Heron, W., G. K. Doane, and T. H. Scott. "Visual Disturbances after Prolonged Perceptual Isolation." *Canadian Journal of Psychology,* 10 (1956), 13–18.

Hertzig, M., M. Bortner, and H. G. Birch. "Neurologic Findings in Children Educationally Designated as Brain Damaged." *American Journal of Orthopsychiatry,* 39 (1969), 437–446.

Hess, E. "Attitude and Pupil Size." *Scientific American,* 212 (1965), 46–54.

Hetherington, E. M., and R. D. Parke, *Child Psychology,* McGraw-Hill, New York, 1975, pp. 354–379.

Hirsch, J. "Behavior-Genetic Analysis." In *Behavior-Genetic Analysis,* ed. J. Hirsch. McGraw-Hill, New York, 1967, pp. 416–453.

Hirsch, J. "Behavior Genetics and Individuality Understood." *Science,* 142 (1963), 1436–1442.

Hobbs, N. *The Futures of Children.* Jossey-Bass, San Francisco, 1975.

Hoebel, E. A. *The Cheyennes Indians of the Great Plains.* Holt, Rinehart and Winston, New York, 1960.

Honzik, M. P., J. W. Macfarlane, and L. Allen. "The Stability of Mental Test Performance between 2 and 18." *Journal of Experimental Education,* 18 (1948), 309–324.

Hostetler, J. A. *Hutterite Society.* Johns Hopkins University Press, Baltimore, 1974.

Imanishi, K. "Social Behavior in Japanese Monkeys, *Macaca fuscata.*" In *Primate Social Behavior,* ed. C. H. Southwick. Van Nostrand, Princeton, N.J., 1963, pp. 68–81.

Itani, J. "On the Acquisition and Propagation of a New Food Habit in the Troop of Japanese Monkeys at Takasakiyama." *Primates,* 1 (1958), 84–98.

James, W. *The Principles of Psychology.* Henry Holt, New York 1890, p. 488.

Janowitz, H. D., and M. T. Grossman. "Some Factors Affecting the Food Intake of Normal Dogs and Dogs with Esophagostomy and Gastric Fistula." *American Journal of Physiology,* 159 (1949), 143–148.

Johns, J. *The Mating Game.* St. Martin's Press, New York, 1970, pp. 40–45.

Johnson, W., ed. *The Onset of Stuttering.* University of Minnesota Press, Minneapolis, 1959.

Jones, N. G. B. "An Ethological Study of some Aspects of Social Behavior of Children in Nursery School." In *Primate Ethology,* ed. D. Morris. Aldine, Chicago, 1967, pp. 347–368.

Kagan, J., and H. A. Moss. *Birth to Maturity.* John Wiley, New York, 1962.

Kawai, M. "Newly Acquired Pre-Cultural Behavior of the Natural Troop of Japanese Monkeys on Koshima Island." *Primates,* 6 (1965), 1–30.

Kendler, T. S., and H. H. Kendler. "An Ontogeny of Optional Shift Behavior." *Child Development,* 41 (1970), 1–27.

Kennedy, W. A., V. Van De Riet, and J. C. White. "A Normative Sample of Intelligence and Achievement of Negro Elementary School Children in the Southeastern United States." *Monographs of the Society for Research in Child Development,* 28, No. 6 (1963).

Kessen, W. "Sucking and Looking." In *Early Behavior,* ed. H. W. Stevenson, E. H. Hess, and H. L. Rheingold. John Wiley, New York, 1967, pp. 147–179.

Kimble, G. A. *Hilgard and Marquis' Conditioning and Learning,* 2nd ed. Appleton-Century-Crofts, New York, 1961, p. 388.

Klinghammer, E. "Factors Influencing Choice of Mate in Altricial Birds." In *Early Behavior, Comparative and Developmental Approaches,* ed. H. W. Stevenson, E. H. Hess, and H. L. Rheingold. John Wiley and Sons, New York, 1967, pp. 6–42.

Klopfer, P. H. "Mother Love: What Turns It On?" *American Scientist,* 59 (1971), 404–407.

Krafka, J. "The Effect of Temperature upon Facet Number in the Bar-Eyed Mutant of *Drosophila:* Part I." *Journal of General Physiology,* 2 (1920), 409–432.

Kruuk, H. *The Spotted Hyena, A Study of Predation and Social Behavior.* University of Chicago Press, Chicago, 1972.

Kummer, H. *Social Organization of Hamadryas Baboons.* University of Chicago Press, Chicago, 1968.

Lack, D. "Darwin's Finches." *Scientific American,* 188 (1953), 67–72.

Lantis, M. "The Social Culture of the Nunivak Eskimo." *Transactions of the American Philosophical Society,* 35 (1946), 153–223.

Lenneberg, E. H. *Biological Foundations of Language.* John Wiley and Sons, New York, 1967.

LeVine, R. A. "Cross Cultural Study in Child Psychology." In *Carmichael's Manual of Child Psychology,* ed. P. H. Mussen. John Wiley and Sons, New York, 1970, vol. II, pp. 559–612.

Lindauer, M. *Communication Among Social Bees.* Harvard University Press, Cambridge, Mass. 1961.

Linton, R. "Marquesan Culture." In *The Individual in his Society,* ed. A Kardiner. Columbia University Press, New York, 1939, pp. 137–196.

London, I. D. "A Russian Report on the Postoperative Newly Seeing." *American Journal of Psychology,* 73 (1960), 478–482.

Lorenz, K. " The Companion in the Birds' World." *Auk,* 54 (1937), 245–273.

Lorenz, K. "Comparative Studies of Motor Patterns of Anatinae." In *Studies in Animal and Human Behavior,* trans. R. Martin. Harvard University Press, Cambridge, Mass., 1971, vol. II, 14–114.

Lorenz, K. "Part and Parcel in Animal and Human Societies." In *Studies in Animal and Human Behavior,* trans. R. Martin. Harvard University Press, Cambridge, Mass., 1971, vol. II. pp 115–195.

Lorenz, K. "Psychology and Phylogeny." In *Studies in Animal and Human Behavior,* trans. R. Martin. Harvard University Press, Cambridge, Mass., 1971, vol. II, pp. 196–245.

Lorenz, K., and N. Tinbergen. "Taxis and Instinctive Action in the Egg-retrieving Behavior of the Graylag Goose." In *Instinctive Behavior,* ed. and trans. C. H. Schiller. International Universities Press, New York, 1957.

Lott, D. F. "Parental Behavior." In *Perspectives in Animal Behavior,* ed. G. Bermant. Scott Foresman, Glenview, Ill., 1973.

McCandless, B. R. *Adolescents: Behavior and Development.* Dryden Press, Hinsdale, Ill., 1970.

McCarthy, D. "Language Development in Children." In *Manual of Child Psychology,* ed. L. Carmichael, 2nd ed. John Wiley and Sons, New York, 1954.

McHugh, T. "Social Behavior of the American Buffalo *(Bison, bison bison)." Zoologica,* 43 (1958), 1–40.

McNeill, D. *The Acquisition of Language.* Harper and Row, New York, 1970.

McNemar, Q. *The Revision of the Stanford Binet Scale.* Houghton Mifflin, Boston, 1942.

Maccoby, E. M. and C. N. Jacklin. *The Psychology of Sex Differences.* Stanford University Press, Stanford, Cal. 1974.

Market, C. L., and H. Ursprung. *Developmental Genetics.* Prentice-Hall, Englewood Cliffs, N. J., 1971.

Marler, P., and W. J. Hamilton. *Mechanisms of Animal Behavior.* John Wiley, New York, 1966.

Mason, W. A. "Early Social Deprivation in the Nonhuman Primates: Implications for Human Behavior." In *Environmental Influences,* ed. D. C. Glass. Rockefeller University Press, New York, 1968, pp. 70–100.

Mason, W. A. "The Effects of Social Restriction on the Behavior of Rhesus Monkeys." *Journal of Comparative and Physiological Psychology,* 53 (1960), 582–589.

Masters, W. H., and V. E. Johnson. *Human Sexual Response.* Little, Brown, Boston, 1966.

Mead, M. *Growing up in New Guinea.* Mentor Books, New York, 1953.

Mech, L. D. *The Wolf.* Natural History Press, Garden City, New York, 1970.

Merei, F. "Group Leadership and Institutionalization." *Human Relations,* 2 (1949), 23–39.

Money, J. "Intersexual and Transexual Behavior." In *American Handbook of Psychiatry,* ed. S. Arieti and E. B. Brody. Basic Books, New York, 1975, pp. 334–351.

Montagu, A. *Culture and the Evolution of Man.* Oxford University Press, London, 1962.

Morris, D. *The Naked Ape.* Dell Publishing, New York, 1969.

Mowrer, O. H. "A Stimulus-Response Analysis of Anxiety and its Role as a Reinforcing Agent." *Psychological Review.* 46 (1939), 553–565.

Munn, N. L. *The Evolution and Growth of Human Behavior.* Houghton Mifflin, Boston, 1965, p. 538.

Murphey, R. M. "Genetic Correlates of Behavior." In *Perspectives on Animal Behavior,* ed. G. Bermant. Scott Foresman, Glenview, Ill., 1973, pp. 72–101.

Peterson, R. S. "Social Behavior in Pinnipeds." In *The Behavior and Physiology of Pinnipeds*, ed. R. J. Harrison, R. C. Hubbard, R. S. Peterson, C. E. Rice, R. J. Schusterman. Appleton-Century-Crofts, New York, 1968, pp. 3–53.

Phoenix, C. H., R. W. Goy, A. A. Gerall, and W. C. Young. "Organizing Action of Prenatally Administered Testosterone Propinate on the Tissues Mediating Mating Behavior in the Female Guinea Pig." *Endocrinology,* 65 (1959), 369–382.

Piaget, J. *The Child's Conception of Number.* Humanities Press, New York, 1952.

Piaget, J., and B. Inhelder. *The Child's Conception of Space.* Humanities Press, New York, 1956.

Piaget, J., and B. Inhelder. *The Psychology of the Child.* Basic Books, New York, 1969.

Premack, A. J., and D. Premack. "Teaching Language to an Ape." *Scientific American,* 227 (1972), 92–99.

Premack, D. "Language in Chimpanzees?" *Science,* 172 (1971), 808–822.

Razran, G. H. S. "The Observable Unconscious and Inferable Conscious in Current Soviet Psychology." *Psychological Review,* 54 (1961), 81–147.

Redican, W. K., and G. Mitchell. "The Social Behavior of Adult Male Infant Pairs of Rhesus Macaques in a Laboratory Environment." *American Journal of Physical Anthropology,* 38 (1973), 523–526.

Riesen, A. H. "Arrested Vision." *Scientific American,* 183, (1950), 16–19.

Riesen, A. H. "Stimulation as a Requirement for Growth and Function in Behavioral Development." In *Functions of Varied Experience,* ed. D. W. Fiske and S. R. Maddi. Dorsey Press, Homewood, Ill., 1961, pp. 57–80.

Rogers, C. R. *Becoming Partners: Marriage and its Alternatives.* Delacorte Press, New York, 1972.

Rowell, T. E. "Forest Living Baboons in Uganda." *Journal of Zoology,* 149, (1966), 344–364.

Sackett, G. P. "Effects of Rearing Conditions upon the Behavior of Rhesus Monkeys (*Macaca mulatta*)." *Child Development,* 36 (1965), 855–868.

Schaller, G. B. "The Behavior of the Mountain Gorilla." In *Primate Behavior: Field Studies of Monkeys and Apes,* ed. I. Devore. Holt, Rinehart and Winston, New York, 1965, pp. 324–367.

Schein, M. W., and E. B. Hale. "The Effect of Early Social Experience on Male Sexual Behavior of Androgen Injected Turkeys." *Animal Behavior* 7 (1959), 189–200.

Schein, M. W., and E. B. Hale. "Stimuli Eliciting Sexual Behavior." In *Sex and Behavior* ed. F. A. Beach. John Wiley and Sons, New York, 1965, pp. 440–482.

Schneirla, T. C., J. S. Rosenblatt, and E. Tobach. "Maternal Behavior in the Cat." In *Maternal Behavior in Mammals,* ed. H. L. Rheingold. John Wiley and Sons, New York, 1963, pp. 122–168.

Schutz, F. "Sexuelle Pragung bei Anatiden." Zeitschrifft fur Tierpsychologie, 22 (1965), pp. 5–103. Cited in A. Manning, "Evolution of Behavior." In *Psychobiology,* ed. J. L. McGaugh. Academic Press, New York, 1971, pp. 1–52.

Scott, J. P. "Comparative Social Psychology." In *Comparative Psychology: A Modern Survey,* ed. D. A. Dewsbury and D. A. Rethlingshafer. McGraw-Hill, New York, 1973, pp. 124–160.

Scott, J. P. "Comparative Social Psychology." In *Principles of Comparative Psychology,* ed. R. H. Waters, D. A. Rethlingshafer, and W. E. Caldwell. McGraw-Hill, New York, 1960, pp. 250–278.

Scott, J. P. "Critical Periods in Behavioral Development." *Science,* 138 (1962), 949–958.

Scott, J. P., and J. L. Fuller. *Genetics and Social Behavior of the Dog.* University of Chicago Press, Chicago, 1965.

Seay, B., and N. W. Gottfried. "A Phylogenetic Perspective for Social Behavior in Primates." *Journal of General Psychology,* 92 (1975), 5–17.

Seay, B., R. Schlottmann, and R. Gandolfo. "Early Social Interaction in Two Monkey Species." *Journal of General Psychology,* 87 (1972), 37–42.

Seligman, M. E. P. "On the Generality of the Laws of Learning." *Psychological Review,* 77 (1970), 406–418.

Selye, H. *The Stress of Life.* McGraw-Hill, New York, 1956.

Sheffield, F. D., and T. B. Roby. "Reward Value of a Non-Nutritive Sweet Taste." *Journal of Comparative and Physiological Psychology,* 43 (1950), 471–481.

Sherif, M. *In Common Predicament.* Houghton Mifflin, Boston, 1966.

Sherif, M., O. J. Harvey, B. J. White, W. R. Hood, and C. W. Sherif, *Intergroup Conflict and Cooperation: The Robbers Cave Experiment.* University Book Exchange, Norman, Oklahoma, 1961.

Sherif, M., and C. W. Sherif, *Reference Groups.* Harper and Row, New York, 1964.

Sherman, M., and C. B. Key. "The Intelligence of Isolated Mountain Children." *Child Development,* 3 (1932), 279–290.

Simon, W., and J. H. Gagnon. "On Psychosexual Development." In *Sexuality: A Search for Perspective,* ed. D. L. Grummon and A. M. Barclay. Van Nostrand, New York, 1971, pp. 67–88.

Simpson, G. G. *The Major Features of Evolution.* Columbia University Press, New York, 1953.

Simpson, G. G., and W. S. Beck, *Life: An Introduction to Biology,* shorter ed. Harcourt, Brace, and World, New York, 1969, p. 479.

Sjostrom, H. *Thalidomide and the Power of the Drug Companies.* Penguin Books, Baltimore, 1972.

Skeels, H. M. "Adult Status of Children with Contrasting Early Life Experiences." *Monographs of the Society for Research in Child Development,* 31, No. 3 (1966).

Slobin, D. I. "On the Learning of Morphological Rules." In *The Ontogenesis of Language,* ed. D. I. Slobin. Academic Press, New York, 1971, pp. 215–223.

Sluckin, W. *Imprinting and Early Learning.* Aldine, Chicago, 1965.

Spitz, R. A. "Hospitalism: An Inquiry into the Genesis of Psychiatric Conditions in Early Childhood." *Psychoanalytic Study of the Child,* 1 (1945), 53–74.

Stewart, M. A., F. N. Pitts, Jr., A. G. Craig, and W. Dieruf. "The Hyperactive Child Syndrome." *American Journal of Orthopsychiatry,* 36 (1966), 861–867.

Tanner, J. M. "Physical Growth." In *Carmichael's Manual of Child Psychology,* ed. P. H. Mussen. John Wiley, New York, 1970, vol. I, pp. 77–155.

Thomas, A., S. Chess, and H. G. Birch. *Temperament and Behavior Disorders in Children.* New York University Press, New York, 1968.

Thorpe, W. H. "Ethology as a New Branch of Biology." In *Readings in Animal Behavior,* ed. T. E. McGill. Holt, Rinehart and Winston, Inc., New York, 1965, p. 38.

Tinbergen, N. *The Curious Naturalists.* Basic Books, New York, 1958.

Tinbergen, N. *The Study of Instinct.* Oxford University Press, London, 1951.

Tryon, R. C. "Individual Differences." In *Comparative Psychology,* ed. F. A. Moss. Prentice-Hall, Englewood Cliffs, N. J., 1942, pp. 409–448.

van Lawick-Goodall, J. *In the Shadow of Man.* Houghton Mifflin, Boston, 1971.

von Uexkull, "A Stroll through the Worlds of Animals and Men." In *Instinctive Behavior,* trans. and ed. C. H. Schiller. International Universities Press, New York, 1957, pp. 5–80.

Washburn, S. L., and I. Devore. "The Social Life of Baboons." *Scientific American,* 204, (1961), 62–71.

Watson, J. B. "Kinesthetic and Organic Sensations: Their Role in the Reactions of the White Rat to the Maze." *Psychological Monographs,* No. 33 (1907).

White, B. L. *Human Infants: Experience and Psychological Development.* Prentice-Hall, Englewood Cliffs, N.J., 1971.

White, R. W. "Motivation Reconsidered: The Concept of Competence." *Psychological Review,* 66 (1959), 297–333.

Whorf, B. L. *Language, Thought, and Reality,* John Wiley and Sons, New York, 1956.

Wolff, P. "Observations on the Early Development of Smiling." In *Determinants of Infant Behaviour,* ed. B. M. Foss. John Wiley, New York, 1963, vol. II, pp. 113–138.

Woodworth, R. S., and H. Schlosberg. *Experimental Psychology.* Henry Holt and Co., New York, 1954, p. 616.

Wright, L. "The Theoretical and Research Base for a Program of Early Stimulation, Care and Training of Premature Infants." In *Exceptional Infant Studies in Abnormality,* ed. J. Hellmuth. Brunner/Mazel, New York, 1971, vol. II, pp. 277–304.

Yarrow, L. J. "The Development of Focused Relationships during Infancy." In *The Exceptional Infant,* ed. J. Hellmuth. Brunner/Mazel, Inc., 1967, vol. I, pp. 427–442.

Yarrow, L. J., J. L. Rubenstein, and F. A. Pedersen, *Infant and Environment,* John Wiley and Sons, New York, 1975.

Young, W. C., R. W. Goy, and C. H. Phoenix. "Hormones and Sexual Behavior." *Science,* 143 (1964), 212.

Index

DATE DUE

8/14/82			

DEMCO 38-297